Dante's Vision and the Circle of Knowledge

Dante's Vision and the Circle of Knowledge

Giuseppe Mazzotta

PRINCETON UNIVERSITY PRESS

PRINCETON, NEW JERSEY

Copyright © 1993 by Princeton University Press
Published by Princeton University Press, 41 William Street,
Princeton, New Jersey 08540
In the United Kingdom: Princeton University Press, Oxford

Library of Congress Cataloging-in-Publication Data

Mazzotta, Giuseppe, 1942–
Dante's vision and the circle of knowledge / Giuseppe Mazzotta.
p.   cm.
Includes bibliographical references and index.
ISBN 0-691-06966-2
1. Dante Alighieri, 1265–1321—Divina commedia.   2. Dante
Alighieri, 1265–1321—Criticism and interpretation.
3. Dante Alighieri, 1265–1321—Knowledge and learning.
4. Creation (Literary, artistic, etc.)   I. Title.
PQ4392.M39   1992
851'.1—dc20   92-5839

This book has been composed in Adobe Janson

Princeton University Press books are printed on
acid-free paper and meet the guidelines for permanence
and durability of the Committee on Production
Guidelines for Book Longevity of the
Council on Library Resources

Printed in the United States of America

1   3   5   7   9   10   8   6   4   2

For Carol

———————————

CONTENTS

PREFACE

THIS BOOK is a critical study of Dante's poetry and thought. Because its aim is to show the new directions Dante imparts to the late medieval debates on knowledge, which to him is rooted in vision, it traverses multiple domains of knowledge (theology, philosophy, the liberal arts, mystical literature, visionary traditions, ethics, etc.) and traces the encyclopedic compass of Dante's imagination.

Many are the scholars—one thinks of Nardi, Gilson, Foster, Contini, Singleton, Petrocchi, Corti, Fumagalli, Sarolli, Freccero—who over the years have scrupulously reconstructed the shifts in Dante's thought or have redrafted the map of knowledge in the Middle Ages. Their research, as well that of other medievalists—van Steenberghen, Michaud-Quantin, Hissette, and Weber, to mention only a few of those who have surveyed the traditional routes of knowledge (the intricate philosophical controversies, the division and classification of the sciences, the role of the universities, such as Bologna, Oxford, and Paris)—is the necessary context for the argument that Dante's poetic thought opens up new spaces of knowledge.

It is a banality to recall here that the fundamental metaphor of the *Divine Comedy* is that of a journey across the desert. I recall this metaphor—and this study will probe its implications in a variety of ways—to suggest that the journey, which is a radical emblem of displacement, figures knowledge not as a fixed and crystallized formal system but as a nomadic movement across disparate realms of spiritual and intellectual experience. More than that, for Dante the journey is poetry itself, the *translatio* of metaphor which affords him with the means to chart the cracks of the terrain he crosses, to cut through its traditional boundaries, and to plot anew its configuration. This process of exploration occurs at all levels. For instance, Dante, who is primarily known for his keen sense of reality, also loves abstractions, and he longs to give them solidity and a place of habitation in his world. The fables and abstractions of philosophy, myths and sciences, politics, theologies and personal memoirs, enigmas of history, visionary flights, and superstitious lore—all are turned into imaginative, idiosyncratic elements that together make up Dante's mosaic of knowledge.

One can read in many medieval texts the sort of lapidary formulation one finds in the *Roman de la rose* to the effect that "poésie c'est travailler en philosophie," which is to be understood as Jean de Meun's insight that the barriers between poetic and philosophical languages are the shallow artifices of academia's objective thinking, partitions quick to tumble at the poet's waving of his magic wand. In the *Divine Comedy*, however, there is

a sustained and rigorous praxis of marking the crossing between heterogeneous and fragmentary regions of knowledge, and between these and what
is not known, so that they communicate among themselves, are joined together, and are part of a global whole. In ancient mythology this privilege
was coextensive with the magic art of Hermes, who, as Vico says, is the god
of the crossroads and is the forebear of Ulysses. There is a scene in *Paradiso*
that is in a way emblematic of the procedures I am here describing, and I
shall briefly focus on it.

In *Paradiso* XXVII (79–87), immediately after the blessed reascend to the
empyrean, the pilgrim, with the sun under his feet, looks back at the earth
across the vast distances of planetary space. In the absolute horizon of his
vision two points of this world's map stand out with infinite precision: the
shore where Jupiter, disguised as a bull, raped Europa in the east, and in
the west the "varco folle" (mad passageway) of Ulysses. The two stories
Dante evokes as his geographical coordinates are both complementary and
antithetical to each other. The archaic myth of Europe's origin and foundation in the violence of the god is symmetrically countered by the epic
hero's tragic transgression of the boundaries of Europe. The god's violence is never thematized in the *Divine Comedy*, but Dante's personal itinerary occurs in the shadow of the philosophical route of Ulysses.

Ulysses' "varco" at the fringe of the West designates his crossing into
another world, his opening of a path into secret and forbidden spaces. His
knowledge has gone astray, and his madness lies in the fact that for him, as
for Adam in the Garden of Eden, knowledge is possible only as transgression. Yet his adventure reveals to us, and to the pilgrim's gaze, that there
are other vast spaces of knowledge and that there are imaginable and possible pathways leading to them. Dante's poetic imagination prowls into
those multiple uncharted regions of knowledge, wanders across the
blurred frontiers of the arts and sciences, and weaves them together into
unexpected, visionary shapes and combinations. In all of this his faith is his
freedom and the rock of his vision.

Such a method of reading the *Divine Comedy*, of heeding, that is, its
visionary energy and resilience as it reinvents the vocabulary and conventions of knowledge, harks back to critical principles voiced by Vico—
whose circuitousness of thought eludes conventional methods—and, later,
by Emerson. In recent times Vico has been frequently recognized as the
ideal point of departure for much of Dante criticism. It has even become
something of a critical commonplace to stress that Vico, who viewed
Dante as a sublime poet, that is to say as a seer and supreme fabulist of the
totality of languages, felt himself to be Dante's kindred spirit. It was Vico's
unique understanding that the poetry of Dante—and of Homer—comes
before philosophy and all poetic and critical arts. From this fundamental
principle it follows that it is an error to believe that their poetry merely

gives expression to Aristotelian or Neoplatonic doctrines, or, to use the terms of current Dante criticism, to Augustinian, Thomistic, and Averroistic ideas. On the contrary, for Vico the poetic imagination gathers together in its light all the shadowy discourses of history.

If Vico's philosophical thought can be said to constitute the general theoretical framework for *Dante's Vision and the Circle of Knowledge*, its interpretive practice is rooted in the philological work of those teachers of mine, among whom I single out here the late Robert E. Kaske and James Hutton, who, for all their differences from each other, habitually thought of knowledge as a totality of relations and as archaeology or, to use a term from mathematicians' understanding of invariants, topology. From their work on *topoi*, which certainly owed much to the findings of Curtius, literature—and above all the *Divine Comedy*—comes forth as a *syntopicon*, as the experience that spatializes history, traces time's memories, and recreates history's multiple rifts and languages. Their philology, to put it in Vico's vocabulary, is the necessary presupposition for critical thought.

I recall their teachings—and those of others—here not simply out of sentimentality toward some more or less idyllic reconstruction of the past but to clarify my critical procedure, which in many ways responds to what is generally perceived as the impasse of literary criticism in our times. Vico's sense of the inseparable unity of philology and philosophy, and, above all, Dante's own poetry, with its inevitable but unpredictable ways of delivering knowledge and vision, force on us the model of what vital critical thinking ought to be.

ACKNOWLEDGMENTS

IN THE spring of 1983, I lectured at the Benedictine abbey in Elmira, N.Y. It was during the unforgettable few hours I spent with that community that I "saw" the shape this book was going to have. But I wrote this book over an extended period of time, and I owe a debt of gratitude to the advice of many friends and to the generosity of many institutions. I am delighted to be able to acknowledge the advice I have received from a number of medievalists and friends who are at Yale and elsewhere: special thanks to Pete Wetherbee for his rare intellectual generosity matched only by his expertise; to Warren Ginsburg for our unforgettable weekly lunches at Silliman College back in 1984 while my encyclopedic project was being laid out; to María Rosa Menocal, who made valuable comments on some later drafts of the manuscript; and to another of my Yale colleagues, Daniel Poirion, for his comments from his perspective as a *médiéviste*. It gives me a particularly great pleasure to acknowledge other friends—Roberto Gonzalez, Mihai Spariosu, and Alfonso Procaccini—for the passionate, endless conversations we have shared over the years.

I must also express my deepest gratitude to several institutions. The faculty of and participants in the Dartmouth NEH Dante Institute, where in the summers of 1985 and 1986 I presented early versions of some of the chapters on the arts of language included here, were very helpful. Thanks are also due to the faculty of Lonergan College, where in a series of seminars in 1986–87 I first fully articulated the general movement of my argument. I will never forget, may I add, the hospitality and kindness shown to me by Principal Doughty, Judy Herz, and the other colleagues. I am equally thankful to two other institutions: first, the Department of Romance Languages at the University of Alberta (above all to my friend and host Massimo Verdicchio), where I again lectured on the medieval history of the encyclopedia; second, the Folger Library, where in a weekly seminar in the fall of 1989 I came to realize that this book was finally completed. Madame Françoise Brito, herself a gifted scholar, proved to me a most valuable research assistant during the compilation of the bibliography.

It is a welcome duty for me to record my indebtedness to Luisa Dato for her incomparable grace and wit while typing or retyping the manuscript.

The book is dedicated to my wife, Carol, whose presence and work have taught me what vision means.

Chapters of this book have appeared in a slightly different form either in professional journals or critical anthologies, and I gratefully acknowledge permission to reprint. Chapter 9 was first published as "Dante and the

Virtues of Exile" in *Poetics Today* 5 (3): 645–67. Chapter 3 was published in a volume to honor R. E. Kaske, *Magister Regis* (New York: Fordham University Press, 1986), pp. 147–61. Chapter 10 appeared in a shorter version in *ACTA: Ideas of Order in the Middle Ages* (SUNY at Binghamton, N.Y.: The Center of Medieval and Early Renaissance Studies, 1990), pp. 1–21. Finally, chapter 11, in a considerably abbreviated form, was published in *Discourses of Authority in Medieval and Renaissance Literature* (Hanover, N.H.: University Press of New England, 1989), pp. 216–35.

NOTE ON DANTE'S TEXTS

Unless otherwise stated, all quotations from Dante's texts and their English translations are drawn from the following editions:

Convivio. A cura di Cesare Vasoli e Domenico de Robertis. In *Opere minori*, vol. 1, pt. 2. Milan-Naples: Ricciardi Editore, 1979. (*Dante's Convivio*. Trans. William Walrond Jackson. Oxford: Clarendon Press, 1909.)

De vulgari eloquentia. A cura di Pier Vincenzo Mengaldo. In *Opere minori*, vol. 2. Milan-Naples: Ricciardi Editore, 1979. (*De Vulgari Eloquentia* [English text]. Trans. A. G. Ferrers Howell. London: Kegan Paul, 1890.)

La Divina Commedia secondo l'antica vulgata. Ed. Giorgio Petrocchi. 4 vols. Società dantesca italiana. Milan: Mondadori, 1966–67. (*The Divine Comedy*. Trans. with a commentary by Charles Singleton. Bollingen Series 80. Princeton, N.J.: Princeton University Press, 1970–76).

Epistole. A cura di Arsenio Frugoni e Giorgio Brugnoli. In *Opere minori*, vol. 2. Milan-Naples: Ricciardi Editore, 1979. (*The Letters of Dante* [emended text]. Trans. with introduction and notes by Paget Toynbee. Oxford: Clarendon Press, 1920.)

Il fiore e il detto d'amore (attribuibili a Dante Alighieri). A cura di Gianfranco Contini. In *Opere minori*, vol. 1, pt. 1. Milan-Naples: Ricciardi Editore, 1979.

Monarchia. A cura di Bruno Nardi. In *Opere minori*, vol. 2. Milan-Naples: Ricciardi Editore, 1979. (*On World Government*. Trans. Herbert W. Schneider. The Library of Liberal Arts. Indianapolis: Bobbs-Merrill Educational Publishing, 1980.)

Questio de aqua et terra. A cura di Francesco Mazzoni. In *Opere minori*, vol. 2. Milan-Naples: Ricciardi Editore, 1979.

Rime. A cura di Gianfranco Contini. In *Opere minori*, vol. 1, pt. 1. Milan-Naples: Ricciardi Editore, 1979. (*Dante's Lyric Poetry*. Ed. and Trans. Kenelm J. Foster and Patrick Boyde. 2 vols. Oxford: Oxford University Press, 1967.)

Vita Nuova. A cura di Domenico De Robertis. In *Opere minori*, vol. 1, pt. 1. Milan-Naples: Ricciardi Editore, 1979. (*Dante's Vita Nuova*. Trans. with an essay by Mark Musa. Bloomington, Ind.: Indiana University Press, 1973.)

Dante's Vision and the Circle of Knowledge

INTRODUCTION

I CONCEIVED and wrote *Dante's Vision and the Circle of Knowledge* as a companion volume to *Dante, Poet of the Desert*. *Dante, Poet of the Desert* is primarily a critical reflection on history, and I still take Dante's sense of history to be both the ground and the core of the *Divine Comedy*. *Dante's Vision and the Circle of Knowledge* presupposes Dante's sense of history as the economy of redemption and as the realm of exile, as the place where contradictory and yet real possibilities of human existence are decisively played out, but it undertakes different paths of investigation. The chief aim of the present volume, to state it plainly, is to explore Dante's radical claims about poetry as nothing less than the foundation of all possible knowledge.

The cluster of problems such a claim for poetry entails and in which the unfolding of *Dante's Vision and the Circle of Knowledge* is rooted is readily apparent: What kind of knowledge does poetry engender? How is poetry for Dante related to knowledge? How does poetry's mode of knowledge differ—if it can be said to differ at all—from other modes of knowledge, such as, for instance, the specific knowledge produced by the discourses of logic or theology? To what extent are these rational or scientific discourses metaphorical displacements of the insights of the poet? And—since the climax of the poem is the vision of God—can Dante's poetry be simply reduced within the narrow confines of conceptual knowledge, or in what way does it open up new imaginative worlds?

This series of interrelated questions punctuates the movement of the present book, but it entails in turn other questions. What exactly does knowledge mean for Dante? Why is it a circle? And what is Dante's idea of poetry? Should the two main terms in my title—knowledge and vision—be construed as marking a logical opposition between vision and knowledge or, on the contrary, as a hendiadys, as if, that is, the conjunction "and" joined together into a symbolic unity poetic vision and the circle of knowledge?

These questions will be confronted by paying close critical attention mainly to the *Divine Comedy* but, when necessary, also to Dante's other works. Throughout I will locate Dante's poetry within the context of the major epistemic models and paradigms—which can be "cosmological" poems, such as, for instance, the *Cosmographia*, or more traditional systematizations of knowledge, such as the theological *summae* and the encyclopedias. For my present purposes these discursive structures are genres seeking to contain and give universal intelligibility to all forms of experience. My point of departure is the commonly agreed conviction that Dante conceives of all contingent experiences within what I would call a context of the whole, within a global network of close-knit relations. The primary model for the representation of a unified totality is the encyclopedia, and my title, in fact, partly translates the Greek *enkuclios paideia*, the Latin *encyclios disciplina*—encyclopedia, a term that designates a "round learning," the cycle of education in the diverse disciplines of the curriculum.

A preliminary synopsis of both the structure and the limits of the medieval encyclopedias (chapter 1 will map more textually the presence of specific encyclopedic works relevant to the *Divine Comedy*) is in order here.[1] The term encyclopedia was made popular in the seventeenth century by John Henry Alsted's erudite compendium of the arts and sciences, which was envisioned both as a pedagogical tool and as the quest for a unified system of knowledge at a time of extaordinary scientific advances. But the term goes back at least to Vitruvius, whose educational ideals reflect the concerns and values of Greek antiquity, including Plato's conviction that the true aim of philosophy is education. The core of the Platonic *paideia*, as Werner Jaeger has shown, is not simply the ingathering of the heterogeneous branches of knowledge but the education of the soul, which is understood as the restoration of unity and harmony to man's fragmentary existence.[2]

This encyclopedic ideal was not always kept at the forefront of erudite encyclopedic projects such as Pliny's or Martianus Capella's. But it was certainly present in later medieval elaborations. As a matter of fact, the Middle Ages—in spite of the theological conviction that man is fallen; that knowledge does not necessarily mean virtue; that grammar might be a diabolical art, for it teaches that the word *deus* can have a plural; that dialectics can be blasphemous because it subjects the tenets of revelation to the rigors of rational inquiry—produced a rich flowering of the encyclopedic practice and promoted complex speculations on the premises and possibilities of the genre.

The striking phenonemon of medieval encyclopedias has long been an object of study. From de Bouard to Michaud-Quantin, from Fontaine to Wagner to Fumagalli, scholars have described the distinctive traits of the "petites encyclopédies" of the twelfth and thirteenth centuries. The explosion of this genre, it is correctly said, is to be attributed primarily to a consciousness of history as a continuous spatial order, wherein the disparate traditions of Greek thought, of biblical revelation, and of Latin as the unifying language of institutions and culture appear to converge simultaneously in giving a global vision of the world. The medieval encyclopedias—Vincent of Beauvais's *Speculum quadruplex* (encyclopedias, let me add in passing, are also called mirrors because, as Vincent says, mirrors induce speculation and imitation); Alexander Neckam's *De naturis rerum*; Bartholomeus Anglicus's *De proprietatibus rerum*; the *Tresor* of Brunetto Latini as well as *La composizione del mondo* by Ristoro d'Arezzo and *L'Acerba* by Cecco d'Ascoli—are certainly repositories of knowledge, but they are also, and fundamentally, emblems (both a fact and a metaphor) of the belief in a unified order of the sciences and of the unity of knowledge.

From a formal standpoint encyclopedias can be defined as a logical space, a framework within which the entities of the world are interpreted and classified. Thus understood, encyclopedic knowledge presents itself as a completed, systematic, and global order (hence the amount of repetitiveness in them), as a closed circle, in fact, because the belief in a revealed theological-symbolic universe is the premise making possible the representation of the totality and unity of knowledge. But, as Dante understood, knowledge is not a static, immobile entity; on the contrary, it is authentically historical and time-bound, and chapter 1 will focus precisely on the inevitable failure of the traditional encyclopedias to come to terms with what, centuries later, would be called "the augmentation of the sciences."

The historical development of the encyclopedic genre betrays the general awareness of the need to update traditional compilations in the persuasion that knowledge is a process of growth in time. The systematic, closed circle of Isidore of Seville's seventh-century encyclopedia could no longer be viewed as a complete and global representation of available knowledge: thus, Vincent of Beauvais's thirteenth-century *Speculum quadruplex* incorporates, in his tabulation of knowledge, citations from authors of the twelfth century, from the philosophers of nature, from astronomy, and from Arab translations and commentaries of Aristotle; by the same token, as Fumagalli points out, *De proprietatibus rerum* of Bartholomeus reflects the historical and cultural changes by its absorption of Aristotelian and Arab lore (above all, the *Analytics* and the *Topics*.)

Although encyclopedias did not originate in the Middle Ages, the main theoretician of the encyclopedia is St. Augustine in his *De ordine* and in his *De doctrina christiana*. In *De ordine* the study of the liberal arts is explicitly linked to the Greek ideal of rationality. The liberal arts—the phrase *artes liberales* was coined by Cassiodorus—are the arts of the *trivium* or arts of language (grammar, rhetoric, and dialectic) and the arts of the *quadrivium* or arts of number (arithmetic, music, geometry, and astronomy).[3] They are called "liberal arts" because their study frees the mind, and they are to be distinguished from the mechanical or adulterine arts (weaving, theater, commerce, navigation, war, etc.). The first aim of philosophy, says St. Augustine in *De ordine*, is to provide a purified, objective perspective from which the soul can contemplate God and his order in the universe; second, the liberal arts provide the preliminary investigation into the true sources of one's blessedness.

De doctrina christiana, on the other hand, is primarily designed to pave the way for a method of allegorical interpretation of scripture in the light of the Ciceronian ideal of education, "sapientia et eloquentia." In order to arrive at a correct reading of the biblical text, which is open to a variety of interpretations, and in order to master the rhetoric of preaching, the Christian must identify and make use, says St. Augustine, of all suitable pagan knowledge. A clear distinction is thus drawn (II, xc) between the pagans' false and superstitious imaginings and the "liberal disciplines." Christians, St. Augustine says, must avoid and detest the worship of idols but must take with them, as did the Jews when they fled Egypt, the pagan treasures and put them to Christian uses. This passage from *De doctrina christiana* exerted an enormous influence in the Middle Ages because, under the guise of an apologetic text, it legitimized the opening of biblical studies and theological speculations to secular wisdom. In short, St. Augustine reversed the outlook of earlier and later apologists, such as Tertullian and Cyprian, who sought to stave off the classics and the study of literature. On the other hand, Hugh of St. Victor and John of Salisbury drew together the biblical text and the available range of pagan authors (Vergil, Ovid, Horace, etc.).

St. Augustine implemented his sense of the importance of the pagan school curriculum as preparatory to the study of the Bible by writing treatises on the arts of the *trivium* as well as on music and arithmetic. A few examples of the impact of this text will have to suffice. St. Augustine's views are the basis of Cassiodorus's *On the Institution of Divine and Secular Letters*; they provided the inspiration for Hugh of St. Victor's *Didascalicon* and Honorius of Autun's *De animae exsilio et patria*, which reflect both on the classification of the secular arts and philosophy and on the techniques of interpretation of the divine scriptures. To be sure, the two treatises of Hugh and Honorius respond to different intellectual challenges. The *Didascalicon*, which is informed by the principles and concerns articulated by *De doctrina christiana*, aims at constructing a formal scheme that would account for the whole of human knowledge, from the fourfold division of philosophy (theoretical, practical, mechanical, and logical) to the soul's possession of divine wisdom. Honorius's *De animae exsilio*, on the other hand, is a map of the topography of the soul's education: the arts are cities scattered in a foreign land through which the soul passes on its way to the fatherland, the citadel of divine wisdom.

But if *De doctrina christiana* theorizes the epistemic presuppositions and methods of the encyclopedias, it was left to Isidore, who compiled in the seventh century an encyclopedia known as *Etymologies* or *Origines*, to embody the genre's most influential and long-lasting practice. The sources of Isidore's remarkable archive of knowledge are well-known classics: Apuleius's catalog of *mirabilia*, Varro's antiquities, Macrobius's philosophical dialogues on the enduring value of pagan thought in the *Saturnalia*, Pliny's *Natural History*, and Gellius's *Noctes atticae* provide the building blocks for Isidore's twenty books of *Etymologies*, which deal with the liberal and mechanical arts, scriptures, liturgy, the Old Testament, philosophical sects, poets, the sciences of nature, geography, and so on. More substantively, the underlying principle of organization of the *Etymologies* is grammar. Knowledge, Isidore believed, is reachable through the archaeology or *etymon* of each word, as if every word contained within itself the fable of its own historical origin and of the archaic depths of its meaning. Because of this belief in the epistemology of grammar and in the fact that etymology is the master category for knowledge, scholars, unsurprisingly, have spoken of grammar as "the totalitarian science" of the *Etymologies*.[4]

This brief exposition of the medieval theory and practice of the encyclopedic genre intends to show that encyclopedias are primarily envisioned as tools of a total education. What clearly emerges from the reflections of St. Augustine, of Hugh, of Honorius, and from the *Etymologies* is the sharp sense of the precarious place literature, and above all the classics, occupies in the pursuit of *scientia* and Christian *sapientia*. *Dante's Vision and the Circle of Knowledge* seeks to bring to the fore the shifts and the configuration of the debate on the "place" of literature within the wide grid of the other sciences. The traditional perspectives on this question are well known, and I will not rehash them in any great detail. For Albert the Great and Thomas Aquinas poetry, as Curtius reported long ago, was "infima inter omnes doctrinas."[5] Like the Scholastics of the thirteenth century, they believed in the epistemological value of logic for expounding theology; they were also intent on preserving the idea of an intrinsic difference between the figurative mode of the Bible and that of poetry, but they opposed grammar, rhetoric, and the *auctores*. For the encyclopedists, on the other hand, poetry or literature was part of grammar, and, as such, it was legitimately considered part of the curriculum. At the same time there was a poetic tradition as well as the tradition of allegorical interpretation of literary texts that vindicated the epistemological value of literature. Various allegorists of the classical texts of, say, Vergil, such as Macrobius, Servius, or Bernard Silvester, asserted with different degrees of emphasis the philosophical value of the *Aeneid*. Poets such as Alan of Lille or Bernard Silvester made their poetry the vehicle by which the mind grasps the essence of the natural order and by which that order can be restored.[6]

These issues will be considered from a variety of angles in the first five chapters of this book. In fact, this study has *grosso modo* a tripartite structure, and its first section (up to chapter 5) focuses on poetry and the arts of language. Together those chapters probe how Dante imaginatively engaged all the epistemological debates of his time and disclosed complicities in the apparently most divergent systems of thought. Chapter 1 examines

Dante's sense of the links between poetry and the encyclopedic genre; chapter 2 comes to terms with the debates over the Bible, which is a veritable encyclopedia, between exegetes and theologians, and it presents the view that grammar—the discipline Thomas Aquinas professedly considered merely ancillary to theology—shapes the discourse of Dante's theological reflections; chapter 3 shows that rhetoric is the unavoidable tool with which to tackle metaphysical questions; chapter 4 deals with the relationship between poetry and justice, and it argues that the equivalences of metaphor uncover complexities about equity and justice that treatises of ethics gloss over; chapter 5, finally, surveys the traditional debates on logic's value (how and whether or not it is the privileged path to rational knowledge), and it reveals Dante's sense of the bonds between dialectics and political power.

To say it more clearly, this book deals with Dante's engagement in all the liberal arts, but it gives prominence to the arts of language because, and the point will be made repeatedly throughout, language is the stuff of poetry. For Dante it was also history, the locus, as etymologists believe, where the properties of things lie hidden; where revelation takes place; where political and moral order can be posited and the shared idiom of history deciphered. But what exactly is the range of these arts of language? How do they affect the questions of knowledge?

It might be useful to recall, first of all, Dante's ordering of the sciences in *Convivio* (II, xiii, 1–30): the sciences of the *trivium* (grammar, logic, and rhetoric) are followed by those of the *quadrivium* (arithmetic, music, geometry, and astronomy), and both are followed by the natural sciences (physics and metaphysics), ethics, and theology, which is the "divine science." To exemplify how the arts of language are traditionally understood and to show why they trigger intense debates on their value and role in the scheme of what is thought to constitute knowledge, it is well to give an overview of them. Encyclopedias, as is to be expected from compilations that are not speculative but give the existing state of knowledge, attempt to draft clear boundaries for the various disciplines, and I shall cull the general definitions given by Isidore of Seville (whose importance and influence, of course, depend on the fact that he is not very original). But I shall later turn to the intellectually more demanding poetic and theological arguments regularly surfacing up to the thirteenth century over the status of the arts of language in the theories of knowledge.

Grammar, for instance, is "the science of speaking well and the origin and foundation of the liberal arts" (Isidore, *Etym.* I, v, 11). Its province, as Priscian and Donatus conceive of it, is the study of reading and writing, rules of orthography, shifts of vowels and letters, etymologies, solecisms, and barbarisms. It is also the science of interpreting poets and historians, as Rabanus Maurus states, and, eventually, it is identified with the rules of

Latin. Dialectics, or logic, on the other hand, examines not how things are said but what is said. Because its primary aim is to investigate the meaning words express as well as the truth or falsehood of an argument, dialectics is defined as the "art of the arts and the science of the sciences, which points the way to the principles of all methods" (*Etym.* II, x, 9). Divided into demonstrative, probable, and sophistical logic, it provides rational, scientific principles for effective argumentation in the form of syllogisms. Whereas the task of logic is to engender knowledge of the truth, the aim of rhetoric is persuasion. Rhetoric's standard definition is "the science of speaking well in civil questions and persuading" (*Etym.* III, v, 24). Ever since Aristotle, Cicero, and Quintilian, rhetoric is subdivided into three general headings, deliberative, judicial, and epideictic, according to its function in, respectively, political assemblies, law courts, or encomiums of individual characters.

In spite of the efforts to delimit sharply the domain of each discipline, it is quickly clear from the foregoing didactic simplification that the distinctions within the *trivium* are neither neat nor immutable. The boundaries betweem grammar and rhetoric continuously overlap, as rhetoric concerns itself with tropes, figures, style, and so on. Grammar itself, beginning with the commentary of Petrus Helias on Donatus and under the influence of the "new Aristotle," turns into a logical science, a speculative discipline that does not merely describe the concrete features of a language but seeks to infer a universal grammar or logic of language, and posits links between the grammatical order of language and the material content of thought. The *Logica nova* investigates grammatical and logical distinctions, such as the properties of terms in metaphysical and theological questions in the assumption that the order of reason is coextensive with the order of reality.

This summary tracing of a shift or broadening of focus in the disciplines of the *trivium* certainly suggests the major role grammar, logic, and rhetoric assume in the epistemological debates of the late Middle Ages. The tabulations of the various liberal arts by Thierry of Chartres, Honorius of Autun, Hugh of St. Victor, and St. Bonaventure reflect the desire to harmonize secular knowledge with the quest for divine wisdom. Yet it should be stressed that at every turn voices can be heard denouncing and rejecting the unqualified assimilation of secular knowledge, embodied by the arts of the *trivium*, to what is conceived as the purity and self-sufficiency of theological discourse. The polemic is recurrent, and it can be found in St. Jerome, Gregory the Great, Smaragdus, and Peter Damian.

A version of this polemic occurs in St. Augustine's *Confessions*. In book I, 18, St. Augustine recalls his delight in the art of eloquence; he then questions the classical theory of education as imitation and custom by turning his attention to the professors of literature who force on him the declamation of poetic fictions and forget the "wine of error" they contain:

Look down, my Lord God, and, as you always do, look down with patience on how the sons of men most carefully observe the agreed rules of letters and syllables which they received from those who spoke before them and yet pay no attention to the eternal covenant of everlasting salvation which they received from you. Indeed it is true that a teacher and learner of these traditional rules of pronunciation would cause more offense if he were to break the grammarians' laws and say "uman being," without the aspirate than if, being a human being himself, he were to break your laws and hate another human being. . . . A man who is trying to win a reputation as a good speaker will, in front of a human Judge and surrounded by a crowd of human beings, attack his opponent with the utmost fury and hatred, and he will take great care to see that by some slip of the tongue he does not mispronounce the word "human"; but he will not be concerned as to whether his rage and fury may have the effect of utterly destroying a real human being.

The central focus in St. Augustine's theological critique of the formalism of grammarians and rhetoricians, who observe rules but not the real referents of those rules, is the sense of what it means to be human. In the radical polarization of his vision two contrasting perspectives confront each other: the rhetorical and the Christian. His aversion to rhetoric and the value it places on style will certainly not keep him from setting down rules of eloquence, diction, and oratorical ornament for the benefit of preachers. He steadily encourages them to master the tools of language with the provision that their eloquence be yoked to wisdom so that Christian truths may be defended against the "fallacious arguments" of opponents. At one level, the mixture of the techniques of pagan science with the content of Christian revelation, especially in *De doctrina christiana*, reflects the syncretism of Augustine's cultural project. It also reflects his awareness that the arts of language by themselves have the power to unsettle the value system embodied by theology and even to obliterate the sense Christians attach to the word "human."

St. Augustine's caveat resurfaced in the intellectual debates flaring up in thirteenth-century Paris. I focus on Paris because, for a variety of political reasons historians have recently analyzed, it had become the place where the most powerful personalities, such as those of St. Bonaventure and St. Thomas Aquinas, among others who engage Dante's imagination in the *Divine Comedy*, converged. Their debates essentially turned, it seems to me, on the role and place of the various disciplines in the general scheme of knowledge. So strong, for instance, were the links between logic and theological speculation and between theology and grammar that in 1277 the bishop of Paris condemned in proposition 183 (under the rubric "Errores in Theologia") the view that theology is founded on poetic fictions ("quod sermones theologi fundati sunt in fabulis"), as well as the opinion (proposition 181) that in Christian dispensation there are fables and false-hoods.[7] These condemnations are steadily brought to bear on my discussion not because it is to be believed that Dante endorses them in the poem or even that he directly responds to them; rather, they are ideological crystallizations of his time. Thus, it can be recalled that the theology of Albertus Magnus and Thomas Aquinas was fiercely contested by the Oxford Franciscans, such as John Peacham, because it deployed the methods of logic for its speculations.[8] It mattered little to the Oxford polemicists that St. Thomas Aquinas was in fact seeking a reconciliation of the twofold source of knowledge, knowledge by faith and knowledge by reason. In the opinion of the Neo-Augustinians, who mistrust the legitimacy of reason, Aquinas's procedure meant the unacceptable subjugation of faith to the sovereign principles of pagan philosophy.

Not everybody agreed with such a rigorist exclusion of the *artes sermocinales* from the edifice of Christian wisdom (which in the past had seen St. Jerome and Odo of Cluny present these selfsame objections). The classic question put by St. Jerome, "what has Horace to do with the Psalter . . . or Cicero with the Apostle?" is the unequivocal symptom of the Christian uneasiness about the moral value of the classics. Historically, the uneasiness was tempered by the revival of humanistic studies at Chartres, Orléans, and Italy.[9] But in the thirteenth century such a grammarian as John of Garland bemoaned the decline of the study of pagan poets, who were neglected not on grounds of their dangerousness to the Christian ethos but, rather, in favor of studies in logic. In this context one could recall the allegorical poem *The Battle of the Seven Arts* by a trouvère of the thirteenth century, Henri d'Andeli, as an example of how these debates on the arts were seen from the viewpoint of a poet.[10]

The poem reformulates the controversy as a personified struggle between Grammar, which in this context means the study of classical authors as it was practiced at Orléans, and Logic, as it was pursued in the faculties of philosophy and theology at Paris. Lady Grammar is provisionally defeated, but Henri predicts the imminent return of the classics and, more generally, of literature to the forefront of what constitutes knowledge. *The Divine Comedy*, which begins by resurrecting—literally by recalling—Vergil from his "long silence," both heeds and fulfills the prophecy. More than that, pace Tempier, metaphors and fables are deployed as the sinew of what for Dante necessarily is poetic theology.

If the substance of the *Divine Comedy*, however, were only the encyclopedic impulse to transcribe, give a critical assessment of, and represent abstract forms of knowledge, which in fact organizes and binds together Dante's vision, the poem would be nothing more than a polymath's idle display of erudite material of mere antiquarian interest. It would perhaps resemble a cento, the congeries of *mirabilia*, or bizarre, esoteric fragments

one reads in, say, Macrobius's *Saturnalia*, Varro's *Antiquitates*, Aulus Gellius's *Noctes atticae*, and maybe in Pliny's *Natural History* or Isidore's *Etymologies*. The *Divine Comedy* is not and cannot be that kind of encyclopedia. Actually it can be argued that Dante's poetry intends to counter exactly
the sort of massive assemblage of erudition available in technical encyclopedias. What rescues the poem from being a patchwork of lifeless anach-
ronisms, a mere reliquary of ghostly glyphs, are, at least, three qualities.

The first is that it is self-evidently a poem. This means that the imaginary unity and global intelligibility of the disparate elements of the world
are made possible and exist solely by virtue of a poetic language that animates the fragments of ancient lore and that perpetually resonates with
prodigious vibrations. To say it differently: in traditional, technical encyclopedias the entries are isolated, fragmentary definitions of words, concepts, and objects; the unity of those encyclopedias is an accidental unity of
disjointed parts in their alphabetical sequence, and no necessary relationship exists between an entry and its adjacent one. In Dante's poetic encyclopedia, by contrast, each word is necessarily wrapped in a network of
infinite resonances, of transversal associations with other words which may
be either proximate or distant from one another. From this standpoint the
meaning of a word in a text can never be definitively fixed or encapsulated:
the mobile sense of words is guaranteed, in effect, by the inexhaustible
imaginative context surrounding them.

The second quality is poetic-political. Dante writes an encyclopedic
poem in the intense awareness of the great historical, political, and intellectual crises of his time: the doctrinal turmoil within the church; the con-
flicts between church and empire; the crisis of fraternal orders; the battle
of the arts at Paris; the reality of civil wars; the earlier but recent discovery
of Aristotle's *De anima*, which, along with Averroes' commentary on that
tract, was the single cultural event triggering divisive debates—this is the
horizon of problems which Dante's *Divine Comedy* confronts and *Dante's
Vision and the Circle of Knowledge* probes.[11] But the poem does not simply
reflect and prolong the deep divisions of its time; on the contrary, as I shall
argue, the poem counters the ruptures of history: Dante's vision consists
exactly in his will to reconstitute the scattered, chaotic fragments of history
into an imaginative order and unity, aware, as he was, that in the world of
time the unity is inevitably experienced in the mode of contingent disjunctions.

The third structural quality that sets the *Divine Comedy* apart from traditional encyclopedias is the central fact that the poem recounts the spiritual
and ethical education of a historical agent, Dante himself, as the pilgrim
who, impelled by love, is engaged in an itenerary of self-knowledge which
coincides with finding the objects of his love, Beatrice and God. The inert
heap of clichés, fables, and prodigies that traditionally passed for erudition

among medieval encyclopedists comes to a focus and is given a firm dramatic plausibility by Dante's intrusion of the historicity of his own life and by the hermeneutics of his own self within the larger pattern of creation.

The intrusion of subjectivity contradicts the idea of a mere objective, forever fixed knowledge arranged according to the arbitrary principle of alphabetical order and/or the neatly divided juxtaposition of entries. The second large division of *Dante's Vision and the Circle of Knowledge* ranges from chapters 6 to 8, and its focus is the internalization of knowledge, for these three middle chapters discuss respectively Dante's poetic dramatization of the imagination, of dreams, and of vision. More generally, whereas the first part of this book deals with what could be called the epistemology of language, the middle section tackles the questions of what is knowledge, how it becomes experience, and how the self is both the locus of and the limit to knowledge; the relationship between love and knowledge; how love leads to self-knowledge and becomes virtue; and, finally, how both love and knowledge are tied to vision.

As we learn from Plato, who asserted the primacy of vision in knowledge, vision (which is also *idea, theoria*) is intellectual. This principle, which stood behind the rationalists such as Aquinas, entails the notion that the will or the affections follow behind the intellect. For Dante, who from this viewpoint owes a great debt to a well-documented contemplative tradition, there was a coincidence between intellect and love. Accordingly, the second part of this study maps the movement of Dante's formulation of the identity and difference between love, knowledge, and vision. St. Thomas Aquinas had fully articulated the role of the imagination in the quest for knowledge. But Dante learned from the poets of the *Dolce stil nuovo* (such as Guinizelli and Cavalcanti) that the poetic imagination produces knowledge; and in his *Vita nuova* he himself put into practice what Arab theorists (Alfarabi, Avicenna, and Averroes) had eloquently formulated: that the knowledge engendered by the poetic imagination both encompasses reason and exceeds the vast boundaries of rational discourse.[12] Thus, it can hardly come as a surprise to learn that Dante's poetry goes beyond the concerns of the arts of discourse, for the visionary power of Dante's voice makes his poetry transcend the enterprise of philosophers and theologians.

Dante altered the thought of philosophers and theologians by bringing together their limited and thus unavoidably contradictory, antagonistic perspectives which, by themselves, were false in the measure in which they were partial. By the same token, Dante connected the partial, relative viewpoints of philosophers and theologians by uncovering the poetic foundation of both philosophical and theological knowledge. And, as he did this, he showed the necessity of poetry in all forms of knowledge. What makes poetry necessary is that it steadily reflects on (and does not just use) language, and, as it curves up on itself, it unveils the rhetorical mechanisms though which we reach knowledge. What makes poetry necessary is that it opens up all the questions and enigmas of man's life in its radical historicity; what is more, poetry is necessary because it opposes and transcends the values and myths of history.

The last three chapters—9, 10, and 11—which constitute the third unit of this study, show the radical shape of Dante's poetic theology and make visible the power of his imagination. The shift to theology, which means the "discourse about divine things" and is the traditional "queen of the sciences" as well as the point of destination of the liberal arts, marks an essential, critical reappraisal of the value of the encyclopedic project and its rational grounding. Chapter 9, more specifically, argues that traditional discursive theology neither provides a closure for Dante's inquiry nor circumscribes Dante's idea of poetry; it also argues that for Dante the language of theology was coextensive with his exilic imagination. Chapter 10, on the other hand, redefines the notion of "encyclopedia" and focuses on the ultimate break between the various epistemic models and Dante's sense of poetic theology. Chapter 11, finally, moves beyond the horizon and representation of the epistemic predicament and locates the foundation of Dante's transcendent vision in the metaphorics of *theologia ludens*.

To state it in a more general way, these last three chapters together retrieve Dante's faith in theological aesthetics. His poetry still recognizes the importance of a rational theology such as Aquinas's, but this cannot mean, for Dante, poetry's subordination to a dominant theological structure other than the one he forges. On the contrary, Dante is engaged in a creative polemic with St. Thomas, who, in many ways, is his privileged interlocutor. Yet, against Aquinas—who relegates poetry to the corner of the merely delightful and inconsequential, in the belief that the depths of the divinity can be fathomed only through the rigor of rational investigation; whose own thought bypasses the Augustinian and Victorine legacy of history and of symbolic theology; who opposes allegory and the mythologizing of knowledge—against Aquinas, Dante writes a poem that retrieves history, the passions of his own life, fables, and theology together in the conviction, first, that poetry is the path to take to come to the vision of God and, second, that the poetic imagination is the faculty empowered to resurrect and glue together the fragments of a broken world.

It is this enigmatic mixture of rigor and visionariness in the *Divine Comedy* that *Dante's Vision and the Circle of Knowledge* seeks to grasp and communicate. Given these large claims for poetry, it is small wonder that in 1335 the Dominican chapter at Santa Maria Novella prohibited the reading of the *Divine Comedy* on grounds that it was a heretical text. It is even smaller wonder that Pietro di Dante, to defend his father's memory, called him a theologian. Because Dante's unsurpassed poetic imagination forever allows and contains these contradictory possibilities, it is nothing less than the divination of man's history and deepest longings.

Chapter 1

POETRY AND THE ENCYCLOPEDIA

IT HAS LONG been acknowledged that the *Divine Comedy* is a poetic encyclopedia or a *summa medievalis*. This conventional view of the poem's encyclopedism is still restated in our own time, and it can even be said to account for the scholarly recognition of the necessity of tools such as the *Enciclopedia dantesca* or the sundry general dictionaries and interdisciplinary volumes meant to provide bald summaries of the themes, concerns, and characters the poem draws from the most disparate sciences. But the definition of the poem's encyclopedic compass is hardly new.[1]

One could mention Guido da Pisa's suggestion that the *Divine Comedy* is best figured by Noah's ark, or Benvenuto da Imola's sense of the poem's "ineffable abundance," which he attributes to the fact that "poetry is counted among the liberal arts because it surpasses all of them and embraces them all together; it excels by rising above all of them." The statement reappears with a slight but significant variation in Cristoforo Landino's preamble to his commentary on Dante. In his preliminary musings on the divine origin of poetry Landino marvels at Dante's (and the other ancient poets') "profound and various doctrine." Yet poetry, he says, cannot merely be classified "as one of those arts the ancients called liberal," because it is something "much more divine" than the liberal disciplines, for it "embraces them all."[2] These assessments—which clearly depend on contrasting theoretical principles—constitute the vital focus and the foundation of the critical traditions on the *Divine Comedy*, and they find an extension in the views of, say, Gravina and Vico, who stress, respectively, the poem's rational encyclopedic structure and its sublime visionariness. But they are of some importance also because, taken together, they point to a sense of disjunction and disparity between classical questions of the poem's logical and rational order and, on the other hand, the problematics of poetic visionariness.

The encyclopedism of the *Divine Comedy* cannot be viewed only as a mere descriptive formula of its complexity, comprehensiveness, and cosmic scale; this view of the poem invests, on the contrary, the interpretive debates on Dante's sense of the value, extension, and limits of the sciences and philosophy; on the relationship between knowledge and desire; and on his lucid understanding of poetry as the breath, as it were, of all knowledge. There is still a strain of Dante criticism, represented by critics who, in the wake of Benedetto Croce, choose to bracket the theological and doctrinal substance of Dante's poetic thought in the assumption that the essence of poetry lies outside the structure of ideas and of systems of thought, and is only an intuitive matter of subjective taste or narrative craft. This traditional skepticism about structure and ideology notwithstanding, the concerns with knowledge are constant in Dante's imaginative world.

The narrative of the *Vita nuova* plunges the reader into the depths of the lover's inwardness and of the nearly destructive excesses of a self-consciousness largely unanchored from the external world.[3] *Convivio*, though left unfinished, tells the story of a philosophical quest for ethical values, and its metaphysical ground is Aristotle's generalized assertion from *Metaphysics* (I,i) that all men naturally desire to know, for knowledge, Dante adds, is the ultimate perfection of the soul.[4] The seven liberal arts are duly acknowledged and placed within a planetary context, but the pursuit of this knowledge is carried out through philosophy, which is to be understood as the "love of wisdom," according to a standard definition, as the mind's effort to grasp all things, visible and invisible.[5] The longing for knowledge, the value of reason as a guide on the path to vision, the tragically deluded transgressions committed to arrive at knowledge (the fall of Adam is a fall into knowledge as guilt—cf. *Par.* XXVI, 114-42), the morass of sophistry, and other motifs are massively intertwined in the fabric of the *Divine Comedy*.

Historians of medieval philosophy and thought, such as Gilson, Nardi, Foster, Mazzeo, Corti, and Vasoli, have scrupulously reconstructed the development of and shifts in Dante's configuration of ideas (i.e., the limits of his rationalism and of his Thomism, the degree of his involvement with radical Aristotelianism, his assumed "palinodes" of beliefs held at the time he wrote *Convivio* or *Monarchia*, his political theology, his sense of wisdom as that in which—to say it with Hugh of St. Victor—"the form of the perfect good stands fixed," etc.).[6] A brief remark is in order here as I address what I perceive to be a limit in the genuinely important contribution of these scholars. Not much is gained by engaging in one of those gratuitous and all too common polemics in which academics revel as a fairly obvious way to self-justification, claiming the necessity of their own work because of the errors presumably perpetrated by their predecessors and rival critics.

The present argument is not meant as a polemic against earlier scholarly positions. It simply draws attention to what I must call the question of poetry (in the belief that poetry is always a question, in the double sense of the word)—a question that is not raised enough and is all too often taken for granted. It seems to me, thus, that the very rigor of these scholars' historical documentation makes of the *Divine Comedy* a shadowgraph of abstract ideas, as if poetry were a mechanical, albeit linguistically inventive, process of versifying established ideas handed down by tradition. These historians' almost exclusive preoccupation with content, their indifference to the formal and unique epistemological value of poetry, necessarily reduces poetry to the irrelevant status of pure ornamentation or of providing documentary evidence.

The main problem to be considered here is, first, the meaning Dante attaches to poetry and to the perimeter of its power and possible extension. Second, I shall document Dante's broad canvas of explicit reflections on poetry's relation to the liberal arts and the encyclopedic tradition. It is impossible, as we all know, to distill in a formula the elusive essence or aura of what constitutes poetry, just as it is impossible to summarize a poem, to give a prosaic paraphrase without annihilating its poetry. A poem's materiality—its sounds, rhythm, word order, likely syntactical or lexical obscurities, syllabic relations—is never separable from what one thinks of as poetry's secret core. For Dante (and one can say the same thing with varying degree also for encyclopedic poets such as Homer and Vergil), poetry is the palimpsest of language's memories; it voices the infinite dimensions of life; it is, to put it in the rhetoric of this book, an encyclopedic art that unifies and underlies all the branches of knowledge.

The celebrated remark by Alan of Lille—"omnis mundi creatura / quasi liber, et pictura / nobis est, et speculum. / Nostrae vitae, nostrae mortis, / nostrae status, nostrae sortis. / Fidele signaculum" (Every creature in the world is like a book and a picture to us, and a mirror. A faithful representation of our life, our death, our condition, and our end)—is certainly a useful, if vague, description of the most general principles on which the poem's encyclopedic structure, its inclusive, expansive representation of the heterogeneity and totality of the world, may be rooted. For Alan's much quoted verse reflects the sense that the whole of creation is a harmonious totality and a symbolic construction of things and words, a book and a mirror, whose alphabet can be deciphered, whose arcane signs can be distinguished and classified, and whose secret allegorical images can be revealed as a faithful representation ("fidele signaculum") of our condition.

But there is substantial textual evidence that allows for thinking of the *Divine Comedy* in encyclopedic terms. One may recall, first off, the poet's sense of his enterprise, to which he refers as "impresa" (*Inf.* XXXII, 7)—a term that belongs to the vocabulary of the epic quest, such as Jason's (and the word reappears in *Par.* XXXIII, 95). The term confers on the poem the expanse and range of the epic mode. More specifically, it suggests that the poet's heroic undertaking lies, and this is the brunt of the exordium of *Inferno* XXXII, in Dante's will to describe the foundation holding together the whole universe: "chè non è impresa da pigliare a gabbo / descriver fondo a tutto l'universo, / nè da lingua che chiami mamma e babbo" (7–9) (for to describe the bottom of the whole universe is not an enterprise to be taken up in sport, nor for a tongue that cries mamma and daddy).

There is a transparently ironic counterpoint in the above tercet: it is through the spare resources of the familiar, child's language—hence the heroics and at once the pathos of the poet's task—that Dante's cosmologi-

cal poem comes into being. At the end of the poem the pilgrim's vision of
the whole cosmos as a volume whose leaves are scattered through the layers
of the material world—"Nel suo profondo vidi che s'interna / legato con
amore in un volume / ciò che per l'universo si squaderna: / sustanze e
accidenti e lor costume / quasi conflati insieme, per tal modo / che ciò ch'io
dico è un semplice lume" (*Par.* XXXIII, 85–90) (In its depth I saw ingath-
ered, bound by love in one single volume, that which is dispersed in leaves
throughout the universe: substances and accidents and their relations, as
though fused together in such a way that what I tell is but a simple light)—
merely confirms both Dante's notion that creation is a book and his imaginative impulse of conflating and reconstituting into a unity the rich, unfolding variety of creation.

In order to establish the evidence of the specific encyclopedic nature of
the poem one could even stress the extent to which Dante mobilizes and
deploys sundry notions or mythical figurations and concerns drawn from
the most disparate sciences. At the cost of slipping into an involuntary
parody of the classifications in Borges's improbable encyclopedias, I will
suggest here the inventory of symbolic rubrics and general chapter headings, as it were, that in their fabulous mixtures make up Dante's poem:
lapidaries, bestiaries, color and number symbolism, optics, apocalyptics
and astronomy, cosmology, references to comets, movements of the heavens, planetary orbits, mythography, angelology, classical myths, chronicles
of ancient and contemporary politics, heresies, family dynasties, Roman
and church history, biblical typologies, toponymastics, ethics, the soul's
immortality, determinism and free will, love and its force, geography, various schools of philosophical thought, the liberal and mechanical arts,
canon and civil law, witchcraft, theological debates, summations of trends
and genealogies in Roman, Provençal, or early Italian literary history, and
compendia of rhetorical forms (hagiography, pastoral, epic, novel, romance). All these semantic registers are rigorously deployed side by side
with gossipy bits on the public or private sins of men and women from the
whole of history.[7]

Such a description of the encyclopedic material available in the poem
does not begin to explain how, exactly, Dante thinks of poetry as encyclopedic and in what explicit ways he uncovers the liberal arts as constitutive
elements of poetry. Poetry ceases to be merely a part of the whole of
knowledge (as it is in Isidore) or a secondary activity as it is for Dominican
theologians, such as Albert the Great and Thomas Aquinas. Very simply,
poetry for Dante contains the world and expresses it. But in order to provide some concrete evidence as to how Dante thinks of poetry in encyclopedic terms, I must turn to the pronouncements Dante makes on poetry in
his various texts, and in the process I shall seek to correlate these partial
formulations into a coherent argument.

The most sustained and perhaps most well-known reflection on poetry is available in the *Vita nuova* (XXV), where, in the middle of the lover's delirious dreams, tremors of the heart, and sense of awe at Beatrice's miracuolus apparition in the streets of the city, Dante breaks the narrative and confronts head-on the nature of poetic metaphor. After staking a claim about the originality of the poetry of his own time (poets of antiquity did not, he says, take the theme of love as a subject for verses), Dante goes on to say that from a rhetorical standpoint the poetry of his time—especially his own—does not differ from that of the past: he speaks of love as though it were a thing in itself. In his figuration love is not only a substance endowed with understanding, but it is also a physical substance. His poetic procedure resembles that of the poets of antiquity: just as the ancient poets—Homer, Vergil, Horace, and Ovid—spoke of inanimate things as if they had sense and reason, and made them talk to one another, and just as they made animate things speak to the inanimate and inanimate things speak to the animate, so Dante speaks of love as if it were a man.

What emerges from the passage is, first, Dante's powerful and steady conviction, which also fundamentally shapes the poetics of the *Divine Comedy*, that poetry is the orphic art that animates the world of inanimate entities and the world of the dead. In the immediate context of the *Vita nuova* this disclosure of the essence of metaphor as the vehicle affording a rhetorical simulation of life accounts for the poet's desire to bring Beatrice to life. Second, the poetic self-reflexiveness of chapter XXV climaxes with Dante's assertion that writing poetry is and ought to be a conscious, rational practice: if a poet is asked why he introduces a rhetorical ornament, he ought to be able to divest his words of their fabulous coverings and reveal their inner meaning. The extraordinary double feature of this idea of poetry—at the same time visionary-orphic and rational—largely depends on the belief that poetry is an absolute, a privileged self-enclosure in the sense that nothing important matters or exists outside of it. In other discursive texts that are openly involved in a radical interrogation of language and poetry itself, Dante feels compelled to expand and in a way justify such a totalizing conception of poetry.

One such text is *De vulgari eloquentia*, where the fact that poetry for Dante is bound to all forms of intellectual and moral experience is cogently derived from his central recognition of language as the absolute foundation of knowledge and history. *De vulgari eloquentia* offers ample proof of Dante's insight that language, in its temporality and alterations, is history, the locus where the hard work of man's knowledge is acted out; that language traverses all realms of discourse and organizes them into a historical totality. The configuration of Dante's theories of language is certainly well known, but a brief recapitulation of their salient aspects will shed light on the issues at hand.

The burden of the treatise, as some scholars have eloquently shown, is to review history through the events of language because language is the archive, as it were, of man's historical activity in its broadest reaches.[8] Thus, any consideration of the language of the angels, who communicate through mirrors of light, is omitted. The omission is of some significance to our concerns. For it signals that for Dante there is a domain of experience that exceeds language, and this reality is best understood as the intellect's unmediated communion with the divinity. The empire of language, however, is vast, and Dante starts off by evoking the utopia of Edenic language within which an unbroken kinship exists between words and things. The first word spoken by Adam in the Garden of Eden, we are told, was "El," the Hebrew name of God, and the name was spoken as either a question or a response to a call. This original language, Hebrew, persisted till the Incarnation, for it is unthinkable that the Reedemer would speak in a corrupt, fallen language, rather than in the language of grace. But Hebrew is no longer the unified or unifying language of mankind.

The event that erases the unity of language and collapses the myth of language's transparency is the construction of the Tower of Babel. As one reads in St. Augustine's *City of God* (XVI, 4), God "confounds" men's effort to have one city and one language—Babylon means "confusion"—in order to punish their impious pride. "As the tongue," St. Augustine comments, "is the instrument of domination, in it pride was punished; so that man, who would not understand God when He issued His commands, should be misunderstood when he himself gave orders. Thus . . . the nations were divided according to their languages, and scattered over the earth as seemed good to God, who accomplished this in ways hidden and incomprehensible to us."[9] In the *Divine Comedy*, as we shall see, Dante certainly shares St. Augustine's sense of the politics of language, of language as power, but in *De vulgari eloquentia* the Tower of Babel marks the beginning of man's diaspora in the wilderness of the world.

As Dante introduces in the treatise the principle of the historicity of languages, their diversity in time and space and their changes in both sound and designation, he underscores the role of grammar or Latin as the discipline tending toward order and universality, as an artificial language governed by unalterable laws. A few years ago Corti proposed the notion that among the influences shaping Dante's views of grammar are the concepts of the speculative grammarians or *modistae* (who were not really "Averroists," as is often suggested.)[10] For all its interest, the problem with the hypothesis of a philosophical grammar is that grammar becomes an abstract, generalized construction that bypasses the historical, contingent experience of spoken language. For Dante grammar, rather, has the power to halt and contain language's mutability, which is fostered by the variables of geography and time. By the same token the vernacular tongue Dante envisions is modeled on Latin, and it is conceived as "illustrious," "cardinal," "courtly," and "curial," because it is the language of literature (it unifies, by selecting the best features of each, the Italian dialects); the medium for political discourse in the royal court, if Italy had one; and the instrument for moral-legal decisions. There is in *De vulgari eloquentia*, in effect, a delineation of the ethics of language, the conviction that political myths and moral values are established and legitimized by the language of art.[11]

The second book of *De vulgari eloquentia* aims at constructing what can be called a grammar of rhetoric.[12] As in a classical *ars poetica* or medieval poetics, from Horace to Geoffrey of Vinsauf to Raymon Vidal, Dante lays down prescriptions about style, genres, meter, lexicon, sounds, and, generally, about poetry. In this sense poetry can be said to be, like history, part of grammar. Yet poetry is defined as "fictio rhetorica musicaque poita" (*De vulgari eloquentia* II, iv) (rhetorical fiction set to music.)[13] There is a serious critical misconception about this definition, for on the basis of this sentence it is erroneously believed that poetry is reduced to the parameters of rhetoric. A closer look at Dante's formulation will reveal a more complex pattern. Poetry is said to be a rhetorical art, but it is also more than that: it is set to music, and, indirectly through issues of rhythm and quantities, it is tied to arithmetic. The detail is of the greatest importance.

The acknowledgment of "soave armonia"—music's sweet harmony—as the finer spirit, so to speak, and the accompaniment of poetry, is commonplace in Dante ever since the *Vita nuova* (XII) or *Convivio* (II, xi). In the pilgrim's encounter with the musician Casella, the friend sings Dante's own love poem (*Purg.* II, 112).[14] The scene nostalgically dramatizes, among other things, the bond (long lost since the poetry of the Sicilians) between music and poetry, and it signals Dante's perception of poetry as the art that uncovers and shapes the hidden rhythm and the inner soul, as it were, of language. But to understand the wide range of associations music entails, we ought to recall its traditional tripartition: there is the music of the universe (*musica mundana*), the music belonging to man (*musica humana*), and that which is instrumental (*musica instrumentalis*).

Dante alludes variously to these subdivisions while he is always aware, for instance, that music is also the "characteristic of the soul," as Hugh of St. Victor puts it (*Didascalicon* II, xii).[15] Within the conventional tabulations of the branches of knowledge, more importantly, music is one of the arts of the *quadrivium*. Boethius in his *Institutio musica* makes poetry a branch of music (I, xxxiv). But from Dante's definition poetry comes forth as a unique art capable of crossing the boundaries between a discipline of the *trivium* (rhetoric) and two of the *quadrivium* (music and arithmetic), as an art capable of harmonizing and joining together words and numbers.

The definition sketches an all-inclusive view of poetry; yet we are never told in *De vulgari eloquentia*, which is left unfinished, whether or not poetic language has the power to shape the discursive practices of political, legal, and theological language in their totality and interactions. Because the aim of the present book is to probe exactly the modality, extension, and implications of such a claim for poetry, it ought to be emphasized at the outset that Dante's treatise makes no explicit statement on poetry's all-inclusiveness. Nonetheless, one can infer from it the idea that poetic language resonates with such a power. Dante's "volgare illustre," to begin with, is envisioned as a language capable of forging the intellectual and moral myths of a culture; second, the discussion on poetry falls within the totalizing structure of history as language; third, poetry is seen as the imaginative space where the historical, dense sedimentations of language—and of the common memories language hands down and preserves—find their crystallized essence.

The casting of poetry in terms of rhetoric has other critical resonances. In the *Epistle to Cangrande*, which I take to be Dante's, Dante is at pains not simply to confuse poetry with rhetoric and not to lapse into a facile identification between the two activities of language. In paragraph 18 of the *Epistle*, more particularly, Dante distinguishes between the mode of exordium deployed by poets and that which is deployed by rhetoricians. Rhetoricians, we are told on the authority of Aristotle's *Rhetoric* (iii, 14), manipulate the preamble to an oration as a way of getting the attention of listeners; poets, however, have need of invocation inasmuch as they have to "petition the superior beings for something beyond the superior range of human powers." Poetry, in short, is not reducible to a flat question of rhetorical techniques and style, or generally to the common measure of man, but it is "divinum quoddam munus"—almost a divine gift.

The statement of a difference in the finalities of rhetoric and poetry makes it clear that there is in the *Divine Comedy* a metaphysical dimension to poetry. The reference to Aristotle's *Metaphysics* (par. 20 of the *Epistle*), in the context of the assertion of the chain of effective causes up to infinity, gives weight to this claim. From a thematic viewpoint the one-sentence summation of the poem's transcendent vision is patently a platitude. Dante, who is the poet of death, confronts in the poem, as he puts it, "the state of the souls after death," and this is the literal subject matter of his narrative. In epistemological terms, however, the bond between poetry and metaphysics forces on us the idea that philosophy lies within the compass of poetry, that poetry is engaged in a steady questioning of what lies at the edge of physical reality and beyond the boundaries of death, that the realm of thought, to say this a bit differently, is part of the purview of poetry.

At the same time it must be stressed that, although Dante insists that poetry exceeds rhetoric's goal of persuading an audience, rhetoric itself is still part of poetry. I read the definition of poetry as both rhetoric and music in *De vulgari eloquentia* to mean that poetry is an art of both "places" (rhetoric) and time (music), that poetry is the art of memory. But memory has a double resonance and value.[16] Its doubleness comes down to us through the complex myth of Memory as the mother of the Muses. The genealogy of Memory conveys the idea that there is primarily a temporal dimension to memory, in the sense that memory is the metaphor of the experience of time as a radical disjunction. From this standpoint, such a perception of time as fragmentation and pastness projects lyrical poetry as a reflection on the heap of ruins time brings into our lives. This understanding of memory is the very paradigm of the *Vita nuova*'s temporality (see further remarks on this in chapter 7), while in the *Divine Comedy* it is figured forth largely through the narrative of the pilgrim's journey in the beyond and its subsequent poetic recollection.

Alongside this temporal aspect of memory there is also a *spatial* or rhetorical aspect, in the sense that memory, as a faculty of rhetoric, is a "palace," a "field," or a "chamber"—the repository of language's *topoi* and commonplaces.[17] The spatial figuration of memory complements the traditional view of history as a process of time; it suggests, more precisely, that history is also space. From the standpoint of rhetoric as memory, then, poetry is the archive of the past, the topography of the layered inscriptions and posthumous legends of history. One can venture to say that poetry is the measure of the unfathomable, stratified depths of language's memories, out of which a poet such as Dante, who is the cartographer of the soul, is enabled to hew out, map, and divine the future of those memories.

Such a strong claim about poetry's all-inclusiveness can be gleaned from another place in the *Epistle to Cangrande*. In paragraph 16 of the letter the poetry of the *Divine Comedy* is inscribed within the orbit of ethics:

> Genus vero philosophiae sub quo hic in toto et parte proceditur, est morale negotium, sive ethica; quia non ad speculandum, sed ad opus inventum est totum et pars. Nam si et in aliquo loco vel passu pertractatur ad modum speculativi negotii, hoc non est gratia speculativi negotii, sed gratia operis; quia, ut ait Philosophus in secundo *Metaphysicorum*; "ad aliquid et nunc speculantur practici aliquando."

> (The branch of philosophy which determines the procedure of the work as a whole and in this part is moral philosophy, or ethics, inasmuch as the whole and the part have been conceived for the sake of practical results, not for the sake of speculation. So even if some parts or passages are treated in the manner of speculative philosophy, this is not for the sake of the theory, but for a practical purpose, following the principle which the Philosopher advances in the second book of the *Metaphysics*, that "practical men sometimes speculate about things in their particular and temporal relations.")

The disparity between the rhetorical-musical definiton of poetry in *De vulgari eloquentia* and the ethical formulation in the *Epistle to Cangrande* is not as sharp as is usually thought. To be sure, this is not the place to show how problematical the relationship between ethics and aesthetics is in the *Divine Comedy*, and, at any rate, chapters 4 and 11 below will probe the tangled complexities of that relationship. In this context it will suffice to remark that ethics describes the fact that the poem charts the characters' vast range of moral acts and moral plights; that it is a perspective from which to summon readers to an awareness of moral choices and to the inexorable consequences of those choices in the making of history; that it gauges the distance between acts and their unintended effects; that it calls attention to the explicit statement in paragraph 8 of the *Epistle to Cangrande*, namely that from the allegorical point of view the subject of the poem is man "according as by his merits or demerits in the exercise of his free will he is deserving of reward or punishment by justice."

In a more general sense ethics is one of the threefold divisions of philosophy, while the other two areas are logic and physics. Isidore of Seville (*Etym.*, II, xxiv, 5), St. Augustine (*The City of God*, VIII, iii), and Hugh of St. Victor (*Didascalicon* III, ii) tell us that the originator of ethics was Socrates, who wrote twenty-four books from the perspective of positive justice. More to the point, in the general classification of the aims of philosophy, ethics is the branch of meditation on the "ordo vivendi" (*Etym.* II, xxiv, 4), a perspective that reverses, as *Convivio* does, Dante's absorption with death chronicled in the *Vita nuova*; it is the science whose practical focus falls on the cardinal virtues—prudence, justice, fortitude, and temperance. In Brunetto Latini's analytic of knowledge the arts that usually comprise logic (grammar, dialectic, and rhetoric) fall under the general definition of ethics.

The point in this sample of contradictory opinions in the schematic organization of the sciences is that for Dante the language of poetry is never closed in upon itself. The myth of poetry as a self-referential entity (an assumption which unavoidably leads to the impasse of aesthetic formalism and to the myth of the "prison-house of language") or as a sort of pure aesthetic language at the fringe of the world and outside the dynamics of history is one that might probably describe the views held by Petrarch, for instance, or those forged by latter-day Romantics. In the *Divine Comedy* Dante reflects constantly and by necessity on poetry: this self-reflexiveness—as opposed to the presumed self-referentiality of language—does not mean the elision of the world of reality, nor does it sever poetry's contact with the world of history. For Dante, further, poetry does not even mimetically double existing discourses (theological, philosophical, political, etc.); it forever reaches into other disciplines and is entangled with other discourses, and yet it exceeds each of them.

The idea that in the *Divine Comedy* poetry embraces all the arts and disciplines and is constituted by their interaction is made manifest by Dante's dramatization of and explicit thinking on encyclopedias and their traditions. To illustrate this point I shall now look at two scenes: the representation of Limbo (*Inf.* IV) and the encounter with Brunetto Latini (*Inf.* XV). There is, let me say at the start, an overt disproportion between an encyclopedia's claim of representing totality and Dante's actual containment and discussion of the encyclopedic mode in discrete, partial narrative units. One infers that for Dante these representations of totality are bound to be defeated, for each representation appears to be but a synecdoche for that totality.

The description of the noble castle in Limbo has long been interpreted as the figuration of the medieval encyclopedia. While it has been fairly conventional to understand it allegorically as the place where natural philosophy is celebrated (Boccaccio) or the philosophy and sciences of antiquity are gathered, the Ottimo commento identifies the castle as philosophy circled by the seven liberal arts (from grammar to astrology—the word for music is missing) and the river that surrounds the castle as the diligence or disposition of the human intellect delighting in these arts: "e per questo vuol mostrare che scienziati erano, e che entrarono per tutte e sette liberali arti."[18] One can extend this commentator's insight, for the scene can be read as a monumental version of intellectual, pre-Christian, and non-Christian history.

The souls sheltered in Limbo are those of virtuous pagans: the wisdom and the magnanimity of the classical and non-Christian world—from Homer to Vergil to Lucretia to the Saladin—are now celebrated in the half-light of this pastoral self-enclosure. The reward for the intellectual and moral achievements of these souls is to be acknowledged and remembered, to have, as the text puts it, "onrata nominanza" (*Inf.* IV, 76)—honored fame. Appropriately, the canto dramatizes this reward: fame, which is the eternity of the name and which accounts for the desire for recognition beyond the boundaries of one's own time, is exactly what these spirits get as the canto turns into an epic catalog or roll call of biblical patriarchs and women and of the poets of Greek and Roman history and thought. The two strains are capped by a list of the most prominent figures in the history of philosophy, the sciences, politics, medicine, geometry, ethics, and so on: Aristotle, Socrates, Plato, Orpheus, Cicero, Galen, Avicenna, Averroes, and others.

But history in Limbo is not dramatized as an open-ended, dynamic reality; rather, it is reduced to the inscription of names, for fame is both the secular prefiguration of and the counterpoint to Christian eternity. At the same time the canto takes on the appearance of an imaginary library, a space where temporal differences among authors drawn from different ages are shattered, while their names are scrupulously written down. No doubt the canto primarily ackowledges the greatness of the past. Nonetheless, Dante's miniature representation of this atemporal imaginary library of the various branches of knowledge is placed at the edge, literally in a liminary position as if to dramatize the fact that all together these figures no longer play a central role in the determination of what for Dante constitutes true knowledge.

A number of dramatic details convey Dante's sure judgment of classical knowledge: Limbo is wrapped in darkness; the souls' knowledge is painfully incomplete in that they lack true knowledge of God; and they live, accordingly, in desire but without hope—two contradictory terms that suggest both unfulfillment and privation of a future wherein their desires might be satisfied. Moreover, the spiritual vision of the heathen sages has led them no farther than the knowledge possessed by unbaptized infants. These infants—and the irony in Dante's deployment of the word "infanti" (30) is made transparent by its etymology from *fari*, to speak—are ironically also housed in this moral area (35–36) as if deliberately to undercut and temper the likely impression of the sages' unqualified distinction.

Dante's ambivalent judgment of classical and non-Christian culture from the viewpoint of Christian theology cannot hide the fact, however, that the pilgrim's own spiritual quest in the beyond begins under the guidance of a soul who belongs to Limbo, Vergil. Vergil's mastery is steadily acknowledged: he is the "maestro e . . . autore" (*Inf.* I, 85) (master and author); later, he is called "savio gentil, che tutto seppe" (*Inf.* VII, 3) (the gentle sage who knew all). I stress, among all other formulas of praise with which Dante invests Vergil, the one from *Inferno* VII because it echoes Macrobius's definition of Vergil as an encyclopedic poet whose knowledge branches out into all directions of learning (*Saturnalia* V, I, 18–19). Above and beyond the vindication of the perennial, though limited, values of the classical tradition, which is embodied in the extraordinary and privileged role played by Vergil, Vergil's presence points to Dante's sense of the necessary transformation of the encyclopedia from a static, ahistorical, and crystallized ensemble to an authentic process of education. The pilgrim's process of education, as has been correctly argued, is the unifying drama of the poem, and its *telos* is the vision of God.[19]

In a way, Dante's emphasis on his spiritual education wills to test (the way Don Quixote, say, can be said to test the truth of the books he reads) the validity of the vast realm of objective encyclopedic knowledge at a time when he is seeking nothing less than his own spiritual salvation. It should also be stressed that the basis for the interaction between a subject's education and the objectivity of knowledge is a Platonic truism, which derives from the conviction that the individual shares in and reflects the great laws of the cosmos and which means that one knows oneself by knowing the world or, and the statement is the mirror image of the earlier one, that one knows the world only if one knows oneself. I shall examine further in chapter 7 the complexities in Dante's poetic representation of the question of subjectivity. For the time being, let me point out the rich historical, medieval traditions behind Dante's mixture of encyclopedic structure and the narrative of the education of self.

There are a number of encyclopedic and didactic poems which certainly stand behind Dante's imaginative elaborations of the questions of knowledge. Poems such as the *Romance of the Rose* and Neoplatonic allegories of education, such as the *Cosmographia* of Bernard Silvester or the *Anticlaudianus* of Alan of Lille, flagrantly enact the dramatic convergence of encyclopedic context and narratives of education.[20] Even a text such as St. Augustine's *Confessions*, which overtly tells the story of a spiritual *paideia*, owes much to the tradition of the liberal arts. The narrative of the *Confessions*, to begin with, is punctuated, first, by the young Augustine's schooling in grammar—Greek and Latin (above all the *Aeneid*, which in the Neoplatonic allegorizations of Bernard Silvester, Fulgentius, and Dante himself in *Convivio* is understood also as a parable of the hero's education). He journeys to Madaura—he tells us in book II of the *Confessions*—to learn grammar and rhetoric, till at sixteen he leaves school for a while.

After achieving great distinction in eloquence (book III), Augustine falls upon a certain book of Cicero, which is called the "Hortensius" and which is an exhortation to philosophy, which he says, repeating a commonplace, is "the love of wisdom." Augustine will eventually become a professor of rhetoric, and during this period (book IV) he consults the mathematicians or astrologers, those who revel in the vanity of superstition and who, in their practice, place the fates of men in the stars. In due course he comes to find out how insufficient in themselves are the categories of secular knowledge and how they need to relate to theology. As in *De doctrina christiana*, where secular learning is taken to be a necessary preliminary instruction to the interpretation of the Bible, in the *Confessions* the arts are propaedeutics to the exegesis of the book of Genesis, with which the autobiographical novel comes to a close.

The *Romance of the Rose*, the *Cosmographia*, and the *Anticlaudianus* are all texts of education, and, as I shall soon show, they are central to Dante's conceptualization of encyclopedic poetry.[21] The *Romance of the Rose* of Guillaume tells the story of the education of Amant in the whole art of love or, as Poirion puts it, his sexual initiation;[22] the second part by Jean de Meun, on the other hand, recounts and digresses over the wide range of medieval thought and science (from Macrobius to Albert the Great) in an effort to mime the "systeme du monde"—cosmology, the moral virtues, the scholastic debates at the university of Paris, views held by Guillaume de Saint-Amour, mythography, and so forth.[23] On the other hand, the

Cosmographia and the *Anticlaudianus*, for all the profound differences between them, are here mentioned together as instances of cosmological poetry in that together they represent and conceptualize questions of matter,
creation, cosmic process, energy, and the turbulent and contradictory role
of man within the harmony of God's creation.

Bernard Silvester's *Cosmographia* tells primarily about Nature's fashion-
ing of man. The Platonic creation myth Bernard envisions is well known.
Nature, child of divine Providence and the principle of life, begs Nous to
give the shape of life to Silva or Hyle, which stands for unformed materiality. After the creation of the universe, the poem tells the story of the fash-
ioning of the *microcosmos*. From our point of view, *Megacosmos* (I, 3) draws
a broad and inclusive picture of the firmament as a book of ciphers to be
explicated: all the events of history are inscribed in this cosmic order, "For
that sequence of events which ages to come and the measured course of
time will wholly unfold has a prior existence in the stars. There are the
scepter of Phoroneus, the conflict of the brothers at Thebes, the flames of
Phaeton, Deucalion's flood. . . . In the stars Vergil composes with grace,
. . . Egypt gives birth to the arts, learned Greece reads, Rome wages war.
Plato intuits the principles of existence, . . . A tender virgin gives birth to
Christ, at once the idea and the embodiment of God, and earthly existence
realizes true divinity."[24]

The providential order of the cosmos never strays far from God's grace.
To complete the original ordering of creation, however, man is needed,
and his creation brings nature itself into a new focus. Bernard, who seeks
to fathom the metaphysical principle of coherence of the cosmos in its
perennial antinomies of disintegration and order, instability and purpose,
explicitly dramatizes the dilemma of two contrary perspectives in which
man is caught. There is, on the one hand, Urania's perspective according
to which man's discipline takes place in the realm of intelligence. Her
speech to Nature is the epitome of her vision of man: "The human soul
must be guided by me through all the realms of heaven, that it may have
knowledge of the laws of the fates, and inexorable destiny, and the shifting
of unstable fortune; what occurrences are wholly open to the determination of will, what is subject to uncertain accident; how, by the power of
memory, she may recall many of these things which she sees, being not
wholly without recollection" (II, 4). On the other hand, as Wetherbee has
eloquently argued, man is implicated in the contingency of a recalcitrant
materiality, which goes contrary to Urania's summons to man's intellectual
perfection and self-dominion.[25]

Alan of Lille's *Anticlaudianus*, finally, tells the story of Nature's effort to
produce the perfect new man. Written against the backdrop of the *Plaint
of Nature*, in which man appears a corrupt creature, the *Anticlaudianus* focuses on the cosmic enterprise of regeneration and the restoration of man's

prefallen state. The new man will have a new body and a new soul, but, whereas his body is made of the four elements (and Alan's dependence on the rational naturalism of Bernard Silvester has long been acknowledged), the soul must come from God. In order to form the new man's soul, Prudence (Phronesis) undertakes a journey to heaven in a chariot prepared by the seven liberal arts.[26] Under the guidance of Reason, Prudence reaches the stars (the domain of astronomy), but true knowledge is provided by theology and by faith, through which the vision of God is granted.

I have described at such length these encyclopedic-didactic poems for a couple of reasons. First, these poems present a mixture of individual education and objective encyclopedic structure, which is also Dante's imaginative resolution. Second, they clearly shape *Inferno* XV, a canto that features Dante's overt reflection on and judgment of a certain type of encyclopedic and didactic literature. I have examined the canto from a somewhat different perspective in *Dante, Poet of the Desert,* and I complement now that reading from the narrow angle of my present concerns.[27] In *Inferno* XV, the canto of the sodomites who have violated the norms of nature, the pilgrim meets his teacher, Brunetto Latini.

The conversation between teacher and disciple ranges from politics (the violence of the civil war in Florence) to the lasting role of Brunetto in Dante's education to less overt questions of intellectual allegiances.[28] But their exchange is not so narrowly academic. Brunetto Latini, the teacher of eloquence and, according to Filippo Villani, of philosophy, and of what could somewhat anachronistically be called civic humanism, translates these questions in terms of his and his disciple's personal experiences. But a mere list of their topics of conversation can never convey the emotional intensity of their encounter.

The pilgrim proudly acknowledges his discipleship to Brunetto and his abiding faithfulness to the memory of that teaching (*Inf.* XV, 79–85); Brunetto, in turn, twice addresses Dante as "son" (31, 37). More than that, when Brunetto asks Dante by what chance or fate he fell down into that pit before his death (46–48), Dante responds that he went astray in a valley and is now being led home (49–54). Brunetto radically misunderstands the purpose and goal of Dante's journey and language. He predicts that, if Dante were to follow his star, he would reach a glorious port (55–57). Unlike Dante, Brunetto lives intellectually in a world of chance occurrences, astrological determinations, and blind fatalities. But the extensive discrepancies between their respective vocabularies ("glory" is certainly earthly fame for Brunetto, but for Dante it has an irreducibly theological resonance; "home" is Florence for one and heaven for the other, etc.) point primarily to the *limit* of personal experience in the act of knowledge. Whereas Ser Brunetto seems intent on establishing an illusory symmetry between his own and Dante's life experience, Dante abandons the teacher's formula-

tions: for him the world is not and cannot be limited to the absolute measure of one's own life and one's own theoretical constructions of it; there
always exist other realms of discourse just beyond one's own experience.

As has so often been remarked, Dante's lines on his going astray in a
valley, which recapitulate the opening verses of the poem, deliberately
echo the beginning of Brunetto Latini's *Tesoretto*.[29] The didactic allegory
of that autobiographical poem recounts Brunetto's exile from the city and
his own educational quest through the stations of the liberal arts for the
intellectual principles of a new order under the guidance of the allegorical
figure of Nature.[30] Nature, which figuratively is shored up with the idiom
and conceptual resonances of Nature from Alan of Lille's *Plaint of Nature*
as well as Lady Philosophy from *The Consolation of Philosophy*, leads
Brunetto through the garden of blindfolded Love and to Science
(Ptolomy). By his response to Dante, Brunetto, himself an object of varieties of dislocations—linguistic, political, and so on—ironically enough
now locates his disciple within the circumscribed horizon of his own
problematics and concerns. He is blind, therefore, to the particularity and
uniqueness of Dante's own subjectivity, which is bound to remain inaccessible to Brunetto. Quite unsurprisingly, given his claims of mastery, by the
end of the canto Brunetto recommends to the pilgrim that he read his
Tesoro (119). This imperative of knowledge and of its necessity wills to
draw Dante within the circle of Brunetto's understanding of knowledge—
knowledge as an encyclopedic system, as the system is embodied by the
Tresor. The *Tresor*, it could be said, is the logical and necessary counterpart
of the *Tesoretto*. If the *Tesoretto* tells the parable of one's own education, the
Tresor, on the other hand, maps the coherence and organization of the
sciences. Dante subjects both to a rigorous critique.

The *Tresor*'s point of departure is the tabulation of knowledge as well as
an account of the text's own organization.[31] The work is divided into three
books. The first book, which falls under the aegis of theoretical philosophy
in that it seeks to grasp the nature of earthly and heavenly realities (theology, physics, and mathematics) surveys the creation of the world and man,
salvation, history, and natural history. The second book belongs to the
practical and logical sphere of philosophy and deals with ethics, economics, and politics. Brunetto also includes in this sphere all the mechanical
arts and the arts of language—grammar, dialectics, and rhetoric. The third
part of practical philosophy, says Brunetto, is logic, which he differentiates
as dialectics, "efidic" (which I take to be the logic of laws), and sophistical
logic. But the the final book of the *Tresor* treats politics as rhetoric and as
the art of government.

Brunetto's organization of the sciences, though it does not deploy a qua-
ternary schematization of knowledge, can still be called Aristotelian. For
he alters and absorbs the more traditional Platonic model of dividing phi-

losophy into three parts—physics, ethics, and logic—by suggesting a division into theoretical, practical, mechanical, and logical. In effect the *Tresor*, with its sense of the importance of the practical arts but without the attention to Arab learning that had entered the West in the twelfth century and that characterizes the Dominican Vincent of Beauvais's *Speculum*, was written under the influence of the Chartrian didascalic texts such as the *Didascalicon* and the *Heptateuchon* as well as humanistic, Ciceronian works such as Alcuin's *Dialogus de rhetorica et virtutibus* and John of Salisbury's *Policraticus*.

Dante's own tabulation of knowledge, as the "encyclopedic" *Paradiso* cantos XII make clear and my chapter 10 below suggests, brings to mind, rather, St. Bonaventure's *De reductione artium ad theologiam*. Bonaventure's "reductio" is to be understood in the sense of a circle, as a circular movement of the soul back to its point of origin and its "home": the work, in fact, articulates a theory of knowledge that embraces the mechanical arts, philosophy (natural philosophy; rational philosophy, which is subdivided into grammar, logic, and rhetoric; and moral philosophy), and, finally, theology, whereby the soul follows the hidden footprints that lead to God. In a way, the theological view of wisdom is the perspective from which Dante mounts a critique of Brunetto's educational ideas. Yet if Dante's critique of knowledge were simply theological, it would be a radical but ultimately predictable, and thus not very interesting, procedure. Dante's critique is powerful because he finds Brunetto's educational ideas intrinsically self-contradictory.

The narrative of *Inferno* XV opens with an evocation of the chaotic, uncontrollable powers of nature: the embankments of this ditch of Hell resemble, the text says, the dikes built by the Flemish between Wissant and Bruges to hold off the destructive fury of the sea as well as those built by the Paduans along the Brenta to protect their towns from the floods. The opening image epitomizes both the overriding energy and disorder of nature and, at least on the face of it, projects sodomy as one form in a larger configuration of the chaos and anarchy of nature. But the image also serves to insinuate a juxtaposition between the allegorical representations of the majesty, fertility, and benevolence of nature (which Brunetto Latini had endorsed and celebrated in the wake of Chartrian rational naturalism) and Dante's sense of the potential destructiveness of nature.

At the same time, it would seem that Brunetto misunderstands another aspect of nature. It can be said that just as his simplified myth of a benevolent nature is a chimera, so his pursuit of an encyclopedic knowledge, which would contain the totality of traditional knowledge, is an impractical and fanciful construction. Patently enough, the claim of a total knowledge is a logical contradiction because it reduces knowledge to a static and sterile ensemble and excludes the possibility of augmenting it. This exclusion amounts to a misunderstanding of the openness of history and time. Within this context one can grasp the sense of Dante's representation of Brunetto as a figure who narcissistically stresses his priority over his disciple, who can come to terms with his disciple's destiny only as a version of his own, and who believes that Dante's extraordinay adventure is already written in Brunetto's own script. And there is a dramatic link, finally, between Brunetto's idea of nature and his ideas of the arts.

As a matter of fact, *Inferno* XV dramatizes the failure of a natural theory of education. Many are the arts and discourses represented here: rhetoric and politics are embodied by Brunetto; his speech is punctuated by astrological references; in addition, the names of two other sinners, among the the clerks and scholars who have violated the norms of nature, the Latin grammmarian Priscian and the jurist Francesco d'Accorso (106–14), signal the presence of various arts—a summary recapitulation of knowledge's division in the *Tresor*—and all together they point to Dante's insight into the metaphysical ground of Brunetto's educational concept. Like rhetoric and politics, grammar and law are arts whose common scope is the ordering of experience according to the principle of imitating nature's abstract order. Alan of Lille's representation of sexual perversions in terms of grammatical errors in the *Plaint of Nature* is too well-known a case of sustained metaphoric relationship between grammar and the ideal order of nature. At the same time, John of Salisbury in his *Metalogicon* (I, 2) stresses how nature is the mother of all the arts and how grammar, though arbitrary and subject to man's discretion, still imitates nature and conforms to it in all respects (I, 14). The universe of nature for Dante is the ground of the arts, but he eschews any idea of mechanical imitation between nature and the arts.

There is another perspective from which Dante critically rethinks and revives the tradition of the encyclopedic project. In effect, Brunetto's and the encyclopedic texts of the thirteenth century were bound to appear to Dante as a symptom of mere nostalgia for a unified culture at a critical time when that spiritual unity was about to disintegrate. The suspicion that encyclopedias were for Dante at once reflections of the perceived unity of knowledge and nostalgic retrievals of a mythical wholeness of knowledge is made plausible by the realities of the intellectual crisis in the thirteenth century, which I shall document as I go along. Dante brought about the resurgence of this tradition. And he did it in the only way that the retrieval was possible—not by choosing one of the conventional and trite options between Aristotelian and Platonic modes of knowledge, but by unleashing the poetic imagination. It is the distinctive trait of his poetry to acknowledge that unity is made up of heterogeneous entities.

It is usually believed that in the Renaissance, with its emphasis on knowledge as both subjectivity and as an adventurous, open-ended discovery, encylopedias could no longer be produced, and that one had to wait for a more reflective time, when knowledge was understood not as a definitive totality but as organically branching out like a tree (such, of course, is the implication of the *arbor scientiae*); one had to wait, it is said, for what is called the Baroque period, when knowledge folded up on itself and compendia were produced, to witness the resurgence of the genre. But the *Divine Comedy*, with its double structure, first, of miming the order and harmony of creation and, second, of providing a paradigm of the ongoing adventure of the soul's growth, embodies the principle of knowledge as radically historical.

As will be seen in the next chapters, Dante's poem is organized by a steady pattern of references to the disciplines of the curriculum—the liberal arts, ethics, and theology. But what makes all knowledge come alive, as I have been arguing in this first chapter, is poetry, which for Dante is neither simply mimetic-icastic (as Aristotle would have it) nor simply fantastic (as Platonists would say). Poetry for Dante has the double, paradoxical nature of being both mimetic and visionary. Yet, for all of Dante's bold efforts to join together the various arts through the sheer force of his poetry, a disjunction does exist between vision and the knowledge available through the arts of discourse.

Dante's visionariness sets his imaginative venture—and in this he recalls both Bernard and Alan—beyond the boundaries of rational knowledge, and it comes to a focus in his "mad" quest for a face-to-face vision of God as well as in his gift of poetry to us. His gift is his insight into poetry's unique privilege as the space of man's invention and man's freedom, wherein the poet can make assertions about the very foundation of the world and can, if he so chooses, transgress those assertions; it is a gift by which he calls on us to have a vision of ourselves in the world, which depends on what we have decided our purposes in the world to be. This sort of poetry or poetic theology, which reflects on and opens up what is calcified or forgotten within the fold of discursive languages, also suggests that all knowledge may be imaginary and that the consistency of the objective world may be a mere poetic figment. This doubleness of poetry makes it the imaginative prolongation of the ever-ambiguous realities of the world of history.

Chapter 2

SACRIFICE AND GRAMMAR

(*PARADISO* III, IV, V)

SINCE THE WORK of Smalley, de Lubac, and Chenu, we are familiar with the polemic which developed in the thirteenth century between the theologians and the biblical exegetes.[1] In essence, the debate revolved around the problem of how to situate the Bible within the larger scheme of the intellectual disciplines, without going so far as to question or misconstrue its fundamental authority. The exegetes took the Scholastics to task for their emphasis on systematic theology. In their view, the theologians' attempt to rationalize and to establish norms for grasping the truths contained in the *doctrina sacra* in point of fact subordinated the Word of God to profane sciences such as grammar and logic. With their dialectical artifices and formal investigations—so went the exegetes' argument—the theologians were guilty of nothing less than trivializing the unfathomable complexity of salvation history.

The debate about the place of the Bible in "the medieval world" is infinitely more complex than the above paragraph suggests. Some critical problems, for instance, lie, first, in the recognition of the *Hebraica veritas*, which concretely addresses the dependence of Christian exegetes, who knew no Hebrew, on Jewish commentators in order to figure out the literal meaning of biblical passages; second, there was a desire by the Christian fathers to emancipate themselves from that dependence on rabbinical commentaries.[2] But even so summarily sketched, the polemic constitutes itself as a variation on the questions raised in the twelfth century at St. Victor, where Hugh, Richard, or a Hebraist such as Andrew of St. Victor restored and gave renewed impulse to the practice of biblical exegesis, subordinating the encyclopedic entirety of the human sciences to the sovereign authority of biblical hermeneutics. Texts such as Hugh of St. Victor's *Didascalicon* and Honorius of Autun's *De animae exsilio et patria* exemplify the belief in the liberal arts as preparatory to the reading of the Bible.[3]

The Victorines' project was one of extraordinary clarity. They vehemently opposed the abstract, formal problematics of logicians and theologians in the conviction that such speculations made short shrift of empirical phenomena and of the concreteness and particularities of history. Because they were faithful to the Augustinian legacy of history and symbolic thinking, the Victorines' gesture of opposition was to reintroduce into their schematizations of knowledge and into their criteria of exegesis the *ordo historiae*, the categories of time and nature, and the sense of the necessity to come to terms with the material contents of the text (they consulted the Hebrew orginal). Indeed, they went so far as to articulate the principles of symbolic representation (which have come to be known as "Victorine esthetics"), thus drawing theological discourse away from subtle ratiocinations into a universe of tangible actualities and expressions.[4]

The thirteenth century, to be sure, did not mark a total abandonment of the Bible as an object of knowledge. Rather, the matter was, as believed the biblicist Hugh of St. Cher, that of an evolution of method. The exclusive adherence to the limitless resonances of the scriptures, which character- ized patristic exegesis, underwent modification and diversification. One might still complain that the structure of Scholastic arguments, with the focus on the rigors of schematic procedures of speculation and disputation, bypassed what, pragmatically speaking, were the factual contents of the Bible. Yet—and this is more like the shadow of an unspoken suspicion falling across the page—the theologians were certainly justified in their search for a rational systematization of the data of the Revelation. For they felt the need both to harmonize reason and revelation and to respond to what they perceived as the interpretive crisis produced by the stubborn contradictions inherent in the biblical text.

Many were the exegetical disputes aiming to establish which of the four possible senses of the Bible—the historical, the allegorical, the tropologi- cal, and the anagogical, or all four—should be applied to various passages of the text. At the same time the catalog of *sic et non* compiled by Abelard, much like Bacon's call for a thorough knowledge of grammar (specifically of Hebrew and Greek, which Sigo, to mention one, had come to know well) and for a recovery of the biblical text in its philological and grammat- ical integrity, is symptomatic of the crisis enveloping biblical exegesis.[5] A caveat is again necessary to temper the impression of a sharp rift between theologians and exegetes. Abelard, in a commentary on the Epistle to the Romans (where St. Paul takes to task the philosophers), says that he does not want to be a "philosopher opposed to Paul," nor an Aristotle separated from Christ.[6] At the same time, both Albert the Great and St. Thomas Aquinas, for all their commitment to a rational systematization of theol- ogy, wrote commentaries, respectively, on the prophets and the Gospels.

In this chapter I do not wish so much to track the tortured windings of the conflict—amply treated by Smalley and de Lubac—between theologi- ans and exegetes, between, say, Abelard and St. Bernard, as to focus on the ways in which this polemic shapes the opening cantos of *Paradiso*. This is not to suggest that in the Heaven of the Moon Dante writes a descriptive sketch of these methodological intrigues; rather, these references consti-

tute the exact context and the means by which Dante vindicates the epistemological value of grammar in theological formulations. More precisely,
in the Heaven of the Moon there comes to light a poetic discourse on
sacrifice which involves the reflections of the theologians and which also
defers, as we shall see, to the ceremonies of sacrificial practices in the Bible.
Finally, I shall argue that the meaning of sacrifice, which is understood as
both a literal and a symbolic action, can be best grasped from the perspective of grammar, the art of discourse which in *Convivio* Dante assigns to the
Heaven of the Moon.

For the sake of clarity I would like to quickly review the salient moments
in the dramatics of cantos III–V of *Paradiso*. The text primarily records the
pilgrim's encounter with Piccarda and the empress Costanza in *Paradiso* II
and III. Piccarda was a nun, under the name of Costanza, and was forced
by her brother Corso Donati to leave the cloister and marry. Costanza was
the mother of the emperor Frederick II and grandmother of Manfred (who
appeared in the corresponding canto III of *Purgatorio*), and according to
the legend she, too, was removed from the cloister in order that she marry
the emperor Henry. Because of their broken vows both of them now exult
in the quiet splendor of the moon. It is inevitable, in a context in which the
poem dramatizes the two nuns' broken promises, to remark how the name
"Costanza" calls attention to the downright reversal of its sense and how,
in a symbolic imitation of her inconstancy, Piccarda passes in silence her
name in the cloister and refers to herself as Piccarda, "I'fui nel mondo
vergine sorella; / e se la mente tua ben sé riguarda, / non mi ti celerà l'esser
più bella, / ma riconoscerai ch'i' son Piccarda, / che posta qui con questi
altri beati, / beata sono in la spera più tarda" (*Par.* III, 46–51) (In the world
I was a virgin sister, and if you search well in your memory, my being more
fair will not hide me from thee, but you will know me again for Piccarda,
who am put here with these other blest and am blessed in the slowest of the
spheres). This self-definition primarily exploits the attributes of the moon
as both chaste Diana and as the shifty planet.

But there is a further irony contained in the name. For Costanza, textually, discloses the temporality of the promise in the sense that the promise,
which is an illocutionary act which promises constancy, entails the foreclosure of the flow of time. To make a promise, in fact, is to be engaged in an
act that projects one's future as the realm under the control of one's present will. The experience of the two women, however, dramatizes the collapse of the promise, and Piccarda's account goes on to trace the reasons
for the failure of her pledge: "Dal mondo, per seguirla, giovinetta /
fuggi'mi, e nel suo abito mi chiusi / e promisi la via de la sua setta. / Uomini
poi, a mal più ch'a bene usi, / fuor mi rapiron de la dolce chiostra: / Iddio
si sa qual poi mia vita fusi" (*Par.* III, 103–08) (To follow her I fled, a young
girl, from the world and wrapped me in her habit and promised myself to

the way of her order. Then men more used to evil than to good snatched me from the sweet cloister. God knows what my life was then).

What Piccarda's account imaginatively summons back is the sort of malignancy, the delirious chronicles of evil, that we have steadily witnessed in *Inferno*. To be reminded in *Paradiso* of domestic violence and of the fragility of sanctuary is to grasp that Dante's Paradise is neither a visionary utopia nor the lotusland of earth. History, its sinister machinations and its complex ambiguities, stands forever at the center of Dante's poetic concerns. Corso's intrusion into the boundaries of the cloister brings with it a world of politics in which men establish alliances, seal contracts, exert their mastery; and in the process it unveils the rude pageants of power as the tragic action of history. More to the issue at hand, Corso's anarchic will—he possesses his sister and disposes of her at will (and, ironically, Piccarda is a sister who had abdicated her will)—and his conviction of the limitlessness of his power are the dramatic backdrop for the exchange between Dante and Beatrice.

On account of Piccarda's and Costanza's inconstancy to their order, as well as their presence in the lowest level of beatitude, the pilgrim puts two questions to Beatrice (*Par.* IV, 16–27). The first dwells on the apparently incongruous relation between fault and desert (Piccarda's low rank of beatitude seems due to the violence perpetrated upon her by others and not the product of her wrongdoing). Dante pointedly asks why, if a man's will never sways from its resolve but is coerced to alter its course by "la violenza altrui" (20) (by somebody else's violence)—why should the measure of one's merit be lessened. In a hierarchical system wherein everything has a place and the place of a thing implies value, the question at its most general focuses on the literalness of the ranking, and this is, in effect, what Beatrice will eventually undertake to explain.

The pilgrim's second question seeks to explore further the apparent hierarchy of beatitude enjoyed by the elect and touches on the problematics of representation in the *Paradiso*. Dante asks if the spectacle of the blessed in the heavens coincides with the truth, that is, if the Platonic *reditus animae* is to be taken as literally true, or whether the spectacle of the souls showing themselves forth in the stars is an allegorical *adaptatio*, a condescencion or accommodation of these events, as those of scripture, to the limits of man's intellectual faculties. Beatrice recognizes that, of the two questions, the one about the relative authenticity of the representation "più ha di felle" (*Par.* IV, 27) (has more gall), while the other "ha men velen" (*Par.* IV, 65) (is less envenomed). Why is the question about representation referred to as being more poisonous than the other? What is the logical link, if any, between the two questions? Beatrice will not linger on these seemingly lateral issues; rather, she proceeds to answer the pilgrim's two questions with punctilious precision, discussing first the theological structure of vows and promises, whether or not they can be dispensed or commuted, and how the authority of the church is required for the reparation of broken pledges.

Her intricate discourse overtly resembles the logical movement of a theological argument. Thus, she starts her exposition with a view of God, who, in his bounty, bestows the greatest gift ("lo maggior don," *Par.* V, 19—the greater gift) to man. The gift is "de la volontà la libertate" (22), the *libertas arbitrii*—a faculty of will and judgement—which is the stamp of rationality angels and men alike share and which is to be understood as a perfection which inspires a man to follow the promptings of God.[7] Within this framework of God's liberality the vow—the "voto"—is primarily a restitution of the gift, an act which establishes a covenant between God and man; the covenant is sanctioned by the sacrifice of free will: "nel fermar tra Dio e l'omo il patto, / vittima fassi di questo tesoro" (28–29) (in the very closing of the pact between man and God, this precious thing is made a victim). That what is consummated in the alliance is a sacrifice is stressed a few lines down in the canto when Beatrice refers to the pledge as a sacrifice, "l'essenza / di questo sacrificio" (42–43) (the essence of this sacrifice).

The shift from the vocabulary of gifts to that of sacrifice to describe free will is not arbitrary: the grammar of Beatrice's language, actually, recalls the standard distinctions available even in Isidore of Seville's *Etymologies*. After contrasting *dona* and *munera*, Isidore juxtaposes *donum* to *sacrificium*: "Donum dicitur quidquid auro argentoque aut qualibet alia specie efficitur. Sacrificium autem est victima et quaecumque in ara cremantur seu ponentur" (*Etym.* VI, xix, 30–38) (A gift is what is presented in gold and silver or in whatever other form; but sacrifice is the victim and whatever is put or immolated on the altar). But for Dante the sacrifice functions as an offering of the will and, as such, the word "sacrificio" carries the same meaning it has in *Purgatorio* XI, 10–12: "Come del suo voler li angeli tuoi / fan sacrificio a te, cantando osanna, / cosi facciano li uomini de' suoi" (As your angels make sacrifice to you of their will, singing Hosanna, so let men make of theirs).

The dramatic linking of the cluster of words—vow, will, and sacrifice— is made possible by one of the two etymologies of the Latin word *votum*, and the conceptual and linguistic field of this stretch of Dante's text, in effect, is organized around the etymological resonances of *votum*. Etymology, which is a category of grammar, provides the impetus for the analysis of vows by St. Thomas Aquinas, who, picking up the definition and inquiry on vows by Peter Lombard, affirms that a vow is "testificatio quaedam promissionis spontaneae, quae Deo et de his quae sunt Dei, fieri debet" (a spontaneous promise, a free act of the will dedicated to God). But his first point is that "the word 'vow' [*votum*] derives from the word for will [*voluntas*], and a man is said to do *proprio voto*, on his own, what he does voluntarily. Therefore a vow consists only in act of will. But to aim is an act of will, while to promise is an act of reason."[8] To be sure, the will, as St. Thomas goes on to argue, moves reason to promise, and his conclusion is that three things are required for a vow: deliberation, resolution of the will, and the promise, "in qua perficitur ratio voti."

From the perspective of St. Thomas's theological musings one can easily understand why the vow is explicitly described as a promise in *Paradiso* III, 105: "e promisi la via de la sua setta" (and I pledged me to the pathway of her sect). Even more one can understand the reason for the canto's insistent discusssion of vows in terms of will. We read, thus, of the "volontà": "se non vuol s'ammorza" (*Par.* IV, 76) (nothing can quench the unconsenting will). Equally clear are Beatrice's references to "volere intero" (*Par.* IV, 82) (whole will) as well as the "salda voglia" (87) (steadfast will) exhibited by St. Lawrence and by the heroism of Mutius Scaevola (82–84). These terms of distinction in the operations and forms of will stage and further articulate the semantic possibilities contained in the etymology of *votum*. The same etymological principle supports the distinction between absolute will (*Par.* IV, 109 and 113), which is the distinctive trait of the heroic temper and never wavers, and the relative, contingent will, which yields to coercion.

The unconditional, strenuous determination of the will is embodied, then, by two Romans: by Lawrence, who endured unto death the pagan persecutions, and by Mucius, who burned his right hand in fire to punish it for its failure to kill Porsenna. In either case the heroic experience, of which the absolute will is the emblem, is to be understood as the knowledge that the sense of one's life is to be sought in one's loyalties and principled actions. Through the example of the two Romans who adhered to their principles, we are told that, to put it in Augustinian terms, we are nothing if not our wills and that it is a grave misconception to attribute one's failures not to oneself but to outside forces. This is the specifically Roman trait of Dante's vision, whereby factors that condition one's assent or dissent from options are translated into the responsibility of one's will.

There is in *Paradiso* IV an obvious fascination with heroic action as a means of transcending the ordinary limits of the will. This fascination reverses Dante's undoing of the heroic myths in, say, *Inferno* XXVIII. As we shall see in chapter 4, the tragic world of Bertran de Born is shaped by a heroic illusion and by the rhetoric of blood deployed by his own war songs. Yet visible underneath Bertran's heroic illusion lies death's destructiveness: his death is stripped of its mythic aura, though Bertran likes us to believe that his suffering is disproportionate to his deeds, that his death makes tragic, not moral, sense. In *Paradiso* IV, however, the heroic energy of Lawrence and Mucius is upheld. In the light of their absolute will, it can be said that there is a moral failure in Piccarda and Costanza, for they both acquiesced to abide in what could have been only a provisional, though severe, test of affliction. But Dante, who certainly is not a poet given to compromises, makes allowances for their limited commitment to their pledge. In the absence of self-pity, in their absolute will, in their constant affection for the veil, Piccarda and Costanza are two heroic figures, whose appeasement can be construed as a rebuke to the savagery they have previously suffered.

Heroic action for Dante is preferable to the wavering of the will, yet he knows how action can issue into a tragic predicament. Piccarda's inaction is explained, in fact, by another grievous ceremony of violence (*Par.* IV, 100–102). Dante evokes the Theban myth of Alcmaeon, who, to avenge his father Amphiarus (*Inf.* XX, 31–36), who had been betrayed by his wife, kills his mother: "per non perder pietà si fè spietato" (*Par.* IV, 105) (not to fail in piety, he became pitiless). This story of tragic revenge again brings us imaginatively to the heart of hell, for it conjures up the satanic world of traitors, figures who by their actions declare the emptiness of all bonds. Avengers are esthetes of violence, in that they are victims of nostalgia who yield to the desire to restore the old order. More than that, the point of recalling the mythical Alcmaeon is to dramatize the paradoxical moral consequences of absolute actions: Alcmaeon's grief turns into cruelty and his pity into pitilessness. So notorius in antiquity was the moral quagmire of Alcmaeon that Aristotle, reflecting on voluntary and involuntary actions in his *Ethics* (III, 1), directs his attention to it and judges the circumstances compelling Alcmaeon to kill as patently absurd. Dante, on the other hand, views the myth as a crystallization of the moral contradictions engendered by actions: there are discrepancies for him even within the absolute will just as there are no direct equivalences between vows and their literal observance.

The elaborate discussion of the absolute and contingent will which takes up *Paradiso* IV turns explicitly to a theological exposition of the sacrifice of free will. The logical quandary Beatrice now confronts is the following: the promissory character of the vow seems merely to entail the hard knowledge that promises and vows are not always kept; yet man is nonetheless bound to fulfill the obligation contracted with God. There are two things, Beatrice explains, that constitute what she calls "l'essenza di questo sacrificio" (*Par.* V, 42–43): "l'una è quella / che si fa, l'altra è la convenenza. / Quest'ultima già mai non si cancella / se non servata" (43–47) (The essence of the sacrifice includes two things: one is the thing promised, the other is the covenant itself; this last one is never canceled, if not by being kept). Whereas the covenant, as the formal bond between God and man, can never be abrogated, the material offering is subject to change. The historical precedent for the substitution of material is to be found in the Bible: "peró necessitato fu a li Ebrei / pur l'offerere, ancor ch'alcuna offerta / si permutasse, come saver dei" (*Par.* V, 49–51) (Therefore it was imperative upon the Hebrews to offer sacrifice in any case, though the thing offered might sometimes be changed, as you should know).

The allusion is to Leviticus, the rigorous codification of God's promises to and somber vigilance over Israel, which is expressed through a glaringly contractual language: "If you walk in my statutes and observe my commandments and do them, then I will give you your rains in their season, and the land shall yield their fruit. . . . And . . . if you walk contrary to me . . . I will bring a sword upon you, that shall execute vengeance for the covenant" (Leviticus 26:3–21). But if the pact, to continue with the logic of Leviticus, is violated, there is the shekel of silver for the sanctuary, the money to be paid to the temple to redeem the unkept pledge: "When a man makes a special vow of persons to the Lord . . . then your valuation of a male from twenty years old up to sixty years old shall be fifty shekels of silver. . . . When a man dedicates his house to be holy to the Lord, the priest shall value it as either good or bad; as the priest values it, so it shall stand. And if he who dedicates it wishes to redeem his house, he shall add a fifth of the valuation in money to it, and it shall be his" (Leviticus 27:1–15).

The main purpose of this text from Leviticus is to dramatize the compact between man and God as a literalized, quantifiable order in which facts and values, promises and observances, words and deeds are bound together in a code of absolute coherence. In the statutes and laws which the Lord makes between himself and Israel there is an exact pricing for all substitutions. From one point of view it can be said that Dante, much like Leviticus, systematically punctuates his discussion on vows with metaphors of legal contracts and economic exchanges. The word "patto" (*Par.* V, 28), to begin with, means, according to Cicero, "conventum" and "lex." The pilgrim wonders, furthermore, whether or not a broken vow may be paid with other services as may secure the soul from suit (*Par.* V, 13–15); at the same time, we are told that man is endowed with God's gift of free will, which itself is a "tesoro" of incomparable worth. The immolation of one's free will is placed within a contractual system guaranteed by God and consistently disrupted by man.

The most urgent dramatic principle in these cantos of the First Heaven—as is revealed by the rhetoric of appropriate exchange—is the principle of equivalence. The thematics of pacts, legal contracts, exchanges of gifts between God and man, and possible permutations and correspondences of value is, as I have been stressing, explicit. But the metaphorical order of equivalences is turned upside down by the antithetical awareness of the consequences attendant upon the faithfulness to promises, as is made clear by the fates of Alcmaeon, Iphigenia, and Jephthah's daughter.[9] Even the metaphorical universe of Piccarda's and Costanza's promises reveals its fragility. The interruption of their seclusion is a crude illustration of the impossibility of imposing closure on the mobility of time. Dante, then, overtly dramatizes his conviction that the literal pattern of values set forth in the biblical text is inadequate.

The reference to the heroic will of Lawrence in *Paradiso* IV (83) exemplifies Dante's distance from Leviticus. The martyrdom of Lawrence by the emperor Valerian occupies a central role in Christian spirituality from Ambrose to Jacobus da Varagine's *Legenda aurea*. But it is above all in Prudentius's *Peristephanon liber* that the passion of this martyr is told in great detail.[10] Lawrence is said to be the keeper of the treasure of the church, and when he is asked by Valerian for the treasure, he presents the poor of the church—the spiritual jewels with which she decks herself. Lawrence's gesture is dismissed as theatrical buffoonery, as a piece of entertainment by a pantomime. But for Prudentius, Lawrence's death is an experience of self-possession in the presence of his enemies' covetousness for literal, material riches. As much for Prudentius as for Dante, value is not a function of literalized quantities: on the contrary, a word such as "treasure" carries radically contrasting senses for Valerian and for Lawrence.

Beatrice's explanation of the will, promises, and vows, then, is characterized primarily by the awareness of a legal code or covenants that regulate them, but the binding legalism of the contract is countered by and is poised against the experience of broken pledges, of actions with tragic consequences, of values which cannot be taken literally, and of perplexities as to what are adequate substitutions for unkept promises. Her exposition, one can say, is marked by an oscillation between what is literal and what is metaphorical. This doubleness is made manifest by the two exhortations in which she warns man not to exchange the material of the vow at one's "arbitrio" (*Par.* V, 56), or whim.

More precisely, the first apostrophe is addressed to all mortals, urging them not to take vows lightly as did Jephthah and Agamemnon (*Par.* V, 64), whose rash promises forced them to execute their innocent daughters. In these two cases the vow reveals itself as a potentially tragic tangle in which a moral imperative slides into the cruelty of an expiatory sacrifice. The tragic death of Iphigenia and Jephthah's daughter comes to coincide, ironically, with a desperate juridical-literal observance of the promise. It is as if the heroic decision to keep faith at any cost to one's word (which in fact suffices to dislocate the metaphoricity of vows into the legality of the letter) is a way of countering and containing what is intuitively felt to be the gods' despotic and capricious rule.

But Christians, and this is Beatrice's second exhortation in *Paradiso* V, are given an alternative which allows them to escape the tragic tyranny of the law. They are, thus, enjoined to abide by the Bible and the teaching of the church:

Avete il novo e 'l vecchio Testamento
e 'l pastor de la Chiesa che vi guida:
questo vi basti a vostro salvamento.

(76–78)

(You have the New Testament and the Old, and the Shepherd of the Church to guide you; let that suffice for your salvation.)

It should be mentioned that the reference to the church in the context of the Heaven of the Moon obliquely alludes to the ecclesial typology of the *mysterium Lunae*, and it casts the church as the *mediatrix* between the light of the sun and the dimness of the earth. More poignantly, in the tercet above there is a clear echo of the formula "extra ecclesiam nulla salus." At the same time the *hysteron proteron* in the injunction "Avete il novo e 'l vecchio Testamento" reverses the temporal pattern of succession of the two texts. The authority and priority of the Old Testament, the reader infers, cannot be taken literally; rather, the alliteration (the fricative sound of *v*) which covers the verse and which continues in line 78 seems to link the two testaments in a harmonious whole. The word "testamento," I might add, extends the semantic grid of covenants and pacts around which the thematic substance of the canto is articulated. "Testamento," which translates the Greek *diatheke*, is itself the pact between God and Abraham, and in II Corinthians (3:6) St. Paul refers to the pact on Mount Sinai as the old testament to which the messianic advent gives spiritual fulfillment. *Diatheke* is translated into Latin also as "foedus," or, as Isidore of Seville has it, "omne pactum et placitum testamentum vocabant" (*Etym.* V, 24).

Beatrice's detailed but austere discourse on vows, which has often seemed to critics to be nothing more than a pointless arid discussion, brings to a theological head a number of problems that have been treated in the preceding cantos of *Paradiso*. The beginning of *Paradiso* IV, for instance, recapitulates the questions at hand as the pilgrim finds himself trapped in an impasse. His predicament, we are told, resembles that of a man who, caught between two equally enticing items of food, cannot choose and starves himself to death. The reference to the crisis of the will—which has been handed down as the story of the Ass of Buridan—is not a gratuitous piece that would argue for the will's inactivity in the act of choice, as an "Averroistic" gloss on the passage by Bruno Nardi argues.[11] The reference foreshadows, on the contrary, the concern with vows as the sacrifice of the will debated in *Paradiso* V. At any rate the pilgrim's indecision at this point of the text is short-lived. If generally throughout the poem Dante is obsessed with the necessity of choices and the implacable consequences of choices, with acts of will and the realities of self-will, here it is Beatrice who gets him out of the deadlock in which the two questions provisionally hold him.

I have been examining these cantos in terms of a tension between, on the one hand, the literal pattern of order and symmetrical correspondences that vows entail and, on the other hand, the radical metaphoricity of sacrifice as a system of substitutions and exchanges. This casting of sacrifice in linguistic terms stems from the text, for Dante understands sacrifice as an act of signification or as a semiotic activity. From this perspective Dante shares in a powerful theological tradition, which runs from St. Augustine to St. Thomas Aquinas and which interprets the sense of the sacrifice as an eminently semiotic act. That this is the case is explicitly stated in book X of the *City of God*, where St. Augustine undertakes the analysis of *latreia* (worship), which, he says, could be called "cultus" only if the word were applied to God and did not include the respect we pay either to the memory or the living presence of men. Part of God's worship is sacrifice. After debating both the Platonists' misunderstanding of what true worship is for the Christians and the common assumption that offerings to God are needed by God (rather than seeing them as means by which men profit), St. Augustine proceeds to define sacrifice.

> And the fact that the ancient church offered animal sacrifices, which the people of God now-a-days read of without imitating, proves nothing else than this, that those sacrifices signified the things which we do for the purpose of drawing near to God, and inducing our neighbors to do the same. A sacrifice, therefore is the visible sacrament or sacred sign of an invisible sacrifice. Hence that penitent in the psalm, or it may be the Psalmist himself, entreating God to be merciful to his sins, says, "If Thou desiredst sacrifice, I would give it: Thou delightest not in whole burnt-offerings. The sacrifice of God is a broken heart: a heart contrite and humble God will not despise." Observe how, in the very words in which he is expressing God's refusal of sacrifice, he shows that God requires sacrifice. He does not desire the sacrifice of a slaughtered beast, but he desires the sacrifice of a contrite heart. Thus, that sacrifice which he says God does not wish, is the symbol of the sacrifice which God does wish . . . if He had not wished that the sacrifices He requires, as, e.g., a heart contrite and humbled by penitent sorrow, should be symbolized by those sacrifices which He was thought to desire because pleasant to Himself, the old law would never have enjoined their presentation; and they were destined to be merged when the fit opportunity arrived, in order that men might not suppose that the sacrifices themselves, rather than the things symbolized by them, were pleasing to God or acceptable in us.

St. Augustine's conclusion is that a true sacrifice is every work which is done that men may be united to God in true fellowship: "For, though made or offered by man, sacrifice is a divine thing, as those who called it *sacrifice* (literally, a sacred action) meant to indicate. Thus man himself, . . .

vowed to God, as a sacrifice in so far as he dies to the world that he may live to God" (*City of God* X, 5).[12]

In a passage of thoughtful attention to the works of religion—vows, sacrifices, offerings, and so on—St. Thomas lingers over the question of the sacrifice, taking as his point of departure St. Augustine's theory of metaphorical signification. An offering, writes Aquinas, cannot be exhaustively accounted for by the price of a killed sheep ("pretium occisi pecoris"); rather, we should be attentive to its "significatio." Quite overtly, St. Thomas in his *Summa theologiae* (IIa IIae, 85) acknowledges St. Augustine's definition that sacrifices are offered in signification of something ("sacrificia in quadam significantia offerentur"), but, quoting Aristotle's *De interpretatione* I, 2, he stresses that sacrificial symbolism, the fact that sacrifice is always an operation of substitution, is modeled on the process of verbal signification. He adds that words, which are the most important signs, do not signify by nature but by convention ("Voces autem, quae sunt praecipua inter signa, ... non significant naturaliter, sed ad placitum, secundum Philosophum").

The coda is meant to prepare the argument that offering sacrifice is required by natural law, and Aquinas submits that natural reason dictates that man use material signs, offering them to God as a sign of due subjection and honor. Like material signs, "which are the fitting mode of human expression, because man derives his knowledge through material signs" whose determination depends upon human agreement ("secundum humanum placitum"), offering sacrifice "belongs generically to the natural law, ... but the particular way in which sacrifices are offered is determined by human or divine institution ("determinatio sacrificiorum est ex institutione humana vel divina"), and this is the reason why they differ." Elsewhaere in the *Summa* (Ia IIae, 102, 3) Aquinas reflects on the sacrificial ceremonies of the Old Testament, and he states that the ceremonies of the old law had a dual purpose: "namely, one literal, according as they were ordained to the worship of God; and another one figurative or mystical, according as they were ordained to prefigure Christ."

The theologians' insight into the symbolic nature of the sacrifice and of the linguistic model that controls it reappears in the complex figuration of the Heaven of the Moon. We have seen above that for Dante sacrifice contains within itself a principle of unalterable legality as well as a variable content: it is the locus of overt metaphoric substitution, and the language of exchange runs through canto V of *Paradiso*: "se con altra materia si converta" (54) (there is no fault if it is exchange for other matter); "Ma non trasmuti carco a la sua spalla" (55) (Let no one shift the burden on his shoulders); "e ogne permutanza credi stolta, / se la cosa dimessa in la sorpresa / come 'l quattro nel sei non è raccolta" (58–60) (and let every exchange be reckoned vain unless the thing laid down is contained in that taken up as four in six). The language of exchange and conversion echoes the technical language of metaphor. Alan of Lille in his *Distinctiones* defines a trope as a "conversio." The trait of figurative speech, he adds, lies in the fact that it "convertitur"—turns round a term from its proper signification.[13] But—and let me make this clear—the claim that Dante, like the theologians, underscores the links between theology and metaphoric discourse does not mean that he merely repeats a discussion which is properly part of the domain of theology. On the contrary, the theologians' admission of the metaphoricity of sacrifice marks the moment when the theologian follows the path of the poet; to say it differently, the project of theological speculation about sacrifice comes to coincide with the metaphorical thinking proper to poetry.

By way of showing the extent and depth of Dante's poetic thought on poetry and theology it should first be pointed out that it is precisely in the Heaven of the Moon that Dante both presents the question of sacrifice and also raises the problematics of allegorical representation—an issue that is nothing less than "velen" to Beatrice's extraordinary lucidity. It should also be added that the two issues of the symbolic nature of sacrifice and of representation are taken up in the Heaven of Grammar. That this is the haven of grammar, in truth, is suggested only obliquely by the *Divine Comedy*, but it is plainly articulated in another major text by Dante. It is well known that in *Convivio*, where Dante assigns the seven liberal arts to each of the seven planets, he links grammar and the Heaven of the Moon:

Dico che 'l cielo de la Luna con la gramatica si somiglia per due proprietadi, per che ad esso si può comparare. Che se la luna si guarda bene, due cose si veggiono in essa proprie, che non si veggiono ne l'altre stelle: l'una si è l'ombra che è in essa, la quale non è altro che raritade del suo corpo, a la quale non possono terminare li raggi del sole e ripercuotersi così come ne l'altre parti; l'altra è la variazione de la sua luminosità, che ora luce da uno lato e ora luce da un altro, secondo che lo sole la vede. E queste due proprietadi ha la Gramatica: chè per la sua infinitade, li *raggi de la ragione* in essa non se terminano, in parte spezialmente de li vocabuli; e luce or di qua or di là in tanto quanto certi vocabuli, certe declinazioni, certe construzioni sono in uso che già non furono, e molte già furono che ancor saranno: si come dice Orazio nel principio de la Poetria quando dice: "Molti vocabuli rinasceranno che già caddero." (II, xiii)

(I say that the heaven of the Moon resembles Grammar because it may be compared with it. For if the Moon is carefully observed, there may be seen in it two things peculiar to it, which are not seen in the other stars; the one is the shadow in it, which is nothing else but the rarity of its substance, upon which the rays of the sun cannot be brought to a stand and reflected back as in the other parts; the other is the variation in its brilliancy, which shines now on one side, now on the other, according as the sun looks upon it. And Grammar has these two properties, because on account of its infinitude the rays of the reason are not brought to a stand in any direction, especially in the case of words; and it shines now from this side, now from that, in so far as certain words, certain declensions, certain constructions are in use which formerly were not, and many formerly were in use which shall hereafter be in use again, as Horace says in the beginning of the *Poetry*, when he affirms that "many words shall revive which formerly have lapsed.")

The link between grammar and the moon, explicitly formulated in the passage above, holds true in the opening cantos of *Paradiso*, where Dante picks up, albeit with some modification, notions formulated in *Convivio*, such as the doctrine of the rarity and density of the moon's matter as well as that of the lunar spots and their relation to the metaphysics of light. That Dante still connects in *Paradiso*, as he did in *Convivio*, grammar and the Heaven of the Moon, however, emerges decisively from the explanation of the principle of allegorical representation by which Beatrice accounts for the souls' display in this sphere and generally in heaven.

The blessed, Beatrice explains in *Paradiso* IV (28–63), are showing themselves to the pilgrim on the moon not because this sphere is allotted to them, "ma per far segno" (38), but to signify the celestial grade to which they experience beatitude. This happens because it is only through sensible perception that the human mind may perceive intellectual truths. This same principle of signification, Beatrice goes on to say, sustains the metaphoricity of the Bible. Dante's formulation of the nature of biblical writing clearly reflects, as is known, the influence of St. Thomas's meditation on biblical metaphor. The Bible attributes, the text says, "e piedi e mano / . . . a Dio, ed altro intende" (*Par.* IV, 44–45) (feet and hand to God, but has a different meaning). In his *Summa* (I, 1, 10) St. Thomas refers to the arm of God ("Dei brachium") to signify *virtus operativa*.[14] On the other hand the phrases "altro intende" (45) and "E forse sua sentenza è d'altra guisa / che la voce non suona" (55–56) (And perhaps his sentence has a different meaning from its sound), which refer respectively to the mode of writing in the Bible and Plato, translate the classical definition of allegory: "aliud enim sonat et aliud intelligitur."[15] In short, we are given the allegorical mechanism for the iconic representations of angels with a human face— a case of *prosopopoeia*—and for the mythic figurations which stud Plato's *Timaeus*.

In this theory of allegorical representation the alliance between *signum* and *res*, sign and thing signified, is ruptured. We are approaching an understanding as to why the question on representation put to Beatrice had "poison" in it. Representation suggests that there is no natural, necessary resemblance between the truth of an essence (for example, intellectual substances like angels), which for Dante is always beyond doubt, and the anthropomorphisms which are its crystallization. Anthropomorphisms—*prosopopoeia* and *fictio personae*, which are the dominant figures of the *Divine Comedy* and which are common to both secular and sacred texts—postulate a mimetic continuity between images and essences, but they also confirm the distance between a given image and its referent. Such a view of the arbitrary link between sign and thing in allegorical representation rises directly from the claims conventionally made for grammar.

Grammar is consistently defined as "the science of speaking and writing correctly—the starting point of all liberal studies." A thorough description of grammar's place in the curriculum by John of Salisbury (who takes the definition given by Isidore of Seville and who, in turn, influences both Walter of Chatillon and Alan of Lille) captures the art's wide perimeter. Grammar, he says, is also

> the cradle of all philosophy, and in a manner of speaking, the first nurse of the whole study of letters. It takes all of us as tender babes, newly born from nature's bosom. It nurses us in our infancy, and guides our every forward step in philosophy. . . . It is called "grammar" from the basic elements of writing and speaking. *Grama* means a letter or line, and grammar is "literal," since it teaches letters, that is, both the symbols which stand for simple sounds, and the elementary sounds represented by the symbols. . . . Since grammar is arbitrary and subject to man's discretion, it is evidently not a handiwork of nature. Although natural things are everywhere the same, grammar varies from people to people. However, we have already seen that nature is the mother of the arts. While grammar has developed to some extent, and indeed mainly, as an invention of man, still it imitates nature, from which it partly derives its origin. Furthermore, it tends, as far as possible, to conform to nature in all respects. (*Metalogicon* I, 13–14)[16]

The tension between convention and nature (*nomos* and *physis*), which figures prominently in the passage above, is the brunt of Dante's treatise on language. *De vulgari eloquentia*, in fact, reproposes, first, that general notion of grammar which appears in the thought of John of Salisbury and Alan of Lille, whereby grammar is the artifice that remedies the wear and tear of words, the self-identical science that stabilizes through the convention of its rules the temporal mutability of language. But grammar, which Dante calls *gramatica*, is also embodied in Latin as well as the new vernacular, historical language Dante imagines as being capable of expressing the values of Italian culture, if the language is sustained by rational rules.

De vulgari eloquentia, however, moves in the direction of presenting itself as a new *ars poetica*, and thus it quickly shifts its ground. Because of his assumption of the natural mutability of all languages Dante coherently proceeds to suggest ways to contain language's shiftiness and recover linguistic stability; his treatise, thus, turns into a project for artificial rules which would make possible a rhetorical organization of language, wherein poetry plays a pivotal role. In a way, Dante reenacts the insight, voiced by Isidore and John of Salisbury and all medieval poetics, that "poetry no more belongs to grammar than to rhetoric." Grammar, we are traditionally told, regulates the use of tropes, which are the special forms of speech whereby "speech is used in a transferred sense that differs from its own proper meaning. Examples of tropes are found in metaphors, metonymy, synechdoche and the like" (*Metalogicon* I, 19). The "like" includes allegory, which is enumerated by Isidore exactly as a trope belonging to the sphere of grammar. The presence of tropes and figures disrupts the literalness and order of the grammatical utterance. Figures are actually viewed as excusable departures from the rule because they occupy an intermediate zone somewhere between grammar and rhetoric, and the injunction is that one must learn to discriminate between what is said literally, what is said figuratively, and what is said incorrectly.

Dante's understanding of grammar and of allegorical discourse obscures the distinction between grammar and rhetoric in that he envisions, let me recapitulate the argument, that tropes are permissible deviations from rules, that there is no necessary kinship between words and things, and that any strict discrimination between the literal and the figurative is called into question. How does this view of metaphorical language (which also concerns the biblical text) shed light on the problematics of sacrifice in the Bible and in theology? The question concerns the epistemology of grammar, and this issue, as has been mentioned in the first chapter, is at the forefront of medieval poetic practices, such as Alan of Lille's *Plaint of Nature*. Right from the start, Alan writes of how barbarisms in grammar dramatize man's moral flaws, how the "active sex shudders in disgrace as it sees itself degenerate into the passive sex."[17] Alan's use of grammar as a tool of moral knowledge is part of an extensive debate on the relationship between grammar and theology that streches, as historians from Chenu to Ziolkowski have shown, from St. Augustine to Smaragdus to Peter Damian to Gilbert of Poitiers and Alan of Lille.[18] Alan's speculations on the Trinity in his *Contra haereticos*, for instance, deploy grammatical arguments: just as the various voices of the adjective *albus* are inflections of the same word, so are the persons of the Trinity not separate gods but manifestations of the one divinity.[19] Dante, too, deploys grammatical categories in the *Divine Comedy* as a way of probing the nature of theological discourse. Such a concern figures prominently, for example, in *Paradiso* XXVI. Thus, before turning back to the questions of sacrifice and allegory, I will make a brief digression on the exchange on language between Adam and the pilgrim in *Paradiso* XXVI, 91–142.

It has often been remarked that the encounter marks a radical reversal of the linguistic theory put forth in *De vulgari eloquentia*. Whereas in *De vulgari* Dante affirms that Adam's language was created by God and that it survived the confusion of Babel, in *Paradiso* XXVI Dante reverses himself on both counts. Adam begins by attributing the cause of the fall from the Garden of Eden not to the tasting of the tree but to his transgression of the bounds set by God. After mentioning the time of his creation, Adam focuses on what he earlier had called "l'idioma che usai e ch'io fei" (114) (the tongue that I spoke and I myself made). The subject and verb in the phrase "io fei" emphatically announce that Adam's language is his own work, that language is human and is rooted in the will and energy of the subject. More precisely, "fei"—from *facere*—is the verb of the poet, as Varro reports, and it casts language as one of the *factibilia*, as an art and an activity of the practical intellect.[20] The art of language, in effect, is Adam's poetic invention.

Adam continues his exposition by introducing the principle of historicity of language. The primal language he spoke, he says, "fu tutta spenta" (124) (was all extinguished) even before Nimrod built the Tower of Babel. It is of interest to note that in the medieval *Liber Nemroth*, Nimrod is a dialectician and an astronomer, a quester for knowledge "ultramodum"—a detail which makes Nimrod, like Ulysses and Adam himself, one who trespasses the frontiers of knowledge.[21] More to our concern, Adam says that language is natural, but words are conventional. The order of grammar follows and seeks to counter the natural randomness of language: in a natural state language is under the aegis of time and desire, which are both categories of impermanence and displacement. Finally, Adam focuses on an eminently theological and grammatical problem, the variations in the name of God:

> Pria ch'io scendessi a l'infernale ambascia,
> I s'appellava in terra il sommo Bene,
> onde vien la letizia che mi fascia.
> E El si chiamò poi, e ciò convene,
> chè l'uso dei mortali è come fronda
> in ramo, che sen va e altra vene.
>
> (133–38)

(Before I descended to the anguish of Hell the Supreme Good from whom comes the joy that girds me was named *I* on earth; and later he was called *El*: and that must needs be, for the usage of mortals is as a leaf on a branch, which goes away and another comes.)

The description of words as leaves that come and go is an allusion to Horace's *Ars poetica* (60–62), which, as we saw earlier in this chapter, Dante also deploys in *Convivio*. The image primarily conveys the idea of language's ceaseless mobility as if it were a natural, living organism. Language is, in fact, a work of nature, yet the determination of signs is *ad placitum* (130–32). Further, there is a technical resonance in the phrase "s'appellava." Appellation (*appellatio*) is a grammatical term, which was brought into logic in Boethius's commentary on Aristotle's *Categories*. In logic *appellatio* differs from *suppositio*. *Suppositio* is a term deployed for existing or nonexisting entities. *Appellatio*, on the other hand, designates existing things, and Peter of Spain uses the term to designate the eternally existing ideas of the Platonists.[22]

In *Paradiso* XXVI the existence of God is beyond question, but the different names used for him do not reveal his essence. The mutations of the name of God—first *I* and later *El*—show that the relationship between words and their referents is not sustained by a necessary etymological bond as one finds in Cratylism, for signs signify "ad placitum." To be sure, etymologies are deployed systematically throughout the *Divine Comedy*; in the *Vita nuova*, further, the principle for this rhetorical category is fully stated: "*Nomina sunt consequentia rerum.*" The statement is commonly taken to mean the positing of a necessary link between words and things. In effect, the phrase, modeled as it is on Justinian's *Institutiones*, suggests that names are part of the things they designate, that they share in the reality of the things by the process of designating them.[23]

At any rate Dante believes, in the wake of Anselm, Thierry of Chartres, and Alan of Lille, that words can properly designate natural entities; yet, when transferred to theology, they are used improperly. In *Paradiso* XXVI the names of God are empty leftovers, ephemeral designations for that which cannot but remain inaccessible. In effect, Adam's recitation makes the "proper" of the proper name vanish, and he thereby annihilates the myth of an Edenic language in which there is a necessary, natural, and stable relation between words and things. It is from the perception of the shattered unity between *res* and *signa* that Dante gets the impulse to establish a poetic order capable of gathering within itself the scattered fragments of language.

The ambiguities which characterize the universe of linguistic signs can be summarized thus: there is a discrepancy between signs and their referents, but words are also part of the realities they represent. Dante's reflections on sacrifices and gifts move within and exploit this double understanding of the relationship between signs and their referents. Gifts, for instance, are gratuitous acts that establish a possible and continuous communication between God and man. Gift-giving is also a description of the metaphoric transaction between words and things, as was intuited by John of Salisbury, who, in a chapter on the transfer of grammatical properties, writes that "this reciprocity between things and words, and words and things, whereby they mutually communicate their qualities, as by an exchange of gifts, is more commonly accomplished by words used in a metaphorical sense than by those of secondary intention" (I, 16). This reflection on gifts—which for Dante, as shown earlier, are coextensive with promises—as a model for language highlights Dante's contrary perception of the arbitrariness and violence inherent in the economy of sacrifices.

Both St. Augustine and St. Thomas Aquinas understood, as has been argued earlier, that sacrifice is patterned on a process of linguistic signification and that its explicit model is that of metaphoric substitution. Dante, as our analysis of *Paradiso* III–V has made clear, accepts the analogy instituted by the theologians. But in his text we witness a daring and radical interrogation of that which hardly surfaces in the theology of sacrifice: linguistic signs and metaphorical structures are regulated by arbitrary and shifty conventions, which, in turn, reveal the sacrifice as a tragic knot of possible errors. More precisely, the arbitrariness of the sign shows how sacrifice may be caught in the arbitrariness of literal violence. From this perspective we can understand how for Dante piety turns into tragic impiety (Alcmaeon, the text says, "per non perder pietà si fè spietato"—*Par.* V, 105); vows ("voti") become the occasion for a dark pun, "perchè fuor negletti / li nostri *voti*, e *voti* in alcun canto" (*Par.* III, 56–57) (because our vows were neglected and voided); and Constance is simultaneously constant and inconstant. The overt paronomasia of "voti," the metonymic contiguity of "pietà" and "spietato," and the ambiguity in the *figura etymologica* of Constance adumbrate Dante's judgment of the arbitrariness and violence in sacrificial rituals.[24]

If the theologians are taken to task for missing the full implication of the epistemology of grammar, does it mean that Dante turns to and endorses exclusively the perspective of the biblical exegetes? To answer this question we must look once again at the two admonitions the poet addresses to mortals, for they dramatize Dante's understanding of the Bible. In the first admonition Dante warns us not to make a vow in sport but to be faithful and keep the promise. To exemplify the importance of this injunction he recalls the story of Jephthah as told in Judges 11:39. Jephthah made a vow to the Lord, saying: "If you deliver the Ammonites into my power, whoever comes out of the door to meet me when I return in triumph shall belong to the Lord. I shall offer him up as a holocaust" (11:30). To keep his promise, Jephthah kills his innocent daughter. From St. Jerome to Peter Comestor, biblical exegetes agree that in vowing, Jephthah was foolish because he did not use discretion, and in keeping the vow he was impious. Because St. Paul in Hebrews 11:32 includes Jephthah among the saints, Aquinas muses that he is a saint "probably because he repented of his evil deed," but thinks that the vow should not have been observed.

Dante equates this biblical story with the story of Iphigenia, who was sacrificed by Agamemnon so that the gods would allow the Greek expedition to embark for the Trojan War (*Par.* V, 68–72). The imperative to keep a promise—not to move like a feather to every wind (74) or, as the Letter to the Ephesians has it, every wind of doctrine—is the foundation of moral order. But as Dante focuses on the tragic role of chance in the sacrifice of Iphigenia and Jephthah's daughter, he shows how the literal observance of each promise, as if it were the letter of the law, unavoidably brings about violence.

In the presence of the series of paradoxes in which every formulation on vows and promises seems to be entangled and which Dante lucidly pursues, it is not surprising to find a second injunction by which he urges us to follow the Bible and by which he announces the ardent vision dwelling in the poet's heart:

> Avete il novo e 'l vecchio Testamento,
> e 'l pastor de la Chiesa che vi guida;
> questo vi basti a vostro salvamento.
> Se mala cupidigia altro vi grida,
> uomini siate, e non pecore matte,
> sì che 'l Giudeo di voi tra voi non rida.
>
> (*Par.* V, 76–81)

(You have the New Testament and the Old, and the Shepherd of the Church, to guide you: let this suffice for your salvation. If evil greed cry aught else to you, be you men, and not silly sheep, so that the Jew among you may not laugh at you.)

The lines, which we have already examined in part, give just prominence to the sovereign authority of the Bible, within whose frame the lacerating contradictions of human promises may be placated. Given the narrative context of the exhortation, we can even construe the reference to the two testaments as as a faint echo of the exegetes' vigorous opposition to the speculations of grammarians and theologians, of the faith in the gospel voiced by those, such as Peter Damian, who were impatient with the dialectical treatment of verb tenses and inventories of accidents and substances. The Word of God was not to be subjected to the banal rules sanctioned by Donatus and Quintilian; on the contrary, their doctrine was extraneous to the comprehension of the truth inscribed in the Bible.[25] Dante's call to follow the Bible is particularly suggestive because it makes the *Divine Comedy* a book about the promise of the book of God.

But the reference to the New and Old testaments takes on an equivocal aspect within the economy of the canto. It would certainly be plausible to read the line "Avete il nuovo e 'l vecchio Testamento" as an affirmation of

the alliance of the two testaments. The temporal inversion in the order of
the two testaments could be read as signaling that the new and eternal
alliance between them is the fulfillment of the prophetic prefiguration of
the law, much as the spirit is the fulfillment of the letter, the reality of the
shadow, and grace of nature.[26] A similar typological reading may be legitimately based on the Pauline hermeneutical principle contained in a verse
from the Letter to the Romans: "the elder shall serve the younger" (9:12).
A long tradition of patristic glosses which imagine the two testaments as
"brothers" embracing or, as one of them puts it, "Novum Testamentum
jungitur veteri fraterno foedere,"[27] supports this reading. The patristic notion of the fraternal unity and reciprocity of the two testaments acts as a
forceful counterweight to the theme of Corso's tragic violation of his
sister.

On the other hand, the verse "sì che 'l Giudeo di coi tra voi non rida"
(*Par.* V, 81), which is doubtless a recognition of the continuing moral authority of the primogeniture of Israel, underlines, with the motif of deri-
sion, the limit of the apparent harmony between the two testaments as if
they were two brothers. According to the figural logic of the Christian
Bible, spiritual sacrifice replaces the contractual legality of Leviticus, much
as the New Testament, in a more general way, completes and surpasses the
terms of the old alliance. Consequently, the line "Avete il nuovo e 'l vecchio Testamento" reflects the patristic awareness of the great distance separating the two texts. A shadow falls, as John Scot puts it, "inter litteram et
spiritum, inter figuram et veritatem, inter umbram et corpus."[28] From this
it follows that in the temporal and ethical reversal of the Old Testament
the language of love, which is the language of substitution, hides a possible
gesture of violence. And there is something of a paradox in this. Quite
simply, the Word of God, as it displaces and replaces the old covenant,
purports to heal divisions only to heighten them; the sinister reciprocity of
love and violence, which is so memorably dramatized in *Inferno* V, resur-
faces in the corresponding canto of *Paradiso*, where the language of love as
surrender and sacrifice perpetuates divisions.

The truth of theology is caught in the trap of grammar, and, as we shall
see in the last three chapters of this book, Dante must rethink and poeti-
cally expand the purview of theology beyond the theologians' range of
vision. At the same time the Bible, which exegetes routinely interpret, enacts for Dante a crisis of signification. Precisely on account of this crisis of
signification the Bible, as much as the *Divine Comedy*, is the space of an
interpretive experience, the textual metaphor of a fundamental errancy, of
wandering, of questions, of that which tales of adventure call the quest.
The territory is one that theologians, grammarians, and exegetes could not
map conclusively, but their theories and speculations are the stuff of

Dante's vision, for he is a poet who eschews the banality of *aut . . . aut* for the harder road of *et . . . et.*

It is this wandering, which for Dante finds its historical form in the fact of exile, this interpretive journey across the vast ambiguity of conventional and natural signs, that generates history. And for Dante history is always the history of infallible promises, errors, and exile. It should come as no surprise, then, that from this perception which controls the opening cantos of the *Paradiso* Dante moves on, in canto VI, to an investigation of that sense of history in which the event of Redemption, the supreme sacrifice of the new Abel, insofar as one can judge the flow of history from a human standpoint, proves futile to check the course of violence. But history is not over. Indeed, because history is a project yet to be completed, Dante gives voice to his stubborn belief in the necessity of a *reparatio* of the fabric of man, to his faith that there is a world to be made over from the leftovers of history's tragedies. The *Divine Comedy* is the book of these promises and of these questions. This undertaking, poised between questions and promises, is the truth of exile.

Chapter 3

THE LIGHT OF VENUS

THE TITLE OF this chapter refers to the passage in the *Convivio* in which Dante classifies the seven liberal arts according to a conventional hierarchy of knowledge. Grammar, dialectics, rhetoric, music, geometry, arithmetic, and astronomy are the disciplines of the *trivium* and *quadrivium*, and each of them is linked to one of the planets in the Ptolemaic cosmology.[1] Venus is the planet identified with rhetoric because the attributes of Venus are those of rhetoric:

> E lo cielo di Venere si può comparare a la Rettorica per due proprietadi: l'una si è la chiarezza del suo aspetto, che è soavissima a vedere più che altra stella; l'altra sì è la sua apparenza, ora da mane ora da sera. E queste due proprietadi sono ne la Rettorica: chè la Rettorica è soavissima di tutte le altre scienze, però che a ciò principalmente intende; e appare da mane, quando dinanzi al viso de l'uditore lo rettorico parla, appare da sera, cioè retro, quando da lettera, per la parte remota, si parla per lo rettorico. (II, xiii, 13–14)

> (And the heaven of Venus may be compared with Rhetoric on account of two properties; one is the brilliancy of its aspect which is more pleasant to behold than that of any other star; the other is its appearing at one time in the morning, at another time in the evening. And these two properties exist in Rhetoric, for Rhetoric is the pleasantest of all the Sciences, inasmuch as its chief aim is to please. It "appears in the morning" when the rhetorician speaks directly of the surface view presented to his hearer; it "appears in the evening," that is, behind, when the rhetorician speaks of the letter by referring to that aspect of it which is remote from the hearer.)

The definition alludes, as is generally acknowledged, to the traditional double function of rhetoric: oratory and the *ars dictaminis*, or letter writing.[2]

What the definition also contains is the notion of the *ornatus*, the techniques of style or ornamentation whereby rhetoric is said to be the art that produces beautiful appearances.[3] The term "chiarezza," one might add, translates *claritas*, the light that St. Thomas Aquinas conceives to be the substance of beauty and the means of its disclosure.[4]

In the *Convivio*, Dante does not really worry about the issue of the beautiful as an autonomous aesthetic category. Although the beautiful can be an attribute of philosophy (Dante speaks, for instance, of "la bellissima Fi-

losofia")[5] or a synonym of morality,[6] the importance of both the beautiful
and rhetoric is decisively circumscribed in this speculative text of moral
philosophy. To grasp the reduced value conferred on rhetoric in the *Convivio*, where it is made to provide decorative imagery, one should only
remember its centrality in *De vulgari eloquentia*. The treatise, which strad-
dles medieval poetics and rhetoric, was written with the explicit aim of
teaching those poets who have so far versified "casualiter" to compose
"regulariter" by the observance of rules and by the imitation of the great
poets of antiquity.[7] This aim reverses, may I suggest in passing, Matthew
of Vendome's judgment. In his *Ars versificatoria*, Matthew dismisses the
lore of the ancient poets, their rhetorical figures and metaphors, as useless
and unworthy of emulation: "hoc autem modernis non licet."[8] But for
Dante rhetoric, which begins with the Greeks, is one of the decisive components, as has been argued in the first chapter, of poetry, or, as he puts it,
poetry is "fictio rhetorica musicaque poita."[9] The concern with style and
taste, which occupies a large portion of *De vulgari eloquentia*, dramatizes
the partial identification of rhetoric and poetry. At the same time, as the art
of discourse, the art of pleading political or juridical causes, rhetoric is also
in *De vulgari eloquentia* the tool for the establishment of political, legal, and
moral authority. In this sense, Dante's notion of rhetoric reenacts the concerns of a cultural tradition that ranges from Cicero to Brunetto Latini.[10]

It comes as something of a surprise that scholars, who have been remarkably zealous in mapping the complex implications of rhetoric in *De vulgari
eloquentia*, have not given equal attention to its role in Dante's other major
works. In the other texts rhetoric is treated as a repertory of figures but not
as a category of knowledge with unique claims about authority and power.
The statement, in truth, ought to be tempered somewhat in the light of the
extensive debates to which the question of allegory in both the *Convivio*
and the *Divine Comedy* has been subjected.[11] Yet even then the relationship
between rhetoric and the other arts or the way in which rhetoric engenders
reliable knowledge and may even dissimulate its strategies has not always
been adequately probed.[12] It is not my intention to review here the research that scholars such as Schiaffini, Pazzaglia, Tateo, Baldwin, and others have carried out on the various influences on Dante's thinking about
rhetoric, or their systematic analyses of the places in Dante's oeuvre where
rhetoric is explicitly mentioned.[13] I shall focus instead on the *Convivio*, the
Vita nuova, and *Inferno* XXVII to show how rhetoric works itself out in
these texts, but I will also submit new evidence that might shed light on
Dante's position in the liberal arts, namely, thirteenth-century polemics
involving the secular masters of theology at the University of Paris and the
antiacademicism of the early Franciscans.

There is no significant trace of this polemic in the *Convivio*. The point
of departure for this unfinished treatise, and the principle that shapes its

articulation, is the authority of Aristotle, who in his *Metaphysics*, which Dante calls "la Prima Filosofia," states that "tutti li uomini naturalmente desiderano di sapere"[14] (all men naturally desire to have knowledge). The reference to Aristotle may well be an enactment of the technique of the exordium—the invocation of an *auctoritas*, the statement of a generalized truth—which rhetorical conventions prescribe. But the reference also announces what turns out to be the central preoccupation of the four books, namely, that knowledge is made available by and through the light of natural reason. This recognition of man's rationality allows Dante to argue that it can be the choice of man to pursue the good life on this earth, that man can choose to work for justice. In spite of the initial *sententia*, the *Convivio* is explicitly modeled not on Aristotle's *Metaphysics*, which deals with pure theoretical knowledge such as the knowledge of spiritual entities, but on Aristotle's *Ethics*. This is, as Isidore of Seville refers to it, the practical "ars bene vivendi" (the art of good living), which casts man in the here and now of historical existence and which demands that man exercise the choices (without which no ethics can be conceived) appropriate to a moral agent.[15]

It is this philosophical optimism about human rationality that accounts for the thematic configuration of the *Convivio*. The narrative is punctuated, for instance, with references to one's own natural language as preferable to Latin, which is at some remove from one's own life; it is clustered with insistent discussions of the moral virtues and whether or not nobility is contingent on birth, wealth, or customs; it focuses on the value of political life and the justice which the Roman Empire, a product of human history, managed to establish in the world.[16] What sustains the textual movement is above all a belief in the allegory of poets as a technique that affords the thorough interpretability of the indirections of poetic language.[17] Running parallel to the notion that poetry can be the object of a full philosophical investigation, there is an insistence on the knowability of the moral and rational operations of man.

This acceptance of the natural order is the principle that lies at the hert of two related and crucial gestures which shape the intellectual structure of the *Convivio*. The first, as Gilson has argued,[18] is the revolutionary rearrangement, within the confines of the *Convivio*, of the dignity of aims: ethics rather than metaphysics is placed as the *summum bonum*. The second is the subordination of rhetoric to ethics. This statement needs clarification. The first treatise actually begins by explaining Dante's own shift away from the *Vita nuova* to the *Convivio*:

> Non si concede per li retorici alcuno di sè medesimo sanza necessaria cagione parlare, e da ciò è l'uomo rimosso perchè parlare d'alcuno non si può che il parladore non lodi o non biasimi quelli di cui elli parla: . . . Veramente, al principale intendimento tornando, dico, come è toccato di sopra, per neces-

sarie cagioni lo parlare di sè è conceduto: e in tra l'altre necessarie cagioni due sono più manifeste. L'una è quando sanza ragionare di sè grande infamia o pericolo, non si può cessare; ... E questa necessitate mosse Boezio di sè medesimo a parlare, acciò che sotta pretesto di consolazione escusasse la perpetuale infamia del suo essilio, mostrando quello essere ingiusto, poi che altro escusatore non si levava. L'altra è quando, per ragionare di sè, grandissima utilitade ne segue altrui per via di dottrina; e questa ragione mosse Agustino ne le sue Confessioni a parlare di sè, chè per lo processo de la sua vita, lo quale fu di non buono in buono, e di buono in migliore e di migliore in ottimo, ne diede essemplo e dottrina, la quale per sì vero testimonio ricevere non si potea. (I, iii, 2–15)

(The teachers of Rhetoric do not allow anyone to speak of himself except on ground of necessity. And this is forbidden to a man because, when anyone is spoken of, the speaker must needs either praise or blame him of whom he speaks; ... However, to return to our main contention, I affirm, as has been intimated above, that a man may be allowed to speak of himself for necessary reasons. And among necessary reasons there are two specially conspicuous. One may be urged when without discoursing about oneself great disgrace and danger cannot be avoided, ... This necessity moved Boethius to speak of himself in order that, under the pretext of finding consolation, he might palliate the lasting disgrace of his exile by showing that it was unjust, since no one else came forward as his apologist. The other necessity arises when from speaking about oneself great advantage to others follows in the way of teaching. This reason moved Augustine to speak of himself in his *Confessions*, because by the progress of his life, which was from bad to good and from good to better and from better to best, he gave us example and teaching which could not be received on any testimony so sure as this.)

The passage is primarily a dismissal of what is known as epideictic rhetoric, one of the three classical divisions—along with the deliberative and the forensic—of rhetoric proper. Epideictic rhetoric, says Cicero in *De inventione*, is the branch of oratory "quod tribuitur in alicuius certae personae laudem aut vituperationem"[19] (which is offered in praise or vituperation of some person). This epideictic mode, quite clearly, is identified with the autobiographical writing of Boethius and St. Augustine. But for all the acknowledgment of the utility and exemplariness of the *Confessions*, Dante's passage is overtly anti-Augustinian: the point of the *Convivio* is that the natural order, of which St. Augustine had too narrow an appreciation, is the locus of a possible moral-social project. More important, the passage marks an anti-Augustinian phase in Dante because it signals the limitations of autobiographical writing in favor of a philosophical discourse that would transcend private concerns and squarely grapple, as the *Convivio* will

do, with the issue of the authority of intellectual knowledge and its relationship to political power.

The departure from the *Confessions* is in reality Dante's way of distancing
himself from his own Augustinian text, the *Vita nuova*, and its rhetoric. It
could be pointed out that in the *Vita nuova* there is an occasional resistance
to the excesses of self-staging: "converrebbe essere me laudatore di me
medesimo, la quale cosa è al postutto biasimevole a chi lo fae"[20] (this would
entail praising myself—which is the most reprehensible thing one can do).
Yet the rhetoric of the self remains the path through which the poet's own
imaginative search is carried out. The exordium of the *Vita nuova* consistently stresses the autobiographical boundaries of the experiences about to
be related:

> In quella parte del libro de la mia memoria dinanzi a la quale poco si potrebbe
> leggere, sì trova una rubrica la quale dice: *Incipit vita nova*. Sotto la quale
> rubrica io trovo scritte le parole le quali e mio intendimento d'assemplare in
> questo libello; e se non tutte, almeno la loro sentenzia.
>
> (In my Book of Memory, in the early part where there is little to be read, there
> comes a chapter with the rubric: *incipit vita nova*. It is my intention to copy
> into this little book the words I find written under that heading—if not all of
> them, at least the essence of their meaning.)

The exordium is a proem, as Dante will call it later in the narrative, in
the technical sense of a *captatio benevolentiae*.[21] One could also point out the
technical resonance of the term "sententia." Although the *Glossarium* of
Du Cange refers only to the juridical sense of the word and neglects the
meaning of moral lesson, which one can find in the *Rhetorica ad Herennium*,
it hints that the text is also a plea for oneself in the presence of one's beloved. But what is central in the proem is the textual presence, which has
gone unnoticed by the editors, of Guido Cavalcanti's "Donna me prega"
(A lady bids me).

As is well known, Cavalcanti wrote his poem in response to the physician
Guido Orlandi's query about the origin of love. Orlandi's sonnet "Onde si
move e donde nasce amore?" (How does love move and whence is it born?)
proceeds to ask where love dwells, whether it is *sustanzia*, *accidente*, or *memora* (substance, accident, or memory) and what feeds love; it climaxes
with a series of questions as to whether love has its own figural representation or whether it goes around disguised.[22] Cavalcanti replies, "in quella
parte dove sta memora / prende suo stato" (in that part where memory
resides, [Love] takes its place)—a formulation which Dante's exordium,
"in quella parte del libro de la mia memoria," unequivocally echoes.

The echo compels us to place the *Vita nuova* as conceived from the start
in the shadow of Cavalcanti's poetry, but it does not mean that the two

texts are telling the same story. The most fundamental difference between them is their antithetical views of rhetoric and the nature of the aesthetic experience. For Guido, memory—which is in the sensitive faculty of the soul—is the place where love literally resides. In his skeptical materialism there is no room for a vision that might relieve one's dark desires.[23] The deeper truth—so runs Cavalcanti's argument—is imageless, and Guido's steady effort in the poem is to unsettle any possible bonds between poetic images and love, or love and the order of the rational soul. The scientism of "Donna me prega" literalizes desire and makes it part of the night: its poetry, with its overt antimetaphysical strains, paradoxically turns against poetry and assigns truth to the idealized realm of philosophical speculation.

For Dante, on the contrary, love reveals its truth only as the child of time—as Venus is—and hence under the sway of mutability and death. The temporality of desire links it unavoidably to memory, but memory is here—and this is the main departure from Cavalcanti—a book or the "memoria artificialis," which is one of the five parts of rhetoric. The parts are usually identified as *inventio, dispositio, elocutio, memoria,* and *pronuntiatio;* memory is defined as "firma animi rerum ac verborum perceptio" (the firm perception of things and words).[24] The rhetoricity of memory turns the quest of the *Vita nuova* into an interrogation of the value of figures. More precisely, memory is not the refuge of a deluded self, the a priori recognition of appearances as illusive shapes, the way Cavalcanti would have it. For Dante, memory is the visionary faculty, the imagination through which the poet can question the phenomena of natural existence and urge them to release their hidden secrets. It can be said that Cavalcanti makes of memory a sepulcher and of death the cutting edge of vision: he broods over the severance death entails, and it thwarts his imagination. He is too much a realist, too much a philosopher, to be able to soar above the dark abyss into which, nonetheless, he stares.

But the poet of the *Vita nuova,* who fully understands the danger of memory in that it affords only knowledge of the past and can foreclose the opening into the future, is impatient with this skepticism, this dead literalism, and from the start he seeks to rescue vision from the platitudes of the materialists. The figures of love are not irrelevant shadows or insubstantial phantoms in the theater of one's own mind, as Cavalcanti thinks when he ceaselessly beckons Dante to join him on the plain where the light of ideas endures. Nor are women part of an infinite metaphorization, always replaceable (hence never necessary), as the physician Dante da Maiano believes, who tells Dante that his dream of love is only lust that a good bath can cure.[25]

The contrivance of the lady of the screen, related in chapter IV of the *libello,* which literally makes a woman the screen on which the lover projects and displaces his own desires, is rejected because it casts doubt on Beatrice's own uniqueness. At the same time, chapter VIII, which tells of the death of one of Beatrice's friends, allows Dante's sense of poetry in the *Vita nuova* to surface. The passage is undoubtedly meant to prefigure Beatrice's own future death. Retrospectively, however, it is also another put-down of the materialists' belief that love is a spiritless experience reducible *to the play and force of attraction of material bodies. Dante refers* to the dead woman as a body without a soul—she is one "lo cui corpo io vidi giacere sanza l'anima" (I saw her body without the soul, lying in the midst of . . .). The poem he then proceeds to write is "Piangete, amanti, poi che piange Amore" (If Love himself weeps, shall not lovers weep), which turns out to be, quite appropriately, a lament over the dead figure, "la morta imagine." But this poet can glance heavenward, "ove l'alma gentile già locata era" (where that sweet soul already had its home).[26] In short, Dante installs his poetry at the point where Cavalcanti's poetry—where most poetry, for that matter—stops: between the dead body and the soul's existence. Images are not, a priori, mere simulacra of death, and the "stilo de la loda" *(style of praise), which reenacts the principles of epideictic rhet-*oric, strives for a definition of Beatrice's felt but unknown essence.

This concern with metaphysics, with the links between rhetoric and the soul, emerges in chapter XXV, where metaphor is said to be the trope that animates the face of the world. The meditation on metaphor, which is the burden of the chapter, is carried out as an attempt to grasp the nature of love. Here we see why Venus should be coupled to rhetoric. The question Dante raises has a stunning simplicity: Is love a divinity, as the Notaro suggests, or is it a mere rhetorical figure, as Guido Cavalcanti states in his *pastorella,* "In un boschetto trova' pasturella" (In a little wood I found a shepherdess)?[27] Dante defines love in only partial agreement with Cavalcanti, for whom love is "un accidente—che sovente—è fero" (an accident that is often unruly), as "accidente in sustanzia" (accident in a substance).[28] The metaphoricity of love is then discussed in terms of a movement from the animate to the inanimate and vice versa:

Onde, con ciò sia cosa che a li poete sia conceduta maggiore licenza di parlare che a li prosaici dittatori, e quei dicitori per rima non siano altro che poete volgari, degno a ragionevole è che a loro sia maggiore licenzia largita di parlare che a li altri parlatori volgari: onde se alcuna figura o colore rettorico è conceduto a li poete, conceduto è a li rimatori. Dunque, se noi vedemo che li poete hanno parlato a le cose inanimate, sì come se avessero senso e ragione, e fattele parlare insieme; e non solamente cose vere, ma cose non vere, cioè che detto hanno, di cose le quali non sono, che parlano, e detto che molti accidenti parlano, sì come fossero sustanzie e uomini; degno è lo dicitore per rima di fare lo somigliante, ma non sanza ragione alcuna, ma con ragione la quale poi sia possibile d'aprire per prosa. . . . Per qesto medesimo poeta parla la cosa che non è animata e le cose animate, nel terzo de lo Eneida, quivi: *Dardanide duri.* Per Lucano parla la cosa animata a la cosa inanimata . . . per Ovidio parla Amore, sì come fosse persona umana. (XXV, vii–ix)

(Since, in Latin, greater license is conceded to the poet than to the prose writer, and since these Italian writers are simply poets writing the vernacular, we can conclude that it is fitting and reasonable that greater license be granted them than to other writers in the vernacular; therefore, if an image or coloring of words is conceded to the Latin poet, it should be conceded to the Italian poet. So, if we find that the Latin poets address inanimate objects in their writings, as if these objects had sense and reason, or made them address each other, and that they did this not only with real things but also with unreal things (that is: they have said, concerning things that do not exist, that they speak, and they have said that many an accident in substance speaks as if it were a substance and human), then it is fitting that the vernacular poet do the same—not, of course, without some reason, but with a motive that later can be explained in prose. . . . This same poet has an inanimate thing speak to animate beings in the third book of the *Aeneid: Dardanide duri.* In Lucan the animate being speaks to the inanimate object. . . . In Ovid, Love speaks as if it were a human being.)

It could be mentioned that "dicitori per rime" and "prosaici dittatori" are phrases that find their gloss in Brunetto Latini's *Rettorica*, which is defined as the science of two aims, one of which "insegna dire" (teaches to speak) and the other "insegna dittare" (teaches to compose).[29] More to the point, metaphor is given in the guise of *prosopopoeia*, the orphic fiction whereby that which is dead is given a voice or, more correctly, a face.

With the actual death of Beatrice, related from chapter XXVIII on, the fiction that poetry is capable of providing a simulation of life is no longer sufficient. To be sure, Beatrice was described as the living figure of love, but now that she is physically dead, the metaphors for her seem to be another empty fiction. If the question while Beatrice was alive was whether and how she is unique, now that she is dead the question is finding the sense of metaphors that recall her. Dante's imaginative deadend at this point (it induces tears, but Dante records no poetry) narrows in the prose to a vast image of general darkness, the death of Christ. An analogy is established between Beatrice and Christ in an effort to invest the memory of Beatrice with a glow of material substantiality. Singleton views this analogy as the exegetical principle of the *Vita nuova*, the aim of which is to portray the lover's growing awareness of the providentiality of Beatrice's presence in his life.[30]

But the tension between the Christological language, the status of which depends on the coincidence between the image and its essence, and the poetic imagination, which in this text comes forth in the shifting forms of memory and desire, is problematic. There is no doubt that the poetic imagination aspires to achieve an absolute stability which only the foundation of theology (which has its own visionariness and its own metaphoricity) can provide. But Dante marks with great clarity the differences between his own private world and the common theological quest. The penultimate sonnet of the *Vita nuova* addresses exactly this predicament:

> Deh peregrini che pensosi andate,
> forse di cosa che non v'è presente.
> venite voi da sì lontana gente,
> com'a la vista voi ne dimostrate,
> che non piangete quando voi passate
> per lo suo mezzo la città dolente
> come quelle persone che neente
> par che 'ntendesser la sua gravitate?
> Se voi restaste per volerlo audire,
> certo lo cor de'sospiri mi dice
> che lagrimando n'uscireste pui.
> Ell'ha perduta la sua beatrice;
> e le parole ch'om di lei pò dire
> hanno vertù di far pianger altrui.

(Ah, pilgrims, moving pensively along, thinking, perhaps, of things at home you miss, could the land you come from be so far away (as anyone might guess from your appearance) that you show no signs of grief as you pass through the middle of the desolated city, like people who seem not to understand the grievous weight of woe it has to bear? If you would stop to listen to me speak, I know, from what my sighing heart tells me, you would be weeping when you leave this place: lost is the city's source of blessedness, and I know words that could be said of her with power to humble any man to tears.)

The sonnet is an apostrophe to the pilgrims who are going to Rome to see the true image—literally a *prosopopoeia*—Christ left on the veil of Veronica. The pilgrims are unaware of the lover's own heartsickness, and the poet's mythology of love—that Beatrice is an analogy of Christ—comes forth as too private a concern. More precisely, the sonnet is built on a series of symmetrical correspondences: the pilgrims are going to see Christ's image and are caught in an empty space between nostalgia and expectation, away from their homes and not quite at their destination. The motif of the *terra longinqua*, of being in a faraway land, which is here applied to the pilgrims, traditionally describes, as in the classical poem of Jaufrè Rudel, the lover's longing for a faraway object of desire. The word "lontana" in the sonnet is the hinge between the pilgrims' quest and the lover's pilgrimage: the lover is in his own native place, but, like the pilgrims, away from his beatitude. But there is another contrast in the sonnet which unsettles the symmetries: the motion of the pilgrims, who are on their way, is in sharp contrast to the poet's invitation that they stop to hear the story of his grief. In the crucial canzone "Donne ch'avete intelletto d'amore" (Ladies who have intelligence of love), the heavens vie with the lover to have Beatrice; now the terms are reversed: the lover seeks to waylay the pilgrims, begs them to stop for a while, a gesture that is bound to remind us of the repeated temptations the pilgrim himself eventually will experience in *Purgatorio*.

The vision of th pilgrims' journey to Rome triggers the last sonnet, "Oltre la spera" (XLI) (Beyond the sphere), which tells of the poet's own pilgrimage. This is an imaginative journey to the separate souls which the intellect cannot grasp, for the intellect stands to those souls, Dante says, "sì come l'occhio debole a lo sole: e ciò dice lo Filosofo nel secondo de la Metafisica" (as the weak eye does in relation to the sun, and this the Philosopher tells us in the second book of the *Metaphysics*). At the moment when a revelation is at hand in this most visionary text, the eye is dazzled by the sun, and the essences remain hidden behind their own inapproachable light. The perplexing quality of the image is heightened by the fact that it was used by both Averroes and Aquinas to describe the separate souls. Doctrinally, the text evokes and is poised between two opposite metaphysical systems.[31] More poignantly, the phrase " 'l sospiro ch'esce del mio core" (the sigh that arises from my heart) echoes "sospiri, / che nascon de' penser che son nel core" (XXIX) (sighs born of the thoughts that overflow my heart), which in turn is patterned on Cavalcanti's "Se mercè fosse amica a' miei disiri" (If Favor were friendly to my desires).[32] Cavalcanti restates the absolute separation of desire and its aim; Dante yokes rhetoric to metaphysics, makes of rhetoric the privileged imaginative path to metaphysics, though rhetoric can never yield the spiritual essence it gropes for.

The *Convivio* picks at the very start the reference to Aristotle's *Metaphysics* on which the *Vita nuova* comes to a close. But Dante challenges, as hinted earlier, the traditional primacy of metaphysics and replaces it with ethics. The move is so radical that Dante dramatizes the shift to ethics in the first song, "Voi che 'ntendendo il terzo ciel movete" (Ye who by thought move the Third Heaven). Written in the form of a *tenso*, a battle of thoughts within the self, and addressed to the angelic intelligences that move Venus, the planet of rhetoric, the poem tells the triumph of the "donna gentile"—Lady Philosophy—over Beatrice. With the enthronement of Philosophy, rhetoric is reduced to an ancillary status: it is a technique of persuasion, the cover that wraps the underlying morality within its seductive folds. The envoi explicitly confronts this issue:

> Canzone, io credo che saranno radi
> color che tua ragione intendan bene,
> tanto la parli faticosa e forte.
> Onde, se per ventura elli addivien
> che tu dinanzi da persone vadi
> che non ti paian d'essa bene accorte,
> allor ti priego che ti riconforte,
> dicendo lor, diletta mia novella:
> "Ponete mente almen com'io son bella!"

(O Canzone, methinks that few shall be those who shall rightly understand thy argument, so wearisome and hard thy speech proclaimeth it. Wherefore if by chance it come to pass that thou goest into the presence of such as seem to thee not to be rightly acquainted therewith, then I pray thee comfort thyself again saying to them, well-beloved song of mine, "Take note at least how beautiful I am.")

The confinement of rhetoric to a decorative role in philosophical discourse is not unusual. From Cicero to Brunetto Latini rhetoricians are asked to link rhetoric to ethics because of rhetoric's inherent shiftiness, its power to argue contradictory aspects of the same question.[33] In a way, it is possible to suggest that the voice of Dante in the *Convivio* is a Boethian voice, for like Boethius, who in his *De consolatione philosophiae* banishes the meretricious muses of poetry to make room for Lady Philosophy, under whose aegis poetry is possible, Dante, too, makes of poetry the dress of Philosophy.

This analogy with the Boethian text stops here, for unlike Boethius, Dante does not seek consolation for too long. Philosophy, says Isidore of Seville, is "meditatio mortis."[34] Dante has no intention of being trapped in the grief that Beatrice's death caused in him. He turns his back on the past in the *Convivio* and ponders ethics, which is not the land of the dead but the "ars bene vivendi."[35] As a matter of fact his voice is that of the intellectual, who, exiled and dispossessed, asserts the authority of his knowledge and seeks power by virtue of that knowledge.[36] This claim to power through intellect obviously did not start with Dante. Its origin lies in the revival of another sphere of rhetoric, the *artes dictaminis* elaborated by Alberic of Monte Cassino and the Bologna school of law and rhetoric, where intellectuals shaped and argued the political issues of the day.[37]

Yet Dante's project in the *Convivio* to cast the philosopher as the adviser of the emperor fails utterly. Many reasons have been suggested by Nardi, Leo, and others as to why the project collapsed.[38] The various reasons essentially boil down to Dante's awareness that a text expounding a system of values cannot be written unless it is accompanied by a theory of being. The text that attempts the synthesis is the *Divine Comedy*.

The point of departure of the poem is the encounter with Vergil, whose "parola ornata" (*Inf.* II, 67) (fair speech), an allusion to the *ornatus* of rhetoric, has the power, in Beatrice's language, to aid the pilgrim in his quest.[39] But if rhetoric is unavoidably the very stuff of the text, rhetoric's implications and links with the other disciplines of the encyclopedia are explicitly thematized in a number of places. One need only mention *Inferno* XV, where, as has been seen in chapter 1, rhetoric, politics, grammar, astrology, law, and their underlying theory of nature are all drawn within the circle of knowledge; or *Inferno* XIII, the canto which features the fate of Pier delle Vigne, the counselor at the court of Frederick II, whose failure can be gauged by Brunetto Latini's reference to him in *La rettorica* as a master in the art of "dire et in dittare sopra le questioni opposte"[40] (speaking and dictating about opposite questions).

I shall focus, however, on *Inferno* XXVII, because this is a canto that inscribes Dante's text within the boundaries of the thirteenth-century debate on the liberal arts and, more precisely, on the Franciscan attack against logic and speculative grammar. The canto is usually read in conjunction with the story of Ulysses that precedes it.[41] The dramatic connections between the two narratives, however superficial they may be, are certainly real. It can easily be granted that *Inferno* XXVII is the parodic counter to *Inferno* XXVI and its myth of style. In *De vulgari eloquentia*, in the wake of Horace's *Ars poetica* and the *Rhetorica ad Herennium*, Dante classifies the tragic, elegiac, and comical styles in terms of fixed categories of a subject matter that is judged to be sublime, plain, or low.[42] In the canto of Ulysses, with its "verba polita," to use Matthew of Vendome's phrase,[43] moral aphorisms and grandiloquence stage the language of the epic hero whose interlocutor is the epic poet Vergil.[44] Ulysses' is a high style, making his story a tragic text, for Ulysses is, like all tragic heroes, an overstater, and hyperbole is his figure: he is one who has staked everything and has lost everything for seeking everything.

As we move into *Inferno* XXVII, there is a deliberate diminution of Ulysses' grandeur. His smooth talk is replaced by hypothetical sentences, such as "S'i'credesse che mia risposta fosse / a persona che mai tornasse al mondo, / questa fiamma staria sanza più scosse" (61–63) (If I thought that my answer were to one who might ever return to the world, this flame would shake no more); hypothetical phrases, "se non fosse il gran prete" (70) (but for the high priest); parenthetical remarks, "s'i' odo il vero" (65) (if what I hear is true); and swearing, colloquialisms, and crude idioms. From the start, Guido's speech draws the exchange between Vergil and Ulysses within the confines of dialect:

O tu, a cu' io drizzo
la voce, e che parlavi mo Lombardo
dicendo: "istra ten va, più non t'adizzo."

(19–21)

(O you to whom I direct my voice and who just now spoke Lombard, saying,
"Now go your way, I do not urge you more.")

Vergil allows Dante to speak to Guido, "Parla tu, questi è latino" (33) (You
speak: he is Italian), because Vergil, too, observes the rhetorical rules of
stylistic hierarchy. There is a great deal of irony in shifting from Ulysses'
high ground to the specifics of the Tuscan Apennines or Urbino and Ravenna. But from Dante's viewpoint the irony is vaster: degrees of style are
illusory values, and Ulysses and Guido, for all their stylistic differences, are
damned to the same punishment of being enveloped in tongues of fire in
the area of fraud among the evil counselors. Even though the image of the
Sicilian bull within which its maker perishes (7–9) conveys the sense that
we are witnessing the fate of contrivers trapped by their own contrivances,
it also harks back to Ulysses' artifact, the Trojan horse.

It could be said that Guido is the truth, as it were, of Ulysses. If the
pairing of their voices, however, can be construed as a confrontation between the epic and the mock-heroic, style is not just a technique of characterizing their respective moral visions. Guido's municipal particularity of
style introduces us to the question of political rhetoric—the rhetoric by
which cities are established or destroyed—which is featured in the canto.
What we are shown, to be sure, is an obsessive element of Dante's political
thought: Guido da Montefeltro, the adviser of Pope Boniface VIII, coun-
seled him how to capture the city of Palestrina, and this advice is placed
within the reality of the temporal power of the papacy. From this standpoint *Inferno* XXVII prefigures St. Peter's invective in *Paradiso* XXVII, and
it also echoes *Inferno* XIX, the ditch of the Simonists, where Pope Boniface
is expected.

As in *Inferno* XIX, we are given the cause of the general sickness: just as
Constantine sought out Pope Sylvester to cure his leprosy (94–99), so did
Boniface VIII seek Guido da Montefeltro to cure his pride. If leprosy suggests the rotting away of the body politic, pride is the fever of the mystical
body; the origin of both is the Donation of Constantine. The chiasmus
that the comparison draws (Boniface is equated with Constantine) points
to the unholy mingling of the spiritual and secular orders and to the role
reversal of the pope and his adviser.[45]

But there is in the canto an attention to political discourse that goes
beyond this level of generality. In a way, just as there was a theology of
style, we are now allowed to face political theology as the politics of theology. We are led, more precisely, into the council chamber—behind the

scenes, as it were—where "li accorgimenti e le coperte vie" (76) (all wiles and covert ways), the art of wielding naked political power, is shown. Here big deals are struck, so big that they focus on the destruction of cities and the salvation of souls. These are the terms of the transaction: by virtue of his absolute sovereignty—an authority that depends on the argument of the two keys, "Lo ciel poss'io serrare e diserrare, / come tu sai; però son due le chiave / che 'l mio antecessor non ebbe care" (103–5) (I can lock and unlock Heaven, as you know; for the keys are two, which my predecessor did not hold dear)—the pope promises absolution for Guido's misdeed.[46] Guido's advice is simply to make promises without planning to keep them: "lunga promessa con l'attender corto / ti farà triunfar ne l'alto seggio" (110–11) (long promise with short keeping will make you triumph on the High Seat).

This advice, I would suggest, textually repeats and reverses Brunetto Latini's formulation in *La rettorica*. Commenting on Cicero's statement that the stability of a city is contingent on keeping faith, on observing laws and practicing obedience to one another, Brunetto adds that to keep faith means to be loyal to one's commitments and to keep one's word: "e dice la legge che fede è quella che promette l'uno e l'altro l'attende" (and the law says that faith is that by which one promises and the other keeps it).[47] The deliberate violation of the ethical perspective, which alone, as Brunetto fully knows, can neutralize the dangerous simulations that rhetoric affords, brings to a focus what the canto of Ulysses unveils: that ethics is the set of values rhetoric manipulates at will.[48] From Dante's viewpoint, however, the arrangement between the pope and his counselor is charged with heavy ironies that disrupt the utilitarian calculus of the principals.

The pope begins by taking literally what is known as his *plenitudo potestatis*, the fullness of spiritual and temporal powers given to him by God, yet he is powerless to act and seize a town. He believes in the performative power of his words, that by virtue of his office his words are a sacramental pledge. Yet he takes advice to say words that do not measure up to his actions. There is irony even in Dante's use of the word "officio," a term which for Cicero means moral duty; its appearance in line 91 only stresses the dereliction of duty. On the other hand, there is Guido, who knows that in the tough political games men play there is a gap between words and reality. Yet he believes in the pope's "argomenti gravi" (106) (weighty arguments)—a word that designates probable demonstration according to logical rules[49]—without recognizing that the pope does not deliver what he promises, which, after all, was exactly Guido's advice to him.

The point of these ironies is that Boniface and Guido thoroughly resemble and deserve each other. Both believe in compromises, practical gains, and moral adjustments, as if God's grace could be made adaptable to their calculus and to the narrow stage of everyday politics. And both are sophists of the kind St. Augustine finds especially odious in *De doctrina christiana*,[50] those who transform the world of political action to a world of carefully spoken words. As a sophist Boniface entertains the illusion that he can control the discourse of others and ends up controlling Guido while at the same time being controlled by him. As a sophist Guido is the character who is always drawing the wrong logical inference from his actions: he mistakenly believes Dante is dead because he has heard that nobody ever came alive from the depths of hell (61–66); he becomes a friar, believing that thus girt he could make amends for this past (66–69).

What exactly does it mean to suggest, as I am doing, that Guido is portrayed as if he were a logician? And how does it square with the fact (to the best of my knowledge it has not been investigated by commentators) that he is a Franciscan, or, as he calls himself, a "cordigliero" (67) (a corded friar)? The fact that Guido is a Franciscan has far-reaching implications for the dramatic and intellectual structure of the canto. It accounts, first of all, for the textual references to the bloody heap of the French (44), a reference to a world at war that is the parodic counter of Franciscan ideals of peace. More substantively, the tongues of fire in which the sinners are wrapped are an emblem more appropriate to a Franciscan like Guido than to Ulysses. The tongues of fire are usually explained as a parody of the Pentecostal gift of prophecy that descended on the apostles at the time of the origin of the church. It happens, however, that the Constitution of the Franciscans established that the friars should convene at the Porziuncola every four years on Pentecost.[51] The reason for this ritual is to be found in the Franciscans' conscious vision of themselves as the new apostles, capable of reforming the world.

Guido's language perverts the Pentecostal gift, and the perversion has put him in touch with the fierce enemies of the Franciscans, the logicians. The possibility for this textual connection is suggested by the canto itself. At Guido's death there is a *disputatio* between one of the "neri cherubini" (black cherubs) and St. Francis over Guido's soul (112–17). The devil wins the debate and speaks of himself as a "loico" (123) (logician). The debate between a devil and St. Francis is not much of a surprise, for as a fallen angel—one of the cherubim—the devil is the direct antagonist of Francis, who is commonly described in his hagiographies as "the angel coming from the east, with the seal of the living God."[52] Furthermore, the reference to the devil as one of the cherubim, which means "plenitudo scientiae" and is the attribute of the Dominicans,[53] seems to be involved obliquely in Dante's representation of both orders of friars. But this is not the hidden allegory of a *quaestio disputata* between Dominicans and Franciscans. What is at stake, on the contrary, is the long debate in which the two fraternal orders were engaged in the thirteenth century—and in which they ended up on the side of their opponents, as Dante implies.[54] The debate centered on the value of the liberal arts at the University of Paris.[55]

In historical terms, the debate saw the preachers and the mendicants opposed by the secular masters of theology. The Dominicans, to be sure, adapted quickly to the pressures of university circles because their order was founded with the explicit intellectual aim of combating heresies. The Franciscans, on the other hand, in response to the call for evangelical practice, believed that their homiletics had to retrieve the essence of the good news without any sophistry.[56] St. Francis was an "idiota," given to the cult of *simplicitas*; Paris, the city of learning, was made to appear the enemy of Assisi.[57]

This stress on simplicity did not mean that the Franciscans kept away for too long from the world of learning. There was in effect a strong Augustinian strand in their attitude toward academic knowledge. St. Augustine, it will be remembered, encouraged Christians in *De doctrina christiana* to make good use of pagan rhetoric in order to communicate the message of the Revelation effectively. Secular wisdom, which was crystallized in the liberal arts and which St. Augustine never quite rejected in the *Confessions*, was viewed as a treasure to be plundered by Christians the way the Hebrews plundered the "Egyptian gold."[58]

The Franciscans—figures such as Alexander of Hales, St. Bonaventure, and Duns Scotus—did move into the universities, but by virtue of their voluntarism they adhered to an essential anti-Aristotelianism. The formal edifice of Aristotelian logic was severely challenged, both as a theory of abstract reasoning and as a doctrine that the universe is a logical system of numbers and mathematically measurable order.[59] In *Inferno* XXVII, as the devil is identified as a logician, logic comes forth as the art that deals with judgments about the consistency or contradictions within the structure of an argument, but it radically lacks an ethical perspective. Appropriately, Guido, who has betrayed his Franciscan principles, is now claimed by one of the very logicians the Franciscans opposed.

But the debate between Franciscans and the secular masters is not left entirely on this academic level in the canto. There are political ramifications which Dante absorbs in his representation. Guillaume de Saint-Amour, a leader of the secular masters, had unleashed an attack in his *De periculis novissimorum temporum* against the Franciscans as the pseudoapostles and heralds of the anti-Christ; in their purely formal observance of the externals of faith they were identified as the new pharisees, who connive with popes under the habit of holiness to deceive the believers.[60] As Congar suggests, the polemic was a clear attempt to contain the power of the pope, for the mendicants, by being under the pope's direct jurisdiction, weakened the *potestas officii* of the local bishops.[61] Largely at stake was the issue of confessions, a source of controversy between local priests and friars, which ironically was given a firm solution in the bull *Super cathedram* by Boniface VIII.[62]

In *Inferno* XXVII, Boniface is "lo principe di'i novi Farisei" (85) (the prince of the new Pharisees); he makes a mockery of confession, "Tuo cuor non sospetti; / finor t'assolvo, e tu m'insegna fare / sì come Penestrino in terra getti" (100–102) (Let not your heart mistrust. I absolve you here and now, and do you teach me how I may cast Penestrino to the ground), and his *potestas* appears as only temporal power. By the same token Guido, who as a Franciscan should believe in the power of confession, settles for a pharisaic formula, "Padre, da che tu mi lavi / di quel peccato ov'io mo cader deggio" (108–9) (Father, since you do wash me of that sin into which I now must fall), and seeks absolution before the commission of sin—an act that makes a mockery of his prior contrition and confession (83). And finally, he is the pope's conniver throughout.

In effect, Guido da Montefeltro never changed in his life. The emblem he uses for himself, "l'opere mie / non furon leonine, ma di volpe" (74–75) (my deeds were not those of the lion, but of the fox), gives him away. The animal images, to begin with, are consistent with the unredeemed vision of the natural world in terms of mastiff, claws, and young lion (45–50). More to the point, the metaphor of the lion and the fox echoes Cicero's *De officiis* (I, xiii, 41), and it may be construed in this context as a degraded variant of the *topos* of *sapientia et fortitudo*.[63] But the fox, Guido's attribute, has other symbolic resonances. In the *Roman de reynard* the fox goes into a lengthy confession of his sin and then relapses into his old ways; for Jacques de Vitry, more generally, the fox is the emblem of confession without moral rebirth. More important for *Inferno* XXVII is the fact that Rutebeuf, who wrote two poems in support of Guillaume de Saint-Amour, uses the fox as the symbol of the friars; in *Renart le nouvel* the fox is a treacherous Franciscan.[64]

These historical events and symbols are brought to an imaginative focus in the digression on the deceits of False Seeming in the *Roman de la rose* of Jean de Meung. Absorbing the antifraternal satire of Guillaume, Jean presents False Seeming as a corded friar, a "cordelier,"[65] who has abandoned the evangelical ideals of St. Francis and lives on fraud. Reversing Joachim of Flora's hope that the fraternal orders were providentially established so that history would hasten to a close, Jean sees the mendicants as symptons of decay: "fallacious is the logic of their claim: religious garment makes religious man."[66] This sense of the friars' deceptiveness ("now a Franciscan, now a Dominican," as Jean says)[67] reappears in *Il fiore*, where False Seeming's steady practice of simulation comes forth as metaphoric foxiness:

I' sì so ben per cuor ogne linguaggio,
le vite d'esto mondo i' ho provate;
ch'un' or divento prete, un'altra frate,
or prinze, or cavaliere, or fante, or paggio.
Secondo ched i' veggio mi vantaggio.
Un'altra or son prelato, un'altra abate:
molto mi piaccion gente regolate,
chè co llor cuopro meglio il mi' volpaggio.[68]

(I know so well by heart every language and I have tasted the lives of this
world, that one moment I become priest, at another friar, now prince, now
knight, now footman, now page. Just as I see my advantage. One time I am a
prelate, another an abbot; I much like monks, for with them I cover better my
foxiness.)

If "ogne linguaggio" hints at and perverts the apostles' knowledge of all
tongues under the power of the Spirit, the sonnet also conveys Jean's insight, namely, that the only fixed principle in False Seeming's shifty play of
concealment (which the technique of enumeration and the iterative ad-
verbs of time mime in the sonnet) is falsification itself.

To turn to the antifraternal satirists such as Guillaume and Jean is not
equivalent, from Dante's viewpoint, to granting assent to their statement
or even giving them the seal of a privileged authority. In *Inferno* XXVII,
Dante endorses the antifraternal rhetoric, for Guido da Montefeltro has
clearly betrayed the paradigm of Franciscan piety. But Dante also challenges, as the Franciscan intellectuals did, the logicians' categories of
knowledge. When the devil, at the triumphant conclusion of his dispute
with St. Francis, appeals to logic's principle of noncontradiction ("ch'as-
solver non si può chi non si pente, / nè pentere e volere insieme puossi /per
la contradizion che nol consente" (118–20) (for he who repents not cannot
be absolved, nor is it possible to repent of a thing and to will it at the same
time, for the contradiction does not allow it), he is using logic only rhetorically: it is a sophistic refutation by which he sways the opponent. But logical conceptualizations, as has been argued earlier in this chapter and as we
shall see more fully in chapter 5, are delusive because they are not moored
to the realities of life and because they establish a de facto discontinuity
between the order of discourse and the order of reality. More important,
the devil is claiming Guido da Montefeltro as his own, whose very experience in the canto unveils exactly how the principle of noncontradiction is
a fictitious abstraction: like False Seeming, the pope, and the devil himself,
Guido is Proteus-like (to use Jean de Meung's metaphor for the friars),
shifty, and always unlike himself.

This rotation of figures and categories of knowledge is the substance of
a canto in which, as this chapter has shown, prophecy is twisted into rheto-

ric, theology is manipulated for political ends, politics and ethics are masks of the desire for power, and logic is deployed rhetorically. From this perception of how tangled the forms of discourse are comes Dante's own moral voice, both here and in his attacks against the sophistry of syllogisms immediately after the Dominican St. Thomas Aquinas celebrates the life of St. Francis.[69]

Because of this movement from theory to practice and back again to theory, and from one order of knowledge to another, it appears that each of the liberal arts can never be fixed in a self-enclosed autonomous sphere: each art unavoidably entails the other in a ceaseless pattern of displacement. Ironically, what Dante condemns in Guido da Montefeltro from a moral point of view becomes, in Dante's own poetic handling, the essence of knowledge itself, whereby the various disciplines are forever intermingled. The idea that the arts cannot be arranged in categorical definitions is not only a poet's awareness of how arbitrary boundaries turn out to be. Medieval textbooks and compendia are consistent, so to speak, in betraying the difficulty of treating each of the liberal arts as crystallized entities. If Isidore views dialectics as logic, John of Salisbury's *Metalogicon* considers *logica* an encompassing term for "grammatica" and "ratio disserendi," which in turn contains dialectics and rhetoric.[70] For Hugh of St. Victor, who follows St. Augustine's *City of God, logica* is the name for the *trivium*.

These references are valuable only if we are ready to recognize that what is largely a technical debate never loses sight of the spiritual destination of the liberal arts. What the technicians may sense but never face, however, is that which rhetoricians and poets always know: that knowledge may be counterfeited. Small wonder that in the *Convivio* Dante would repress rhetoric—in vain. But in the *Vita nuova* and the *Divine Comedy* we are left with the disclosure that rhetoric, in spite of its dangerous status and, ironically, because of its dangerousness, is the only possible path for the poet to tread on the way to metaphysics and theology respectively. Poetry, very simply, is the imaginative locus encompassing all the arts in their heterogeneous mobility. Whether the poet delivers genuine metaphysical and theological knowledge or dazzles us with luminous disguises is a question which lies at the heart of Dante's poetry.

Chapter 4

METAPHOR AND JUSTICE

(*INFERNO* XXVIII)

THERE CAN BE little doubt that the unifying thread of the *Divine Comedy* is the question of justice and, more generally, of ethics. Justice, as has been correctly said in a study on Dante's conception of it, "lies at the heart of the *Commedia*,"[1] but it also plays a central role in most of Dante's other texts. The argument by Etienne Gilson about the sovereignty of ethics in the *Convivio*, as we saw in the preceding chapter, depends on the link Dante posits between ethics and the Primum Mobile (*Conv.* II, xiv, 14).[2] In Aristotle's thought ethics is, like politics, a practical science, and, in this sense, it occupies a lower place in his scheme of knowledge than do the theoretical branches of philosophy—metaphysics or theology, physics, and mathematics. By placing ethics in the Primum Mobile, Dante confers on ethics primacy over metaphysics. Further, we ought to recall that Dante had planned to treat the subject of justice in the fourteenth book of *Convivio*. As a way, no doubt, of laying the theoretical foundations for the projected dissertation, he describes justice, in the wake of Aristotle's *Ethics*, as "the most distinctively human" virtue, which exists only in the rational part of man, in his will (*Conv.* I, xii, 9–10). In *Monarchia*, on the other hand, where the primary concern is the structure of the political relationship of laws to the good of the state and universal happiness, Dante defines "right," (*jus*), following Cicero's *Rhetoric*, as that which, maintained, preserves society, and, infringed upon, destroys it (II, 5, 3–6).

These references to Dante's general theory and understanding of ethics and justice in *Monarchia* and *Convivio* as the totality of political relations, whereby individuals can best develop and actualize themselves, paradoxically, by taking on universal forms, certainly do not even begin to convey the sense of Dante's familiarity with the technical debates on issues such as natural and legal justice. One finds in *Convivio* citations from the *Infortiatum* and the *Old Digest* to the effect that "written law is the art of well-doing and of equity" (IV, ix, 87); in *Monarchia*, on the other hand, the concrete categories of the jurists are found wanting, for they do not teach "what the essence of Right is" (II, v, 6–9). The essence of right for Dante is encapsulated by the philosophers of natural law, such as Thomas Aquinas.[3] The foundation of right, Dante says in *Monarchia*, is inseparably bound to the provisions of nature and to the natural order in things (II, vii,

1–22), or, to say it in the language of his sixth *Epistle* and of the theorists of natural law, the best laws are those which are in harmony with natural law.[4]

These ethical questions will all appear in the *Divine Comedy* not as abstract categories of thought but as a concrete constellation of concerns, as one gathers from some explicit statements in a letter that is conventionally taken to be Dante's introduction to the poem. In the *Epistle to Cangrande*, in fact, Dante assigns the *Divine Comedy* to the moral sphere of philosophy, "morale negotium, sive ethica," on the grounds that the poem's aim is not speculation but "opus inventum," a term which, by extrapolation, designates the totally human and historical domain of actions, behavior, laws, and values. This overt inclusion of poetry within the larger domain of ethics implies that we as readers of the poem have the freedom to choose and to shape our lives, and that we are accountable for our choices. The ethical claim accurately describes the *Divine Comedy* as a poem that dramatizes the range of moral possibilities and actions, asserts the value of political actions, and probes questions of their purposes. This ethical finality of the poem is stressed in the *Epistle*'s assertion that "taken literally the subject of the whole work is the state of the souls after death . . . if the work is to be understood allegorically, the subject is man, as he is liable to rewarding or punishing justice, according as he is worthy or unworthy in the exercise of the freedom of the will" (par. 8).

The voice and the thematic substance of the *Divine Comedy* are rooted in these ethical claims. It is clear that Dante's radical indictment of the world's chaos and of the divisions within self and history, which are the bounds of his imaginative experience, comes to a sharp focus through the prism of justice and stems from his unique ethical concerns. It is equally clear that the moral order of Dante's *Inferno* is shaped by Aristotle's *Ethics*.[5] Canto XI of *Inferno*, which both traces and recapitulates the rationale for the pattern of crime and punishment in hell, transparently evokes Aristotle's moral categories and vocabulary. The pilgrim and his guide have just entered the City of Dis, and after meeting the heretics who are entombed along the walls of the city, they tarry their descent. So that their time may not be lost, Vergil explains the principles by which the moral system of *Inferno* is organized. Obliquely, and in a grotesque perversion of the ideal interrelation between ethics and politics, ethics is now made to appear as the science regulating the moral topography of evil.

Of all kinds of malice that triggers heaven's abhorrence, Vergil tells the pilgrim in *Inferno* XI, the aim is "ingiuria" (22). The word, etymologically from *non-ius*, means injustice, and Cicero uses the word in this sense in *De legibus* (I, vi, 19). Aquinas himself, quoting Isidore's *Etymologies*, derives *justice* from *jus*, and this etymology emphasizes the Roman code underneath Dante's representation of justice in hell.[6] This injustice, canto XI goes on to expound, consists, to couch it in the language of St. Thomas

Aquinas, in an injury inflicted on others by intention or choice, by force or fraud. Manifestly, this general subdivision of sins does not account for either the souls punished outside of Dis or the way in which usury can be said to offend the "Divine Goodness" (94–96). These omissions perplex the pilgrim. In response to Dante's queries, Vergil recalls Aristotle's *Physics* (101), where human art is said to imitate the reproductive processes of nature, which is God's art and child, so that usury, which is an action of sterile symbolic reproduction, violates the fecundity of the natural order.[7] To explain the reasons for the place assigned to the souls punished outside of the City of Dis, on the other hand, Vergil recalls the tripartite moral order put forth by Aristotle's *Ethics*, where "la tua Etica pertratta / le tre disposizion che 'l ciel non vole, / incontenenza, malizia e la matta / bestialitade" (*Inf.* XI, 80–83) (your *Ethics* treats the three dispositions which heaven wills not: incontinence, malice, and mad bestiality).

The explicit reference to Aristotle's *Ethics* forces us to give a brief historical synopsis of the sundry polemical strains and interpretive traditions stemming from the reading of this text in the thirteenth century. In effect, the translation by Robert Grosseteste (1246–47) succeeded, among other things, in triggering intense and renewed debates on the limits and extensions of the Aristotelian moral theories. The debates largely focused on the possible autonomy of ethics, as a philosophical theory of virtue operative in this life, from theological faith in and Platonic adherence to a supreme Good. As is known, it was in 1366 that the *Ethics* became part of the university curriculum, in the recognition that Aristotle's philosophical theories were central to man's moral education. But before its inclusion in the curriculum, Albert the Great wrote two commentaries shaped by the conviction that Aristotle's text deals exclusively with natural virtues and the domain of philosophical ethics, whose sole practical purpose, Albert maintains, is to make men good.

Aquinas's commentary on the *Ethics* (1271–72), on the other hand, corrects Albert's interpretation and further develops Aristotle's theories from a theological perspective. Intellectual history has certainly exaggerated the opposition between Plato and Aristotle, and, at any rate, medieval commentators on and translators of Aristotle sought to reduce the sense of too drastic a contrast between them. St. Thomas belongs to this tradition. Because Aristotle confines the treatment of ethics to the economy of the *polis* and because for him actions are to be determined as if there were no God, Aquinas complements his philosophical views from the Neoplatonic and Augustinian theological standpoint of the *civitas Dei* and the knowledge of man's ultimate ends. From this perspective justice, as the primary moral virtue, is conceived as a direction of the will toward Christian love. Aquinas's harmonization of philosophy and theology is in large measure a reaction to the commentaries by the radical Aristotelians, such as Siger of

Brabant and Boethius of Dacia, who wrote, respectively, the *Liber de felicitate* and *De summo bono*, and who understood the "right life" as the philosophical life.[8]

For Dante, as for St. Thomas, ethics deals with the world of man (the "ordo vivendi" or the art "bene vivendi"), but theology is its decisive premise. This is not to say, however, that the ethical questions staged in the *Divine Comedy* are to be circumscribed exclusively within these speculative parameters of philosophy and theology. There are in the poem, as scholars such as the late Judson Allen have shown, specifically literary-moral concerns that recall the traditions of the twelfth-century commentaries on Ovid by the likes of Arnulf of Orléans or the fourteenth-century moralization of the *Metamorphoses* by Giovanni del Virgilio.[9] Arnulf's exegetical principle that the *Metamorphoses* deals with exterior and interior change and that Ovid's intention in presenting the changes in the material world and in the soul "ethice supponitur" (is a question of ethics) and even the more generalized practice of biblical exegesis, which is founded on the fourfold sense of scripture and which Dante acknowledges in the *Epistle to Cangrande* as the dramatic paradigm of the poem ("The letter teaches the facts, the allegory what you are to believe; the moral what you should do, the anagoge where you are to strive for"), offer further evidence of how paramount the questions of ethics are for Dante and for medieval poetics.[10]

In a primary way, the present chapter explores some complications in the kinship between poetry and ethics that Dante establishes in the *Epistle to Cangrande*. There are massive historical reasons, as I have just indicated, for linking the two activities of the practical intellect. There is another compelling reason for viewing them together. In the formal structure of knowledge drafted by Brunetto Latini, for instance, the term "ethica"—as one of the three general classifications of philosophy, along with the theoretical and the mechanical subdivisions—comprises grammar, rhetoric, and dialectics. But the relationship between ethics and poetry is not understood by Dante the way medieval *accessus ad auctores*, who are the moralizers of poetry and superimpose allegorical meanings on the letter of the text, understand it. Arnulf of Orléans, to take a case we have just mentioned, believes that by presenting the changes in the material world Ovid wants to teach us to despise temporal things, which are unstable and transitory, and to urge us to a single devotion to our Creator. On the contrary, Dante's *Divine Comedy*, in which the questions of justice and ethics are the very substance of the representation, moves into the space of problems opened up by the ethical reflections of Plato, Aristotle, and St. Thomas Aquinas.

Dante's point of departure in the *Divine Comedy* is the conviction that, as one of the four cardinal virtues, justice is part of ethics. Like St. Thomas, Dante, however, knows that the two terms—justice and ethics—cannot be seen as purely synonymous. There is a gap separating them, which both Aquinas and Dante seek to bridge but which Dante ultimately widens. In a way, just as in *Convivio* theology and ethics do not coincide, they are not shown to coincide in the *Divine Comedy*—for if they did, it would be easy to give up theology in favor of ethics. At its most general, the difference between ethics and justice can be simply formulated. Ethics, which is grounded in justice, designates the sphere of the duties and obligations attendant upon man's concrete actuality; but justice is not simply equated with the sphere of human actions. There is a Platonic theory of the Good and of Justice operative in Dante's imagination, as there is in Aquinas's. For Dante this means that the cosmos itself is regulated by a transcendent justice. The belief in a harmonious scheme of things, which had been asserted by Pythagoreans and Platonists (and which Chalcidius's commentary on the *Timaeus* again made available in the Middle Ages), depended on the mathematical arrangement of the world.

To examine the claims here advanced, I shall discuss in some detail *Inferno* XXVIII, where Dante raises the issue of the operations of God's justice in hell through a poet, Bertran de Born. Why through a poet? Is Dante saying that God's justice *is* poetic justice, and what exactly is the relationship between God's justice and poetic justice? Before answering these questions, let us look closely at this canto of the schismatics and sowers of scandal and discord, "seminator di scandalo e di scisma" (35), which comes to a close in the pilgrim's encounter with this Provençal poet, Bertran de Born.

Bertran, who fomented a rebellious war between the young king Henry and his father, is now punished by having his own body mangled: he carries his head, severed from his trunk, by the hair, and he walks as if he were "due in uno e uno in due" (125) (two in one and one in two). In Bertran's own textual account there is a typological correspondence between his action and that of Achitophel, who, according to the biblical narrative, instigated Absalom to rebel against his father, King David (II *Kings* 15:7–17:23). But, whereas the counselor Achitophel expiates his sin by hanging himself, Bertran, who has breached the due course of succession and the sanctity of bonds of consanguinity, is requited so that the punishment fits the crime, or, as he says, "Così s'osserva in me lo contrapasso" (142) (Thus is the retribution observed in me). In linguistic terms the "contrapasso" is rendered by the deployment of the same verb in lines 139 and 140 to describe both Bertran's act and the punishment he suffers: ("Perch'io *partì* così giunte persone, / *partito* porto il mio cerebro") (Because I parted persons thus united, I carry my brain parted from its source).[11]

The "contrapasso," which translates what St. Thomas Aquinas in his commentary on Aristotle's *Ethics* and in the *Summa theologiae* calls "contrapassum," is the ethical principle of justice that establishes the symmetrical correspondence between a sin and the suffering for that sin.[12] Because it announces that each man should justly suffer what he has inflicted, this ethical structure of just reciprocation also enacts the biblical *lex talionis*. This law is to be understood to mean the retaliatory balance of measure for measure, and it governs the unfolding of divine justice itself. The link between the philosophical terminology of Aristotle and the biblical moral design is forged by St. Thomas himself, who writes that "contrapassum" denotes equal passion repaid for previous action ("aequalem recompensationem passionis ad actionem praecedentem"). Retaliation demands, "for instance, that if a man strike, he be struck back. This kind of justice is laid down in the law (*Exodus* 21:23, 24): *He shall render life for life, eye for eye,* etc."[13]

This retributive pattern, which is generally taken to be the principle that lies at the heart of Dante's moral system in hell, receives, on the face of it, an appropriate exemplification in Bertran de Born's sin. Dante has a way of demanding, as we know, the highest standards of conduct from those who occupy the highest offices. It seems appropriate, then, that Bertran, the poet-counselor who encroached on the king's political authority, should paradoxically become an emblem of the authority of the divine law and have his own body become a metaphor for the disruption he incited: his head, cut off from his body, literally bears witness to his revolt against the figurehead as well as to the objective collapse of the metaphor of the body politic.

As anyone can gather from a primer of medieval political theology, the unity of both civil society and the church is conventionally envisioned in terms of an analogy between both institutions and the organic unity of the natural body.[14] St. Paul (I Cor. 12:14) applied the metaphor of the human body as the symbolic reflection of the *corpus mysticum* of the church, whose head is Christ. The schismatics, unlike the heretics who hold a faith other than that professed by the Catholic church, hold the same faith and even practice the same worship, but violate the unity of the mystical body. The word "schism"—which was used by St. Paul to signify a tear in the fabric of the Corinthian church—Aquinas says, quoting the etymology of Isidore of Seville, derives "from a scission of mind."[15] The schismatics are properly so called because they willfully and intentionally take pleasure in the disunion of the community. Because, as Cicero says in *De officiis* (I, 7), the purpose of justice is to hold men together in a community, the schismatics violate the fundamental aim of justice. A secular version of the Pauline corporate doctrine of the church is available in John of Salisbury's Plutarchian description of the republic in the *Policraticus* (V, 2). The body politic, *corpus politicum*, is a metaphoric structure of order, a whole made of living, interdependent parts, with the head as "the citadel," in the language of Macrobius, and with feet, eyes, and limbs standing for different dignities and offices in a hierarchy of fixed functions.[16]

As a sower of discord Bertran de Born has violated the hierarchy and unity of civil society; more than that, his sinful act has fractured the organic unity of what paradoxically is known as "the king's two bodies." There is a formula by Baldus, a late fourteenth-century Neapolitan jurist, which crystallizes the long-accrued legal wisdom sanctioning both the laws of inheritance and of dynastic continuity: "Pater et filius unum fictione iuris sunt."[17] The unity of the two, father and son, is a fiction which has the weight of law and which, as such, subtends the principle of continuity of the royal line of succession: Bertran has divided the unity against itself and goes now as "due in uno e uno in due." It can be said, since the material symbol of the unity is the authority and perpetuity of the crown, that Bertran, by willing the king's authority to be usurped, has abrogated the authority of the figurehead.

The punishment which is meted out to Bertran depends on the reparative operation of justice, which properly belongs to the sphere of commutative justice. St. Thomas Aquinas, closely following Aristotle's *Ethics*, discusses the parts of justice and identifies its two main operations as distributive and commutative.[18] In either case the essential aim is to achieve what Aquinas calls "aequalitas" (equality), for an act of justice is to render unto each what was his own. In commutative justice equality is achieved according to an arithmetical mean; in distributive justice, which has reparation as its specific province, the desired equality is attained through geometrical proportionality, by rearranging the balance between the whole and its parts. Or, in the words of St. Thomas, "in distributive justice something is given to a private individual, in so far as what belongs to the whole is due to the part, and in a quantity that is proportionate to the importance of the position of that part in respect to the whole. Consequently, in distributive justice a person receives all the more of the common goods, according as he holds a more prominent position in the community."[19] The just mean, in other words, is observed not according to equality between one thing and another but according to proportion between things and persons. It is possible to suggest that the task of carrying out God's distributive justice in the *Divine Comedy* is assigned to Fortune—the other face of Nature—which is figured in *Inferno* VII as the blind but purposeful intelligence which apportions the economy of limited goods according to a pattern of providential order but without an apparent adjustment for merit and prosperity. It is this gap that makes unaccountable and illusory, in the explicit formulations of *Inferno* VII, Fortune's steady shifts.

In commutative justice the specific aim is always equality, "so that one person should pay back to the other just so much as he has become richer out of that which belongs to the other." In this case there is a necessary equalization of thing with thing which is sustained, as said earlier, by an arithmetical mean: "Thus 5 is the mean between 6 and 4, since it exceeds the first and is exceeded by the second by 1. If each has 5 to start with, and one receives 1 from what belongs to the other, he will have 6 and the other will be left with 4. Justice will be served when both are brought back to the mean" (*Summa theologiae* IIa IIae, 61, 2).

The principle of counterpassion, the form that divine judgment takes, belongs to the domain of commutative justice because it deals with equality between thing and thing or between passion and action. Equality between passion and action cannot always be achieved in an exact manner, and St. Thomas must grant that there is a "certain proportionate standard of measurement," which properly belongs to distributive justice, in equalizing passion and action. "Take the case, to begin with, of a subordinate who injures his superior; his action," St. Thomas explains, "is more serious than a like action done on him in return. And so he who strikes a ruler is not only struck back, but also much more severely punished" (IIa IIae, 61, 4). It is clear, then, that commutative justice aims at restoring justice; but it is also clear that equity and justice are not identical terms. That they do not always coincide is openly stated by Aquinas's reference to Aristotle's assertion in his *Ethics* V, 5, that the just is not always the same as counterpassion, because reciprocation is the result of proportion and not of equality:

> Some people believe with the Pythagoreans that the just in the unqualified sense is reciprocity, for the Pythagoreans used to define the just without any qualification as "suffering that which one has done to another." Now, reciprocity corresponds neither to just action as distribution nor to just action as rectification; . . . for there are many cases in which reciprocity and the just are not identical, e.g. if a magistrate, while in office, strikes a man, he should not only be struck in return but should, in addition, be punished. Moreover, there is a great difference between voluntary and involuntary action.
>
> But in associations that are based on mutual exchange, the just in this sense constitutes the bond that holds the association together, that is, reciprocity in terms of a proportion and not in terms of exact equality in the return.

On the face of it, Dante does not worry about the degree of possible arbitrariness in the transactions lodged at the heart of the relationship between equality and justice. Within his vision of human history the world is represented as given over to darkness because justice, as the crown of the virtues and a moral habit, is exiled from it. The eclipse of justice from the world notwithstanding, Dante repeatedly affirms throughout the poem the triumph and just measure of God's law in inflicting punishments. In *Inferno* XXIX, immediately after the exchange the pilgrim has with Bertran de Born, Dante refers to the punishments of the falsifiers administered by "la ministra / de l'alto Sire infallibil giustizia" (55–56) (the ministress of the High Lord, infallible Justice); or, more specifically, one can easily find a line such as "perché sia colpa e duol d'una misura" (*Purg.* XXX, 108) (so that fault and grief may be of one measure), and in *Paradiso*, "E in sua dignità mai non rivene, / se non riempie dove colpa vota, / contra mal dilettar, con giuste pene" (VII, 82–84) (and to its dignity it never returns unless, where fault has emptied, it fill up with just penalties against evil delights). In *Inferno* XXVIII, however, it is possible to catch more than a glimpse of Dante's perception of disparity in the workings of justice. But let there be no misunderstanding: this perception does not suggest a tragic recognition of the futility of suffering or the miscarriage of justice, as a character such as Job would have it. At stake, rather, is the difficult question of determining what the identifying principle of justice may be, and the extent to which moral judgments are in fact aesthetic judgments and vice versa.

The repeated statements of a measurable bond between a crime and its punishment are put to the test in *Inferno* XXVIII as if Dante meant to probe Aristotle's and Aquinas's insight on the possible aporia between justice and equality. Thus, it is not surprising that this stretch of the text should be so heavily punctuated by a rhetoric of balanced correspondences, equality, numbers, and measurements, which, taken together, have primarily the effect of dramatizing the irreducibility of justice to a system of quantifiable values. Let us see how this mathematical pattern, which is, as we have seen, the model of justice, works out in the canto.

At the start, the poet announces that if he were to "narrar più volte" (3) (to narrate many times), he would not be able to relate the ghastliness of the schismatic's suffering; he also states that no description could "aequar . . . / il modo de la nona bolgia sozzo" (20–21) (equal the foul fashion of the ninth pouch). Later, after the pilgrim sees Bertran walking as if he were "due in uno e uno in due" (125) (two in one and one in two), Bertran draws attention to the excess of his suffering:

> . . . 'Or vedi la pena molesta,
> tu che, spirando, vai veggendo i morti:
> vedi s'alcuna è grande come questa.
>
> (*Inf.* XXVIII, 130–32)

(See now my grievous penalty, you who, breathing, go to view the dead: see if any other is so great as this.)

From Bertran's viewpoint the principle of just measure has been violated. Dante, on the other hand, will continue to probe the sense of possible equality in God's justice. At the very exordium of *Inferno* XXIX the text records again how for the pilgrim the encounter with Bertran is a vision of deepest pathos. The lacerated figure of the Provençal poet so enthralls Dante's sympathy that Vergil must warn him not to gaze insistently but be ready for the fresher horrors of the falsifiers' imminent tortures. Vergil even wonders whether Dante was attempting to count the mutilated shades: "Tu non hai fatto sì a l'altre bolge; / pensa, se tu annoverar le credi, / che miglia ventidue la valle volge" (*Inf.* XXIX, 7–9) (You have not done so at the other pits. Consider, if you think to count them, that the valley circles two and twenty miles).

The unique mathematical detail about the architectonic construction of hell prepares the allusion to the archetypal architect of antiquity, to Daedalus's flight from the labyrinth later in the canto (116). But it also brings into focus the metaphoric connection between arithmetic and justice. Since the *Timaeus*, justice has been figured as a mathematical harmony, because the order itself of the cosmos is founded on the virtue of numbers in whose likeness all things have been made. Or as the *Book of Wisdom* has it, "omnia in mensura, numero, et pondere fecisti" (11:21) (you formed everything according to measure, number and weight), a statement which elicits Isidore's gloss, "tolle numerum in rebus omnibus, et omnia pereunt" (*Etym.* III, 4, 4) (take away the number in all things and all things perish). In this context it could be added that justice is referred to in the numerical symbolism of the Pythagoreans, as Macrobius reports in the *Commentary on the Dream of Scipio*, by the number eight, because eight is the product of equals: "two times two times two. Since it is the product of even numbers and may be divided equally, even down to the unit, which does not admit of division in mathematical computation, it deserves to receive the name Justice."[20]

But for Dante there are no definable, mechanical categories which can account for the judgments Minos gives, and, ironically, in *Inferno* XXVIII the "two" of justice may call attention to the uneven works of justice. More literally, the numbers "two in one and one in two" refer to the fact that the very unity of Bertran's individuality, which etymologically means that which cannot be divided (*in-dividuum*), is broken. More important, the point of the canto's extended language of computation is to dramatize the disparity as the unlikeness of justice to anything but itself. There is another passage at the beginning of canto XXIX that questions the principle of justice's equality. This is the passage in which Vergil explains that while Dante was brooding over the halved figures, a kinsman of his, Geri del Bello, was pointing threateningly at him. Dante adds that Geri, whom he calls, "un spirto del mio sangue" (*Inf.* XXIX, 20) (a spirit of my own blood), died of a violent death which still lies unavenged: "O duca mio, la violenta morte / che non li è vendicata ancor,' diss'io, / per alcun che de l'onta sia consorte, / fece lui disdegnoso; ond'el sen gio / sanza parlarmi, sì com'io estimo: / e in ciò m'ha el fatto a sé più pio" (31–36) (O my leader, I said, the violent death which is not yet avenged for him by any who is partner in the shame made him indignant; wherefore, as I judge, he went on without speaking to me, and thereby has he made me pity him the more).

The concern of the narrative here is with the mechanism of revenge as an accepted moral procedure. More precisely, Dante recalls a blood feud, as the phrase "un spirto del mio sangue" implies. A blood feud entails the moral duty of a retaliatory action: inflicting on the murderers of a kinsman a punishment equal and symmetrically corresponding to that murder. Although in recent times there have been commentators, such as Isidoro del Lungo, who read the line about the death which "non li è vendicata ancor" to mean that Dante shares Geri's ethics of revenge, Francesco da Buti, Iacopo della Lana, and l'Ottimo Commento agree that Dante is here challenging the Florentine practice of revenge, the economy of an eye for an eye and a tooth for a tooth.[21] Let me add that the adjective "pio," which conveys the pilgrim's attitude of mercy, signals that the pilgrim turns away from the code of revenge, the *lex talionis*, which has its sanction in the natural belief in the organic bonds joining members of a family in one living, corporate whole. Exactly like the *contrapasso*, private revenge depends on a law of nature, of cause and effect, or the principle whereby every act has a consequence and the consequence is commensurate with that act.[22]

As Dante turns away from this practice, one cannot but be struck by the overt contradiction between the daughters of God, mercy and justice, or, to put it differently, between Dante's Christian conduct of renouncing violence and the principles of God's justice, which are akin to revenge and seem to perpetuate violence. The sense of a paradox between mercy and justice has traditionally been the object of intense theological speculations from the eleventh century on. The paradox cannot be dismissed, as Peter Damian, Anselm, and other theological writers were to discover, as a simplistic juxtaposition between the morality of the Old Testament and the morality of the New Testament, whereby with Christ the law of love does away with the law of divine wrath, which had threatened to break with Moses.[23] Justice and mercy are acknowledged as God's attributes even in the Old Testament. As Psalm 101 has it, "I will sing of mercy and judgement unto thee."

What is more likely is that Dante recognizes that vengeance does not belong to man but is a prerogative of God's justice and even its synonym. The idea of God as the Avenger is quite conventional, and it ranges from the Bible to Lactantius's objection to Stoic and Epicurean characterizations of God as a remote benevolence incapable of wrath, to Aquinas's sense that by God's wrath a sin will be transformed into a moral good.[24]

From this standpoint it is possible to view man's involvement in revenge as an act which harbors within itself an immense pride, the pride that one can play God and punish the guilty, the pride that one's own world of schemes and plots can eclipse public laws. Thus, two incompatible forms of justice—private revenge, which is ungodly, and counterpassion, which is God's law—seem to be used to sustain the rationale of the uniqueness of God's justice. Yet it is difficult to escape the suspicion that Dante is questioning here all forms of revenge under the guise of rejecting the way it is practiced by men bound to the observance of the law of nature. For revenge is a tragic experience in that it never restores the condition of the world to what it was before violence set in; rather, it is an act by which the killer yields to and invites his own destruction. More important, the phrase "la violenta morte / che non li è vendicata ancor" and other phrases about God's "living justice" allowing vengeance for God's own wrath (*Par.* VI, 88–90) and favoring "vendetta . . . de la vendetta del peccato antico" (92–93) (vengeance for the vengeance of the ancient sin, said of Titus's God-willed destruction of the temple) make clear, revenge always doubles the crime and perpetuates it. The adverb "ancor" suggests, further, the temporal pattern of revenge and discloses the avenger's subjection to the tyranny of the past. Though revenge appears as an act of self-assertion, by it the avenger is caught in the past and always ends up resembling the very enemy he plans to destroy.

But as Dante approaches this genuine ethical impasse, whereby God's justice appears excessive to Bertran or is like the revenge the pilgrim renounces in his life, there is an impulse to bracket it. What seems to be a perplexing ethical predicament, as in cantos XXVIII and XXIX of *Inferno*, is generally retrieved either as part of the pathos of the narrative or as the affirmation of an order whereby evil chaos is never allowed to prevail. In point of fact, Dante will explicitly acknowledge that man can never presume to plumb the depth of justice's enigma. The issue is raised with great clarity in *Paradiso* XVIII and XIX, and we must turn to these two cantos.[25]

This is the Heaven of Jupiter and of Geometry, and, unsurprisingly, it is in this context that Dante discusses justice. Jupiter is appropriately called the "temprata stella" (*Par.* XVIII, 68) (temperate star), both in the sense that it is free from extremes of heat and cold and in the musical sense that it is harmonious. After the pilgrim sees the warriors in the cross of light—among whom are Joshua, Maccabeus, Charlemagne, Roland, and the crusader Godfrey of Bouillon—the souls of Jupiter arrange themselves in letters and spell out the first verse of the *Book of Wisdom*: DILIGITE IUSTITIAM QUI IUDICATIS TERRAM (90–93) (Love justice, you who judge the earth), a line which admonishes that justice must be the object of a ruler's love. On the M of the fifth word, TERRAM, innumerable sparks form the figure of an eagle (94–108). In brief, justice shows itself forth as biblical discourse and as a painterly figure. In an overt extension of his musings on justice, in

Paradiso XIX the pilgrim wants to know why a man who is born on the banks of the Indus and has never heard of Christ but lives without sin and dies without faith should be punished: "ov'è questa giustizia che 'l condanna? / ov'è la colpa sua, se ei non crede?" (77–78) (where is this justice which condemns him? Where is his sin if he does not believe?). The answer is that there is no salvation without faith in Christ (103–8). The logical answer to the query, formulated a little earlier in the canto, is that the human eye is to eternal justice as the eye is to the sea: the bottom can be seen at the shore, but in the open sea the eye cannot perceive what the depth conceals (58–63). And as if to stress the unfathomable quality of God's justice, *Paradiso* XX lists among the blessed two pagans—the emperor Trajan (43–45), who is the Roman emperor exemplary for his justice and pity (*Purg.* X, 93), and the obscure but just Ripheus the Trojan (67–69)—both born outside of the Revelation and providentially saved.

To grasp Dante's understanding of justice as the absolute and unfathomable metaphysical principle of the cosmos, we must examine his reasons for linking justice with geometry. An encyclopedist such as Hugh of St. Victor reminds us that there are three types of geometry (planimetry, altimetry, and cosmimetry) and, of the three, cosmimetry provides the measure of the universe (*Didascalicon* II, 14). More specifically, geometry is concerned with space and with immobile magnitude, and, as he puts it, is "the contemplative delineation of forms" by which the limits of every object are shown. That there is an essential relation between the idea of geometry and the idea of justice was formulated by Plato in order to convey his conviction that, like geometry, justice is neither adventitious nor is it vulnerable to chaotic vagaries and to the inconsistencies of opinion. Like geometry, which is based on the law of inference, whereby one point in space entails other points, justice joins together the individual soul to the city and to the entirety of the cosmos. Like geometry's, justice's mode of existence is absolute, its perfection supreme, its order exact. The power of Plato's stunning vision, as has been suggested earlier, affected Aristotle, St. Thomas Aquinas, and Dante, who all dramatize justice in terms of mathematical relations and proportionalities. Dante, however, radicalizes Plato's vision and places divine goodness beyond all categories and predicaments of knowledge.[26] At the end of *Paradiso*, as the pilgrim approaches the vision of God, his failure to see how the image conforms to the circle is rendered through the figure of the geometer who fails to square the circle (*Par.* XXXIII, 133–38).

This awareness of the discrepancy between absolute justice and the seeming inequalities in its workings does not lead Dante to an impasse. On the contrary, the critical insights he has gained in the ethical debate he has staged are neither repressed nor irresolutely concealed. The perception of the disparity in justice will turn into a starting point for further critical questions about poetry and its power to capture adequately the moral and political order. As we shall presently see, Dante's interrogations will have a tortuous flow and will take a detour through the specifically poetic realm of metaphor and rhetoric. This detour is not a gratuitous drifting into questions of style and craft. Its necessity lies in the fact that ethics and politics, which are founded on metaphoric correspondences, have concealed the power of metaphor: political theory, as we have seen, enacts the metaphor of the body politic; the schismatics violate the metaphor of the mystical body. In this perspective, only a detour can unveil what the solid body of the ideologies has forgotten. As for divine justice, in and of itself it is likened to an unfathomable sea surface, yet the way we know it is through its visible effects, which are proportion, exchange, measure, restitution, and so on. What does this terminology mean?

In truth, this terminology of reciprocity reflects primarily a preoccupation with what Aristotle and Aquinas would call political economy, the type of justice which may provide a sufficiency for a community and which carries out the economy of the natural order. That there is a literal coupling of justice and economy is quite clear in the case of distributive justice. Just as the meditation on commutative justice comes to a head in Bertran, the meditation on distributive justice in *Convivio* climaxes with the praise of Bertran de Born's liberality and is introduced by a passage on the acquisition and keeping of riches. Covetousness, which can be defined as an inequality of the measure in the things man possesses, is considered by Dante an imperfection in which "nulla distributiva giustizia risplende" (there shines no distributive justice).[27] But the economy of commutative justice cannot be viewed in literal terms, because its aim is not the distribution of things among people; it is, rather, the equality of thing and thing, the correspondence of an action to another. This metaphoricity of justice is not unusual in philosophical speculations. Suffice it to say that Aristotle, in a different context, calls justice metaphorical when he writes that "metaphorically, and in virtue of a certain resemblance, there is a justice, not indeed between a man and himself but between certain parts of him." Such a definition is picked up by St. Thomas, who writes that "by a figure of speech justice is said to operate within one and the same man in that his reason commands his desirous and spirited emotions, and these obey, and also in general that each of his parts is fittingly composed. Aristotle entitles this justice in the metaphorical sense of the term."[28] In *Inferno* XXVIII the possibility of yoking poetic metaphor and the ethics of commutative justice is the dramatic substance of the text.

The protasis of the canto articulates the predicament of the poet in his effort to find metaphors adequate to portray the hideous spectacle of the mutilated bodies he sees.

Chi poria mai pur con parole sciolte
  dicer del sangue e de le piaghe a pieno
  ch'i'ora vidi, per narrar più volte?
Ogne lingua per certo verria meno
  per lo nostro sermone e per la mente
  c'hanno a tanto comprender poco seno.
S'el s'aunasse ancor tutta la gente
  che già, in su la fortunata terra
  di Puglia, fu del suo sangue dolente
per li Troiani e per la lunga guerra
  che de l'anella fé sì alte spoglie,
  come Livio scrive, che non erra,
con quella che sentio di colpi doglie
  per contastare a Ruberto Guiscardo;
  e l'altra il cui ossame ancor s'accoglie
a Ceperan, là dove fu bugiardo
  ciascun Pugliese, e là da Tagliacozzo,
  dove sanz' arme vinse il vecchio Alardo;
e qual forato suo membro e qual mozzo
  mostrasse, d'aequar sarebbe nulla
  il modo de la nona bolgia sozzo.

(1–21)

(Who could ever fully tell, even in unfettered words, though many times narrating, the blood and the wounds that I now saw? Surely every tongue would fail, because of our speech and our memory which have little capacity to comprehend so much.

Were all the people assembled again who once in the fateful land of Apulia bewailed their blood shed by the Trojans, and those of the long war that made so vast a spoil of rings—as Livy writes, who does not err—together with those who felt the pain of blows in the struggle with Robert Guiscard, and those others whose bones are still heaped up at Cerperano, where every Apulian was false, and there by Tagliacozzo where old Alardo conquered without arms; and one should show his limb pierced through, and another his cut off, it would be nothing to equal the foul fashion of the ninth pouch.)

The burden of the passage is to acknowledge the poet's inability to give an adequate representation of what he witnesses, and he does so by listing the battles fought at different times in one war theater. The grim metonymic sequence of episodes drawn equally from classical and medieval history—Rome's war with the Sannites, the Punic wars, and two other contemporary medieval wars—would still fall short, however, of the heap of dismembered parts and bodies stuck together in the vast landscape of death the pilgrim beholds. Recalled here for this tableau of horrors are chronicles and annals of warfare, but there is no encompassing metaphor for the chaotic, random accumulation of bodies. The *praeteritio* of the first six lines, which pull together the authority of several texts, the *Tristia*, *Aeneid*, and *Convivio*, dramatizes, ironically, the poet's disclaimer.

The text's major echo, though still a distant one, is from a passage in *Convivio* where Dante discusses two possible ineffabilities and attributes them to the weakness of the intellect to grasp the nature of his love and to the "cortezza del nostro parlare" (shortness of our speech).[29] This rhetoric of authorial modesty is picked up at line 20, where the failure of the poetic metaphor is restated through the word "aequar": no metaphor can equal the foul reality of the ninth pouch. The primary aim of the disclaimer is to convey a sense of the utter artlessness of language, of dumbness in the presence of the unspeakable magnitude of horror in what paradoxically is such a crammed space. But a more compelling reason forces itself on us, a reason which makes the pilgrim's initial pathos slide toward the poet's tragic insight. There is, actually, a double sense of one word that Dante exploits. The word, "aequar," is, first of all, a term of grammatical comparison deriving from "aequus" (and "aequus" is the synonym, as Du Cange's *Glossarium* and Isidore's *Etymologies* report, for "justus").[30] Second, Dante's "aequar" is etymologically related to *aequalitas*, which is the aim of commutative justice. By this buried semantic resonance of the word, in short, it is as if Dante obliquely wants to draw us within a domain wherein aesthetic and ethical concerns, poetic and theological ideas of justice, must be brought together. This initial authorial modesty, however, jars sharply with the reference, toward the middle of the passage, to the authority of Livy, "che non erra" (12) (who does not err).

The attribution of infallibility to Livy reverses the poet's *praeteritio*, his sense of inability to render adequately the scene of horrors. Livy's infallibility dramatizes the force of sheer fact, the power writing has to posit history and to become its documentary evidence. This oscillation within metaphor, its power to constitute itself as fact and its powerlessness in confronting and comprehending the fragmentary, confused materiality of bodies is not an isolated feature of the canto. I have shown earlier how the representation of justice wavers between the quantifiable and the incommensurable. One can add that the human body itself, evoked as a metaphor of order for church and state, appears in the canto as a series of fragmented and disjointed parts: the intestines, chin, foot, heart, hair, head, and brain are itemized, emptied of the symbolic purposeful value they would have in the corporate ideology of John of Salisbury. The organic and metaphoric unity and symmetry of the body collapses as Dante shows schism as the disintegrative, literal experience of war.

There is a rationale, generally neglected by scholars, why war should be

the privileged metaphor in the canto of the schismatics and sowers of discord. The rationale is provided by St. Thomas Aquinas, who in a passage
of his *Summa theologiae* (IIa IIae, 39, 1) generally cited by Dante scholars
only to draw attention to the differences between schism and heresy, joins
war and schism, along with strife and sedition, as vices contrary to the unity
and peace of the church and of civil society.[31] It is within these conceptual
boundaries that we can understand the poet's insistence on war throughout
the canto. I have already examined the catalog of battles given in the opening lines of *Inferno* XXVIII. Yet all the pilgrim's other encounters in this
canto evoke the violent world of war, betrayals, tyranny, and piracy. Mohammed, for instance, gives a prophecy of war to be relayed to Fra
Dolcino: "Or di a fra Dolcin dunque che s'armi, / tu che forse vedra' il sole
in breve, / s'ello non vuol qui tosto seguitarmi, / si di vivanda, che stretta
di neve / non rechi la vittoria al Noarese" (55–59) (Tell Fra Dolcino, then,
you who perhaps will see the sun before long, if he would not soon follow
me here, so to arm himself with victuals that stress of snow may not bring
victory to the Novarese).[32]

The reference to Mohammed as a prophet of war deserves a special
gloss. The medieval mythology about him is utterly imaginary: in the
Chanson de Roland Mohammed is seen as a god of the Moslems; in
Brunetto's *Tresor* he is a cardinal of the church; in other sources he is
always a heretic. All of them (and Dante's text is consistent with this tradition) bypass Islam's otherness in relation to Christianity. These rampant
legends were largely inspired by fear of what was conceived to be Islam's
military expansion as well as by a desire to promote the Crusades, but there
is an exception to these raw fantasies of violence. Peter the Venerable, who
was a friend of Bernard of Clairvaux and who embodied the ideals and
values of the Cluniac monastic order, wrote his *Liber contra sectam sive
haeresim Saracenorum* in the belief that the expansion of Islam had to be
countered not by the coercion of arms but by the peaceful power of intellectual persuasion.[33] Dante, whose vision is rooted in the spirituality of
Bernard, is close to Peter's ideals of peace and to St. Francis's premature
effort to preach in the "proud presence" of the sultan (*Par*. XI, 100–105.)
The statement, on the face of it, jars with the point that Dante certainly
gives due recognition to the scientific work of the Arabs, and yet he, much
like Peter the Venerable and St. Bernard, also exalts crusaders such as
Godfrey of Bouillon and Cacciaguida. The fact is that to him the Crusades
are a response to the doctrinal divisiveness and to the war brought about,
as appears from *Inferno* XXVIII, by Mohammed's violation of the unity of
the church.

Dante's view of war is central to the figuration of *Inferno* XXVIII and the
schismatics. The canto's references to Fra Dolcino and Mohammed are
followed by the recollection of an episode from Lucan's *Pharsalia*, the

story of Curio, whose tongue is now cut off in his throat but who "a dir fu così ardito" (102) (was so daring in his speech). The allusion is to Curio's urging Caesar, at the time when he took up arms against the republic but hesitated in crossing the Rubicon, to leave legality behind and to seek the arbitrament of war. Civil war, in effect, is the secular counterpart of ecclesial division. This pattern of war and words, which involves Mohammed's prophecy, Fra Dolcino's own preaching, and Curio's political counsel, stretches to the representation of Bertran de Born and his rhetoric of war.

It is well known how in the second book of *De vulgari eloquentia* (II, ii, 7–8) Dante identifies the three great arguments of poetry, the *magnalia*, in "armorum probitas" (prowess in Arms), "amoris accensio" (the fire of Love), and "directio voluntatis" (the right direction of the Will). He then singles out the three troubadours who have excelled in the treatment of these exalted themes: "Circa quae sola, si bene recolimus, illustres viros invenimus vulgariter poetasse; scilicet, Bertramum de Bornio, arma; Arnoldum Danielem, amorem; Gerardum de Bornello, rectitudinem" (And, if we duly consider, we shall find that the illustrious writers have written poetry in the Vulgar Tongue on these subjects exclusively, namely, Bertam of Born on Arms; Arnauld Daniel on Love; Gerard of Borneil on Righteousness).

In the context of *De vulgari eloquentia*, the tragic voice of Bertran stands for the martial prowess and passions that, as Dante laments, cannot yet be found among the Italian poets. Among these, war is at most a metaphoric register for love, as one finds in Cavalcanti's "Donna me prega" (A lady begs me). But in Dante's perception what is still missing is the heroic imagination, the call to bold action that is the sheer power quickening Bertran's *sirventese*. In what is an overt displacement of erotic myths, Bertran is one who, he says, finds no pleasure in peace and sings the sinister beauty of war, the excitement of battle, as the experience which alone can incite the young—and the thematic strain of youth steadily appears in his poetry, as is clear from Dante's reference to the "re giovane" (135) (young king)—to questing, magnanimous deeds.[34]

But in *Inferno* XXVIII we have Dante's farewell to arms. The esthetic passion for martial heroics is no longer recognizable: nor is war a noble act which fashions the world and transfigures man's moral values. Very simply, war is now stripped of its seductive aura. As Dante witnesses the fury and futility of war, he bursts open Bertran's aesthetic illusions and heroic myths. More precisely, what Dante is dramatizing is the gap between his poetic judgment of Bertran as a unique war poet and the present ethical judgment, whereby he seals the tragedy of the heroic style of a will that incites division. In *De vulgari eloquentia*, for instance, the spiritual value of the poetry of arms is asserted by the assumption that it corresponds to the impulses of the vegetative faculty of the soul, whose power is to provide self-preservation. Ironically, that poetry appears now as one that far from preserving life inexorably issues forth from wasted lives.

The suggestion of a split between Dante the aesthetician at the time of his literary judgments in *De vulgari eloquentia* and Dante the stern moralist within the confines of the *Divine Comedy* may seem to provide a pleasing and acceptable exegetical scheme. It would indeed be tempting to establish a correspondence between, on the one hand, the thematics of schism and, on the other, the split between the two roles of the poet as aesthetician and moralist. In a sense, this is a real element of Dante's representation. There is a paradox, for instance, between Dante's moral judgment of Bertran's poetics of war and the fact that *Inferno* XXVIII still resonates with echoes from Bertran's poetry. The description of Mohammed—"tra le gambe pendevan le minugia; / la corata pareva e 'l tristo sacco / che merda fa di quel che si trangugia. / Mentre che tutto in lui veder m'attacco, / guardommi, e con le man s'aperse il petto, / dicendo: 'Or vedi com'io me dilacco'" (25–30) (His entrails were hanging between his legs, and the vitals could be seen and the foul sack that makes ordure of what is swallowed. While I was all absorbed in gazing on him, he looked at me and with his hands pulled open his breast, saying, "Now see how I rend myself")—recalls the gore of corpses cloven through the trunk from "Miei sirventes vuolh far de ls reis amdos." The opening lines of the canto, "Se s'adunasse ancor tutta la gente. . . . E qual forato suo membro e qual mozzo / Mostrasse, da aequar sarebbe nulla," echo "Si tuit li dole e. lh plor e. lh marrimen," the lament for the "jove Rei englés." The presence of these textual reminiscences in *Inferno* XXVIII shows that Dante's acknowledgment of Bertran's poetic achievement is undoubtedly undiminished since *De vulgari eloquentia*, though the beauty of the language is now undisguised as evil and is tied to a moral reality that Bertran could neither envisage nor control.

Clearly, the split is not only between the intellectual positions of *De vulgari* and those of the *Divine Comedy*: the split is now internalized within the narrator himself. Through this strategy of dramatizing his inner division, Dante would seem to suggest that aesthetic judgments and moral judgments are separable. But the *Divine Comedy* also goes a long way in undoing the illusion that there can ever be an aestheticism conceivable as an abstract form of beauty which can be isolated from the rules of ethics. The prominent sinners in *Inferno* XXVIII have one thing in common. Fra Dolcino, as a leader of the Fraticelli and a self-styled emissary of the Holy Ghost, makes prophecies which would fulfill the expectations of the everlasting gospel; Mohammed is the warrior involved in apostasy, which is viewed by l'Ottimo Commento as the fraudulent luring of his people away from the laws of Christ; Curio instigates Caesar into transgressing the boundaries of the law and is punished by having his tongue cut off; Bertran is paying for his political eloquence. They are all sinners whose words are equivalent to actions or immediately cause an action. Insofar as words are performative, and are bound to reality, there is an ethics of words which is the ethics of action. For Dante, then, the boundary between the ethical and the aesthetic seems to fade, and the two overlap into one.

In the downfall of these sinners, and especially Bertran's, we view the power of words and of poetry to open up a crack in the unity of the political body, to usurp authority and create a value system that would replace and double the existing ones. From this viewpoint, Dante's wonder at the sight of Mohammed and his fascination with the shade of the troubadour, which Vergil sensed at the beginning of *Inferno* XXIX, are all too understandable: these schismatics, in their paradoxical belief in the unity of words and actions, have variously reduced the idea of the body politic and of the mystical body to arbitrary metaphorical constructions they can manipulate, violate at will, and duplicate. More specifically, Bertran, the poet-counselor, whose tragic end is heightened by the similar fate incurred by Curio or, in the preceding canto, by another corrupt counselor, Guido da Montefeltro, is for Dante an image of what he himself could be with his own claims of political authority and his own resentful polemics against literary traditions and political institutions.

Unlike Bertran, Mohammed, and Curio, however, Dante writes a critique of language and of poetry, which is understood only as a rhetorical construct. His strategy, in fact, is to pull back into authorial modesty and to claim that he is unable to comprehend the material fragments of bodies into a metaphoric totality. At the same time, however, he does violence to Bertran's text. As he dismembers its integrity and severs lines from the Provençal poet's poetic corpus, he usurps its authority and, in effect, doubles Bertran's own violence. By these oscillations Dante allows us to see that the poetic metaphor conceals deep within itself a scandalous breach: it has power in the full sense of the word, power to foment rebellion and power to renounce power and to undo all claims of power, its own included; it posits the generality of the discourse of order but is dumb in the presence of the random disarticulation of bodies. Metaphor to Dante is the unified locus of contradictory pulls. From this perspective it could be said that a poet has political power when he does not seek it, and loses his head, as Bertran literally does, when he usurps authority.

It would go against the grain of Dante's own poetic argument in *Inferno* XXVIII to suppose that the ambiguities of metaphor, which he explicitly confronts (metaphor's characteristic of being two things at the same time and of being divided against itself), describe simply Dante's own poetics as opposed to Bertran's poetics of power. What Dante says about the doubleness of poetic metaphor unavoidably involves all the structures that have a metaphoric foundation, such as the body politic and the mystical body. But he circumvents and challenges Bertran's reduction of ethics and justice to questions of rhetoric and mere power play. In their violation of the metaphors of the *corpus politicum* and of the *corpus mysticum* Mohammed, Curio, and Bertran have, in fact, severed the unity of poetry and ethics, and have beheaded poetry and ethics from their theological sources. The outcome of their acts is that they have declared null and void the principle of unity, and, thereby, they have made war the basis of life and have sealed, as war always does, the collapse of discourse.

Through the representation of these sinners as well as the sinners in *Inferno* XXIX who double the economy of nature, Dante, who is not a manufacturer of theological pieties or of empty moralistic formulas, faces the crisis of the principle of unity, which is the core of his mature vision (and of the encyclopedic project he constructs). How does he move beyond the impasse figured by the schismatics? He certainly knows that the world is the stage of God's judgment, but he also knows that the workings of justice remain always beyond his grasp, as they are beyond ours. On the face of it, in *Inferno* XXVIII, as the principle of commutative justice is announced, justice seems dimmed by the horror it administers.

In the Renaissance tragic texts, the disproportion of suffering and the randomness of violence force on us, as they did on those who wrote those texts, a sense of how cruel and unacceptable the scheme of things must be, if it allows so much grief. But Dante knows better. He affirms, as Bertran could not understand but as Plato and Thomas Aquinas did, both that ethics is rooted in justice and, more important, that justice is not merely an object one may be said to master or possess but is alien to the self and is irreducible to the measure of oneself. In effect, the providential salvation of Trajan and Ripheus has only shown that Dante's idea of justice is the Platonic idea of the Good, dwelling in a realm beyond and fulfilling all categories of knowledge and rational ethics. From this absolute perspective all constructions, Dante's own included, are arbitrary and violable. This idea of justice accounts for what Gilson, in the wake of Sarolli, has correctly called Dante's theological humility.[35] Finally, this sense of justice's radical otherness, which, as chapter 9 below will argue, is figured as justice's exile, literally calls one to will it in one's soul, to track its tracings in history, and so to constitute oneself as an ethical agent.

Chapter 5

LOGIC AND POWER

"BY ITSELF, logic is practically useless." So states John of Salisbury toward the end of his *Metalogicon* (IV, 28). He quickly goes on to add that "only when it is associated with other studies does logic shine, and then by a virtue that is communicated by them." John's perplexity over the intrinsic utility of logic as an end in itself or as a tool that retards or promotes progress in philosophy or encourages verbosity has to be understood in terms of his broad concern over the *trivium*, under attack by "Cornificius" and the detractors of the liberal arts.[1] Logic to John of Salisbury, in fact, means two things. First, it designates the narrow science of systematic, argumentative reasoning (*ratio disserendi*), which discloses manners of disputation and analyzes the construction of proofs. Second, it is an overall heading describing all the arts of language.

John of Salisbury's doubts about the practical usefulness of this discipline are actually to be explained as a way of criticizing the practice of severing logic from the other liberal arts. This practice, which threatened the conviction of the unity of all the arts, had already been challenged by John's own teacher, Thierry of Chartres. But John certainly agrees with (and cites) St. Augustine's assessment in *De ordine* (II, 13): "For dialectics teaches both how to teach and how to learn. In dialectics, reason discloses its own identity, and makes manifest its nature, purpose, and potentialities. Dialectics alone knows how to know, and it alone both wills and has the power to make men learned" (*Metalogicon* IV, 25).

These statements by a thinker such as John of Salisbury allow us to gauge Dante's own ambivalent attitude toward what in this context I choose to call logic. As we have seen in chapter 3, Dante does not waver in his attacks against sophistry, which cunningly affects the appearance of wisdom, shuns its reality, and revels in the fog of fallacies. But this judgment cannot be construed as Dante's final, unequivocal appraisal of logic. His complex sense of the value and limit of this art of language is made manifest by two contradictory, polarized statements which figure in close succession, respectively at the end and the beginning of cantos X and XI of *Paradiso*. In the Heaven of the Sun, which is the planet of arithmetic, St. Thomas Aquinas directs the pilgrim's attention to a spirit in the wheel of the blessed, Siger of Brabant. Siger is described as he who "leggendo nel vico de li Strami / sillogizzò invidiosi veri" (lecturing in the Street of Straw demonstrated invidious truths) (*Par.* X, 137–39).

The reference, as is known, is to Siger of Brabant, Aquinas's contemporary and a teacher of philosophy in the 1260s in the Faculty of Arts at the University of Paris. I shall attempt to gloss these verses and the scene involving Siger in some detail later in the chapter. For now, let me stress that the truths Siger taught ("veri") render and translate the Latin *vera*, which is the object and purpose of logic. Logic teaches, in fact, "vera loqui," and, as Isidore, Rabanus Maurus, and Alcuin, among others, say, it separates "vera . . . a falsis."[2] And let me also stress that although the precise sense of Aquinas's characterization of Siger is not yet entirely clear, it is undebatable that Aquinas now admires his opponent's work on logic. By a sudden textual twist, on the other hand, *Paradiso* XI begins with Dante's apostrophe against syllogisms, laws, and medical aphorisms: "O insensata cura de' mortali, / quanto son difettivi sillogismi / quei che ti fanno in basso batter l'ali! / Chi dietro a iura, e chi ad aforismi" ("O insensate care of mortals, how vain are the reasonings that make thee beat thy wings in downward flight! One was going after law, another after the *Aphorisms*" (*Par.* XI, 1–4).

Dante's negative assessment of and abrupt reversal about logic, law, and medicine (two arts that, although modeled on the principles of nature, are constructed along logical paradigms) can be accounted for in terms of the immediate narrative context of canto XI. In the case of Siger, St. Thomas gave a positive valorization of logic, as if logic, this most Aristotelian science, provided indeed the method of all the sciences. At the outset of *Paradiso* XI, instead, logic is said to shape the discourses of law and the medical aphorisms of the likes of Taddeo Alderotti; more cogently, its main feature is identified as the syllogism (1). The word describes the pattern of thought as a deduction from two premises (such as the sorites and the enthymeme). But the adjective Dante deploys to qualify the syllogistic shape of arguments—"difettivi" (2)—casts syllogisms as dialectical fallacies.[3] One can legitimately infer that there may even be in Dante's apostrophe an oblique allusion to Siger's own *Impossibilia*, which are a series of self-contradictory syllogisms akin to empty sophisms, and are thus "difettivi silogismi."

It is more likely, however, that in stark contrast to the final lines of the preceding canto, the poet's own apostrophe at the beginning of *Paradiso* XI prepares this canto's new scene: Thomas Aquinas is about to deliver the hagiography of St. Francis, who opposes as useless all sophistical and contentious exercises because they are not after the truth but only the appearance of the truth. In a way, through the apostrophe against logic's fallacies, paralogisms, and deceptive arguments (which is what sophisms usually are), Dante acknowledges and shares, as chapter 3 above has argued, the Franciscan skepticism toward and opposition to the formal abstractions of the Aristotelians. Accordingly, he even alludes to logic's complicities with *iura* (4), and the allusion points to his sense, which I shall examine further on in this chapter, of the historical links between jurisprudence and logic. It also suggests that the aim of logic's subtle reasonings is power, or the manipulation of the law and, more generally, of the principles of nature. At any rate, Dante's reversal signals the presence of a far from clear, and even contradictory, perception of the value of logic. This ambivalence actually emerges from the whole corpus of his works. There is considerable irony, of course, in Dante's entertaining a contradictory view of logic, which is conventionally seen as the hegemonic "ars artium et scientia scientiarum." Logicians arrogate for themselves and their art the privilege to test the coherence or contradictoriness of statements: the ambivalent view of logic undercuts its claim to be the superior standard of intellectual judgment. In this chapter I shall isolate Dante's explicit reflections on and uses of the rhetoric of logic in some of his texts. But it may be well to remark at the outset that the logical sciences in Dante's work would not seem to be so important or even to figure much, if one were to judge from the roughly ten lines devoted to them in the appropriate entry in the *Enciclopedia dantesca*.[4]

To grasp Dante's sense of the ambiguities that characterize his understanding of logic (both admired and found limited), it is appropriate that one start by looking at the description of the art that is made available in *Convivio*, where dialectics is assigned to the Heaven of Mercury:

> E lo cielo di Mercurio si può comparare a la Dialettica per due proprietadi: che Mercurio è la più piccola stella del cielo, chè la quantitade del suo diametro non più di dugento trentadue miglia, secondo che pone Alfagrano, che dice quello essere de le ventotto parti una del diametro de la terra, lo quale è di seimila cinquecento miglia; l'altra proprietade si è che va più velata de li raggi del sole che null'altra stella. E queste due proprietadi sono ne la Dialettica: chè la Dialettica è minore in suo corpo che null'altra scienza, chè perfettamente è compilata e terminata in quello tanto testo che nell'Arte Vecchia e ne la Nuova si trova: e va più velata che nulla scienza in quanto procede con più sofistici e probabili argomenti che altra.

(II, xiii, 11–12)

(And the Heaven of Mercury may be compared to Dialectic on account of two properties, for Mercury is the smallest star in the sky, because the magnitude of its diameter is not more than two hundred and thirty-two miles, according to Alfraganus, who affirms that it is one twenty-eighth of the diameter of the earth, which is six thousand, five hundred miles. The other property is that in its course the rays of the sun veil it more than any other star. And these two properties exist in Dialectic, for Dialectic is less in its substance than any other science, because it is perfectly summed up and brought within the limits of such a text as is contained in *Ars Vetus* and *Ars nova*; and it is much more veiled in its course than any other science, inasmuch as it proceeds by sophistical and probable reasonings more than any other science.)

The linkage between the various planets and the arts is certainly not new. Dante in *Convivio* understands the word "ciel" (heaven) as *science*, as he glosses the first line of the song opening the second book: "Voi che 'ntendendo il terzo ciel movete." An antecedent for this sort of connection appears in texts such as the fifth-century *Marriage of Philology and Mercury* by Martianus Capella and even in the thirteenth-century *Composizione del mondo* by Ristoro d'Arezzo.[5] Because Mercury-Hermes, as one reads in Cicero's *On the Nature of the Gods*, is the inventor of letters, he is traditionally cast as the god presiding over all the arts. In the passage from *Convivio*, however, the specific connection between Mercury and dialectics stems from a mythographic history which is fairly standard. Isidore of Seville interprets Mercury from the Greek Hermes, which means "sermo vel interpretatio."[6] There is, in addition, a traditional mythic representation of Mercury with the head of a dog, which refers to Mercury's *ratio*, for the dog is considered the wisest of animals. At the same time, John of Salisbury in his *Metalogicon* understands dialectics, on the authority of Martianus Capella, as the outcome of the union of eloquence (Hermes) with Philology, who is the sister of Philosophy and Philocaly (IV, 29).[7]

Because my own chapter title manifestly mentions logic, while Dante speaks of dialectics in this passage from *Convivio*, as do Martianus and his commentators in their works, it is imperative that I account for the apparent discrepancy between the two terms. As I do so, I shall draw from the authoritative studies of Michaud-Quantin, Garin, and Weisheipl.[8] At the beginning of the twelfth century *dialectica* was the almost univeral designation of the discipline that controls the exercise of reason. Hugh of St. Victor, however, employed the term *logica* as the fourth division of philosophical knowledge. "Logic," Hugh said, "is separated into grammar and the theory of argument" (*Didascalicon* II, 28). He also believed that logic should occupy the most exalted position among the liberal arts, since without it no treatise of philosophy could be explained rationally. This view was endorsed by Robert Grosseteste as well as by the two Dominicans Albert the Great and Thomas Aquinas.

In fact, in the thirteenth century *logica* was described, as Albert the Great put it, as a form of knowledge. This sense of the word occurred at a time when Scholasticism raised dialectics over the other liberal arts and invested it with a sovereign epistemic value in theological arguments. But it is John of Salisbury's discussion in the *Metalogicon* (II, 4), where he picks up Hugh's arguments, that can begin to clarify Dante's restricted meaning in *Convivio*. "Dialectic," says John, quoting the pseudo-Augustine's *De dialectica*, "according to Augustine, is the science of effective argumentation." John excludes from dialectics both the demonstrative and sophistical varieties, while he thinks the goal of the dialectician is to prove or disprove something probable by alleging reasons. Following the authority of Aristotle, who is the founder of this understanding of dialectics, John locates the substance of the discipline in "disputation" concerning what has been said (II, 4).

The two terms—dialectics and logic—are identical for Peter of Spain, though traditionally they have different applications. Logic is the general term and is so called, as Hugh of St. Victor says in the *Didascalicon* (I, 11), "from the Greek word *logos*, which has a double sense. For *logos* means either word (*sermo*) or reason, and hence logic can be called either a linguistic (*sermocinalis*) or a rational science. Rational logic, which is called argumentative, contains dialectics and rhetoric. Linguistic logic stands as a genus to grammar, dialectic and rhetoric, thus containing argumentative logic as a subdivison." Hugh's idea of the all-encompassing, linguistic sphere of logic reappears in John of Salisbury, who says that logic derives its name from the fact that it is rational, "for it both provides and examines reasons" (*Metalogicon* III, 3). On the other hand, dialectics, which comes from *lecton*, "the Greek word for something said" (Isidore), has a technical, more specialized sense, the way Boethius understands it, for "demonstrative arguments" which can engender knowledge and arrive at the truth. However, because dialectics is a part of probable logic, it also includes rhetoric, "for both the orator and the dialectician, trying to persuade an opponent and a judge, are not too much concerned about the truth or falsity of their arguments, provided only the latter have likelihood."

The substance and scope of Dante's definition extend to the *logica antiqua*, which is distinguished in the thirteenth century from the *logica moderna*. The *logica antiqua* embraces the *logica vetus* and the *logica nova*. The old art is comprised of Porphiry's *Isagoge*, the *Praedicamenta*, and the *Perihermeneias* of Aristotle. The "new art" includes the *Analytica priora*, the *Analytica posteriora*, the *Liber sex principiis* of Gilbert de la Porree, *Topics*, and *Elenchi*.[9] From the brief discussion in the *Convivio* it can be said that Dante does not grant logic the cognitive primacy given to it by John of Salisbury or by Peter of Spain, whose twelve books of the *Summulae logicales* are explicitly mentioned in *Paradiso* XII, "dodici libelli" (twelve treatises) in which the logician now shines ("luce") (135).

There is no apparent awareness in the passage from *Convivio* of any relation between proof and tropes, thought and persuasion, logic and rhetoric, which will figure in Dante's other texts. The figuration of dialectics through the attribute "velata," however, grounds the significance this art has for Dante in a tradition that highlights its intellectual difficulty and imperviousness. The adjective "veiled" actually has a technical force in the allegorical representations of Dialectics by Martianus Capella and Alan of Lille, who, by and large, repeats the figuration of his predecessor. In general, "velata" designates the obscurity and sphinxlike logical riddles in Aristotle's works. For Martianus Capella, Dialectics speaks an unintelligible and covert idiom; in effect, the rhetoric of hiding thoroughly characterizes her appearance (she hides under her cloak a poisonous snake and a hook.)[10] By the same token, and more cogently for Dante's description, Alan of Lille refers to Aristotle's "veiling" his knowledge with "the veil of words" in order to shelter the secrets of the sciences from ever growing cheap and common in his general representation of Logic. Because the *Anticlaudianus* is a sourcebook in Dante's *Paradiso* and because, as will be evident later, Alan's metaphors for logic shed light on Dante's own language, I shall cite Alan's description of the second maiden who, following immediately after Grammar, helps in constructing the car of Prudence:

> Here by dress, carriage, leanness and pallor she indicates the the working of a never-sleeping mind, proclaims that Minerva is sleepless and the lighted lamps ever keep watch with her. Her hair, struggling in a kind of dispute, twists its way far down and unruly strands indulge in a tasteless brawl. No comb restrains it, no clamping buckle holds it fast, no scissors' bite cuts it short. Her eyes rival the stars and seem aglow. The eagle's sight yields her prior place and the lynx's power of vision reverences such eyes. . . . He shows how the power of logic flashes its two edged sword and when the face of truth has been maimed, cuts down the false, refusing to allow falsehood to be hidden beneath the appearance of truth; why the pseudo-logician, thief and corrupter of art, liar and hypocrite, clandestine plunderer and sophist, imitates the outer aspect of logic and relying on certain stunts, tried to sell falsehood packaged as truth; . . . it defines, collects, unites each and everything which it embraces to its ample bosom; how the art of logic, like a road, a gate, a key, points to, unlocks, opens the secrets of Sophia. . . . A series of pictures there gloriously displays the logician of renown to whom fame grants unending life when it does not bury those whom earth covers. . . . There Porphiry constructs an unwinding bridge and points out the path by which the reader may enter the depths of Aristotle and make his way to the heart of the book. Our friend Aristotle, the disturber of words, is here: he disturbs many of us by his turbulence and rejoices that he is obscure. He . . . so veils everything with the veil of words that scarce any toil can unveil it. He drapes his words with such covers so as not to prostitute his secrets and by passing on his mysteries, makes them finally grow cheap and common. (*Anticlaudianus*, III, 20–95)

There is, clearly, an ambivalence in Alan of Lille's understanding of logic: against the logic of the pseudologicians he juxtaposes the speculative efforts of Zeno and Boethius, who manage to cast light where the dark reigns. Dante follows Alan's ambivalent judgment about logic. For instance, in *Paradiso* XII he presents the logician Peter of Spain wrapped in light (135), and Siger is the "luce eterna" (*Par.* X, 136) (eternal light). In passing may I suggest that the figuration of logic's light resonates with the very language deployed by John of Salisbury in his defense of logic's utility.[11] In *Convivio* dialectics does not convey a luminous, crystalline knowledge but only the dimmed light of probabilities. The inference is unequivocal: dialectics in *Convivio* is not raised to the status of a science or a metaphysics; it is, rather, a body of methods, a set of technical procedures by which consistent and clear thought can be achieved. This restricted conception of dialectics, wherein Dante follows the assessment of encyclopedists such as Martianus, Cassiodorus, and Isidore, should not be construed as a sign of dialectics' unimportance in Dante's works. On the contrary, logic, as a structure of thought and as a tool of rigorous rational thinking, is deployed in most of Dante's discursive and poetic texts, and, to begin with, I would like to turn briefly to the most obvious cases that have already received considerable critical attention, the *Quaestio de situ et forma aquae et terrae* and *De vulgari eloquentia*.

The *Quaestio de situ et forma aquae et terrae*, whose attribution to Dante has been challenged by Nardi, belongs to the philosophical/literary genre of the exercise in logical argument, the so-called *quaestio disputata* as was conventionally deployed in Scholastic doctrinal debates.[12] Dialectics is central to this form of knowledge, and in this short treatise written in 1320 in response to an academic controversy disputed in Mantua, Dante displays the vocabulary and argumentative techniques appropriate to this level of philosophical discourse. Pastore-Stocchi has illustrated for the *Enciclopedia dantesca* the text's concerns with medieval cosmology, the sublunary world of elements and its rhetorical-logical structure. Here I will limit myself to the style of this philosophical controversy, which is conducted in the assumption that logic is the way to objective, formal knowledge of the universe and that the laws in the physical realm are intelligible to the mind.

The point to be debated is whether or not the earth is higher than water, and there are thus no empirical issues of history, subjectivity, or society raised in the text. On the contrary, because Dante's aim is to assert the systematic self-evident order of the natural world, his scientific language appears stripped of personal inflections: in a series of twenty-four short chapters/paragraphs he proceeds by drawing a series of distinctions as if his were a real debate; he begins by citing Aristotle's *Predicaments*; he then catalogs the opponents' opinions about the point of contention and shows the fallacies in their syllogisms ("Maior et minor principalis sillogismi . . . dimittebantur") (IV).

If in the *Quaestio de situ et forma aquae e terrae* the involvement with logic's mode of analysis is overt, in *De vulgari eloquentia*, which, as we saw earlier, focuses both on the origins of language and on a project to constitute the paradigmatic grammar of the vernacular, there is an oblique concern with what is called *grammatica speculativa*. The history of this philosophical grammar that would deal with the absolute and universal structures of language and not with specific languages' concrete features, erosions, and accidents, has been frequently sketched in recent years. Let me only stress how in the twelfth century Peter Helias and Peter of Spain forged an abstract grammar which joined together logical and grammatical categories. In the thirteenth century, with the likes of Robert Kilwardby, the status of grammar radically changes. Its concerns are no longer either its history or sundry empirical questions of style, vocabulary, phonology, and so on. The Modistae, who are the speculative grammarians, philosophize about language as a system of logical order and knowledge—its *modus essendi*, *modus intelligendi*, and *modus significandi*.[13]

Corti has suggestively proposed that the theoretical frame of *De vulgari eloquentia* resonates with the *modi significandi* of the speculative grammarians, such as Boethius of Dacia. It is in Boethius's treatise *Modi significandi sive quaestiones super Priscianum minorem* that, according to Corti, is to be found Dante's distinction between the "inventores gramatice facultatis," who are the philosophers probing the "prima principia" of language, and the "gramaticae positores," who establish rules for specific languages.[14] Corti's effort to locate Dante's linguistic thought within the context of the radical Aristotelians has been chastised by empirically minded critics from the standpoint of what could be called language's "stratigraphic" history, its grounding in the facticity and in the fluctuating, crude forms of natural language. The objections to Corti's inquiry are strong; yet, however problematic, her inquiry into Dante's philosophical-Scholastic vocabulary shows how for Dante the experience of language is absolute and transcends all the relativities of specific languages.

Logic for Dante is not simply an ancillary discipline subordinated to other epistemic finalities, as the above brief recapitulation of Dante's two treatises may suggest. To understand his sense of how logical knowledge is linked to other disciplines and to the world of action, we must turn to *Paradiso* VI, which is the Heaven of Mercury and is, thus, according to the definition provided in *Convivio*, the planet of dialectics.

The burden of the canto is Roman law and the justice of the Roman Empire: the principal of the canto is Justinian, the lawgiver and compiler of the *Corpus iuris*, an activity to which he refers as follows: "d'entro le leggi trassi il troppo e il vano" (12) (I removed from the laws what was in excess and vain). To raise the issue of laws in the Heaven of Mercury is not odd, for Mercury is the figure of interpretation and reason, as well as the god who, after slaying Argus and fleeing to Egypt, "gave laws and the art of writing to the Egyptians" (Cicero, *The Nature of the Gods*, III). In logic, reason or *ratio* is the faculty of judgment, the power to discriminate and distinguish with certitude that which is firmly established. In effect, in *Paradiso* VI, laws are ratified as rational, and, in the measure in which they are inspired by God, they are the concrete extensions of universal reason.

But dialectics does not figure in *Paradiso* VI merely through these oblique resonances. At the start of the canto Justinian recalls his conver-

sion, because of Agapetus, from the Eutychian heresy.[15] This heresy holds
that divinity and humanity were not both present in Christ. What
Agapetus, Justinian says, held by faith, "vegg'io or chiaro sì, come tu vedi
/ ogni contradizione e falsa e vera" (20–21) (I now see as clearly as you do
that every contradiction is of false and true). The lines contain the definition of logic as the art that separates truth from falsehood on the principle
of noncontradiction and that determines whether "two contradictory
propositions can be simultaneously true" (Aristotle). The brunt of Justinian's account is that Agapetus's faith, in which Justinian came to believe,
coincided with logic's analytical distinctions. Contradiction means that if
one proposition is true, the other is false, and this principle is the ground
on which Justinian's change of mind from error to truth lies.

This reference to dialectics for a theological end has a number of implications for the dramatic substance of the canto. It echoes, to begin with,
the Scholastic procedure of yoking the discourse of theology to the methods of logical investigation. More precisely, it recalls, I would like to suggest, Boethius's treatise *Contra Eutychen*, written against the heresies "de
personis atque naturis" of Eutyches and Nestorius. The importance of the
Boethian tract in the history of logic is apparent by the references John of
Salisbury makes to it in his *Metalogicon* (II, 20). For Boethius, the phrase
"consist of two natures . . . is an equivocal or rather a doubtful term of
double meaning." The content of Christian faith, clearly, is that the same
Christ is both man and God. For Dante as well as for Boethius this theological assertion is the ultimate logical paradox which, in fact, disavows
logic's principle of noncontradiction. The analogy between the truth ar-
rived at by dialectics and the truth of theology breaks down: faith, in short,
is placed outside and against the power dialectics has to discern the truth.

But dialectics is also yoked to politics, law, and history in the canto, and
the link is of some moment in Dante's thought. I shall leave out the question of history, which I discussed in *Dante, Poet of the Desert*. Suffice it to
say in this context that Dante's evocation of the world of history functions
as a necessary testing ground for the validity of the abstract logical propositions. Dialectics, in short, is empty unless it is grounded in the realities of
history. I shall primarily focus on the relationship between dialectics and
jurisprudence, which in *Paradiso* VI is only hinted at, but which is openly
present in *Monarchia*.[16] That the two disciplines should be thought of as
linked together (and there is a substantial historical tradition to document
the alliance between them) was made inevitable by the assumptions law and
logic share. The rules of law, like those of logic, are fundamentally rules of
reason. At the same time both disciplines concern themselves with questions of form, action, verification of reasonableness, and judgments of
plausible arguments. At any rate, the work of glossators such as Irnerius,

Accursius, and Placentinus is replete with paraphrases of Boethius's *In cate-gorias*. In their legal-philosophical speculations law is the "vera philoso-phia" in that it connects words and deeds and it translates the generality of abstract principles into the contingent particularities of justice. This his-torical tradition is fully deployed in *Monarchia*, and I turn to it.

The treatise presents itself as a theoretical inquiry into the feasibility of political order, which is the sphere of human action. Its central argument is that reason is the way to arrive at a model for politics. Consistently, the text's construction follows the deductive method of starting from a general axiom and deducing from it secondary corollaries. The specific argument of book I, that justice is at its strongest only under a monarch and that, therefore, there is a necessity for empire if the world is to attain perfect order, is carried out through the authority of Gilbert de la Porrée, the "Master of the Six Principles":

> Justice is the most powerful in the world when located in a subject with a perfect will and most power; such is the Monarch alone; therefore Justice is at its most potent in this world when located in the Monarch alone. This prepar-atory syllogism is of the second figure, with intrinsic negation, and takes the following form: All B is A; only C is A; therefore only C is B.

After demonstrating the proposition that all concord depends on the unity of wills and that mankind is at its best in a state of concord, Dante exemplifies the feasibility of his political project by a synopsis of Roman history (book II). His specific aim is to inquire whether or not the logical truth he has just discovered in book one can be translated into reality. In effect, Dante moves within the humanistic tradition of John of Salisbury. Conscious of the predictable objection that logic is a series of abstractions, John of Salisbury and Dante make logic more than mere analytical specula-tion and word-chopping. If logic were left to the analysis of propositions, it would be, however rigorous, a vain, bloodless exercise, a sophistry voided of concern with values and history.

John of Salisbury, in truth, hedges: he states, on the one hand, that dia-lectics in unlike rhetoric, for "dialectics neither aspires to the weighty au-thority of teaching, nor does it become the plaything of political currents." Yet he also insists, as we have seen, that if logic were divorced from other studies, it would be useless. The virtue that must accompany logic and is the crown of all the liberal arts, say respectively John of Salisbury and Alan of Lille, is prudence or Fronesis. "Since the subject matter of prudence is truth (for prudence is concerned with comprehending the truth), the ancients conceived of Prudence and Truth as sisters, related by a divine consanguinity. Thus perfect prudence needs must contemplate the truth, from which nothing can separate it" (*Metalogicon* IV, 14).[17] Dante in both

Paradiso VI and *Monarchia* makes jurisprudence the discipline that changes logic from being a pure theoretical science to one that aims at action and is tied to history.

In both *Paradiso* VI and *Monarchia* history is a history of power and violence. In either text the ostensible purpose is to show that the violence of Roman history is part of God's plan to secure justice and peace to the world. In *Monarchia* the view that the Roman jurisdiction over the world occurred by right and not by usurpation is also subjected to a logical analysis:

> And it must be noted that the argument . . . shows itself really compelling if we translate it into a syllogism of the second figure and then reduce it to a syllogism of the first figure with its antecedent unchanged. This reduction would then read: "Every unjust action is approved unjustly; Christ never gave approval to injustice." If we retain the antecedent, it reads: "Every unjust action is unjustly approved; Christ approved certain unjust actions; therefore Christ approved unjustly." (II, x, 9–10)

This vindication of the legitimacy of the Holy Roman Empire is the point where Dante turns against the invalid syllogisms and false inferences of the "presumptuous jurists," the Decretalists, who minimize the power of the emperor and who use the law to justify the supremacy of papal authority over secular matters. Book III of *Monarchia* makes a frontal attack against the Decretalists' claim that the successor of Peter may impose binding laws upon secular government. Their syllogism about the Donation of Constantine (Constantine donated the seat of the empire to the church, therefore no emperor can assume imperial authority unless he receives it from the pope) is equally discredited by questioning the "major premise of their argument."

The deployment of dialectics in *Paradiso* VI and *Monarchia* is primarily a tool to give Dante's convictions a conceptual coherence and to guarantee the rational consistency of his speculations. From this perspective, logic announces the power of reason, of the *logos*, to counter the willful errors and legal machinations of the Decretalists with a tighter, more rigorous rational construction than theirs. But the rational truth Dante's own logic provides in *Monarchia* is not self-evident. His view of Roman history is highly selective, as a comparison with St. Augustine's version in the *City of God*, which Dante mentions (*Monarchia* III, iv), would show. If his interpretation of Roman history is partial, the logical truth he presents is partisan. In fact, Dante is battling for a substitute version of power relationships: he calls for the equality of state and church against the hierocrats' claim of the church's supremacy over the empire. The metaphor of battling I have just used is not arbitrary. Dante describes his dispute through metaphors of athletics and duels: "Having drawn these distinctions in the present chapter we may base two effective arguments upon them in favor of our theses, one from the athletic contest and the other from the duel between champions. Each of them will be developed in turn in the following chapters" (II, vii).

The metaphor of warfare is a direct extension of the generally polemical tone of the treatise. But it also points to the fact that there is a disparity between logic and reality: logic does not reflect the real order of things but is a weapon of power and a strategy of persuasion. To say that it is also an art of persuasion is to imply that there is no necessary continuity between logical representations and the reality of power. Logic is not just a tool by which to know the abstract configuration of reality, but it is a rhetorical weapon to control and manipulate it. This is not simply a question of suggesting that, say, Hugh of St. Victor borrows and mixes together the terminology of the rhetorical tradition with that of logic. The unity of all the arts for the sake of knowledge, as I have indicated earlier, is a fundamental principle for Hugh of St. Victor, Aquinas, or Thierry of Chartres. In Dante's treatise, on the other hand, logic is applied rhetorically and appears veiled, as if it were under the cloak of rhetoric.

In effect, *Monarchia* is above all a text of political rhetoric aiming at altering the existing power play. Medieval historians have long argued whether or not it is shaped by an Averroistic or Thomistic vision of politics.[18] I submit that *Monarchia* is certainly not an "Averroistic" text, for Averroes' political thought appears to Dante as a theory of division and as a thought that posits the radical rupture of the self and of the polis. Let me illustrate this point. What Dante understands as political "Averroism" can be gleaned from his reading of Guido Cavalcanti's "Donna me prega," a poem briefly treated above in chapter 3. Guido's metaphysical view of love as a dark power descending from the fiery complexion of the planet Mars and as a passion in turn capable only of engendering further strife in the lover's mind; Averroes' theory of the intellect seizing the individual self and dividing him from his senses; the belief in the "double truth," which insidiously encroaches upon the unity of the truth—all these elements go directly counter to the ideal of historical unity and peace *Monarchia* pursues.

One can add that Dante stares squarely at and gives a critique of the "Averroistic" version of political experience in *Inferno* X. *Inferno* X, a canto of the horrors of civil war, is also the canto of the Epicureans—Farinata, Cavalcanti, Frederick II.[19] There is a poetic principle at work in Dante's text that bears a plain formulation: the metaphors of any canto shed light on and interpenetrate one another, and in the process they together alter and expand the boundaries of signification of each one of them. Just as war is the fundamental metaphor for the schismatics in *Inferno* XXVIII, in the poetic space of *Inferno* X civil war is the obverse side of the "Averroistic" theory of love. More precisely, the metaphor of civil war unveils Dante's sense of the tragic, divisive realities deriving from the conceptual foundation of his so-called Averroism, while, at the same time, the textual allusions to Guido Cavalcanti's "Donna me prega," which from a narrow viewpoint can be construed as the analytical representation of Averroistic theories of love, seal love as an inner war.

Whereas the politics, as it were, of a love poem such as "Donna me prega" end up in chaos, Dante's *Monarchia* is a text that posits a link between knowledge and power and wills to dismiss and replace the hierocratic structure of order. Nardi and Gilson have advanced the view that *Monarchia* opens a breach in the unity of Christian wisdom in that—by the claim that the spiritual and the temporal exert their respective functions each autonomous from the other—the order of nature and grace (or philosophy and theology or state and church) are no longer integrated in a hierarchical synthesis of ascending functions and orders.[20] That unity, I would respond, had already been breached by the Decretalists' manipulation of logic for the ends of power. What *Monarchia* does do, however, is to denounce the violence that occurs when knowledge is translated into action.

Paradiso VI dramatizes this tragic insight in a way that *Monarchia* cannot, if the treatise is to keep its political character. In *Paradiso* VI, however, Dante is not hampered by political considerations. The emperor Justinian celebrates the providentiality of the empire, but the figure of Romeo de Villeneuve, the exiled counselor of the prince, on whom the canto comes to a close, seals the disjunction between knowledge and power. There is considerable irony in the speech of praise (a case of epideictic rhetoric) Justinian voices:

> E se 'l mondo sapesse il cor ch'elli ebbe
> mendicando sua vita a frusto a frusto,
> assai lo loda, e più lo loderebbe.
>
> (*Par.* VI, 140–42)

(And if the world knew the heart he had, begging his bread by morsels, much as it praises him, it would praise him more.)

This belated justice Justinian restores to the name of Romeo only heightens how unjust justice can be on the great stage of the world. The courtiers of Raymond Berenger of Provence by "parole biece" (136) (crooked words) forced the count to "dimandar ragione a questo giusto" (137) (reckoning the accounts of this just man and good) from his seneschal. "Dimandar ragione" means to call to account, but the word "ragione" translated primarily *ratio*. In the context of John of Salisbury's logic, *ratio* or reason is the force, "a power to discriminate and distinguish material and immate-

rial entities, in order to examine things with sure unvitiated judgement"
(*Metalogicon* IV, 15). In Dante's narrative, however, the word is both *ius*
and *ratio*. The juridical burden of the term, may I add, is the more ironic
because of its proximity to "questo giusto" in the same line—this just man.
In the heaven of logic and jurisprudence the disfigurement of "ragione"—
in every sense of the word—is complete. As reason is turned upside down
and is inscribed in a field of violence, which reason itself may foster, reason's predicament is the more radical in that its harmonious coincidence
with power occurs outside of history. Dante's response to the perception
of this split between the power of the prince and the knowledge of the
counselor is Romeo's exile, "persona umile e peregrina" (135) (a man of
low birth and a stranger), the experience by which one places oneself outside the scheme of power.

The wisdom of exile is the essence of Dante's poetry. This wisdom is
what Dante opposes to abstract logical knowledge as well as to the belief
that knowledge can turn to action. The encounter with St. Thomas Aquinas in *Paradiso* X focuses on the issue at hand, and it manages to transform
the rigidity of the laws of deductive reasoning into what I call the nomadic
thought of poetry. Dante's encounter with the intellectualist Thomas
Aquinas, as we have seen, takes place in the Heaven of the Sun, where the
wise spirits dwell. In *Convivio* Mercury was said to be veiled by the light of
the sun, and dialectics was said to be veiled. The inevitable inference is that
dialectics has a secret and hidden knowledge. But in *Paradiso* X, set in the
Heaven of the Sun, the emphasis on the light of Siger, the logician who
demonstrated "invidiosi veri" through syllogisms, dispels the shadows and
sheds the veils of that secrecy. Knowledge is here made explicit, its value
retrieved, as it stands in the transparent clarity of the sunlight.

The science that is assigned to the sun is arithmetic, the science of numbers binding all things with a harmonious bond and, thereby, revealing the
existence of a universal plan of creation. Arithmetic, in fact, is the discipline that discloses the rationality and intelligibility of the world as a
system of number relations which have a necessary connection among
themselves. This principle of the mathematical relatedness of the universe
implies that the world is a unified whole. This science accounts for the
harmonization, as will be seen in some detail in chapter 10 below, that is
the distinctive trait of the encounters in this heaven. More to our present
concerns, arithmetic, the science of Pythagoras who is fathered by Apollo,
as *Convivio* tells us, is the luminous knowledge of true numbers, and, as
such, it is the model for the necessary principles of demonstrative logic.
The affinity between the two arts (which possibly accounts for the language of logic in the Heaven of Arithmetic, which is the "power of number") is postulated by Dante, who may have been aware of the extended
comparison drawn by Hugh of St. Victor, among others, in a paragraph in

which he reflects on how all the arts tend toward the single end of philosphy, and yet they do not take the same road, but have each their proper orbits by which they are distinguished from one another:

> Logic treats of concepts themselves in their predicamental framework, while mathematics treats of them in their numerical composition. Logic, therefore, employs pure understanding on occasion; whereas mathematics never operates without the imagination, and therefore never possesses its object in a simple or non-composite manner. Because logic and mathematics are prior to physics in the order of learning and serve physics, so to say, as tools—so that every person ought to be acquainted with them before he turns his attention to physics—it was necessary that these two sciences base their considerations not upon the physical actualities of things, of which we have deceptive experience, but upon reason alone, in which unshakable truth stands fast, and that then, with reason itself to lead them, they descend into the physical order. (*Didascalicon*, II, 17)

For Dante, within this Apollonian space of heaven, logic appears to have an undisputed value, as Aquinas and Siger, who had fiercely fought in life, stand together.[21] With them it seems that theology and logic, an alliance contested by the biblical exegetes, are finally reconciled. It is clear that for Dante and for St. Thomas Aquinas, as Dante figures him, Siger of Brabant never adhered to (or late in his life he had stopped adhering to) the theory of the double truth, the theory, that is, whereby there are contradictory truths, the truths of scriptures and the truths of philosophy. Dante's evaluation of Siger happens also to agree with the views advanced by scholars such as van Steenberghen, Hissette, Weber, Wippel, and others.[22] Their views may be technically accurate; nonetheless, from the standpoint of Dante studies they are seriously limited, for they completely fail to account for the complex transaction Dante's text negotiates between theology, logic, and poetry. The narrative of *Paradiso* X, as a matter of fact, confronts the general positions of the three great Parisian masters who are now circling in a dance: Aquinas, Siger, and a neo-Augustinian such as Bonaventure. What is also present in this figuration is what had always been excluded from the circle of knowledge or had been denied any cognitive dignity: poetry itself. It is clear, however, that the canto dramatizes Dante's conviction that logical and theological problems are given an authentic foundation in poetry, which alone guarantees their unity.

Aquinas begins by giving a pithy recollection of Siger's life. We are told the most contingent, historical details of that life, such as the man's profession and address. "Vico de li Strami" accurately translates "rue du Fouarre" or, as it was known later, rue Paillet and today rue Dante, the Parisian street where practitioners of the liberal arts, logicians, and poets such as Jean de Meun (as Iacopo della Lana and Benvenuto da Imola inform us) mingled with the merchants of straw for horses. (The commentators' detail about intellectuals and horses conveys, no doubt, their not involuntary sense of what could be called a parodic *pastiche* of words and things.) More to the point, Dante's precision in the topographical reference catches Aquinas's linguistic rigor, the rhetorical powers of the man who, ironically, entertained a vigilant suspicion of grandiloquence and rhetoric. Aquinas's "discreto latino" (*Par.* XII, 144) echoes both his discernment and his linguistic *discretio*, the rhetorical abilities of the theologian and logician also adept in the art of *eutrapelia* and alien from bombast and murk.[23] The address for Siger's place of teaching also illustrates Dante's famed realism, giving the impression of such an intimate familiarity with Paris to the point of making historians posit the yet unproven theory of the poet's sojourn in that city of philosophy.

In Paris, in the rue du Fouarre, Siger spent his time "leggendo" (*Par.* X, 137), reading in the technical sense of *lectio*, university lectures, scholia, and glosses as a hermeneutics or commentaries on authoritative philosophical texts. The *lectio*, it may be added, is the first stage on the journey to wisdom. Because the narrative is focused on the activity of reading and interpreting, it would be a disservice to Dante's ever alert sense of metaphor if one were not to interpret the inference of the address. One should perhaps resist the temptation of reading "strami" in an overdetermined manner as the straw, or *palea*, with which St. Thomas, at the end of his own life and works, as I shall point out again in chapter 9, identified and dismissed his theological probings. The Parisian logicians—and to the extent to which St. Thomas himself and Siger of Brabant believed that logic provides universal principles of certainty, also they—were actually dealing in straw. Yet it is the word "vico" that must be read in its full metaphorical implication. The word occurs twice in the *Divine Comedy*. In *Purgatorio* XXII it refers to a dark alley or dead end in the topography of pagan knowledge where the poets—Terence, Plautus, Persius—stumbled and are said now to be in Limbo with the other poets and philosophers (*Purg.* XXII, 99). The other time is in *Paradiso* X, and it designates the place where Siger taught. The same word is used for the poets and for a logician.

We are all too familiar with the conception of philosophy as a journey, a search and a quest, and we are equally familiar with the *topos* that articulates philosophy's pursuit of the truth, paradoxically, as a challenge to what is familiar: that *topos* is the path or route of thought—the route of Parmenides, the search of Heraclitus, the quest of Odysseus, the *Republic*'s "dialectical journey," or Honorius of Autun's voyage of education through a foreign soil. The metaphor is also central to Dante's poetic quest and vision. This commonplace of knowledge as a quest casts the revelation the philosopher or the poet reaches as a movement from bondage, be it bondage to ignorance or to mere opinion, to the point where the bright light of truth shines. It also implies that the thinker does not sit complacently at home; thought, on the contrary, is itself an event or adventure, for it implies the risky possibility of the mind wandering far afield from itself and going astray.

For a thinker such as St. Thomas Aquinas, who searched the meaning of *via*, as opposed to *modus*, and wrote on the hazards of the "quinque viae"; for a philosopher such as Siger of Brabant, who is praised here for his work in logic, the "scientia scientiarum ad omnium methodorum principia *viam* habens"; and for a poet such as Dante, for whom domicile and the road are always spiritualized—the word "vico," used in the sense of road, figures Siger in a spiritual itinerary, on his way to full knowledge, following the "vestigia Dei." "Vico" can be the dead end of error and vision, as it was for the Roman poets. But for Siger "vico" refers to the open space where he was "sillogizzando invidiosi veri."

In a canto where the etymologist Isidore of Seville stands by and listens to what is being said, one can't but wonder what the secret core of words expresses. For Dante, in a way, not the speculative grammar of the logicians such as Boethius of Dacia but etymology, which is a concrete grammatical category, becomes the vehicle of knowledge. From this standpoint the word "pensieri" (*Par.* X, 134) (called "grave" to designate the absorption of thinking) should give us pause. Etymologically the word implies suspension, hanging, with the possible intimation of an impasse for the mind, of the paradoxes or undecidables or horns of a dilemma in which, say, the Ass of Buridan gets fatally caught (cf. *Par.* IV, 1–6). Yet Siger's thoughts place him, so to speak, on the way; actually, Dante suggests that thought is a path, a path into the unfamiliar, seductive terrain of truth.

The etymology of the word "verum"—from the Greek *heron*—means "secure and stable or certain and clear," says John of Salisbury, "in imitation of the Stoics, who are much concerned about the etymology or resemblance of words" (*Metalogicon* IV, 34). The "veri" Dante refers to are, in historical terms, the questions of the eternity of the world and the unity of the intellect or monopsychism, and the relation of necessity and free will, condemned by Bishop Tempier as heretical in 1270. These propositions for Aquinas were not philosophically demonstrable; they were a matter of faith. Why, however, does Dante qualify these truths as "invidiosi"? This attribute, which has given rise to considerable controversy, is conventionally said to mean unpopular, unwelcome, as if Siger's convictions about the autonomy of philosophy from theology were destined to incur, as they in fact did, envy and hatred.

The adjective certainly carries this meaning: Siger's tragic death in Orvieto in 1284 is a proof of the bitter passions his name aroused. But the web of meaning of the qualifier "invidiosi" also extends to blindness, as one gathers from its standard etymology from *non-video*, which Dante may have found in the etymologies of Hugutio of Pisa and which he deploys in the representation of the envious sinners as blind (*Purg.* XIII). As such, the adjective, considered in its grammatical function, implies that the knowledge logic generates is not certain, self-evident knowledge. In point of fact grammar, the traditional ally of logic, here subverts and circumscribes logic's claims in that it reveals that logic and syllogism deal not with the truth but with probability and hypothesis. Logic is the discipline of demonstrable propositions, a method of analytical investigation in metaphysical and theological debates, but it is incapable of yielding the deeper meaning of their principles. Its value for Dante lies exactly in its speculative and not dogmatic character. A gloss by a logician, John of Salisbury, can clarify, I think, this etymological resonance.

In a passage from his *Metalogicon* (II, 13) in which John reflects on logic's role of providing the other sciences with a *methodos* or rational principles to discriminate between the true and false, he distinguishes, in the wake of Boethius's *De differentiis topicis* (i), between dialectical principles which are probable and the demonstrative ones which are necessary:

> The great difficulty with absolute demonstration is apparent, as the demonstrator is always [and solely] engaged in the quest of necessity, and cannot admit of any exception to the principles of the truth he professes. If it is a difficult matter to perceive the truth, which (as our Academicians say) is as indefinite in outline as though it lay at the bottom of a well; how much energy is not required to discern, in addition to the truth, the hidden secrets of necessity itself? Is it not easier to recognize what exists than to decide what is possible? . . . One who wishes to become a master of the science of demonstration should first obtain a good grasp of probabilities. Whereas the principles of demonstrative logic are necessary; those of dialectic are probable. The dialectician, for his part, will shun theses which seem likely to none, lest he become suspect of insanity. On the other hand, he will refrain from disputing about principles that are already self-evident, lest he seem to be "groping in the dark" (. . . unde et dialecticus ab illis abstinebit, quae *nulli videntur*, ne habeatur insanus). He will limit himself to the discusssion of propositions which are [well] known to all, or to many, or to the leaders in each field.

"Invidiosi," thus, designates Dante's sense of the limits of the science. To the traditional (scholarly) debate on the "double truth" and the possible contradictions therein—the truth of reason and the truth of faith—Dante responds with Aquinas and John of Salisbury that faith, defined by St. Paul as the substance of things unseen, is itself a mode of vision and a virtue that determines what one sees. Knowledge can lead to the preambles of faith; faith is the primary and fundamental prerequisite for understanding the truth.

To grasp more fully the metaphoric pattern woven around these questions in the representation of Siger of Brabant, let me recall the metaphors in the symmetrically opposite canto X of *Inferno* where Dante meets the

Epicureans. Blindness and insanity, as I have argued in *Dante, Poet of the Desert*, are the traits characterizing these heretics who deny, like the radical Aristotelians, the belief in the immortality of the soul. By sharp contrast, in *Paradiso* X Siger, after his death, shines in the eternal light of beatitude: within this context, the word "eterna" even suggests that Dante makes the Brabantine master stand for his belief that the soul is immortal and eternal, as he had argued in his *De anima intellectiva* in 1272 against positions staked by Averroes. Second, unlike the heretics who uphold the primacy of choice and reason, Dante casts Siger as one for whom the truths logic gropes for remain hidden to the eye of reason. The attributes of logic's obscurity, the veils in which logic is shrouded and which Alan of Lille and Dante stressed, are dispelled by the radiance of bliss. Logic itself appears still as a rigorous method of scientific and critical investigation into the disguises of language, yet the source and substance of being remain elusive and concealed from its scrutiny.

In effect, Dante wills to unveil the essential kinship between the poet and the thinker, as he radicalizes the possibilities of either. As we saw earlier, a text such as *The Battle of the Liberal Arts* posits an antagonism between logic'c pursuit of pure knowledge and, on the other hand, grammar and rhetoric, between Paris and Orléans. The dream of a pure, rational intelligibility of Being and of man's being—disengaged from rhetoric and the grammar of language—persists even in the works of Aquinas, who always has intimations of the elusiveness of truth as well as of the necessary inconclusiveness of the quest and who, nonetheless, believes in the possibility of a correct, rational representation of the totality of being. At the same time, theorists of knowledge such as Hugh of St. Victor or John of Salisbury, as they attempt to present knowledge as an ordered, coherent synthesis or a holistic and intelligible totality, carefully separate and distinguish—though their efforts may not always be consistent—the functions and spheres of the various disciplines. Dante wills to reverse this tradition of analytical thinking, as if he remembered St. Augustine's insight into the primordial, buried sense of thinking—reflective, meditative thinking—as gathering and collecting.

The kinship between logic and poetry is made possible by Dante's practice of poetry as the hermeneutics of all discourses, as the commentary on the entire field of knowledge. It is also made possible by the fact the two forms of knowledge are joined by a common reflection on language. Less idealistically, one can say that Dante's will to establish this kinship depends on his desire to vindicate the epistemology of poetry. More historically, several efforts had been made to bridge the gap between the *desideratum* of logic to elaborate a transparent language of truth, which would be voided of ambiguities, and the metaphoric language of poetry, which revels in ambiguities and which rethinks the traditional relations between truth and falsehood. The gulf between logic and poetry had steadily yawned wide, as logic sought to repress poetry's free and imaginative movement. Yet they had always been complicitous, as is made apparent by Aquinas's systematic deployment of the rhetoric of analogy at the core of the architectonics of his theological *Summa*. The debates on "imaginative or poetic syllogisms"—syllogisms that do not demand intellectual assent but an imaginative recognition of the validity of a metaphoric utterance—belong to a common effort to link logic and poetics. These probings figure prominently in medieval Arabic commentaries by Avicenna, Alfarabi, and Averroes on logic and on Aristotle's *Rhetoric* and *Poetics*.[24]

In a context which is immediately relevant to Dante's concerns—the controversies at the University of Paris and Tempier's condemnation of 219 propositions in 1277—it is noteworthy that Siger of Brabant himself had argued in defense of the uses of *fabulae* in philosophy and religion. In a way, his defense of fables may strike us as simply an acceptance of commonplace wisdom about the philosophical value of myths, integuments, and *narratio fabulosa* popularized by the humanists of antiquity (Cicero, Macrobius) and by twelfth-century Chartrian humanists, such as Guillaume de Conches and Bernard Silvester. Yet the value of Siger's statement emerges in full clarity from Bishop Tempier's condemnation of the opinion that "fabulae et falsa sunt in lege christiana, sicut in aliis." As has been shown by Maurer, the phrase "fabulae et falsa" seems to echo Siger's expression *fabulosa et falsa* to define the presence of fables in religion.[25] For Siger—as for Dante—the logical truth of a proposition is not the whole truth, even when it is adequate to some form of reality. There is a deeper truth of which the mind has only vestiges and which can only be the object of vision and faith, and which determines, in turn, all the truth of logic.

Dante's systematic reflections on the arts of language, in effect, lead him to an epistemic predicament. It can be said that for the poet the limit of logic lies in the fact that the knowledge a logical argument delivers is already determined by the formal rules that generate it and never exceeds that which is contained within the terms of the proposition. By contrast, poetic metaphor shatters and exceeds the conventions of univocal meanings and derives its energy from vision. Siger of Brabant—like Boethius in his exile (*Par.* X, 129)—is a figure of the intellectual's predicament in history. In his passion for thinking he, also like Boethius, appears to have undertaken a journey of metaphysical exploration. The endless exploration of rational knowledge at its boundaries is the space of Dante's visionary poetry. The next three chapters will turn by necessity to an analysis of the modalities of Dante's vision.

Chapter 6

IMAGINATION AND KNOWLEDGE

(PURGATORIO XVII–XVIII*)*

In *Purgatorio* XVII the pilgrim is passing through the circle of wrath, and we are told that because of the hour of the day (it is dusk) and because the terrace is covered by a cloud of black smoke—an overt literalization of the biblical cloud of wrath—his physical vision is blurred. The difficulties the pilgrim experiences in seeing are presented in the opening lines of the canto in an address to the reader:

> Ricordati, lettor, se mai ne l'alpe
> ti colse nebbia per la qual vedessi
> non altrimenti che per pelle talpe,
> come, quando i vapor umidi e spessi
> a diradar cominciansi, la spera
> del sol debilmente entra per essi;
> e fia la tua imagine leggera
> in giugner a veder com'io rividi
> lo sole in pria che già nel corcar era.
>
> *(Purg.* XII, 1–9)

(Recall, reader, if ever in the mountains a mist has caught you, through which you could not see except as moles do through the skin, how when the moist dense vapors begin to dissipate, the sphere of the sun enters feebly through them, and your imagination will quickly come to see how, at first, I saw the sun again, which was now at its setting.)

The address is marked by a series of metaphorical symmetries. The image of the Alpine heights, which, ever since St. Augustine, have been conceived of as a spot of possible vision, is reversed into the picture of the mole burrowing into the depths of the earth. The heavy solidity of the natural world bends into the immateriality of mist and sky, just as the mist and dying light of day are countered by the appeal to the reader's memory. For memory, as the traditional iconographic motif has it, is the *oculus imaginationis*, the eye of inner vision cutting through the shadows and airy shapes of this twilight landscape.[1] This inner eye of vision is, in turn, counteracted by a discrete double figuration of blindness. One is the blindness of a mole, "the blind laborious moles," in the language of Vergil (*Georgics* I, 183), which "dig out chambers" underground (*sub terris*). The other is the allusion to the eye blinded by wrath. This blindness, which finds its authoritative text in Psalm 30, "conturbatus est in ira oculus meus," extends a number of direct references to the perplexed and impaired sight of the sinners in the preceding cantos of *Purgatorio*, and it also characterizes the moral substance of this ledge where the sin of wrath is purged. Even the initial address to the reader, which signals the will to a bond between the reader's ordinary perception of daily life and the lonely experience of the pilgrim, is balanced by another apostrophe. As soon as the poet has evoked the misty scene, he appeals to the imagination, the "imaginativa" (13), as the visionary faculty which leads the mind astray from the perception of the material world:

> O imaginativa che ne rube
> talvolta sì di fuor, ch'om non s'accorge
> perchè d'intorno suonin mille tube,
> chi move te, se 'l senso non ti porge?
> Moveti lume che nel ciel s'informa,
> per sè o per voler che giù lo scorge.
>
> (13–18)

(O imagination, that do sometime so snatch us from outward things that we give no heed, though a thousand trumpets sound around us, who moves you if the sense affords you naught? A light moves you which takes form in heaven, of itself, or by a will that downwards guides you.)

This elaborate set of figurative symmetries, parallels, and antitheses conveys a sense of impasse in which Dante as a poet is caught. The formal polarities of the passage, which aim at picturing the landscape within which the pilgrim finds himself, in fact, arrest the narrative flow. But it is also the pilgrim who is at a standstill here: "Noi eravam dove più non saliva / la scala sù, ed eravamo affissi, / pur come nave ch'a la piaggia arriva. . . . Se i piè si stanno, non stea tuo sermone" (*Purg.* XVII, 76–84) (We stood where the stair went no higher and were stopped there, even as a ship that arrives at the shore. . . . If our feet are stayed, do not stay your speech). The pilgrim's deadlock, however, is only provisional, for, in dramatic terms, the apostrophe to the power of the imagination introduces a series of three images of punished wrath that appear in the mind, which is said to be restrained within itself.

From a formal viewpoint, the downward movement of the imagination from a light above—the word deployed is "giù" (downward)—harks back, one might add, to the figure of the setting sun, its rays already dead on the low shores, and of the mole underground. But it also reverses the upward movement suggested by the picture of mountain climbing at the exordium of the canto. More substantively, the imagination discloses, first, the image of Procne avenging the violation of Philomela by Tereus (19–21); second, that of Haman, who was hanged on the gallows he had prepared for Mordecai (25–30); and, finally, the image of Amata, who flew into a fit of grief and rage on hearing the news of Turnus's death, and hanged herself (33–39). The three images quickly fade out as soon as the pilgrim's face is struck by the light, the way, to paraphrase the text, sleep is broken when light strikes closed eyes (40–45).

I shall have occasion in the next chapter to muse again on the metaphor of sleep as the state that prepares and allows visionary experiences. I shall stress here, where the narrative focuses on the abrupt interruption of sleep, that sleep designates the mind's state of passivity, and that the simile the poet deploys for the pilgrim's sudden vision underscores the fact that the images he perceives are not mere objects of ordinary experience, which Dante mimetically duplicates or evokes, nor are they figures of his rational will. The mind is acquiescent and nonresistant as it surrenders to the imperious powers of the "imaginativa." In the opening lines of the canto the pilgrim's gaze hovers over the materiality of a landscape which is at the edge of becoming invisible. Now the "imaginativa" has no contact either with the reality of sense experience or with the claims of the will, and it triggers an inner vision which has the effect of swiftly seizing the mind away from the outside reality.

The power of the mind's self-absorption and removal from the surrounding contingencies and sensory impressions, because of its complete bondage to one of the senses, has been highlighted a few cantos earlier in *Purgatorio* IV (1–18). The pilgrim, who has just met Manfred and has been absorbed by the marvel of this encounter, has not noticed the passage of time. The experience prompts Dante to ponder (and this is the brunt of his meditation at the opening of canto IV) the question of the unity of the three powers of the soul—vegetative, sensitive, and rational—which are all involved when a faculty receives pain or pleasure. The view reflects Aristotle's ideas from his *De anima*, and it also echoes Dante's explication of *De anima* in *Convivio*.[2] But the only time that the "imaginativa" is invested with the attribute of autonomy from the world of the senses occurs in *Purgatorio* XVII, a strategic point if there ever was any, for this is the central canto of the *Divine Comedy*.

Traditionally, scholarly glosses on the passage point out that the "imaginativa" renders the *vis imaginativa* or *phantasia*, the imagination as the passive or receptive faculty of the mind.[3] More recently the apostrophe has been taken to be the basis, along with other features of the purgatorial canticle, such as dreams and art images, for a description of Dante's mode of vision. The dramatic articulation of *Inferno* takes place through a *visio corporalis*; *Paradiso*'s through a *visio intellectualis*; *Purgatorio*'s through a *visio spiritualis*, a vision, that is, achieved through sensible forms and images.[4] But these glosses do not begin to account for Dante's central claim for the power of the imagination, nor do they address the complex set of interrelated problems which hinge around the issue of the imagination. These are problems of moral knowledge which Dante develops from canto XVI to XVIII of *Purgatorio*, and I will give a quick synopsis of them.

Purgatorio XVI focuses on the question of free will ("libero arbitrio," 70–72). To the pilgrim's query about the cause of iniquity in the world, whether it is to be sought in the stars or in man (58–63), Marco Lombardo responds by upholding the principle of moral responsibility. The thesis of astral influence on man's will is clearly incompatible with the tenet of the freedom of the will resolutely affirmed by Christian doctrine, and Bishop Tempier condemned in 1277 the proposition that "voluntas nostra subiacet" to the power of celestial bodies (art. 154; cf. also art. 156).[5] The belief in astral determinism has been associated by Giles of Rome with Alkindi and, more generally, with Averroes, while Siger of Brabant and Aquinas believed, as Dante did, in the indirect influence of the stars on the will.[6] Accordingly, Marco Lombardo asserts that man is given an inner light of choice between good and evil, and thus he dismisses the belief in material determinism and in the direct influence of the stars on the actions of men. If the heavens were to move all things by necessity, Marco Lombardo explains, then free will would be destroyed and there would be no justice in happiness for good nor grief for evil. By a powerful ludic image to which I shall return in chapter 11, the soul at its creation is said to be like a child that sports and goes astray if its inclinations are not guided or curbed.

By a paradoxical formulation human beings, then, are free subjects ("liberi soggiacete") (80). From this paradoxical premise of a necessary combination of freedom and restraint, which defines the essence of laws, Marco Lombardo consistently moves on to evoke the crisis of the law. By the logic of the exposition laws are identified as moral principles binding each individual's moral autonomy to the stability and order of the general body politic. But because the laws are neither enforced nor observed, the unity of the polity is mutilated; the two "suns" of Rome (106)—the two institutions ordained by God, church, and state—have eclipsed each other, that is, have confused the spheres of their respective operations (127–29) and have left the world blind. As is common with the *Divine Comedy*, general moral concerns—figured, as they are, through the same metaphorical language of curbs, blindness, and so on—are transposed into the historical and political realm, which is the locus where abstract propositions are tested. More than that, Marco's historical awareness makes the questions of free will and imagination not just issues of individual psychology and morality but also central concerns of history.[7]

In *Purgatorio* XVII, after the apostrophe to the imagination, Vergil expounds the theory of love shaping the moral order of *Purgatorio*. The problem of free will figures prominently in his discourse. Love, which is the principle and seed of every action, is said to be either instinctive or elective. Whereas instinctive love, the natural impulse that binds all creatures, never errs, the love of choice entails the possibility of moral error. One sins because of excessive or defective attachment to the objects one chooses to love or because one chooses the wrong object. Vergil's exposition triggers new perplexities in the pilgrim: How do we know, in effect he asks, what to love? Or, to put it in the terms of the philosophical debate between voluntarists and rationalists in the thirteenth century, what is the relationship between desire and knowledge? Must one love so that one may know, or must one first know an object in order that one may then love it? To answer this question Dante etches in *Purgatorio* XVIII what amounts to a theory of knowledge whose foundation lies in the imagination.

The mind, Vergil says, quick to love, naturally seeks happiness and is drawn to those objects that promise it. The mechanism of the mind in love starts off when the faculty of perception takes from the material world of objects an image and unfurls it within, so that the mind inclines to it. This inclination is love. In the words of the poem, "Vostra apprensiva da esser verace / tragge intenzione, e dentro a voi la spiega, / sì che l'animo ad essa volger face; / e se, rivolto, inver' di lei si piega, / quel piegare è amor, quell'è natura / che per piacer di novo in voi si lega" (*Purg.* XVIII, 22–27) (Your perception takes from outward reality an impression and unfolds it within you, so that it makes the mind turn to it; and if the mind, so turned, inclines to it, that inclination is love, that is nature, which by pleasure is bound on you afresh).

The mind, then, perceives particular objects through the "intenzione," a term which has the force of a cliché: it alludes to the "intentiones imaginatae," an object of thought in Aristotle's *De anima* and its Scholastic commentaries.[8] On the face of it, Dante's definition of the process of knowledge can be brought within the parameters of St. Thomas's theories. "Nihil est in intellectu quod non sit prius in sensu"—the intellect knows nothing except by receiving sense impressions, Aquinas says in the *De veritate*, and he adds that the intellect reaches understanding only through the mediation of the materiality of the imagination. Aquinas's phrase, may I add, which is of Aristotelian origin (*De anima* 432a, 7–8) occurs also in a variety of Dante's texts.[9]

This view of the role the imagination plays in the production of knowledge in no way disrupts man's moral sense; the imagination, actually, is the ground on which the possibility of conceptualization as well as the exercise of moral judgment rest. Such a formulation, which is Dante's, ushers in a logically consistent query by the pilgrim: If love is an inclination toward an object of pleasure, a ceaseless movement of desire which acquiesces only when "la cosa amata il fa gioire" (33) (the thing loved makes it rejoice)—a phrase which is the reversal of Cavalcanti's love anguish—how can man judge and determine what is good or bad love? The predicament is self-apparent, since love is kindled in us by the perception of an outside reality and is offered to the intellect by the workings of the imagination. The argument circles back to *Purgatorio* XVI and centers on the principle of free will, which Dante now calls both "innata libertate" (*Purg.* XVIII, 68) (innate freedom) and "libero arbitrio" (*Purg.* XVIII, 73–75), freewill, the faculty that counsels and holds the threshold of assent.

So obsessive is Dante with questions of moral choices and their consequences throughout the *Divine Comedy* that this insistence on free will cannot come as a complete surprise. As is known, "liberum arbitrium" is acknowledged to be the substance of the whole poem in the *Epistle to Cangrande*: "Si vero accipiatur opus allegorice, subiectum est homo prout merendo et demerendo per arbitrii libertatem iustitie premiandi et puniendi obnoxius est" (par. 11) (If the work is taken allegorically, the subject is man according as by his merits or demerits in the exercise of his free will he is deserving of reward or punishment by justice).[10] The assertion of free will in *Purgatorio* XVIII marks primarily the dismissal of the blindness of those people (34–39), the Epicureans one infers, who hold every love praiseworthy in itself because its matter appears to be always good. This charge against the Epicureans, against whom Dante articulates his conviction that man has the power to exercise intellect and will, cognition and desire, the conjunction of which is "libero arbitrio," rehashes Cicero's critique in *De finibus* (I and II). More precisely, the Epicurean claim about the sameness of all loves is for Dante "blind": it is a delusory figment of the mind, a style of thought which effaces all distinctions of value and the possibility of moral choice.[11] But as the centrality of moral choice is unquestionably vindicated, the origin of the two faculties of the intellective soul, intellect and will, remains unknown, just as always unknown in the *Divine Comedy* are the first causes: "Però, là onde vegna lo 'ntelletto / de le prime notizie, omo non sape / e de' primi appetibili l'affetto" (55–57) (Therefore whence comes the knowledge of first ideas and the bent to the primary objects of desire, no man knows).

I have been referring to "liberum arbitrium" as an intellectual operation involving the power of both judgment and choice (free will), and as an operation of the will. The two terms are not interchangeable. The decision to adopt either entails a prior decision as to whether freedom is an act of rational knowledge or an act of the will. In *Monarchia*, in the wake of Boethius, Dante refers to "liberum arbitrium" as "de voluntate iudicium."[12] The definition means that free will is the free judgment about the will, or, to state it clearly, free will does not reside in the will, as the Franciscans believe; rather, it resides in the intellect, which can make determinations about what one wills. Such an understanding of the intellect's primacy over the will means the will's servitude to reason. In the light of this text from *Monarchia*, historians of philosophy have argued that Dante, against Duns Scotus, sides with the Averroists in holding that the *liberum arbitrium* is the "free judgement of reason, unimpeded by the appetites, about actions to be undertaken."[13] More than that, on the basis of this very passage in *Monarchia*, Nardi has argued that Dante doubts the existence of free will in *Paradiso* IV, the canto where, as has been shown in chapter 4, the pilgrim is caught in a provisional impasse and his will is inert in making judgments.

Nardi's suggestion depends on his espousal of the Augustinian theologians who asserted the primacy of the will in the act of knowledge. From their perspective St. Thomas Aquinas's own orthodoxy was questioned, and, along with Averroes' theses, he was condemned in 1277 (art. 157, 158, 159).[14] Aquinas had no doubts that "choice is an act of the will and not of reason; for choice is accomplished in a certain movement of the soul toward the good which is chosen. Hence it is clearly an act of the appetitive power."[15] He even wrote that it is the will that moves the intellect, since the will's aim is action. But he also believed that will and reason are always interacting, that election is a desire proceeding from counsel, and that the intellect provides deliberation and judgment about the objects of the will. Such a moderate rationalism made him vulnerable to charges of heresy by the voluntarists.[16]

In his formulation of how the mind comes to know and judge its desires, Dante largely follows, as I have said before, Aquinas. Like Aquinas he is rigorously empirical in the conviction that all knowledge derives from the materiality of sense experience and that objects produce images in the mind. For all its apparent flatness, however, the statement that the imagination follows empirical perception and is contained within and subdued to the sovereign authority of reason is a radical reversal of a number of positions Dante previously staked.

It is, quite clearly, a reversal of the "imaginativa," the faculty that in *Purgatorio* XVII is said to have no bondage to the realm of nature and has the trait of an illumination coming from above. It also alters the concerns of the *Vita nuova*, a narrative which starts off under the aegis of memory, seeks to recapture its sensuous signs, probes the opaque folds of the mind, and is punctuated by hallucinations, dreams, ghostly appearances, and seizures. These fits constitute the dramatic counterpart of memory's effort to resurrect the past, for they lie outside of the will, and, however refractory they may appear to be to reason's decipherment, they are objects of the poet's sustained rational inquiry. More generally, by recalling the Thomistic perspective that the intellect cannot reach understanding without the mediation of phantasms and images, Dante focuses on the issue which is crucial to him as a poet: the value of the representations of the imagination—a question which is the pivot of the debate between St. Thomas and Siger of Brabant.

The text which is central to this discussion is the *De unitate intellectus contra Averroistas*, a polemical tract St. Thomas wrote during his second stay in Paris, where he was teaching as a master (1268–72). Though it is not clear whether St. Thomas was opposing Siger of Brabant—who, as we have seen in the preceding chapter, was the leader of the so-called radical Aristotelians in Paris—or some other prominent figure of Siger's philosophical school, the burden of the treatise is to refute two views which Averroes put forth in his commentary on Aristotle's *De anima*. One is the view of the possible intellect as an incorruptible and separate substance. The other is the view of the possible intellect as one for all men. This is to say that the intellect is not a substantial form of the body and, thus, cannot be thought of as an individualized entity. The logical consequence of this doctrine is the denial of personal immortality, for only the one, general intellect survives death. It also denies the existence of a free will, since the act of judgment is a rational operation entailing the conjunction of will and reason. As I have indicated earlier in this chapter, these inferences were drawn, along with other propositions, by Bishop Tempier in the condemnations of 1277.[17]

Aquinas's quarrel with the Averroists springs from a variety of concerns. He objects to the view that the intellect is a simple and incorporeal substance, whose function is to grasp universal and not concrete entities. From Aquinas's perspective, Averroes' theory of separateness, in short, precludes the possibility of individualized knowledge, or, to put it differently, Averroes makes man the object of the intellect's knowledge and not the subject of knowledge. It also precludes the possibility of moral life. More important, the positing of the unity of the possible intellect appears to Aquinas as patently absurd, because it does not account for diversity of opinions, rational disagreements, and, generally, the fragmentation and subjectivity of knowledge. Were the possible intellect one, it would then follow that there must be one common act of understanding and of willing and, paradoxically, free choice would be the same for all. "If, therefore, there is one intellect for all," Aquinas writes, "it follows of necessity that there be one who understands and consequently one who wills and one who uses according to the choice of his will all those things by which men are diverse from one another. And from this it further follows that there would be no difference among men in respect to the free choice of the will, but it (the choice) would be the same for all, if the intellect in which alone would reside pre-eminence and dominion over the use of all other (powers) is one and undivided in all. This is clearly false and impossible. For it is opposed to what is evident and destroys the whole of moral science and everything which relates to the civil intercourse which is natural to man, as Aristotle says."[18]

In response to Aquinas's critique, Siger of Brabant insists that epistemological differences between men are to be attributed not to the intellect but to the diverse and contradictory experiences men have of phantasms, to the "intentiones imaginatae," which mediate between the separate intellect and the diverse individual acts of knowledge: "It is by these phantasms that the knowledge of this man and the knowledge of that man are diverse, in so far as this man understands those things of which he has phantasms, and that man understands other things of which he has phantasms." Aquinas quotes these lines of Averroes and challenges their validity. For him "the phantasms are preparations for the action of the intellect, as colors are for the act of sight. Therefore the act of the intellect would not be diversified by their diversity in respect to one intelligible. . . . But in two men who know and understand the same thing, the intellectual operation itself can in no way be diversified by the diversity of the phantasms."[19] The source of the Averroists' problem lies in their failure, finally, to distinguish between the things that are outside of the mind and their phantasms.

It is clear that such a debate shapes Dante's theory of knowledge and moral choices in *Purgatorio* XVIII, where he underwrites sundry notions about the imagination. The first is that the imagination, which is the property of the sensitive soul, is neither corporeal nor incorporeal but shares in corporeality and incorporeality. The second is that the imagination by itself neither inquires nor knows if the shadows of objects it apprehends are true or false. It is the office of the understanding to know and judge their truth or falsehood. But it is also clear that for all their ideological divergences, Dante unveils the fact that Averroes, Siger of Brabant, and Aquinas actually agree that the imagination is the central path to knowledge. Yet they circumscribe the powers of the imagination within the perimeter of reason. Their insight into the imagination, which speculative philosophers and theologians share but from which they turn away, forces Dante, who always installs himself imperiously at the center of the most complex intellectual debates of the thirteenth century, to reflect on the value and threatening powers of the imagination. Lest this be seen as an idealistic claim about the privilege and uniqueness of poetry over the mode of knowledge made available by the discourses of theology and philosophy, let me stress that each of these theoretical discourses reveals particular aspects of and has access to the imagination. Dante's poetry does not bracket or elide these particular viewpoints; rather, it is the all-embracing framework within which theological and philosophical discoveries about the imagination are grounded and are given a concrete focus. By themselves, neither

theologians nor philosophers are especially equipped to make pronouncements about the imagination, which is the province of aesthetics, the path
of knowledge, and the home, as it were (and the import of the metaphor
will be evident later), of the poet.

The claim is not unwarranted for the *Vita nuova*, which, moving around
the double focus of love and intellect, delves into the seemingly limitless
horizon of the imagination as well as the effort of binding it. It is a story of
nightmares, apparitions, rapid alterations of the mind, deliriums—all
shapes and seductive images that turn out to be erratic, but to which the
poet-lover succumbs—and these together are the *terra incognita* of love and
poetry themselves. The text is also organized around what the poet calls
"ragioni," prose chapters which attempt to grasp rationally the sense of the
ghostly landscape his poems obsessively conjure up.[20] The prescriptions of
reason are steadily observed throughout the narrative as a way of making
both poetry and the lover's experiences, which are beyond ordinary paradigms, intelligible. But the lyrical essence remains elusive, as images are
neither memories nor thoughts, and the world is the theater of solitary
fantasies in which matter vanishes, in which bodies are astral bodies and
dazzling emanations of light. Written as a visionary account of love for
Beatrice, the *Vita nuova* is directed to Guido Cavalcanti, whose poem
"Donna me prega" casts love as a tragic circle under the cloud of unknowing.[21] Deploying Averroistic and scientific-medical materials, Guido conceives of love as a child not of Venus but of Mars, as a violent experience
which vanquishes the mind. The mind, in turn, separated from the shadows of desire, understands only the abstract essence of love which has been
purified of all individualized concreteness (figures, colors, shapes).

As I have argued earlier, the *Vita nuova* takes to task Guido's literalization of the spirits as material substances and asserts, on the contrary, the
visionary power of the imagination. By the end of the work memory, which
is an interrogation of the past, is reversed into an expectation of the future.
The reversal of memory takes place in the light of the vision of Beatrice
sitting in glory that the lover has at the end of the narrative. One sense of
this "libello" is available from a sonnet Dante wrote to Cino da Pistoia
which can be understood as a recapitulation of the dramatic experience
related in the *Vita nuova*: "Io sono stato con Amore insieme / da la circu-
lazion del sol mia nona, / e so com'egli affrena e come sprona, / e come
sotto lui si ride e geme. / Chi ragione o virtù contro gli sprieme, / fa come
que' che 'n la tempesta sona, / credendo far colà dove si tona, / esse le
guerre de' vapori sceme. / Però nel cerchio de la sua palestra / libero arbitrio già mai non fu franco, / sì che consiglio invan vi si balestra. / Ben può
con nuovi spon' punger lo fianco, / e qual che sia 'l piacer ch'ora n'ad-
destra, / seguitar si convien, se l'altro è stanco" (I have been together with
love since my ninth circulation of the sun and I know how love spurs and

bridles, and how under his sway one laughs and wails. He who urges reason
or virtue against him, he acts like one who raises his voice in a storm,
thinking to lessen the conflict of the clouds, there where the thunder rolls.
Thus within his arena's bounds free will was never free, so that counsel
loses its shafts in vain there. Love can indeed prick the flank with new
spurs; and whatever the attraction that is now leading us, follow we must,
if the other is outworn).

If in this sonnet moral knowledge and free will are shown to be overwhelmed by love's passion, and in the *Vita nuova* the imagination of love
is its incandescent core, in *Purgatorio* XVII and XVIII Dante centers on the
moral value of love. The vibrations of the heart, every virtue, every good
action and sin are reduced to love, the substantial and formal principle
joining together heart and mind, sensitive and rational souls, in an intuition of the good. In strictly Thomistic terms Dante's doctrine holds that
the natural appetite tends to a good existing in a thing, and the will tends
to what is apprehended as good, for evil is never loved except under the
aspect of good. The mind inclined to love is a captive of pleasure (*Purg.*
XVIII, 25–27), yet there is always a free will to make choices.

Vergil's rational exposition of love exemplifies, in itself, the vision of an
intelligible order governing creation: his discourse displays a recognition
of the availability of such an order to the mind of natural man. Yet, the
apostrophe to the imagination in *Purgatorio* XVII, "O imaginativa che ne
rube / talvolta sì di fuor," disrupts, on the face of it, the rational scheme
Vergil puts forth. More precisely, the apostrophe acknowledges the imagination as a power, a figure of personification that arrives like a thief ("che
ne rube"), dispossessing one of one's consciousness of the world outside of
experience. There is also an implied violence (it is the *vis imaginativa*) in
the operation of the imagination, which Dante mutes by the omission of
the *vis* in the phrase. For all its violence, however, the imagination does not
have a spontaneous motion: the power is said to come from God or from
the stars. But what exactly is the "imaginativa"? And what does the disjunction "or" mean in the reference (18) to the origin of the imagination (a
light moves the imagination, which takes form in heaven, by itself *or* by a
will that guides it downward)?

In technical terms the *imaginativa* is one of the five interior senses that
Aristotelean psychology (the textbook for subsequent speculation is Aristotle's *De anima*) locates in the sensitive part of the soul. The arrangement
is not uniform, but the order of faculties and functions of the mind most
consistently repeated is Avicenna's. In the structure he envisions there is
(1) *fantasia sive sensus communis*, which occupies the first chamber of the
brain and which receives the impressions conveyed by the five senses; (2)
imaginatio, which is located in the anterior chamber and retains the im-

pressions; (3) *imaginativa sive cogitativa*, which is known as *virtus formalis* and composes images; (4) *aestimativa*, whose role is to apprehend impressions; and (5) *memorialis sive reminiscibilis*, which is in the posterior chamber of the brain and represents in the mind, from the storehouse of impressions, that which has been absent.[22]

The phrasing of *Purgatorio* XVII effectively blurs the mechanical, clear-cut distinctions of traditional psychology. The canto opens with an address to the reader's memory and imagination ("Recall, reader, if ever in the mountains . . . and your fancy [*imagine*] will quickly come to see") (1–9); there is immediately after a reference to the "imaginativa" (13), which is followed further down by a reference to the "alta fantasia" (25) (high fantasy). These terms are traditionally understood as different inner senses, but they are deployed by Dante (as they are by Aquinas) to describe various aspects of the same process of representation. To be sure, Dante maintains throughout the poem a hierarchy of imaginative states, and the hierarchy of vision, it can be said, is the life principle of the *Divine Comedy*. Such an assertion of an imaginative hierarchy is for Dante a way of restoring connections between diverse areas of human psychology. It is also a way of challenging specific philosophical theories about rational moral freedom to be attained by affirming the empire of reason over the forces and impulses of the imagination. Dante's contention is that psychologists and theologians, who claim that moral freedom can be reached by reason's overcoming of the sensuous realm of passions, in fact restrict the sphere of the imagination's powers and circumvent the possibility of imagination's dialogue both with experiences that lie above the grasp of reason and with those that he assigns to the darkness of unreason.

The theologians' concern is to safeguard the operations of reason from the erratic intrusions of the imagination, to subdue this vagrant faculty, always impatient of restraint, under the authority and rigor of moral sense. This concern is so generalized that it involves prominent figures such as St. Bonaventure and Albert the Great as well as Hugh and Richard of St. Victor. All of them, and especially Richard of St. Victor in his *Benjamin Minor*, acknowledge the visionariness of the imagination, such as in mystical experiences, though they never confront its contradictory powers.

St. Bonaventure urges that the imagination be not allowed to go astray and to take over at the expense of reason, because "it is likely to disturb the freedom of the will." Albert the Great in *De apprehensione*, which draws heavily from Aristotle, Augustine, and Avicenna, understands the imagination as a faculty of retention and preservation of images, and it is said to differ from fantasy, which is the free play of the imagination, in that it enables one to imagine, say, a man with the head of a lion. Because it is the locus of vain imaginings and chimeras, because it is a faculty that may preclude or corrupt the workings of the mind by involving it in immoderate absorption with the "intentiones" it affords, fantasy, so the argument goes, must submit to reason.

In these texts the general insight is that imagination, insofar as it depends on material perception of reality, is to reason as shade is to light, as Hugh of St. Victor puts it. But in the *Benjamin Minor* by Richard of St. Victor (whom Dante acknowledges, as will be shown more extensively in chapter 8 below, in the *Epistle to Cangrande* as one of his authorities) the imagination is not simply excluded from the arc of light shed by reason, nor is it banished to the peripheral activity of manufacturing dark delusions of the heart. Richard of St. Victor's point of departure is an allegory of reason and imagination, which are related as a mistress and a handmaiden who keeps in contact with the servants, the senses. But the imagination is an "evagatio," a pilgrim spirit, always capable of error and coming into play when the mind fails to realize its highest goal of contemplation:

> it is manifestly concluded that reason never rises up to the cognition of the invisible unless her handmaiden, imagination, represents to her the form of visible things. . . . But it is certain that without imagination she would not know corporeal things, and without knowledge of these things she would not ascend to contemplation of celestial things. For the eye of the flesh alone looks at visible things, while the eye of the heart alone sees invisible things. . . . Bala (imagination) is garrulous; Zelpha, drunken. For not even Rachel, her mistress, can suppress Bala's loquacity, and not even the generosity of her mistress can completely quench Zelpha's thirst. The wine that Zelpha drinks is the joy of pleasures. The more of it she drinks, the greater is her thirst. For the whole earth does not suffice to satisfy the appetite of sensation. . . . Now the imagination makes noise in the ears of the heart with so much importunity, and so great is its clamor, as we have said, that Rachel herself can scarcely, if at all, restrain her. It is for this reason that often when we say psalms or pray we wish to banish phantasies of thoughts or other sorts of images of things from the eyes of the heart, but we are not able to do so. Since even unwillingly we daily suffer a tumult of resounding thoughts of this sort, we are taught by daily experience of what sort and how great is the garrulity of Bala. She calls to memory everything, whether seen or heard, that we ourselves have done or said at some time or another. . . . And often when the will of the heart does not give assent to hearing her, she herself nevertheless unfolds her narrative although, as it were, no one listens.[23]

The allegory continues with a distinction between a rational imagination and a bestial imagination. The imagination is rational when from those things which we know by means of bodily sense we fabricate something else; for instance, we have seen gold and we have seen a house, and we picture a gold house. The imagination is bestial, on the other hand, when

"with a wandering mind we run about here and there without any usefulness, without any deliberation concerning those things which we have seen
or done."[24] This type of imagination will not be consulted by Rachel. Val-
ued by Richard, however, are the two children of Bala, Dan and
Naphtalim; Dan knows nothing save through the corporeal and can bring
before the eyes of our hearts infernal torments; Naphtalim can see the
walls of the heavenly Jerusalem made of precious stones.

Richard's notion of the double power of the imagination, which can deal
with the satanic and the heavenly, which wanders off or attends on the
needs of reason, may well be construed as an ideal anticipation of Dante's
sense of the ambivalence of the imaginative faculty. Dante's sense of the
imagination's ambivalence can only in part be accounted for in doctrinal
terms. It is certainly true that for Dante the origin of the "imaginativa," for
instance, is not clearly stated. The images are said to descend into the mind
either from God, whose will directs them downward, or from a light
formed in the heavenly intelligences. The disjunction has forced scholars
to solve the issue of causality either in astrological terms of dream visions,
of a natural origination (and this is Nardi's view), or in supernatural terms
(as Singleton does), since God is the maker of the ecstatic visions the pilgrim beholds.[25] But the imagination is ambivalent for Dante in a more
essential and radical way.

In *Purgatorio* XVII, 13–18, the "imaginativa" is represented in a language that suggests simultaneously its passive and active traits: it is moved
from above, and yet it has the power to snatch us from outward things; it
is personified as if it were an alien feminine force, yet it is contained in the
mind; it is the eye that sees when, paradoxically, all the lights of the natural
world have gone or are going out. The mind's cognitive process in *Purgatorio* XVIII depends on imagination's power to represent objects to the
point that imagination is the ground of all knowledge. But in *Purgatorio*
XVII the imagination is not the ground; it dislodges us, rather, from the
ground. It is within this context that we can begin to understand the figurative discrepancies that characterize the exordium of canto XVII, which I
have analyzed at length at the beginning of this chapter. The temporal
dislocation figured by memory, the spatial dislocations figured by the Alps,
the reversal of the mountain heights into the mole's depth and of light into
darkness, the metaphoric interplay of vision and blindness, which actually
starts in *Purgatorio* XIII—all show that the imagination is a figure of rever-
sals in which immobility turns into action and actions are frozen as images.
It is a trope that is always other than what it seems to be.

The logical and conceptual implications of imagination's steady displacement and self-displacement can be gauged by considering its narrative function in *Purgatorio* XVII. Why does Dante address the imagination
directly as he introduces the sins of punished wrath? What does this prox-

imity between *ira* and the imagination disclose about either? *Ira*, as one
gathers from Aquinas's discussion of vices, is a passion of the sensitive
appetite, which is swayed by the irascible and which, as it flares up, dims
the light of understanding and impedes the judgment of reason.[26] "Ira per
zelum turbat rationis oculum," says St. Gregory the Great, and the *ira
caeca*, a formula that obviously accounts for the blindness of the purgatorial ledge, does not differ from madness. John Chrysostom, for instance,
refers to anger as *furor* and *insania*.[27] In the analytic of the passion the heart
is said to be inflamed with the stings of its own anger, the body trembles,
the tongue stammers, the face is fired, the eyes blaze; more precisely, anger
is accompanied by a *fervor*, the heat of the blood around the heart, and this
is the opposite of the heat produced in love. Since all sins in *Purgatorio* are
forms of perverted love, the sins of anger are cases of mad love.

The first tragic figuration of anger represents what medical authorities
starting from Avicenna to Bernard of Gordon in his *Lilium medicinale* have
called *amor hereos*, literally the disease of the imagination, a love that alters
reason's judgment, for it corrupts the *vis aestimativa* which presides over
and binds the imagination.[28] The examples of punished wrath the pilgrim
beholds (*Purg.* XVII, 19–39) bear out this claim. The details of the Ovidian
story of Procne and Philomela are well known: Tereus is a descendant of
Mars, and his marriage to Procne takes place under the aegis of the Furies.
When Tereus meets his sister-in-law, Philomela, he is taken with her,
schemes to possess her, and rapes her. Philomela accuses Tereus of confounding all natural feelings, of making her her sister's rival. Angered by
her words, and to prevent her from revealing his transgression, he cuts out
her tongue. Philomela reappears years later at the feast of Bacchus and
weaves a pictogram telling the story of the violation she had suffered.
When Procne discovers the horror, in a fury of madness she kills Tereus's
son and serves him up as a meal.

The story can certainly be taken as Ovid's poetic parable of the relationship between art and violence. Art for Ovid reveals and displaces violence,
for it relates the shift from voice to vision back to voice, as the three principals are metamorphosed into nightingale, swallow, and hawk. The shift,
more to the point, discloses how the melic lure of the birds' song transfigures and possibly conceals a plot of madness. The metaphor of metamorphosis, finally, conveys the essence of the image as a figure of dislocation
and of alterations of identity.

There are other dimensions of meaning common to these three images.
Much as the story of Tereus, the other two stories—of Haman, who was
hanged on the gibbet he had prepared for Mordechai, and of Amata, who
not to lose Lavinia to Aeneas commits suicide on hearing the false news of
Turnus's death—dramatize the element of foreignness, the intrusion of a

stranger as a figure throwing into havoc one's familiar world. And in all three cases the stability of the social world is crushed by the destructiveness of the characters' unaccommodated imaginings. More important, all three images are traversed by the shadow of Mars: Tereus is Mars's descendant; Haman plots the destruction of the Jews; and Amata's raving madness ("mad she utters many wild things in moaning frenzy") is triggered by the madness of war. The implicit reference to Mars in the three examples of punished anger must be accounted for in terms of the traditional links existing between Mars and the irascible appetite, the faculty of action seeking to possess the object it desires. In this context one should add that the angel's voice the pilgrim hears as soon as the images vanish, *"Beati/pacifici, che son sanz'ira mala"* (*Purg.* XVII, 68–69) (*beati pacifici* who are without sinful anger), seals, by contrast, the imaginative bond Dante envisions between war and wrath. By this link Dante draws wrath into the dark night of desire or, to put it in the vocabulary of Dante's own poetic experience, into the space celebrated by Guido Cavalcanti and the Epicureans wherein love is war. He also draws it into the public world of political realities, which the fury of war annihilates.

To link wrath and war as versions of mad love, as the *Purgatorio*'s moral system explicitly enables the reader to do, means to root them in the inconsistency of the phantasms which seize and darken one's own judgment and social values. The madness of Tereus, Procne, Haman, and Amata lies in their transgression of reason's bounds as they will to control events and to impart to them the direction of their desires. But they are above all mad because they have yielded to the *vis*, as it were, to the violence of their phantasms; they have literalized the phantasms and have succumbed to them by suppressing reason and, in the case of Procne, language itself. In this sense wrath, which is an active appetite and leads to action, is the passion that mediates between the imagination (of which it is a form gone astray) and the *liberum arbitrium*, which is a principle of action. Small wonder that Dante discusses imagination, love, and moral knowledge in the context of wrath, for wrath is their metonym and their threat, in the sense that it mimes and distorts the individual operations of each one of them.

But there is another, more fundamental reason why Dante should discuss the mysterious workings and origins of the poetic imagination in the context of wrath. The proximity between divine madness and inspired poetry is a given for Plato; and Dante, to put it at its most general, recognizes that the poet, in treading the paths of knowledge, needs both the flight of the imagination and the ceaseless dialogue between imagination and reason. This link is not kept at the level of mere abstraction. The loop between wrath and poetry is suggested by Dante himself in *Inferno* VIII. In this infernal scene, against the stoical ideals of the imperturbability of the sage, he pits the *laudabilis ira*, the just indignation that the pilgrim, like an angry prophet, voices against the savage violence of the "ombra . . . furiosa" (48) (furious shade) of Filippo Argenti.

Dante's own wrath in the canto where wrath is punished (*Inf.* VIII) is consistent with his commitment to his visionary calling, to his steady impulse to yoke moral knowledge and vision. Unlike the images of punished wrath—where the characters surrender to the sovereign call of the imaginings that possess them and, thereby, enter the strange and demonic world of unreason—Dante yields to the imperious summons of the imagination free from restraint and yet, at the same time, yearns to bring his vision within the compass of reason and the demands of reality. By the same token, the world of reality is transposed into the light of visionary figurations. This convergence of visionariness and reality, which is the equivalent of the quandary of freedom and necessity articulated by Marco Lombardo in the oxymoron "liberi soggiacete" (*Purg.* XVI, 80), is the work of art itself, which is the outcome of imagination and the rules of reason and which, inasmuch as it is work and production, entails the desire to engage in a dialogue with others and is, thus, the negation of destructive madness. Central to Dante's work of art is the resolute conviction that his own moral knowledge is rooted in and flows from the extraordinary vision that has been granted to him.

The aesthetic-moral unity of the *Divine Comedy* effectively depends on the poet's astonishing power to hold together two principles that, on the face of it, are irreconcilable. At the very center of the *Divine Comedy* Dante presents the imagination variously as a dazzling poetic faculty autonomous from the rigors of the discourse of reason, as inseparable from the tragic errors of madness, as the path to love, and as the instrument of reason's judgments. To exert a moral judgment, which is simultaneously will and knowledge translated into action, imagination's excesses must be sacrificed and held at bay. To yield to the unrestrained promptings of the imagination is to lapse into the fantastic realm of mad violence. Yet, sacrificing the excesses of the imagination to the order of rationality is tantamount, by the inexorable logic of Dante's text, to renouncing the very visionariness which shapes the poem.

There is, then, at the heart of the *Divine Comedy* a doubleness which is deeper than the determination of how much of St. Thomas Aquinas or how much of Averroes' value systems get absorbed in the text. This doubleness is that of the imagination, as has been described above—a complex, forever ambivalent, and protean faculty which theologians and philosophers never confront in all its problematic implications. Dante is not alone, however, in confronting the doubleness of the imagination as both the portal to a knowledge of reality and as exceeding the domain of material reality. Another poetic text, one that is legitimately viewed as the foundation of Dante's own poetic-moral apprenticeship, directly confronts the question of the ambiguity and potential deceptiveness of images.

The poem is Guinizelli's "Al cor gentil," which is an extended meditation on the effort to establish analogies between the secret essence of love and the world of nature. More to the point, Guinizelli's song seeks to cast—much as Dante does in the *Vita nuova*—the figure of a woman as an irreplaceable and unique image of love. The poem ends with an imagined encounter between God and the poet. God chides the poet for his presumptuous claim about the woman's divinity and for comparing her to God. The comparison, from God's view, is a sin of pride, but the poet replies that he should not be held accountable for the fault: to him the woman does have the semblance of an angel.

Dante goes well beyond Guinizelli's insight into the deceptive effects of images, just as he goes beyond Aquinas's and Siger's formulations. Dante's sense of the primacy of the imagination, in fact, allows him to draw their respective perceptions within a space where ideological contradictions and differences of opinion can be harmonized, for in his construction the apparent contradictions depend on something prior to them: the doubleness of the imagination. This doubleness Dante, who is the visionary poet of history, makes the core of his work.

The awareness of the two operations of the imagination accounts for the vital tension in the *Divine Comedy* between the uncertain vision in the world of immanence and the clarity of knowledge the pilgrim incessantly pursues. In *Purgatorio* XVI the origin of evil is said to rest in the confusion of the secular and spiritual orders:

> Dì oggimai che la Chiesa di Roma,
> per confondere in sè due reggimenti,
> cade nel fango, e sè brutta e la soma.

(127–29)

(Tell henceforth that the Church of Rome, by confounding in itself two governments, falls in the mire and befouls both itself and its burden.)

In *Purgatorio* XVII Vergil, after his exposition of the nature and power of love, turns the issue of confusion around:

> ciascun confusamente un bene apprende
> nel qual si queti l'animo, e disira.

(127–28)

(Each one apprehends confusedly a good wherein the mind may find rest.)

In the first passage the confusion in the social and moral structures of the world is unequivocally condemned. Political order depends on the observance of hierarchical differences and distinctions between institutions. Yet the imagination apprehends confusedly the objects of desire: this confused apprehension of the good textually recalls the Augustinian opening statement of the *Confessions*: "inquietum est cor nostrum donec requiescat in te" (Restless is our heart till it rests in thee). The Augustinian echo places us in history as the land of longing, where all knowledge is—to put it in the metaphors that introduce the apostrophe to the imagination in *Purgatorio* XVII—a *cognitio vespertina*, a twilight knowledge.

The double value the word "confusion" acquires in these two cantos draws attention to Dante's obstinate assertion of the moral necessity of order in the world of man. It also conveys his insight into the confused perceptions the imagination makes available to reason's judgment. In this world veiled by fogs of desire we see as does the mole in its winding maze. Dante, the poet of vision, knows well both the role blindness plays in arriving at knowledge (this is the myth of Tiresias) and how blind knowledge can be. But even as we are in a world of confused shadows, we also can see, in the language of the first letter to the Thessalonians, as the children of light and of the day do, for we belong neither to darkness nor to the night. This mode of vision is rendered by Dante's understanding of contemplation. Such an understanding affords him the notion that poetic vision is not simply the outcome of the pilgrim's journey toward knowledge; vision precedes and gives a shape to that outcome. The primacy of vision, as chapter 8 will show, depends on the pilgrim's *intuition*, the form of immediate cognition in which the imagination incorporates and yet exceeds the mode of knowledge supplied by the rational faculties.

Chapter 7

THE DREAM OF THE SIREN

(*PURGATORIO* XIX–XXXI)

THE PRECEDING chapter has shown two basic points. First, the imagination is not simply a mimetic faculty but is the foundation of knowledge; second, because of the centrality of the imagination Dante stakes a unique claim for himself as a poet. Not the philosopher or the theologian but the poet, who is installed in the world of the imagination—dreams, memories, visions, representations—plays a crucial role in determining the shape of knowledge.

At face value, such a radical claim for the poetic imagination marks an abrupt shift from dominant epistemological theories such as those of St. Thomas Aquinas and Siger of Brabant. History duly records—and chapter 6 has briefly brought to light—the bitterness of their philosophical debate on the function of the possible intellect. In part, at least, their debate can be summarily said to focus on the nature of the relationship between the subject and the act of thinking. The burden of this complex argument can be thus recapitulated: Siger maintains that the subject is the object of a thought that exists separately from matter and, thus, comes to one from the outside. This proposition stands in dramatic contrast to Aquinas's belief in the subjectivity of knowledge.[1] For Aquinas the subject's mind is the active source of thought, and this proposition accounts for the concrete diversity of thoughts. But notwithstanding these fundamental differences on the question of the status and powers of the subject, from Dante's viewpoint the philosopher and the theologian agree in casting rational thought as the reliable path to absolute knowledge.

The assumption that rationality is the secure basis of true knowledge has traditionally justified the expulsion of poetry from Plato's *Republic* as well as from the Christian palace of wisdom. The objections leveled against poetry by Christian and rationalist philosophers alike follow closely Plato's classical critique (*Republic*, X) of the immorality, illusionism, and irrationality of the poetic experience. Because—so runs the argument—it indulges in lust, madness, and sundry such phantasmatic projections of *amor sui*, poetry warps the intellect, unless its powers be controlled by and subjected to the hegemony of reason.[2]

Dante turns around this tradition of thought. As I have been arguing in this study, the poetic imagination cannot be bracketed as a secondary, ancillary activity, the way Aquinas would want it. The central task of poetry for Dante consists in its being able to provide a global, all-embracing framework in order to represent the rich and contradictory phenomena of existence—the sediments of language; the memories, inventions, hopes, ideas, and passions of private selves; and the history of man. Or, to say it succinctly, poetry for Dante both entails and sustains the vast scope of knowledge. Yet Dante is not unaware of the difficulties of making poetry the basis of knowledge, for he knows how tricky is the poetic imagination, how uncertain and subjective is its knowledge, how dangerous are its simulations and opinions. How, then, does he distinguish between "good" and "bad" poetry, between an epistemologically reliable sort of poetry and, on the other hand, a poetry that never attains cognitive status? These questions, clearly, restate the debate on the double value of the imagination studied in the preceding chapter as well as Plato's old dilemma in the *Republic*. The present chapter will address them by an analysis of two related scenes in *Purgatorio* XIX and XXXI.

The first scene is the account of the pilgrim's dream of the Siren (*Purgatorio* XIX, 1–36), which comes straight out of the theoretical concerns on the interactions between imagination, love, knowledge, and moral choices articulated in the two previous cantos (*Purgatorio* XVII and XVIII) already discussed. In many ways, the dream refocuses on those questions from what I would call an existential perspective. Whereas cantos XVII and XVIII of *Purgatorio* probe the realm of the imagination as it brings forth the forms of things unseen by the physical eye, the dream of *Purgatorio* XIX plunges us deep into the shadowy folds of the pilgrim's mind, beneath, as it were, the lids and layers of discursive reason, to the inner, subjective world of dreams and phantasms.[3] The closing lines of *Purgatorio* XVIII, in point of fact, dramatize the transmutation of thought into a dream ("pensamento in sogno trasmutai"—line 145) as they evoke, first, the pilgrim's somnolence (88), later the rambling of the mind from one thought to another (139–41), and finally the dream replacing thinking, with the suggestion that the dream can lead on the path of knowledge.

The dramatic shift in the movement of the text from rational inquiry to the domain of self has a logical necessity. At stake, in effect, is the redefinition of knowledge, which for Dante is never merely or solely a question of bloodless abstractions nor is it a dialectical exercise for grasping the general principles by which the mind reaches understanding. Because knowledge is ultimately self-knowledge—and self-knowledge, as Cicero writes in a tantalizing passage of his *Tusculan Disputations*, is the soul seen by itself (I, xxii)—it must be realized as one's own concrete existential experience. Dante invests the word "esperienza" with extraordinary overtones. The word implies an irreducibly individualized knowledge extracted from one's own practice, witnessing, pleasure and/or suffering. The epistemological value of one's own experience was brought to focus by the Augustinian tradition of medieval thought: St. Augustine's *Confessions*, St. Bernard's *Sermons on the Canticles*, the meditative self-analyses of the Victorine mystics, and, above all, by St. Bonaventure's *Journey of the Mind to God*.[4] A sign of the necessary transformation of knowledge into experience at this juncture of the poem is the autobiographical thrust of the passage which relates a personal dream.

> Ne L'ora che non può 'l calor diurno
>   intepidar più 'l freddo de la luna,
>   vinto da terra, e talor da Saturno
> —quando i geomanti lor Maggior Fortuna
>   veggiono in oriente, innanzi a l'alba,
>   surger per via che poco le sta bruna—
> mi venne in sogno una femmina balba.
>   ne li occhi guercia, e sovra i piè distorta,
>   con le man monche, e di colore scialba.
> Io la mirava; e come 'l sol conforta
>   le fredde membra che la notte aggrava,
>   così lo sguardo mio le facea scorta
> la lingua, e poscia tutta la drizzava
>   in poco d'ora, e lo smarrito volto,
>   com' amor vuol, così le colorava.
> Poi ch'ell' avea 'l parlar così disciolto,
>   cominciava a cantar sì, che con pena
>   da lei avrei mio intento rivolto.
> "Io son," cantava, "io son dolce serena,
>   che' marinari in mezzo mar dismago;
>   tanto son di piacere a sentir piena!
> Io volsi Ulisse del suo cammin vago
>   al canto mio; e qual meco s'ausa,
>   rado sen parte; sì tutto l'appago!"
> Ancor non era sua bocca richiusa,
>   quand' una donna apparve santa e presta
>   lunghesso me per far colei confusa.
> "O Virgilio, Virgilio, chi è questa?"
>   fieramente dicea; ed el venìa
>   con li occhi fitti pur in quella onesta.
> L'altra prendea, e dinanzi l'apria
>   fendendo i drappi, e mostravame 'l ventre;
>   quel mi svegliò col puzzo che n'uscia.

lo mossi li occhi, e 'l buon maestro: "Almen tre
voci t'ho messe!" dicea, "Surgi e vieni;
troviam l'aperta per la qual tu entre."

(*Purg.* XIX, 1–36)

(At the hour when the day's heat, overcome by Earth and at times by Saturn, can no more warm the cold of the moon—when the geomancers see their *Fortuna Major* rise in the East before dawn by a path which does not long stay dark for it—there came to me in a dream a woman, stammering, with eyes asquint and crooked on her feet, with maimed hands, and of sallow hue. I gazed upon her: and even as the sun revives cold limbs benumbed by night, so my look made ready her tongue, and then in but little time set her full straight, and colored her pallid face even as love requires. When she had her speech thus unloosed, she began to sing so that it would have been hard for me to turn my attention from her.

"I am," she sang, "I am the sweet Siren who leads mariners astray in mid-sea, so full am I of pleasantness to hear. Ulysses, eager to journey on, I turned aside to my song; and whosoever abides with me rarely departs, so wholly do I satisfy him." Her mouth was not yet shut when a lady, holy and alert, appeared close beside me to put her to confusion. "O Virgil, Virgil, who is this?" she said sternly; and he came on with his eyes fixed only on that honest one. He seized the other and laid her bare in front, rending her garments and showing me her belly: this waked me with the stench that issued therefrom. I turned my eyes, and the good master said, "I have called you at least three times: arise and come, let us find the opening by which you may enter.")

This dream, which is the second in a series of three dreams in *Purgatorio*, occurs in the ledge where the sin of *acedia*, sloth, is expiated.[5] The moral context within which the scene unfolds is of some moment in conveying the sense of the passage. *Acedia*, which is one of the seven deadly sins, is a term describing the somnolence, sickness, spiritlessness, and despondency of the mind. The condition has many names—indecisiveness, sluggishness, apathy—and they all suggest at least two main traits that characterize this spiritual-moral weariness. The symptoms of *acedia*, first off, point to a crisis of the will, as if the object of desire has lost its consistency and luster, and also to the passivity and torpor that traditionally is said to precede and follow a visionary experience. From this standpoint it might be added that the reference to Saturn (3)—which, as we shall see more extensively in the next chapter, is the planet of contemplation and melancholy—makes of *acedia* the negative version of contemplation. *Acedia* signals, as it were, the contemplation of nothingness. From this viewpoint, the dream-vision triggered by sloth is the parodic mirror image of the mystic's ecstasy. Second, in the typology of the deadly sins, sloth describes the temptation of the "noon-day devil," the dangerous time of the stagnation of the soul when the mind of the monk experiences emptiness, and his body yields to lust. For Dante the Siren is the lure of that emptiness, and she appears as the demon of dawn. More to the point, *acedia* accounts for the dramatic contour of the passage, its configuration of lust and dream.

The reader should hardly be surprised by Dante's redeployment of a dream in this stretch of the text. The technique, as has so often been remarked, is commonplace in medieval literature, and the list of texts centered on dreams as the vehicle to conjure up and deliver visions ranges from the *Romance of the Rose* to the *Book of the Duchess*, from the *Vita nuova* to the *Amorosa visione*. But let us be clear about this far too common literary phenomenon. The poets dream, but, as they dream, they always keep their eyes open. And as they do so, they convey to us their visionary, astonished knowledge of the wondrous possibilities of life, of the constant intersections that could plausibly occur between the natural world and the afterlife or, generally, the supernatural realm. Yet the symbolic value of dreams cannot be merely circumscribed within such generalities.

Because a dream presupposes sleep, more than ever before in *Purgatorio* we are now asked to muse on the metaphoric link between sleep and poetry. As we learn from later Romantics (e.g., Keats's Chaucerian "Sleep and Poetry"), sleep is a favorite state of the poets because of its power to engender unwilled and, thus, at least in theory, portentous visions. What is unwilled and lies beyond the voluntary, conscious acts of the subject may well be a random occurrence, but a poet such as Dante assumes that it has (and he looks for) its own unexpected and prodigious significance. Like the young man's gratuitous first two encounters with Beatrice in the *Vita nuova*, the dreams punctuating this autobiographical text seem to arise spontaneously, in the dark depths of the lover's mind, beyond the volition and vigilance of the "I."

In their apparent contingency, dreams and encounters alike bear the paradoxical mark of a secret necessity. In point of fact, like Dante's first view of Beatrice, the dreams of the *Vita nuova* jolt the complacencies of the mind enmeshed in the ordinary appearances of the natural world; they mobilize the mind's faculties and force it to grasp the elusive sense of that strange occurrence. In short, the experience of the dream compels the dreamer to *interpret* whether it is an empty fantasy or a wondrous, enigmatic sign to be explicated. In *Purgatorio* XIX, the reference to the geomancers and to their figuration of Fortuna Major (4) alludes precisely to their practice of astrological divination/interpretation. The geomancers are diviners who, on the assumption that knowledge is coextensive with divination, seek from fortuitous figures and from lines drawn at random on earth to unfold the concealed contours of fate.

That dreams are allegories that may be interpreted, fabulous narratives veiling a hidden truth, is the brunt of the most influential dreambook of the Middle Ages, Macrobius's *Commentary on the Dream of Scipio*. In book I, 3, of this encyclopedic volume, Macrobius, in the wake of Artemiodorus, drafts an extensive table of dreams and classifies them under five general headings. There is, he says, "the enigmatic dream, in Greek *oneiros*, in Latin *somnium*; second, there is the prophetic vision, in Greek *horama*, in Latin *visio*; third, there is the oracular dream, in Greek *chrematiamos*, in Latin, *oraculum*; Latin *insomnium*; and last, the apparition, in Greek *phantasma*, which Cicero, when he has occasion to use the word, calls *visum*" (87–88).

For Macrobius nightmares and apparitions, which occur in conditions of physical or mental impairment, such as love passions and drowsiness, are insubstantial, diseased fabrications of the mind akin to madness and, thus, without any prophetic significance. On the other hand, oracular dream, prophetic vision, and enigmatic dreams are endowed with the power of divination and cannot be comprehended without skillful interpretation. But if for Macrobius the dream of Scipio partakes of these three types, the pilgrim's dream of the Siren eludes the neat, classificatory pigeonholing set up by Macrobius. Making use of Macrobius's own categories, one can say that the dream of the Siren is at the same time a nightmare and a phantasm, for it exemplifies, respectively, a deceitful love-dream as well as the false imagination of specters wandering about and the enigmatic dream, "which conceals with strange shapes and veils with ambiguity the true meaning of the information being offered, and requires an interpretation for its understanding" (90). Rhetorically, this dream is an enigma, which, as one reads in Isidore of Seville's *Etymologies*, is a trope of dark meanings and is a variety of allegory.[6] Dante's scene is an enigma which also enacts the interpretation of the opaque phantasmic event.

The dream, we are told, takes place at dawn—a detail that conventionally charges the dream with a heightened prophetic significance. Its point of departure, however, is the sudden apparition of a stammering figure of a woman, with eyes asquint, maimed hands, sallow hue, and crooked or bent feet who is referred to as "una femmina balba" (7). In the poetry of the Sweet New Style, say, in the *Vita nuova*, the extraordinary, ghostly apparition of the woman is the epiphanic event that breaks the shadowy, ordinary texture of reality. The surreal scene the poet evokes is well known: Beatrice's beauty is a prodigy of light that makes the air tremble, induces a stupefied silence, dazzles the eye and bewitches the mind of the lover. In *Purgatorio* XIX, by contrast, the "femmina balba" is the ghostly embodiment of hideousness. I will remark later in the final chapter of this book on Dante's deployment of what I would like to call the aesthetics of the ugly. For the present purpose, suffice it to point out the sudden metamorphosis of the woman under the transfiguring power of the dreamer's gaze: "Io la mirava e come il sol conforta / le fredde membra che la notte aggrava, / così lo sguardo mio le facea scorta / la lingua, e poscia tutta la drizzava / in poco d'ora; e lo smarrito volto, / com' amor vuol, così le colorava" (10–15).

The imagining, in effect, takes on the appearance of an erotic dream, in which at first the dreamer is not the subject but an object, in the sense that the oneiric image, as the text says, comes to him without his willing it. The dreamer's passivity is short-lived. It is his own gaze that invests the repulsive figure with an alluring power—and the remarkable grammatical shift from the self as indirect object ("mi venne") (7) to the pilgrim's subjectivity expressed through the pronoun "I" (10) signals the occurrence. Finally, the Siren attempts to draw the dreamer within the magic circle of her song. While the alliteration of words, " 'Io son,' cantava, 'io son dolce serena.' " (19), unveils the seductive euphony of her song, the adjective "dolce" (19), by which she describes herself, also connotes the Siren's musical charm. The musical resonance in her representation is meant to project the Siren's song primarily as a song of temptation. Her honeyed words seek to drag the pilgrim within the illusory, enchanting world of romance, within the epic horizon of Ulysses, who is the steady point of reference for Dante's own quest.

How can one define the exact nature of the Siren's temptation? Early commentators, such as Iacopo della Lana and the Ottimo Commento, among others, have glossed Dante's Siren either as a Circe or Calypso or as a mixture of the two, and they have explained her as the allegory of the attraction of false earthly pleasures.[7] The deployment of terms from magic practices, such as "dismago" (20) and later "quell'antica strega" (58), partly accounts for the commentators' evocation of the mythic enchantresses. More recently, Dante's Siren has been interpreted as an emblem of philosophical pride or as the temptation of false knowledge, a knowledge which cripples the intellect because it takes place without divine revelation.[8] It has also been suggested by Grandgent, in the light of Boethius's *De consolatione philosophiae*, that the Siren's "sweet voice" constitutes a specifically poetic temptation. Regrettably, Grandgent's pithy insight on the Siren as signifying the moral threat of poetry has been discarded or generally neglected on the dubious grounds that poetry for Dante never constitutes a moral threat.

I believe that the Siren is a composite figure of eros and song and that all these views are part of the myth, but I claim that the song of temptation of the Siren, this fabulous hybrid of woman-fish, stands chiefly for the mask of death. That song of temptation is the temptation of nothingness. To say it more clearly, the pilgrim's dream is the dramatic context within which Dante figures primarily an esthetics of imaginary phantasmic pleasures which are signs of death. As the pilgrim yields to the temptation of the dream, the poet in fact discovers that the lure of the imaginary is tantamount to the attraction of death. Dante's imagination steadily focuses on the thought of death: he stumbles against it or exorcises it in both the *Vita nuova* and the *Convivio*. In the *Divine Comedy* death, and what lies in its heretofore uncharted domain, is the sinew of the text and the very horizon of Dante's representation. The encounter with the Siren is a version of death's pull on and temptation for the pilgrim. Traditional mythographic accounts link the Siren with the sweetness of the story and only obliquely with death, but Dante foregrounds these dimensions of the myth.

It is well known that in *De finibus* (V, xviii) Cicero interprets Homer's story of Ulysses' encounter with the Sirens not as a parable of the hero's yielding to the "sweetness of their voices or the novelty and diversity of their song" but as a metaphor for the temptation of encyclopedic knowledge. In line with the Neoplatonic construction of Ulysses' journey as the allegory of the education of the soul, Cicero regards with incredulity the fable of a Ulysses spellbound by the Siren's idle song. Against Cicero and against the tradition which represents the Greek hero's victory over the Sirens' temptation—he hears their enigmatic song but he is not destroyed by its enticement (*Odyssey* XII, 39ff.)—the Siren of *Purgatorio* XIX claims to have enchanted and waylaid him. Her claim is false, but the point of the hero succumbing to the irresistible power of her song is quite consistent with Dante's account of the shipwreck of Ulysses' quest in *Inferno* XXVI as I have interpreted that canto in *Dante, Poet of the Desert*.[9]

In an important study on the iconography of death and Latin Neoplatonism, Pierre Courcelle has richly documented the mythic associations between the song of the Siren and the music produced by the harmony of the spheres. The point of origin of the belief in the Sirens' musical powers is to be found, no doubt, in Plato's *Republic* (X, 617B), which is cited by Macrobius's *Commentary on the Dream of Scipio* (II, 3). This strain is recalled by Boethius in his representation of the Sirens as meretricious muses of poetry in *De consolatione philosophiae* (I, 1), a text which as has often been said to be and, as we shall soon see, indeed is the source for the whole dream of *Purgatorio* XIX. Within a specifically Christian tradition St. Jerome also views the Sirens as demons "dulce cantantes et decipientes homines" as well as the "carmina poetarum."[10] Such a poetic-musical interpretation reappears discreetly in St. Augustine's *De beata vita* and *De ordine*, but it is a stock element in a popular encyclopedic work, and as the *Bestiaire* of Pierre de Beauvais, "La seraine," Pierre writes, "a si doux chanz qu'ele decoit ceux qui nagent en mer et atrait a lui par grant doucor de son chant et lor fait oblier si qu'ils s'endorment."[11] Alongside this central component of the allegory of the Siren there is a Neoplatonic tradition depicted on Christian sarcophagi and cenotaphs and documented by Wilpert, Cumont, and Courcelle.[12] In these allegorical representations Ulysses is cast as the soul of the dead who, in its ascension to the heavenly fatherland, escapes the Sirens summoning it to its death. The Siren's song, pleasurable to the ear, ends up engendering death, and this motif, as we shall soon see, ap-

pears overtly in Boethius's *De consolatione philosophiae*. Let me first recapitulate the textual events.

In *Purgatorio* XIX, at the point when the pilgrim's seduction by the
Siren's song is almost complete, a "donna" suddenly enters the dream,
summons Vergil, rips open the Siren's gown, and by that gesture reveals
the filth of her womb. The *odor feminae*, the stench that emanates from her
body, breaks the dreamer's fascination. He wakes up and sees by his side
Vergil, who urges him to continue winding along the steep path of his
journey (26–36). With the intrusion of this "donna" the dream takes on the
shape of an allegorical *psychomachia*, with the two women as two antithetical impulses of the mind or two *personae* of a spiritual drama in which they
vie for the soul of the pilgrim and make two irreconcilable, absolute demands on him. The text's lexicon stages most clearly the contrast between
them. Whereas the Siren is called a "femmina" (7)—and the term denotes
the sheer physicality of the figure—her antagonist is called a "donna" (26),
a term denoting an as yet unspecified lordship over the pilgrim. The sweetness of the Siren's song is countered by the rudeness of the woman's
speech; and while the song of the Siren induces sleep, the woman's voice
wakes the pilgrim from his slumber. If the Siren stands for an aesthetic
temptation of embracing figments that arise when the soul experiences
emptiness, how are we to understand the other figure, and who exactly is
she?

The general configuration of Dante's dream in *Purgatorio* XIX, as I have
been suggesting earlier in this chapter, depends on a text Dante scholarship knows only too well: the opening scene of Boethius's *De consolatione
philosophiae*. The scene is a *planctus* in which the philosopher relates his
spiritual misery: as he lies sick in bed, the muses ("lacerae Camenae"), who
gave him joy in his youth, give solace to the now weary old man. While the
despondent philosopher begins writing his complaint, a woman of "grave
countenance, glistening clear eye . . . her color fresh and bespeaking una-
bated vigor" and her garment cut by the violence of some enters the scene.
The description and force of this woman shapes Dante's representation of
the "donna." In the economy of Boethius's narrative this sceptered woman
is Lady Philosophy, who tosses the poetical Muses from the philosopher's
side: "Who," saith she, "has permitted these tragical harlots (*scenicas mer-
etriculas*) to have access to this sick man, which not only not comfort his
grief with wholesome remedies, but also nourish them with sugared poison? For these be they which with the fruitless thorns of affections do kill
the fruitful crop of reason, and do accustom men's minds to sickness, instead of curing them. . . . Get you gone, you Sirens pleasant even to destruction (*exitium*), and leave him to my Muses to be cured and healed."

Boethius's text clearly recasts the ancient quarrel between poetry and
philosophy dramatized in book X of Plato's *Republic*. Like Plato, who attacks mimetic and hedonistic poetry (that poetry which merely induces

pleasure and is a travesty of the truths of reason) and juxtaposes to it the rigor of philosophy, Boethius excludes the pleasure-seasoned Muses in favor of Lady Philosophy. The purely aesthetic and musical relief the philosopher initially seeks from the weight of his perturbations is not a solution to his grief; on the contrary, it deepens the philosopher's malaise and engenders his death. The muses of poetry are unreliable, Boethius suggests, because they are theatrical and meretricious: they dissemble, appeal to the senses, and, in their meretriciousness, they give themselves to all. Just as much as Plato, however, Boethius does not altogether banish poetry from the quarters of reliable knowledge. Plato forges in his *Dialogues* a new poetical mythology that would replace the worn-out sciences of the Homeric encyclopedia. Boethius discusses the mind's exclusive self-absorption in the destructive, aesthetic pleasures of poetry and opposes to it a philosophical poetry that would probe and give expression to the mind's concerns.

This Boethian quarrel between the Muses and Philosophy shapes the dramatics of *Purgatorio* XIX with a crucial difference. The "donna" who, imperious and with authority, tears the Siren's gown to reveal her in her naked truth, as it were, is not exactly Lady Philosophy. As is well known, Dante had represented this Boethian figure in his eminently Boethian text, *Convivio*, in the guise of the "donna gentile" who comforts Dante's grief for the death of Beatrice.[13] In *Purgatorio* XIX, however, the Siren and the "donna" do not stand for the traditional dilemma between philosophy and poetry. What they stand for, rather, is two alternate modes of viewing poetry and viewing oneself. What are these two modes, which roughly echo the two versions of the imagination treated earlier? And how is it possible to distinguish between them?

Plato's and Boethius's dilemma opposing the two disciplines is not, as I have suggested earlier, all that clear-cut, and at any rate that dilemma would be a logical impossibility for Dante, who does not conceive of poetry as wholly distinct from the other sciences or from philosophy. Dante does privilege, to be sure, the specific mode of the language of poetry in the belief that the metaphors of poetry enact a radical disclosure of man's essence as uprooted and homeless, above and beyond the desirable accommodations of political life. He believes that poetry reveals a knowledge deeper than any philosophy because it retrieves the common memories buried in the language and because in poetry the imaginary and the real are indissolubly connected. From this standpoint it can be inferred that the mind's philosophical and objective constructions of the world are governed by a principle whereby the self is a sort of Cartesian subject and master of that world. At stake in the dream of *Purgatorio* XIX is exactly Dante's rethinking of two interrelated issues: the question of poetry and the question of self, which will have to be viewed from the standpoint of what is not the "self."

In the description of the pilgrim's awakening and moving away from the Siren, Dante primarily sketches, much as Boethius, Jerome, and Paulinus of Nola did, a critique of aestheticism.[14] The Siren appears as an image of dissemblance, and her promise of pleasure is equally deceptive. Her song seems to encourage desire, but in fact she presents herself as the object and end of all desires, as the illusory point of destination, which in truth would be a shipwreck for Dante as it would have been for Ulysses. From this standpoint it can be said that the stench emanating from her body is certainly a sexual *odor feminae*, but it is also the unmistakable stench of death forever lurking at the heart of the suspended, self-enclosed circle of romance. Finally, as a figure that belongs to the mind's slumber and entices the pilgrim into forgetfulness and death, the Siren is the ghost of the past suddenly resurfacing from the depths of the mind's reveries; she is the material sign of the enigma the "donna" wills to rip open.

The Siren's antagonist is doubtless Beatrice, and we must turn to *Purgatorio* XXXI, to the scene of the pilgrim's encounter with her, for the interpretive gloss on the dream of *Purgatorio* XIX. Many are the textual links—largely inversions—binding these two sections of the poem. In *Purgatorio* XXXI Beatrice vehemently reproaches the pilgrim so that, as she says, he can be stronger in his future encounter with the Siren (44–45); whereas the Siren promises pleasure, in *Purgatorio* XXXI the pilgrim disavows his past attachment to false pleasure. When Beatrice appears in *Purgatorio* XXX, her words "guardaci ben! Ben son, ben son Beatrice" (72) certainly echo the opening words of the Siren's song, "'Io son,' cantava, 'Io son dolce serena.'" But in order to grasp the full sense of the opposition between the Siren and Beatrice we ought to examine closely the scene of *Purgatorio* XXXI:

> Piangendo dissi: "Le presenti cose
> col falso lor piacer volser miei passi,
> tosto che 'l vostro viso si nascose."
> Ed ella: "Se tacessi o se negassi
> ciò che confessi, non fora men nota
> la colpa tua: da tal giudice sassi!
> Ma quando scoppia de la propria gote
> l'accusa del peccato, in nostra corte
> rivolge sè contra 'l taglio la rota.
> Tuttavia, perche' mo vergogna porte
> del tuo errore, e perche' altra volta,
> udendo le serene, sie più forte,
> pon giù il seme del piangere e ascolta:
> sì udirai come in contraria parte
> mover dovieti mia carne sepolta.
> Mai non t'appresentò natura o arte

piacer, quando le belle membra in ch'io
rinchiusa fui, e che so' 'n terra sparte;
e se 'l sommo piacer sì ti fallio
per la mia morte, qual cosa mortale
dovea poi trarre te nel suo disio?"

(Purg. XXXI, 34–54)

(Weeping I said: "The present Things, with their false pleasure, turned my
steps aside, as soon as your countenance was hidden." And she: "Had you been
silent, or had you denied that which you confess, your fault would not be less
noted, by such a Judge is it known. But when accusation of the sin bursts from
one's own cheek, in our court the grindstone turns itself back against the
edge. Still, that you may now bear shame for your error, and another time,
hearing the Sirens, may be stronger, lay aside the seed of tears and listen: so
shall you hear how in opposite direction my buried flesh ought to have moved
you. Never did nature or art present to you beauty so great as the fair members in which I was enclosed and now are scattered to dust. And if the highest
beauty thus failed you by my death, what mortal thing should then have drawn
you into desire for it?")

The scene is quite literally the pilgrim's *confiteor* or confession, and the
word, which figures prominently in the text (6 and 38), derives from *confit-
eri* and means, among other things, acknowledging one's guilt. Scholars
from Grandgent to Paolini still debate whether Dante's confession is to be
taken as the reenactment of the sacrament of penance and conversion (and
according to the liturgical sequence of *contritio cordis*, *contritio oris*, and *sa-
tisfactio operis*) or, instead, as I think is the case, as a literary mode in the
tradition of St. Augustine's autobiographical *Confessions*.[15] The autobiographical mode in Dante's text, in fact, is at this point unmistakable.
Accordingly, this confessional scene, as well as Beatrice's reproach in *Purgatorio* XXX, recapitulates the contours of the pilgrim's past from the perspective of what he now takes to be the central event of his life: his encounter with Beatrice, his love for her and her subsequent death. In *Purgatorio*
XXX it is Beatrice herself who recalls Dante's spiritual and poetic parabola,
which was the narrative burden of the *Vita nuova* and which is viewed as
the preamble to the pilgrim's present. She quickly summarizes the unfolding of his life from her first apparition to him in his youth "vita nova"
(115), her death, his forgetfulness of her, and his turning, while spiritually
adrift, to the "gentile donna" (*Vita nuova* XXXV–XXXVII)—"immagini di
ben seguendo false" (31). The exchange between the two lovers muses
primarily their respective senses of time.

   In *Purgatorio* XXXI, just before Dante is to be immersed into the waters
of Lethe, Beatrice forces on him the memory of the past and urges him to
recover it by disavowing it in a public confession. This focus on memory

is crucial to the scene. The retrieval of the past, which is also the starting point of the *Vita nuova*, projects love as primarily an incessant commemoration, a self-commemorative act by which the pilgrim revives his rootedness in the particularity of that love, beyond the superficiality of concerns, beyond the masks of deception and self-deception to which he once fell prey. As he is forced to remember by Beatrice, Dante goes over the paths he traversed in his youth, and the hidden realm of his own self now stands revealed.

The pilgrim's self-recognition is not carried out with the cool detachment of a man who supposedly has found a firm foundation to his life and has finally attained an objective, transcendent standpoint from where his own self and his world appear intelligible. The truth is that Dante is never the disengaged, Cartesian *spectator* of the drama that is being played out. The myth of Narcissus, which is obliquely recalled in *Purgatorio* XXX, 76–78, right after Dante's own name has been mentioned, is central to the scene. Ovid casts the myth of Narcissus in terms of knowledge and death. The narrative is framed in the *Metamorphoses* (III, 316–520) by the story of Tiresias, the mythical figure who alternately experienced his life both as man and as woman and who is asked by Narcissus's mother whether the boy would live to a ripe old age. Tiresias answers: "Yes, if he never knows himself." The unfolding of Narcissus's life bears out precisely Tiresias's prophecy.

Worn from the heat of hunting, Narcissus tries to quench his thirst in a pool where he sees his image, and, not knowing what he sees, he falls in love with his own reflection and tries to reach it till he drowns. One implication of the myth is clear: Narcissus dies when he knows himself, or, to say it differently, to know oneself is to know one's own mortality. Another implication is that love and knowledge do not coincide in Narcissus. Yet the pilgrim is unlike Narcissus, in the sense that he is not involved in the pure and tragic self-contemplation of Narcissus at the fountain. Quite to the contrary, in the self-reflection of *Purgatorio* XXXI Dante apprehends himself as troubled by and enmeshed in confusion, tears, shame, and guilt—as if these were the passions that lead to a genuine self-knowledge.

We could, no doubt, explain this display of emotions the way the Romantics would, as a sign that the lover is always guilty in the eyes of the beloved, that the lover's innocence, now that paradoxically he is in the Garden of Eden, has been forever lost. More than that, this text's insistence on the pilgrim's grief makes grief (and not, for instance, just pleasure, which in the dream of the Siren is said to induce self-forgetfulness) the privileged path to knowledge and the thoroughfare by which impersonal, objective thinking turns into "lived" and subjective experience. Grief is always valorized, for instance, in the *Vita nuova*'s acquisition of knowledge in the belief that it authenticates knowledge and makes it an irreducible mark of the ravage of the lover's spirit.

But grief, for all its concreteness, is not for Dante, as the next chapter will suggest, a final experience. Dante must learn that he must turn against mourning, that the mind's grievous self-absorption with the shadows of the past is a trap from which he is to free himself. For now let us stress that the self that is constructed and unfolds through this scene of suffering is not an abstract entity who is removed from the accidents of time and from the passions that are under the sway of time, but it is himself engaged in the fragmentations of time. More precisely, by this traditional vehicle of the *jugement d'amour* Dante stages his guilt and shame for his past errors. If guilt is the mark of a deep division within his own mind, of the radical contradiction between what he was and the moral consciousness of what he ought to be, shame, which is the public counterpart of guilt, acknowledges that he sees and judges himself the way he is seen and is judged by Beatrice. The pattern of metaphors dramatizes Dante's awareness of a self-doubling, of an otherness within the individual self. This pattern is also central to Dante's new configuration of subjectivity and, ultimately, to his insight into the ethics of love.

Contemporary readings of the *Divine Comedy*, which are basically Hegelian and which have been fairly prevalent ever since the time of Francesco De Sanctis, tend to stress the poem's indubitable sense of unity and order as well as the poet's "Romantic" celebration of heroic individuality. These views are certainly correct, but they are incomplete. They are incomplete because they miss the vital counterpoint which is interwoven with Dante's passion for unity and order and which can be thus summarized: the pilgrim and the poet's imagination present man as a wanderer and as a stranger on earth. In Dante's and in the medieval framework of thought the self is defined in terms of the place it occupies and its relation to the hierarchical scheme of the *communitas*. At the same time, however, Dante plumbs the depths of the authentically Hebraic understanding of man as a spiritual exile, variously part of an exilic *communitas* (the church), estranged from God, and distant from the objects of his desire.

The radical tension between order and exile (which can be understood in a variety of ways: politics and theology, idolatry and prophecy, knowledge and historicity) is all-encompassing. There is a structural feature of the *Divine Comedy* that graphically conveys this double impulse of Dante's imagination: in the prodigious architecture of the *Divine Comedy* everything is firmly in place (the sinners are where they should be, and so are the blessed, or everything tends toward a definite place, *Purgatorio*). There is, however, an odd element to this global structure of order: the pilgrim, as well as the poet, is *always* out of place, always *in via*; he never ceases wandering, nor does he settle down in the ceremonies and customs of familiar life. This trait of the pilgrim's existence characterizes the conceptual structure of the poet, who decisively questions the apparently secure, generally taken-for-granted categories of knowledge and values.

Even Dante's own self is never enclosed or wrapped in the confines of a self-sufficient subjectivity, but it is rooted in the predicament of time. In the confessional scene in *Purgatorio* XXXI the pilgrim is not simply involved in a Hegelian, recapitulative retrospection of his shameful past. On the contrary, the sentence Beatrice passes on the pilgrim's past is symmetrically balanced by an intimation of openness to the future. The recollection of the past error—of his yielding to some newfangledness, she says— serves to strengthen his resolve in the possible encounters with the Sirens that lie ahead (44–45). The Sirens, in effect, are his future possibilities brooding over the present and yet are incommensurable with the present. They are the ghosts of the memory of the past that is always ahead of oneself and could always return. All this notwithstanding, unlike the Siren in *Purgatorio* XIX who wills to transform the flow of history into the stillness of a romance, who lures the pilgrim to forsake the journey, foreclose it and settle along the way in the figments of the imagination, Beatrice forces on the pilgrim the principle of time as an open-ended process. Beatrice also forces on Dante an idea of a decentered self and a new understanding of love, which is in sharp contrast to the temptation of the Siren. The thought of Beatrice forces on the pilgrim a new type of poetry, just as in the *Vita nuova*, but this new poetry, as Beatrice acknowledges, forever resonates with and is flanked by the song of the Sirens.

Beatrice's love, however, is the perspective which makes possible the pilgrim's self-knowledge.[16] It is Beatrice, appropriately enough, who constitutes the pilgrim in his concrete, irreducible individuality as she calls— and the occurrence is unique in the poem—Dante by name (*Purg.* XXX, 55). Unlike the Siren, for instance, who tempts the pilgrim into believing that his wishing to surrender to her reenacts Ulysses' fate, Beatrice harshly judges Dante's past and forces him to a self-examination that practically repeats her charges. No reader ought to be surprised by Beatrice's tone (which certainly echoes the tone of the woman in *Purgatorio* XIX whose identity is veiled and who herself unveils the Siren's false promises). Beatrice's harshness in *Purgatorio* XIX, XXX, and XXXI asks the sleeping pilgrim to awake, to move out of the land of false shadows and make his moral decisions. Let me stress in passing that the motif of falseness runs through these portions of the text: the Siren's fake beauty covering the horror of her filth; the false account of Ulysses' yielding to her song; the false images of the good (*Purg.* XXX, 131); the false pleasures of the present time (*Purg.* XXXI, 35). Falseness describes the array of illusory appearances that Beatrice wills to dispel. More than that, falseness designates the illusory *hiding* of the discrepancies between appearances and reality, the mistaken belief that the mask is the thing. Ultimately, falseness designates the foreclosure of an ongoing knowledge.

Beatrice's harshness is the necessary counter to falseness, for her harshness (which is opposed to the Siren's sweet song) puts in relief the contours of the ethics of love she embodies. Far from inducing illusory, false complacencies, love as Beatrice understands it is ethical because it unveils and valorizes the dislocations within the self and the disjunctions within the world of appearances; it dispossesses one of oneself because the foundation of this love rests on the principle that one reaches oneself in a detour through the mind of the beloved and one sees oneself through the viewpoint of the beloved, which transcends one's own. Beatrice's love is for Dante that viewpoint, the look which allows him to overcome the temptation to reduce the world to the measure of his own narcissistic subjectivity and of his own imaginary delusions, as if the world were a mere tangle of objectified entities there for him, for his mastery and purview.

Finally, the dream of the Siren discloses Dante's fascination with death, his temptation to yield to the insubstantial world of phantasms or, to say it differently, to be swallowed in the eddies of the imaginary, which seems free of all moral constraints but, because it is a pure figment, is the world of bondage to death. Beatrice's reproach, by contrast, twice confronts her mortality (*Purg.* XXX, 124–29; XXXI, 43–51), where she refers to her buried flesh and her scattered dust, as if what the pilgrim must now learn is to resist the powerful illusion of death's finality and dominion. We can surmise what this fascination with death must have meant to Dante once and what it must mean to him now. In the *Vita nuova* Beatrice's death is the inexorable event that causes the lover's despair, tears apart his reason, and triggers his betrayal of her with the "donna gentile." Retrospectively, that betrayal has come to mean Dante's acquiescing in the instability of time; more poignantly, the betrayal—as we saw earlier in chapter 3—designates the belief in nothingness: to betray means that one has given up all trust, in the persuasion that all bonds are illusory and null and that the world is a mere figuration of insubstantial shadows. To betray the memory of Beatrice is tantamount to accepting death's sway on all bonds. What the lover must learn, as Beatrice harshly impresses on him atop the Garden of Eden, is that love, though born of time, as the myth of Venus's birth from the foam of the sea shows, is not subjected to the dominion of time and death. The language of Beatrice's love, then, is necessarily harsh, for her love does violence to narcissistic constructions of the self, mobilizes the various faculties of the poet's mind, wakes it up, forces one to think about and to interpret the encounters and phantasms in one's life.

The ethical value of love Beatrice upholds in the Garden of Eden sheds light both on the debates staged in the *Vita nuova* and on the various perspectives of that "poets' conversation," as I think the *Dolce stil nuovo* ought to be called. The *Vita nuova* tells primarily the story of a spiritual and poetic self-apprenticeship under the compulsion of love.[17] Love, as the young lover discovers, cannot be reduced to a mere materiality of bodies or to a question of balance of humors, as physicians and empiricists believe. Nor is it necessarily a deranging passion to be renounced, as Cavalcanti urges Dante to do in favor of embracing the security of the mind's immutable ideas. At the heart of the *Vita nuova* there is the poet's urgent discovery that minds cannot be partitioned from bodies, that bodies, by themselves, are corpses, that substances are spiritualized and essences incarnated, and that finally love and intellect—as the pivotal "Donne ch'avete intelletto d'amore" (Ladies who have intelligence of love) exemplifies—must be thought of together.

The formal structure of the *Vita nuova*—the alternation of poems and of prose glossing the poems—dramatizes the interdependence of love and knowledge.[18] We find a compelling version of this issue in *Purgatorio* XXVI, where, appropriately, Dante meets the father of the Sweet New Style, Guido Guinizelli. Their exchange focuses on poetry, and the sinners are under the symbolic aegis of the hermaphrodites. The hermaphrodites (who, because of the witchcraft of Venus, join in themselves man and woman) take their name from Hermes and Aphrodite—intelligence and love. For Dante the hermaphrodites are not purely aberrant figures of grammar and material order, as they are for Alan's *De planctu naturae* (I, i). Because in their practice they attempt to efface the differences between the sexes, the hermaphrodites embody a false, illusory unity of the sexes, but that false unity points to the unity of love and knowledge their poetry pursues.

In the two purgatorial scenes of cantos XIX and XXXI the unity of love and knowledge is brought to a focus by the figures of the Siren and of Beatrice, but, as this chapter has shown, Dante insists on the absolute difference between them. The superiority of Beatrice over the Siren depends on her claim that what binds together love and knowledge is virtue. Beatrice forces on the pilgrim the need to transform love and knowledge into virtue, which, as its name for St. Thomas implies, means "some perfection of power" (*Summa theologiae* I–II, 55, 2), and it must be understood as a virtue of the intellect and a perfection of the will. At the same time the whole of the *Divine Comedy* tells us that the aim of the pilgrim's quest is not abstract knowledge, which, as the inextricable tangle of sophistry and ratiocinations, is by itself vain. Because, as St. Paul states, "scientia inflat," Dante looks not merely for *scientia* but for the wisdom which, as St. Augustine says in *Contra academicos* and Aquinas repeats with only a slight variation, is a life of blessedness and "rerum humanarum divinarumque scientia" (LXIII).[19] True knowledge, then, does not necessarily amount to transgression, as Adam and Ulysses believed. True knowledge must first become self-knowledge; to be a reliable, concrete experience, to say it exactly, it must turn into a virtue, for, indeed, in the language of later humanists from Erasmus to Vico, *sapientia est pietas*.[20]

It is within the context of concerns just described that one can begin to understand Dante's exhortation to abide within the human limits of knowledge: "Matto é chi spera che nostra ragione / possa trascorrer la infinita via / che tiene una sustanza in tre persone. / State contenti, umana gente, al *quia*" (*Purg*. III, 34–37) (Foolish is he who hopes that our reason may compass the infinite course taken by One Substance in Three Persons. Be content, human race, with the *quia*). Dante's belief in the boundaries of human knowledge is certainly real, just as it is correct to see in the pilgrim's recitation of the penitential psalm "Misere di me" (*Inf*. I, 65) an echo of the apothegm that the beginning of wisdom is the fear of the Lord. But the pilgrim's self-binding, as we saw in the preceding chapter and as we shall explore more fully in chapter 10, is the obverse side of the poet's visionary impulse, which climaxes with the pilgrim's desire to see God face to face.

Vision, in effect, is the experience that binds the dual aspect of the imagination, and it is also the fulfillment of both love and knowledge. We know too well that love, according to the codifications of courtly love and the practice of the Stilnovists, is tied to the eyes. He who is blind, we are told, cannot love. We also know that love, though itself blindfolded, opens the lover's eyes. What we are probably less familiar with is the insight that was overtly formulated by no less an intellectualist than St. Thomas Aquinas. Among all the senses, sight is the one the lover values most: "ubi amor ibi oculus."[21] More than anything else—as even the story of Psyche spying Eros asleep reminds us—he who loves wants to see the beloved. Seeing is privileged because it is never partitioned, but, on the contrary, it affords direct, immediate perception of the whole.

Appropriately enough, the *Vita nuova* ends with Dante's "mirabile visione" of Beatrice, who, dead, sits in glory at the foot of God's throne.[22] This vision of love triggers the journey of the lover's poetic imagination to explore unknown but possible worlds in the beyond. More poignantly, in *Purgatorio* XXX (121–23) and XXXI (36) Beatrice's love is formulated as the showing of the radiance of her face to the lover. Even in the Proustian scene of Marcel watching Albertine asleep there is a flicker of the discovery that the perfect joy of the lover lies in seeing the beloved. Whereas the Proustian voyeur, who is a degraded version of the divinity, objectifies and sequesters the beloved, Beatrice looks back at the pilgrim at the moment when she is seen; more than that, her face and glance stand for what can never by appropriated or reduced to an object by the lover.

That vision, finally, is also the perfection of knowledge is a fact that reverberates throughout the *Divine Comedy*. From a summary survey of the concordances to the poem we know that Dante thinks of knowledge in terms of taste (the pun *sapore/sapere* occurs in a variety of languages), of grasping in its wholeness (comprehension—*cum prendere*), of touching as a coming in contact with the real, and so on. Knowledge is above all tied to and depends on wonder, *admiratio*, especially in *Paradiso*, where the pilgrim's *paideia* turns into a journey of discovery. But, as the next chapter will show, true knowledge is contemplation of God.

Chapter 8

LANGUAGE AND VISION

(*PARADISO* XXI AND XXII)

IN ITS CONCLUDING paragraphs (28ff.) the *Epistle to Cangrande* highlights and glosses the poet's predicament, advanced in the prologue to *Paradiso*, that the pilgrim saw things in heaven which he that descends from it has neither the knowledge nor the power to tell again, "perché appressando sè al suo disire, / nostro intelletto si profonda tanto, / che dietro la memoria non puó ire" (*Par.* I, 7–9) (for our intellect, drawing near its desire, sinks so deep that memory cannot follow it). The central concern of this poetic statement is to mark the limits of speech and, generally, of the representation of the pilgrim's visionary experience: because of the absolute nature of his vision, the vision remains both inaccessible to memory's retrieval and irreducible to language. Nonetheless, the realm of the sayable, as *Paradiso* I goes on to state (10–12), is not totally forfeited: the subject matter of the third canticle will be the shadow of the light the pilgrim gazed at and treasured in his mind.

To elucidate the difficult point the poem makes of a gulf existing between intellect and memory, vision and language, spiritual experience and representation, the *Epistle to Cangrande* outlines with admirable economy, suitable to such a general prefatory conclusion, so to speak, as the *Epistle* is, a wide array of visionary analogues to the *Paradiso*. Prophetic visions from the Old Testament, ecstatic raptures from the New Testament, and patristic treatises of mystical and contemplative theology are bundled together as the heterogeneous context for the poet's own visionary claims.[1] The paradigmatic text in the series the *Epistle* marshals is II Corinthians (12:2–5), where St. Paul tells of his rapture to the Third Heaven: "I know a man in Christ who fourteen years ago was caught up in the third heaven—whether in the body or out of the body I do not know, God knows . . . and he heard things that cannot be told, which man may not utter." Whereas the Pauline passage lays emphasis on the necessary disjunction between vision and its narrative, the references to Ezekiel's penetration into the *arcana Dei*, to the three disciples witnessing the transfiguration of Christ (Matthew 17:1), or to Nebuchadnezzar's dream underscore the ineffability of visions veiled and accompanied by forgetfulness. Yet all together these texts are designed to define the end of vision, which is the climactic formulation of the *Epistle*. As one gathers from the *visio Johannis*, the final paragraph says, the truth of vision consists in the beatitude of the soul that sees God.

The *Epistle*'s argument that visionariness is the distinctive feature and the foundation of the *Divine Comedy* is in itself unsurprising. Scholars have long acknowledged the poem's radical visionary-prophetic impulse, its claim that the poet's voice stands in the line of the biblical prophets as he denounces and reads the movement of history from the perspective of God's redemptive promises. The authority of the poet's prophetic voice rests on the premise that he has been singled out by God's grace to undertake a journey through the beyond so that he may deliver his vision of justice to a world that makes a mockery of God's laws.[2] If anything, there is an apparent incongruity in the *Epistle*'s final paragraphs that has largely gone undetected. At the very moment when the focus of attention is the failure of speech to grasp the essence of vision, the *Epistle* evokes the power of the prophet's word. How are the two, visionariness and prophecy, related to each other? Given the *Epistle*'s rhetorical status as a guidepost for travelers-readers into the uncharted seas of *Paradiso*, one cannot expect it to delve analytically into the tensions between prophetic and mystical claims.

The apparent incongruity, however, is not the consequence of Dante's lack of argumentative rigor. On the contrary, what appears as incongruity in fact suggests a deliberate co-implication of prophecy and mysticism in what I would call the *relationality* of Dante's poetic thought. On the face of it, prophecy and mysticism are two alternate modes of experience and being: mystical ineffability is the sign of the mystic's entanglement within the solitary, asocial boundaries of one's own private vision; the prophet's language, born of exile, originates in a self-alienation from the community, but it is rooted in history and it is decisively directed to the empirical world of man. Dante collapses this simplified dualism between prophecy and mysticism and treats them as modes of questioning institutional discourse.

Alongside the biblical texts, he mentions in the *Epistle to Cangrande* three patristic works of spiritual contemplation as analogues to the pilgrim's quest for the vision of God. The first is Richard of St. Victor's *De contemplatione*, an all-encompassing title for his various books on the soul's contemplative ascent. These books were recognized as classics of Christian spirituality by St. Bonaventure in his *De reductione artium ad theologiam*, and Richard himself is greeted by Dante's Bonaventure as one who "a considerar fu più che viro" (*Par.* X, 132) (in contemplation was more than human). The technical sense of the word "considerar," as we shall see further down, emerges from the second treatise on contemplation Dante mentions in the *Epistle to Cangrande*: Bernard of Clairvaux's *De consideratione*. The third item is St. Augustine's *De quantitate animae* (The greatness of the soul).

How do these works shed light on Dante's visionariness? What are they exactly about? In a most general way they can be said to focus on the stages man's mind should follow in preparing for a genuine spiritual existence. *The Greatness of the Soul*, which is a dialogue between Evodius and Augustine, argues for the immateriality of the soul and seeks to define its powers and capacities. Deploying a geometrical-mathematical vocabulary (quantity and unity of the soul, width, breadth, etc.) as a metaphoric representation of the soul's inner space, the dialogue maps seven degrees or levels of its powers, which include animation, sensation, the arts, understanding of truth, and, finally, the contemplation and vision of truth. Of the other two works, Richard's *De contemplatione* focuses on varieties of contemplative experiences in terms of the imagination, reason, and intuition; Bernard's *De consideratione* probes the interdependence between prophecy and mystical contemplation, which is the heart of Dante's idea of poetry.

"Contemplation," says Richard of St. Victor, "is the free, more penetrating gaze of a mind, suspended with wonder concerning manifestations of wisdom."[3] The chief figure of contemplation, as one gathers from his elaborate allegory of the *Twelve Patriarchs*, is Jacob's second wife, Rachel, whose name means "vision of the principle" and who stands for the withdrawn life of prayer and asceticism. By contrast, Leah (whose meaning is *laboriosa*) is given to the active life of service. Rachel is assisted by her handmaid, Bala, who personifies the imagination and whose loquacity in the ears of the heart cannot be controlled. But Rachel resists the disruptions made by Bala's garrulousness, and contemplation is eventually experienced as an interior vision of light, as the unveiling of realities hidden to the ordinary gaze yet shown by the mirror of the soul: "When the mirror has been wiped and gazed into for a long time, a kind of splendor of divine light appears to shine in it, and a great beam of unexpected vision appears to his eyes. . . . Therefore, from the vision of this light that it wonders at within itself, the soul is kindled from above in a marvelous way and is animated to see the living light that is above it."[4]

Readers of the *Divine Comedy* need hardly be reminded of Dante's standard figuration of the active and the contemplative life through Leah and Rachel. In the dream of *Purgatorio* XXVII, Leah gathers garlands of flowers and refers to Rachel as the one who "mai non si smaga / dal suo miraglio, e siede tutto il giorno. / Ell' e' de' suoi belli occhi veder vaga, / com' io de l'adornarmi con le mani; / Lei lo vedere, e me l'ovrare appaga" (*Purg.* XXVII, 104–9) (never leaves her mirror and sits all day. She is fain to behold her fair eyes, as I am to deck me with my hands: she with seeing, I with doing am satisfied). Possibly more poignant to the poem's visionariness is Richard of St. Victor's claim that the contemplative quest climaxes with Jesus' transfiguration. The scene of Jesus clothed in light also occurs in *Purgatorio* XXXII, but Dante gives it a significant twist. After the pilgrim has a vision of the apocalyptic procession, he wakes up and recalls the witnessing of the vision by Peter, John, and James.

> Pietro e Giovanni e Jacopo, condotti
> e vinti, retornaro a la parola
> Da la quale furon maggior sonni rotti
> E videro scemata loro scuola
> cosí di Moise' come d'Elia.
>
> (*Purg.* XXXII, 76–80)

(Peter and John and James came to themselves again at the word by which deeper slumbers were broken, and saw their company diminished alike by Moses and Elias.)

The apostles' revelation of Jesus' divine essence, which to Richard is an experience of plenitude, turns for Dante into an awareness of the gap between vision and words. To awake from the supreme ecstasy into the light of the visible world is to be diminished, to be cognizant that the luminous perfection of the transfiguration has vanished.

The close continuity between prophecy and contemplation is at the forefront of Bernard's *De consideratione*. Addressed to Pope Eugene III, who had been one of Bernard's former students, the treatise (which is the last he wrote) has an avowedly pedagogical purpose. The pope, who stands at the unique point of convergence of practical and spiritual authority and who is chained to the obligations of his public office, is urged to overcome the cares and fragmentations of worldly business and busyness which unravel the life of the soul and into which the spirit sinks. The treatise, thus, maps the way for the mind's withdrawal from the occupations of outer existence, in the conviction that they devastate the spirit. Concerns with privileges, legal wrangles, pettifoggers, flatteries, quarrels over property, abuses of the temporal office, financial affairs, and so on are deemed unworthy of the servant of God. This realm of concrete and finite particularities is oppressive because it makes trivial ends into absolutes and because their pursuit brings about forgetfulness of oneself. To remedy this spiritlessness Bernard calls for a spiritual journey, a journey of self-discovery, the destination of which is the contemplation of God.[5]

De consideratione, which combines the Benedictine current of the contemplative quest with the spirituality of the desert fathers (Antony, Cassian, etc.), examines the contrast and the dialectical relationship between reflective self-absorption and contemplation.[6] The idea that contemplation is a process, a voyage through the desert, is made dramatic for Bernard by the recent failure of the Second Crusade, to which he refers as a spiritual pilgrimage to Jerusalem. More to our concern, the title, *De consideratione*, comes from Gregory the Great's *Regula pastoralis*, but Bernard seeks to delimit the word's orbit of meaning:

> And first of all consider the word [*consideratio*]. I do not wish it to be regarded as exactly synonymous with contemplation, because the latter is concerned with the certainty of things, the former more fitly with their investigation. Accordingly, contemplation may be defined as the soul's true unerring intuition [*verus certusque intuitus animi*], or as the unhesitating apprehension of the truth. But consideration is thought earnestly directed to research, or the application of the mind to the search for truth [*cogitatio intensa ad investigandum verum*]; though in practice the two terms are indifferently used for one another. (II, ii)[7]

The objects of consideration are oneself and the things below, around, and above oneself. Contemplation, however, has no purpose beyond itself: it cuts through the disguises and illusions of *negotium* and transcends the impatient, restless entanglements of practical life.

Bernard's understanding of contemplation as the perfection of analytical and conceptual knowledge is a commonplace of twelfth-century spirituality. But Bernard, much as Hugh and Richard of St. Victor and, later, Bonaventure do, invests the contemplative experience with a radical function: to them, this *askesis* primarily marks the destination of the soul's ultimate quest for beatitude.[8] At the same time, contemplation is the absolute foundation of all knowledge and praxis, and it is the perspective making knowledge possible. This view of contemplation's foundational role, which is central to Dante's poetics, was prevalent in the Benedictine monasteries. As Leclercq has shown, such an insight shaped the "monastic humanism of the cloisters, where the study of Scripture was systematically practiced along with the study of classical literature and patristics."[9]

The contemplative life, then, has priority over active life, but the two are not sharply separated from each other. Contemplation, which is a call to inwardness and purification from worldliness, is never, in fact, inaction. Consistently with this principle, *De consideratione* forges a link between the vision of the contemplatives and the moral action of prophetic language. The text is replete with prophetic concerns: the attention to the pope's proper burden of service, the attacks against canon law and decretals, the dismissal of dialectics (an obvious reference to Abelard) as a useless wandering in a labyrinth of abstractions, the reminder that Peter's chair ought to be the watchtower for the church's spiritual well-being, the quotations from the prophets—these are some of the textual elements which overtly recall Dante's own prophetic utterances and topics and which for Bernard bind together language and vision.

Dante's poetry moves within the broad coordinates drawn by the rich contemplative traditions the *Epistle to Cangrande* conjures up. His sense of both interaction and hiatus between language and vision is dramatized, appropriately enough, in his encounter with the contemplatives (*Par.* XXI and XXII), who are housed in the Heaven of Saturn. Two figures move centerstage in these cantos: Peter Damian and Benedict.[10] Through them Dante evokes the tenets and history of Benedictine spirituality and literature. His recalling of two other major contemplatives, Macarius and Romualdus (*Par.* XXII, 49), of whom Peter Damian wrote a biographical account; his oblique references to both Benedict's *Regula* and to Gregory the Great's life of Benedict—these are the symptoms of Dante's will to probe the essence of the Benedictines' attitude, to grasp the intersections between the disengaged, contemplative attitude and the world of action.

Paradiso XXI opens with an image designed to introduce the specific tension in Dante's understanding of vision. The pilgrim, who has just heard the eagle's discourse on the enigma of predestination (*Par.* XX, 130ff.), fixes his eyes on Beatrice's face. The contemplation of her beauty completely absorbs his mind, but he is perplexed that she does not smile at him (*Par.* XXI, 1–4). Were she to smile, Beatrice says, the pilgrim would be turned to ashes as Semele was (4–6). Her beauty, which grows the higher they ascend through the heavens, must be tempered—"temperasse"(10)—to safeguard Dante's mortal powers. The scene constitutes an apt preamble to the destructive effects of vision.

The allusion to Semele recalls Ovid's *Metamorphoses* (III, 235–315), the fable of the girl who loves and is loved by Jupiter.[11] Enraged by jealousy, Juno, referred to as "Saturnia" (271), disguises herself and instigates Semele to ask Jupiter to show himself to her in his divine splendor. Jupiter complies with the girl's request, but the power of his lightning destroys her. The story, which partly reenacts the allegory of Eros and Psyche, encapsulates Dante's and the contemplatives' insight that love is the source of vision, just as vision in courtly literature is the source of love; even more, it captures the notion that vision is love's perfection. At the same time, the Ovidian tale signals the inexorable dangers lurking when gods and mortals are brought face to face, when mortals strive to be the equals of the gods. For Dante, on the other hand, the myth is a reminder that he, as a pilgrim, is still treading the path of mortals, whose knowledge is necessarily to be filtered through shadowy screens and mirrors.

Juno's identification of herself as "Saturnia" in Ovid's account of Semele's fated love is an oblique and ironic counter to the Heaven of Saturn. If Juno and Jupiter embody the corruption of the world, the planet, by contrast, takes its name from Saturn, the god under whom the world was chaste and every wickedness lay dead (25–28). A more pressing question, however, is why do the contemplatives show themselves forth to the pilgrim in Saturn, which is the Heaven of Astronomy? What do the mythography of Saturn and astronomy, the last step in the ladder of the liberal arts, have to do with contemplation? To begin to answer these questions, it may be well to turn, once again, to *Convivio*, where Dante explicitly couples Saturn with astrology and deciphers their secret affinities:

> E lo cielo di Saturno hae due proprietadi per lo quale si può comparare a l'astrologia: l'una si è la tardezza del suo movimento per li dodici segni, chè ventinove anni e più, secondo le scritture de li astrologi, vuole di tempo lo suo cerchio; l'altra si è che sopra tutti li altri pianeti esso è alto. E queste due proprietadi sono ne l'Astrologia: ché nel suo cerchio compiere, cioé ne lo apprendimento di quella, volge grandissimo spazio di tempo, sì per le sue dimostrazioni, che sono più che d'alcuna de le sopra dette scienze, sì per la esperienza che a ben giudicare in essa si conviene. E ancora è altissima di tutte l'altre. Però che, sì come dice Aristotile nel cominciamento de l'Anima, la scienza è alta di nobilitate per la nobilitade del suo subietto e per la sua certezza." (II, xiii, 28–30)

(And the heaven of Saturn has two properties whereby it may be compared with Astrology: one is the slowness of its movement among the twelve signs, for, according to the writings of the astrologers, it requires twenty-nine years and more to complete its revolution; the other is that it is high above all the other planets. And these two properties exist in Astrology, for in completing its circle, that is to say, in the learning of this Science, a very long space of time is wanted, both on account of its demonstrations which are more numerous than in any of the above-mentioned Sciences, and on account of the experience which is required for forming a right judgement on it. And, moreover, it is far higher than any of the others, because, as Aristotle says in the beginning of the book *On the Soul*, Science is lofty in respect of nobility both on account of the nobleness of its subject and on account of its certainty.)

To grasp the sheer range of the term "astrology" (which Dante conflates with "astronomy"), it is useful to recall a couple of definitions of this science. In the *Didascalicon* (II, 10), Hugh of St. Victor deploys Isidore of Seville's conventional explanation and writes:

> "Astronomy" and "astrology" differ in the former's taking its name from the phrase "law of the stars," while the latter takes it from the phrase "discourse concerning the stars"—for *nomia* means law, and *logos*, discourse. It's astronomy, then, which treats the law of the stars and the revolution of the heaven, and which investigates the regions, orbits, courses, risings, and settings of stars, and why each bears the name assigned it; it is astrology, however, which considers the stars in their bearing upon birth, death, and all other events, and is only partly natural, and for the rest, superstitious; natural as it concerns the temper or "complexion" of physical things, like health, illness, calm, productivity and unproductivity, which vary with the mutual alignments of the astral bodies; but superstitious as it concerns chance happenings or things subject to

free choice. And it is the "mathematicians" who traffic in the superstitious part.

Hugh's sense of the complementarity in the paired concepts of astronomy and astrology, which goes back to Ptolemy, also figures in Albert the Great's *De fato*: "there are two parts to astronomy, as Ptolemy says; one is about the locations of superior [*heavenly*] bodies . . . the other is about the effects of the stars on inferior [terrestrial] things."[12] But Albert, whose overall aim can be characterized as the systematic reformulation of the Aristotelian encyclopedia, seeks to correlate in a coherent whole the two parts of astronomy. His commentary on Aristotle's natural philosophy (*Physics, De coelo, On Generation*) and the influence of Ptolemy's *Almagest* and of Macrobius, Grosseteste, and Michael Scot have a counterpart in his belief—shaped by the work of Ptolemy's (*De natiuitatibus*), Firmicus, and Avicenna, among others—in the existence of symbolic bonds of solidarity joining stars and the human soul. Accordingly, Albert believes that accidents of reality—such as the theory of the four humors, free will itself, natural portents, comets, floods, and births (which are the province of the astrologers' vision as genetechnologists, who believe that the shape of an individual life can be foretold from the configuration of the heavens at the time of its conception)—can be explained in terms of astrological causes and influences.

Historians of science from Orr to Gizzi have clarified the elaborate presence of Dante's astronomy in the architectonics of *Paradiso*. Somewhat more problematical, from a moral viewpoint, is Dante's concern with astrology. *Inferno* XX, the canto of the soothsayers, ends with the astrologers Guido Bonatti (118) and Michael Scot, who "veramente / de le magiche frode seppe il gioco" (116–17) (truly knew the game of magic fraud). Astrology and magical divination appear here as a diabolical form of knowledge, a way of determining by formulaic incantations the illusory pattern of correspondence between the world of reality and empty figures of wax.[13] In their fraudulent effort to affect the real with herbs and images these astrologers recognize the hidden marvels of natural objects, but they are wrong in believing that nature has no higher purpose than to be manipulated for their subjective trivial ends. In *Purgatorio* XVI, as shown above in chapter 6, Dante, much as Albert the Great, rejects the belief in the crippling astrological determination of human acts but acknowledges the influence of the stars in the making of choices.

The conceptual shape of *Paradiso* XXI and XXII, on the other hand, is sustained by astrological concerns. Peter Damian begins, first of all, by explaining to the pilgrim the principle of predestination (*Par.* XXI, 83–102). Any human presumption to fathom the abyss of God's inscrutable plan, he says, is doomed to failure. In effect, Peter Damian's insistence on an infallible divine order of election, which is destined to remain hidden to the gaze of mortals, discredits the astrologers' claim that they have the power to decipher the "Book of Life." But there are other elements of astrological lore in these cantos. At the end of *Paradiso* XXII, for instance, Dante gives his own horoscope. His sign, as we are told by a periphrasis, is Gemini, which is the House of Mercury: "O gloriose stelle, o lume pregno / di gran virtù, dal quale io riconosco / tutto qual che si sia, il mio ingegno, / con voi nasceva e s'ascondeva vosco / quelli ch'è padre d'ogne mortal vita, / quand'io senti' di prima l'aer tosco; / e poi, quando mi fu grazia largita / d'entrar ne l'alta rota che vi gira, / la vostra region mi fu sortita" (112–120) (Oh glorious stars, Oh light impregnated with mighty power, from which I derive all my genius, whatsoever it may be, with you was rising and with you was hiding himself he who is father of every mortal life when I first felt the air of Tuscany; and then, when the grace was bestowed on me to enter the lofty wheel that bears you round, your region was assigned to me).

That astrology (not in its narrow focus) constitutes the symbolic matrix and model for Dante's metaphoric organization of the Heaven of Saturn is evident from a quick survey of the mythography of Saturn.[14] The primary connection of Saturn is with the golden age of the world, the age when wickedness, as Dante says (*Par.* XXI, 25–27), lay dead. This myth of the golden age, when Saturn was the ruler, stands behind and casts Dante's figuration of the cloister as a "paradisus deliciarum" in that, to put it in terms of a conventional exegetical tradition, the peace of the cloister foreshadows on earth the delights of heaven.[15] Yet, just as the golden age has vanished, so has the cloister sunk into degeneracy (*Par.* XXI, 130–35; *Par.* XXII, 73–78). But the planet Saturn has other, and more important, resonances for Dante's understanding of the contemplatives.

Saturn is traditionally collated with Chronos as Father Time, for the god who eats his children is nothing less than the figure of time devouring all it engenders. The myth of Saturn, yoking eternity and time, discloses Dante's insight into the sense of contemplation. Etymologically, as Varro states in *De lingua latina* (VII), contemplation derives from *templum*, the space marked out by the seer or, to paraphrase Varro, by his divining rod as a location for his observation.[16] Twice does Dante use in these cantos of the contemplatives inflected forms of the word. Peter Damian refers to the seasons of his worship spent in "pensier contemplativi" (*Par.* XXI, 117) (contemplative thoughts). St. Benedict points out to the pilgrim the other souls as "contemplanti uomini" (*Par.* XXII, 46) (contemplative men). Varro's etymology of contemplation in terms of a closed-off space is imaginatively extended by Dante to image, first, the monks' interior space, which they perpetually reenter and where they map out their distance from God. Second, the etymology accounts for the topographical description in both Peter Damian's and Benedict's speeches. They refer, respectively, to the consecrated places at Catria (*Par.* XXII, 110) and Cassino (*Par.* XXII, 37) as hallowed spots for worship and vision. But, etymologically, contemplation resonates also with time. *Templum*, space, comes from *tempus*, as the privileged spot of time, the *kairos*, which blots out the randomness of time and joins together time and eternity.

In *Paradiso* XXI and XXII Dante fully exploits the spatial and temporal reverberations of contemplation. The contemplatives live in space and time, but they must struggle *against* the engulfment of space and time. The references to Cassino and Catria as privileged, circumscribed grounds of worship signal primarily the value of the *stabilitas loci*, Benedict's injunction in his *Regula* that monks be not *gyrovagi* (wanderers).[17] Their adherence to a fixed monastic place implies their steadfast heart: "qui son li frati miei che dentro ai chiostri / fermar li piedi e tennero il cor saldo" (*Par.* XXII, 50–51) (here are my brethren who stayed their feet within the cloisters and kept a steadfast heart). But the cloister can become a spiritual trap for the monks, who neglect climbing Jacob's ladder of contemplation (70–72) and, by a sharp reversal of the metaphoric feet of the soul, keep their feet on the ground (73–74). The monks' error, in short, lies in their premature obliteration of time, in their mistaking their present comfort for the eschatological joy.

More specifically, the temporal predicament of the contemplatives is suggested by the musical language of the two cantos. The two cantos are framed by the metaphor of "tempering" (*Par.* XXI, 10, and XXII, 145), and the word refers, respectively, to the softening of the light in Beatrice's smile and of the brightness of the planet Jupiter, where the temperance of justice is celebrated. The word also carries a musical resonance, and it describes the measured time which subtends and produces the harmonious turning of the spheres. Here the sweet symphony of Paradise (*Par.* XXI, 58–60) goes unheard by the pilgrim; the song of the blessed, like the smile of Beatrice, would transmute him (*Par.* XXII, 10). The play of sound and silence suggests their shadowy reenactment in the unbroken liturgy of the hours, the cycles of prayer and work, silence and chants which scan the day of the contemplatives and suspend it in the pure perfection of divine worship.[18] The word Peter Damian uses for the incessant rituals of the contemplatives is "latria" (*Par.* XI, 111) (worship), a *hapax legomenon* in the poem, which casts time not as a blurred flux of heterogeneous events but as the simultaneously intermittent and continuous duration of the liturgy.

There is another property of Saturn that is thematically relevant to the construction of the two cantos. I mention it last, and out of proper order, but it poignantly lays open to us the central terms of the relation between prophecy and contemplation, language and vision. This is Saturn's specific planetary influence: melancholy. An early commentator on Dante, Iacopo della Lana, recognized, in the wake of Aristotelian, Neoplatonic, and Ara-

bic speculations on stellar influences and humoral pathology, the double
and contradictory traits of Saturn. On the one hand, because of its quality
as an earthen, slow, heavy, cold, and dry planet, Saturn produces people
who greatly value material goods and riches and are best suited to the hard
work of husbandry and farming the land. On the other hand, through its
position as the highest planet, Saturn has the power to produce the most
spiritual people, such as prophets and contemplatives. Saturn presides over
"kings, rulers and founders of cities" and even "magicians, philosophers, as
well as excellent soothsayers and mathematicians (that is to say, astrologers), who always prophesy correctly, and whose words possess, as it were,
divine authority."[19] In the *Commentary on the Dream of Scipio* Macrobius
holds that the highest faculties of the human soul, namely rational and
speculative thought, originate in Saturn's sphere.[20]

A number of both central and marginal textual details in *Paradiso* XXI
and XXII are fully intelligible only in light of this complex burden of Saturn's mythography. In contrast to Saturn's slow gyrations, for instance,
Dante's contemplatives circle around in free flight with marvelous quick-
ness. The ascetic practice of both Peter Damian and Benedict jars with the
monks' attraction to wealth and the *bona temporalia* (*Par.* XXI, 130–35;
XXII, 88–93).[21] More cogently, the souls of the contemplatives find themselves in the absolute presence of God, while Peter Damian begins his
explanation of the limits of earthly vision by remarking how he now sees
the supreme essence: "Luce divina sopra me s'appunta, / . . . la cui virtú, col
mio veder congiunta, / mi leva sopra me tanto, ch'io veggio / la somma
essenza de la quale é munta" (*Par.* XXI, 83–87) (A divine light is directed
on me, . . . the virtue of which, conjoined with my vision, lifts me above
myself so far that I see the Supreme Essence from which it is drawn). At the
same time, the vision of the contemplatives is countered by their prophetic
utterances.

It ought to be remarked how the intensity of the souls' mystical illumination is at first stressed by the silence which cloisters, as it were, this wheel
of Paradise. Yet, in a sudden reversal of the silence, which seems to be the
necessary condition of pure inwardness to bring about vision, language is
fully retrieved. Peter Damian begins by explaining the principle of predestination, and he then goes into a prophetic utterance against the degeneracy of the monastic orders. His prophetic proclamation is a direct indictment of the ease and comfort in the life of the modern shepherds (*Par.*
XXI, 131), and it climaxes with a prayer that God's patience may not last
much longer (135). Damian's prophetic indignation, which acknowledges
the authority of the apostolic tradition (127–28), is picked up by Benedict
in *Paradiso* XXII. The apostle Peter, St. Benedict says, began his fellowship
in poverty as Francis did. The lines encapsulate a central theme of Benedictine spirituality, which has as its focus the commitment to total poverty,

as rule 33 states: "Let no man . . . have anything whatsoever as his own, absolutely nothing, not a book, nor tables, nor a style, in a word, nothing at all, because it is not permitted to them to have in their power either their body or their will." But the monks have violated Benedict's *Regula*, turning it into a waste of paper and their abbeys into dens of thieves (75–78). This sense of spiritual decay triggers Benedict's promise of an imminent wondrous ("mirabile") divine intervention that is expressed in the language of Psalm 113: "The sea saw it and fled; Jordan was driven back" (*Par.* XXII, 94–96).

On the face of it, the presence of this extended prophetic strain in the Heaven of Contemplation affirms, as in Bernard's *De consideratione*, the bonds joining the life of contemplation to that of action. Such an assertion obliquely implies that the cloister is not the emblem of either the negation of history or the escape from it. The life of Peter Damian, first spent in a hermitage and, later, devoted to pastoral action (*Par.* XXI, 113–26), exemplifies and reinforces Dante's sense that contemplation is not merely a self-defining realm of inner concentration attainable by severing one's inextricable ties to history. What is truly deadly in Dante's ethics is the retreat into inaction, into the belief that one's own authentic spiritual life is a self-defined autonomous realm of subjectivity. The "great refusal" of a Benedictine pope, Celestine V (*Inf.* III, 59–60), defined—and confined—the inner reality of his own self as essentially distinct from the wider context of the shared life of activity. Dante steadily deflates the picture of an absolute self removed from the sphere of contingency. Contemplation, as has been argued in the foregoing pages, is an experience of time, which yet seeks to break out of time; it is the pure thought of God, and yet it is yoked to moral action; it is, to say it with Richard of St. Victor, the penetration "into the difficult things of secret knowledge and into places inaccessible to all human activity," but is, at the same time, the locus of prophecy.[22]

The binding of prophecy and contemplation is a common element in both mystical and scholastic theological traditions. Thomas Aquinas, in the questions he devoted to prophecy, defines the prophets as seers (the prophet, he says, following Isidore's mistaken etymology, is so called from "*pro* for *procul*, far off, and *phanos*, appearance, because some realities which are far off appear close to them," (*Summa theologiae* IIa IIae, 171, 1).[23] Prophecy is a form of knowledge which surpasses natural reason; the prophecy that derives "from a pure contemplation of the truth . . . is more effective than that which derives from images of bodily things" (IIa IIae, 174, 2r). Following Maimonides, Aquinas believes that Moses surpasses all prophets because he had an intellectual vision of God's very essence (IIa IIae, 174, 4).[24] By the same token, Richard of St. Victor, who systematically analyses the manifold stages by which the mind, being breathed upon by divine inspiration, can pass beyond the bounds of natural knowledge, writes: "Every kind of prophecy, if it happens without alienation of mind, seems to pertain to this third stage of raising up (i.e., above nature). For is it not above human nature to see concerning past things that do not now exist; to see concerning future things that do not yet exist; to see concerning present things that are absent from the senses; to see concerning the secrets of another's heart that are not subject to any sense whatsoever; to see concerning divine things that are above sense?"

Yet, for all the bonds joining prophecy and contemplation, a hiatus exists between them. The aim of contemplation is ecstasy, a Greek word which in Latin means *excessus mentis*, a carrying away of the mind, as the *Glossa ordinaria* explains.[25] The word describes the experience of the mind unable to restrain itself and, "being elevated above itself, goes over into alienation" (*The Mystical Ark*, V, v). This alienation of the mind from itself occurs when the mind in a "dance of sweetness" completely forgets what it is and what it has been. Understood in this sense, contemplation implies the exercise of both intellectual and affective powers, for, insofar as it is divine love that causes ecstasy, it is like the lover's rapture. St. Paul's rapture to the Third Heaven is understood by Aquinas in exactly these terms.[26] Contemplation, however, exceeds the bounds of prophecy: the prophet's mind is enlightened to pass judgment, to speak out in place of and to interpret what the Holy Spirit intends in visions, words, or even deeds, but this does not imply that the prophet sees God's essence. In fact, the prophet speaks, but he may not always know what he says (as with the soldiers who divided the garments of Christ and understood not the meaning of what they did) (*Summa theologiae* IIa IIae, 173, 4).

In *Paradiso* XXI and XXII Peter Damian, Benedict, and the contemplatives have climbed Jacob's ladder (*Par.* XXII, 71), which is the *topos* of the visionary ascent; by their prophetic speeches Dante dramatizes the unity between prophecy and vision and, indirectly, his totalizing idea of poetry as simultaneously earthly and heavenly. Yet for the pilgrim a gap is opened up between seeing and hearing. The pilgrim sees and hears, but his hearing and seeing are said to be those of a mortal: "Tu hai l'udir mortal sì come il viso" (*Par.* XXI, 61) (You have the hearing as the sight of mortals). The discontinuity between what is seen and what is said structures the whole movement of *Paradiso*. Dante's poetic representation is articulated within this gap where vision and words are distinct from each other. Nonetheless, he will attempt to retrieve the original vision in order to generate the vision in his readers.

The idea of casting poetry as the source of vision has at least one notable precedent. At the end of his treatise on contemplation, Richard of St. Victor recounts the story of Elisha the prophet, who, when he was asked for the word of the Lord, feeling that at the time he did not have the spirit of prophecy, had a minstrel brought to him. With the help of the minstrel's song, Elisha immediately drank in the prophetic spirit and soon opened his mouth with words of prophecy (II *Kings* 3:18; 3:15).

> "Perhaps," Richard adds, "some person may ask what it means to him that according to the historical sense a Prophet of the Lord sought a minstrel and received the spirit of prophecy because of his singing." Now, we do know this: that in an ordinary state of mind, a secret harmony is accustomed to gladden the heart and to recall its joy to memory for it. Without doubt the more strongly anyone's love affects his soul, certainly the more deeply the harmony that is heard touches affection. The more profoundly he is touched by affection, the more effectively he is renewed with respect to his longings. Therefore, what else is it proper to feel about the prophetic man except that for him an external harmony brought back to memory that interior and spiritual harmony, and the melody that was heard called back and raised to customary joy the mind of the one listening? However, why should we not feel with respect to spiritual and true delights what we demonstrate by daily experience with respect to corporeal and empty delight? For who does not know how the mere memory of carnal delights can carry the carnal mind away into delight? . . . . And so the melody that was heard by the Prophet—what else was it other than a kind of ladder that raised him to customary joy?[27]

Richard's belief in the power of the song to awaken the prophet's dormant spirit belongs entirely to a theological-aesthetic conception that I call *theologia ludens*, which is largely shaped by Victorine esthetics and which I shall analyze at length in chapter 11.

What does not occur to Richard of St. Victor, however, is that his own claim can mean that the prophet's vision can be an aesthetic delusion, that the playing of music and the song can be another name for counterfeit prophecy and, more precisely, for the astrologer Michael Scot's game of insubstantial magic divination. Dante, as will be shown later, squarely confronts what Richard's optimism brackets. For the present, let us focus on a crucial episode in this portion of the poem. It is exactly here, immediately after the encounter with the contemplatives, that Dante discovers the origin of his poetry and his destiny as a poet.

> O gloriose stelle, o lume pregno
> di gran virtú, dal quale io riconosco
> tutto, qual che si sia, il mio ingegno.
>
> (*Par.* XXII, 112–14)

(Oh glorious stars, oh light impregnated with mighty power from whom I derive all my genius, whatsoever it may be.)

His sign, we are told by a periphrasis, is Gemini, which is the House of Mercury. His "ingegno" (*Par.* XXII, 114) comes from these stars. The word translates "ingenium," which is a technical term for the inborn gift of poetry.[28] More than that, the word refers to "ingenium," which, along with eloquence, astrologers and glossators claim to be the qualities of Mercury.[29]

Why does the disclosure of the gift of poetry take place here in the Heaven of the Fixed Stars? Plainly, the recognition of a bond between the power of poetry and the virtues of the stars is not to be seen as a lapse into astrological determinism, which is discarded on grounds that it annihilates free will (*Purg.* XVI, 66–81). What the apostrophe to the stars conveys, rather, is the poet's sense of his predestined mission as well as his desire to make his voice originate within the cosmic pattern of nature ("con voi nasceva e s'ascondeva vosco / quelli ch' è padre d'ogne mortal vita, quand' io sentì di prima l'aere Tosco" (115–17) (with you was rising and with you was hiding himself he who is father of every mortal life when I felt the air of Tuscany). But there is another fundamental reason why the poet's self-recognition occurs at the point of demarcation of the seven planets from the expanse of the heavens beyond.

The opening of *Paradiso* XXII (1–2) records the pilgrim's astonishment and stupor at the deep cry of the blessed, which his mind cannot comprehend. His bewildered consciousness is in stark contrast to the contemplatives' clarity of vision, but by the end of the canto the bewilderment is over, as the pilgrim sees all the planets till, finally, at the outer edge of the universe the earth appears as a peripheral globe in the vastness of God's space. The planets are all recalled through their mythical genealogies. The list ranges from the "figlia di Latona" (139) (the daughter of Latona) to the sun, periphrastically referred to as Hyperion's son (42); Mercury and Venus are recalled through their mothers Maia and Dione (144), while Saturn and Mars are named, respectively, father and son of Jupiter (145–46).

The genealogical pattern is chiefly designed to dramatize and prolong the metaphor of the poet's self-origination presented a few lines earlier. In formal-rhetorical terms, however, the genealogical periphrastic construction, or "circuitus eloquendi," as Quintilian calls it, betrays primarily the preciosity of the poetic *ornatus*.[30] In effect, the technique of circumlocution is flagrantly meant to foreground the workings of poetic metaphor by which the proper name of each planet is both revealed and hidden. Dante's sense of himself as a poet, in short, occurs at the outer frontier of the planets because poetry for him has the power to grasp the literally global framework of creation and make intelligible its origins; his poetry can be characterized as having the two aspects of Saturn, simultaneously earthly and heavenly; more than that, poetry is for him the crucial enterprise that gains access to the unexplored realm of the planets and comprehends the essence of the sciences each of them stands for.

This view of the world as a totality of internal relations rooted in and recapitulated by poetic metaphor has a number of logical, interconnected extensions. It marks, first of all, Dante's awareness of Peter Damian's paradigm of knowledge. It is well known that Peter Damian dismisses in his polemical works the *litterarum studia* and the profane sciences from the absolute standpoint of his religious vision. Texts such as *De sancta simplicitate*, addressed to a young hermit who regrets not having studied the liberal arts, warn against *scientia inflans* as well as against the heretics, as Damian calls the dialecticians, only in the measure in which they induce forgetfulness of God.[31] To these he juxtaposes the simplicity of Benedict's rules, with their emphasis that life must be lived within the demands of spiritual goals and with an idea of the context of the whole of life. By this focus on the primacy of contemplative vision Peter Damian denies the primacy of epistemology and asserts, to put it in a somewhat abstract formula, that epistemology is founded in metaphysics: his is a critique of the sciences as categories closed in and circumscribed within themselves. In Dante's dramatization, Peter Damian is the contemplative who, paradoxically, shifts his gaze to the earth, and his prophecy, which is a form of imaginative and intellectual knowledge, is the translation of knowledge into moral action, a remembering of history's memories and hopes spoken to us from the standpoint of his vision.

Second, as the pilgrim, miming the contemplatives' retrospective view, looks at the earth, "l' aiuola che ci fa tanto feroci" (*Par.* XXII, 151) (the little threshing-floor which makes us so fierce), it would seem that the world is constituted by his poetic glance, that poetry is the central activity around which all the sciences revolve, and that his poetic self is the imaginative ground of intelligibility for the entities of the world. In the poet's attainment of this purified, transcendent perspective, the world—it would seem—is simply reduced to a spectacle for the founding self. On the face of it, then, Dante's distance from Peter Damian's views is unbridgeable: for Peter Damian contemplation is the closure of knowledge; for Dante poetry is the foundation of all knowledge. In effect, Dante's glance, as much as Damian's prophecy, radically redefines and challenges the belief that the world's existence depends on one's view. His glance "places" him between heaven and earth, and, by the look he casts to the earth from the perimeter of the physical universe, he reenters the earth and becomes part of its ferocities: the adjective "feroci"—the prodigy of alliteration reminds us—has the personal pronoun, "ci," in it. Above and beyond the abandoning of an external, detached vantage point for the pilgrim, there is a tension in Dante's thought that complements Peter Damian's vision. By making poetry the founding mode of knowledge, Dante makes epistemology the path to vision. Poetry itself, in turn, is founded on vision, as a brief examination of some salient aspects of *Paradiso* XXXIII shows.

The question of the pilgrim's vision, on which the *Divine Comedy* climaxes, ought to be considered first within the context of arguments as to
whether or not it is possible to see God.[32] I Timothy 6:18 affirms the invis-
ibility of God, whereas in I John 3:2 it is said that the saints will see God
as he is; the speculations of the theologians of the thirteenth century were
caught within the horns of the question, and even the University of Paris
intervened in the debate. Dante boldly brackets the theological discussions
(as he tells of his own vision of God face to face while still alive) and retrieves the Cistercian modality of vision—the conviction that God can visit
the soul—which is embodied by St. Bernard. *Paradiso* XXXIII opens with
the prayer—the "santa orazione" (*Par.* XXXII, 151)—Bernard addresses to
the Virgin. The term "orazione" is rife among the contemplatives, and it
acquires a special force. Guillaume of St. Thierry—the Benedictine abbot
and Bernard's disciple—distinguishes between *lectio*, *meditatio*, and *oratio*;
oratio is the practice of transforming the will of the monk into love and,
thereby, of gaining access to a spiritual joy.[33]

The substance of Bernard's prayer, in point of fact, is a love song in its
radical carnality. The story of the Incarnation, evoked in the very first line
of Bernard's speech, "Vergine madre, figlia del tuo figlio" (*Par.* XXXIII, 1)
(Virgin mother, daughter of your son), which is explicitly an experience of
love rekindled in the Virgin's womb (7); the textual echoes from Bernard's
commentary on the *Song of Songs*, with its focus on the dialogue of love
between the bride and the bridegroom on the wedding night; the attribute
of the Virgin as the noonday torch of charity (9–10); the reference to the
pilgrim's affections, "affetti suoi" (36), that they may be preserved sound
after his vision; the insistence on the pilgrim's burning desire to see God
(48), wherein desire is not to be understood as want, the way St. Augustine
would, but as a form of love, the way Bernard does; the emphasis on the
heart (63) as the chamber within which drops the sweetness of the vision;
the idea of the whole universe, finally, as a book kept from falling asunder
by love (85–87), and of love as the force moving the sun and the other stars
(145)—this is the dramatic horizon within which the pilgrim's vision of
God takes place.[34]

The pilgrim's gaze is conjoined to the infinite light (80), and as his vision
reaches deeper into the heart of the light he sees, first, bound by love "in
un volume, / ciò che pe l'universo si squaderna" (86–87) (in one single
volume, that which is dispersed in leaves throughout the universe) and,
second, three circles of light, each reflected by the other, "come iri da iri"
(118) (as rainbow by rainbow). This vision induces *gaudium*, joy: "mi sento
ch'io godo" (93) (I feel my joy increase). What exactly is this joy, which is
conveyed, through the first-person pronoun, as a subjective experience?
Joy primarily comes through as the truth and the fulfillment of desire.
From this standpoint this sense of joy turns around much amatory rhetoric

about love's grief (which is also grief's love), the belief (punctuating the mourning for the loss of the beloved in the *Vita nuova*, Cavalcanti's idea of love's agonies torturing the mind, etc.) that love's wounds give love the aura of authenticity it forever seeks; more than that, grief lures the lover in the persuasion that to really know love and to really learn one must suffer for it. By contrast, joy denounces grief's shallowness in that grief makes severance and loss the essence of love.[35] More substantially, this joy is ecstasy as the essence of love, which ravishes the mind and by which the self goes out of oneself and returns to oneself.

Dante's dramatization of vision as love comes to him, no doubt, from the mystics' insight into the unity of all creation.[36] The pseudo-Dionysius, who deeply influenced both Franciscan and Dominican contemplatives, understands the Incarnation—Christ's emerging from the hiddenness of his divinity to take on human shape—as God's love for the frailty of the flesh. What holds the universe together, he writes in *The Divine Names*, are goodness, beauty, love, and ecstasy. Because of his goodness the "cause of all things loves all things . . . [and] holds all things together"; beauty "unites all things and is the source of all things"; by the ecstasy the divine yearning brings, "the lover belongs not to the self but to the beloved."[37] By the same token, St. Bernard of Clairvaux, who, like all the Benedictines and Cistercians, seems least affected by the pseudo-Dionysius, writes in texts such as his *Sermons on the Song of Songs, On Loving God*, and *On the Steps of Humility and Pride* that the "kiss of the mouth" is an emblem of the embrace between creatures and creator.[38] More fundamentally, in Bernard love is the very depth of knowledge the soul seeks. This view is developed by William of St. Tierry, for whom love coincides fully with knowledge. This equation is formulated in a variety of ways: "amor ipse notitia est," "amor intellectus," or even—and every reader of Dante's "Donne ch'avete intelletto d'amore" will find the phrase arresting—"intellectus amoris."[39] William's insight into knowledge as love and into the intellection of love shapes also Bonaventure's mystical spirituality.[40]

For them, as for Dante, to know, then, is to love, to love is to see, to see is to know. Love, knowledge, and vision, each the foundation for the other, each the truth of the other, implicate and explicate each other in the infinite circulation of their identities and differences. This trinity, or, if one prefers, this triad, is the luminous and obscure substance of the poetry of the *Divine Comedy*. There were adumbrations of this triad in the *Vita nuova*, which can be called Dante's "sentimental education," the apprenticeship of love and of writing, first, under the aegis of the eye of memory and, later, in the promise of a future quest for beatitude under the summons of vision. In spite of the final vision, the *Vita nuova*, which starts as an interrogation of the past, remains caught within the compulsive decipherment of the elusive and yet powerful hieroglyphics of the love passion.

To love is to read the stars' prodigious conjunctions, to will to understand
the seemingly chance encounter of a boy and a girl within the architecture
of magic correspondences. To love, the *Vita nuova* at bottom says, is to
interpret the hidden signs emitted by the beloved. *Convivio*, also, lays out
the love of knowledge according to the common path of the philosophers
and according to the predetermined principles of Aristotle's systematization of the sciences. *Monarchia* itself expatiates on how love can be put to
action, in the assumption that if one wants peace one has to work for
justice.

What underlies all these efforts to make sense of the world, as the final
vision of the *Divine Comedy* uncovers, is the mystics' insight into the vital
unity and interconnection of all things kept together by a knot of love. It
matters little whether Dante "really" has a mystical experience or rhetorically concocts it as the overarching discourse of his poetry. It matters even
less that mystical discourses, which forever stumble against the inadequacy
of all discourses to contain the ineffable vision, edge, as skeptically minded
historians believe, toward pathology: the "madness" of the mystics is nothing more than an acknowledgment of the free circulation of language
across the boundaries of sensible knowledge. As the pilgrim—dazzled by
the light—forgets what he has seen and is unable to say what he saw, the
poet posits the essential identity between poetic metaphor and mystical
writings: both displace light into darkness, nearness to God into distance,
presence into absence, totality into fleeting traces and scattered vestiges,
which, as St. Bonaventure fully knows, can turn into a ladder of love.

The paradoxes, which inform the knowledge of the mystics and which
are the most notable feature of Dante's figuration of Mary in *Paradiso*
XXXIII, inform the pilgrim's perspective as well. In fourteenth-century
encyclopedias and in speculations on optics and light by the likes of Bacon
and Grosseteste (who largely follow Averroes' commentary on Aristotle's
Physics and Arab Neoplatonism) *perspectiva* is recognized as an optical science.[41] This science is said to partake of the *quadrivium* and, above all, of
geometry, which is the science of pure intellectual and abstract vision. The
debates on this science assume vision's primacy over discursive knowledge.
Its sphere of study is the examination of how objects change according to
the distance and the viewpoint of the observer. In *Paradiso* XXXIII the
perspective of the pilgrim, however, is neither fixed nor completely detached from what he sees, as if the universe were reduced to an imaginary
spectacle for his gaze. More than ever before, the poet is now wary of
objectifying the world as if it were an entity constituted by his glance. This
objectification would sanction the lordship of his own self, as if he were the
subject around which revolve the objects of the world.

The oblivion of his vision, for instance, is rendered through the evocation of the twenty-five centuries that have lapsed since the enterprise of

Jason's *Argo* that made Neptune, the god of the sea depths, wonder at the shadow it cast over the surface of the water (94–96). Along with the temporal distance, which is its chief burden, the image conveys a spatial distance. More than that, it dramatizes the god's perspective on the human voyager. Further, both viewer and object of vision change together (112–14); later (133–38), geometry, the theoretical science of the measurement of boundaries and shapes, is the term of reference for the pilgrim's perplexed vision: just as the geometer cannot square the circle, the mind's eye of the pilgrim cannot see how the image conforms to the circle. The failure of Memory— the mother of the muses and the eye of the imagination—consigns poetry's vision to the movement of time. At the end, the pilgrim is back on earth longingly looking up at the stars and sun moved by love's compulsion (145).

The shadow of the noonday light the poet preserves in his mind will become the basis for Dante's radical and creative invention of an aesthetic theology. Accordingly, the next three chapters will focus on theology, which is traditionally the "place" where the movement of the liberal arts leads. Theology, however, cannot be understood merely as a turning away from questions of knowledge and history. On the contrary, theology is rooted in history and knowledge and marks a rethinking of them from a perspective that transcends the circle of immanent concerns.

Chapter 9

THEOLOGY AND EXILE

(*PARADISO* XXIV, XXV, XXVI)

IN HIS *Trattatello* Boccaccio devotes a substantial portion of the narrative to a description of the political turmoil that led to Dante's exile from Florence.[1] With an effort at impartiality that somewhat tempers the hyperboles of this essentially hagiographic text, Boccaccio does not shy away from remarking that Dante himself, with his stubborn arrogance, was not entirely free of responsibility in the tragic turn his personal life went on to take. After these statements, which, perhaps because they are slightly unflattering, have the appearance of factual truth, the flow of the narrative is interrupted. In a tone consistent with his stance throughout, Boccaccio proceeds to berate his public, the Florentine contemporaries to whom the text is addressed, for keeping Dante in exile even after their poet has long been dead and passionately urges them to retrieve his ashes from Ravenna.

The generous appeal clearly went unheeded, for Dante's ashes still lie away from his native city. Yet Boccaccio's failure to persuade the Florentines to perform this act of mercy and justice, which would have signaled the reconciliation of the city's divisions in the name of its poet, can in no way surprise us. If anything, one may be struck by a certain naïveté in his belief that he could effect what Dante himself had failed to accomplish. At any rate, the fidelity with which Boccaccio paraphrases the exordium of *Paradiso* XXV, where Dante utters the hope that he return to Florence to take the poetic crown, shows his conviction that the poet's genuine, if frustrated, desire was to see the end of his exile.

The literalism in Boccaccio's understanding of Dante's voice is exemplary, for it prefigures countless subsequent efforts to bring the spirit of the poet "home." As is well known, these efforts range from the innocuous mock trials periodically held to establish Dante's guilt or innocence during the civil war of Florence to deliberate maneuvers to claim him as the founder of latter-day political ideologies. It can doubtless be shown that these gestures to domesticate Dante, whether motivated by the benevolence of a kindred soul, inconsequential playfulness, or a dark calculus, are blind, for they sorely miss the point of Dante's radical insight into the nature of exile. Let me briefly illustrate this point.

In *Inferno* XV Dante encounters his teacher Brunetto Latini. Brunetto asks his disciple by what fortune or chance he is journeying through the beyond and who it is that shows him the way. The pilgrim replies:

"Là sù di sopra, in la vita serena,"
rispuous' io lui, "mi smarrì in una valle,
avanti che l'età mia fosse piena.
Pur ier mattina le volsi le spalle:
questi m'apparve, tornand' io in quella,
e reducemi a ca per questo calle."

                                                        (49–54)

("There above, in the bright life," I answered him, "I went astray in a valley,
before my age was at the full. Only yesterday morning I turned by back on it.
He appeared to me, as I was returning into it, and by this path he leads me
home.")

Brunetto goes on uttering the prophecy of Dante's exile from Florence
cin terms that echo the pronouncements made earlier in the poem by
Ciacco and Farinata (*Inf.* VI and X, respectively). He also reassures him
that if he follows his star, he will not fail to win a "glorioso porto" (*Inf.* XV,
56) (glorious port). The teacher's promise of success for his disciple's quest
is a flagrant misunderstanding of all that is essential and unique in Dante's
journey home, "a ca." The phrase "glorioso porto," as the poet's destination that Brunetto predicts, is a way of drawing the pilgrim within the
confines of the teacher's own experience, of assuming that his accessible
goal, like Brunetto's, is the laurel of fame humanists seek, and, in effect, it
is a way of thinking that Dante's poetry can be domesticated. But this is the
canto where blindness holds sway: Sodom is conventionally understood in
patristic exegesis as "caecitas,"[2] and ironically the whole exchange between
teacher and disciple measures the discrepancy between their respective visions, shattering the impression of gentleness and dignity that lies at the
surface of their encounter. Thus to Brunetto's prophecy of a contingent,
historical exile to be later crowned by glory, Dante counters with an
oblique correction:

"Se fosse tutto pieno il mio dimando,"
rispuous 'io lui, "voi non sareste ancora
de l'umana natura posto in bando;
che 'n la mente m'è fitta, e or m'accora,
la cara e buona imagine paterna
di voi quando nel mondo ad ora ad ora
m'insegnavate come l'uom s'etterna:
e quant' io l'abbia in grado, mentr'io vivo
convien che ne la mia lingua si scerna.
Ciò che narrate di mio corso scrivo,
e serbolo a chiosar con altro testo
a donna che saprà, s'a lei arrivo."

                                                        (79–90)

("If my prayers were all fulfilled," I answered him, "you would not yet be banished from human nature, for in my memory is fixed, and now saddens my heart, the dear, kind paternal image of you, when in the world hour by hour you taught me how man makes himself eternal; and how much I hold it in gratitude it behooves me, while I live, to declare in my speech. That which you tell me of my course I write, and keep with a text to be glossed by a lady who will know how, if I reach her.")

The lines are quite clearly an acknowledgment of the values of humanistic education, but in the same breath the tribute recognizes the teacher's spiritual perspective as limited. For the aim of education, to teach man how he can make himself eternal, is at odds with the whole point of Dante's own journey. After all, the pilgrim's experience is meant to show that man can become eternal, can transcend the fragmentation of time ("ad ora ad ora"), not through an illusory project of man's own making, as Brunetto would want it, but through God's grace. The discrepancy between the two modes is lost on Brunetto, who, oblivious of Dante's reminder that he is irrevocably exiled from humanity, still clings to the belief that he can go on living in the *Tresor*, the text he recommends to the pilgrim at the last farewell between them, as if to confirm his discipleship.[3] Against Brunetto's delusion, surely legitimate within his secular and didactic viewpoint, that the text is the locus where the self perpetuates its life, Dante evokes a view of writing, not as a self-enclosed and definite entity, but as an experience that exceeds the boundaries of "home." More textually, he responds by a reference to the activity of writing and glossing, as if the words he writes down transcend the perimeter of the literal and need a commentary: writing is an allegory, as it were, the sense of which will be disclosed by future glosses.[4]

If the teacher misunderstands, at least in part, the theology of exile that is the horizon of Dante's vision, it is small wonder that Dante's disciple Boccaccio, as well as the humanists that follow him, do not seem to see much further. In truth, there is in Boccaccio's *Trattatello* something other than a banal encomium or literal-minded domestication of a Dante in pursuit of the laurel crown. Florence, Boccaccio argues, ought to be like the myriad cities of Greece that compete for the honor of being acknowledged as the birthplace of Homer.[5] Yet this is not the central concern of the story. Its brunt is that Dante's virtue goes unrecognized among his own people and that even while living within the bounds of his city, he was engaged in a steady meditation on and experience of forms of exile. Dante is accorded the highest merit, for instance, for bringing back the Muses to Florence from their banishment; at the same time, the poet emerges from the legend as a solitary man who, though not rootless and uncommitted in private and public passions, keeps an essential distance from what surrounds him and leaves behind "ogni . . . temporale sollecitudine" (all temporal concerns), uncaring for, in words that overtly recall Dante's *Purgatorio* XXIX, 37–38, "fami ... freddi o vigilie" (hunger, cold or vigils) in order to fathom the secrets of philosophy and theology.[6]

What gives the account extraordinary power, however, is Boccaccio's sense that Dante should be remembered solely by virtue of his being a poet. The claim is such that Boccaccio is almost apologetic about shifting from the pathos of the narrative to a digression on poetry's role in shaping man's common awareness of the world. Deploying arguments that partly appear in his *Genealogy of the Gentile Gods*,[7] Boccaccio dismisses the conventional notion that poets are liars given to the cultivation of a hollow craft. By evoking the mythic foundation of the world, he states that it was the task of the poets to fashion and inaugurate man's knowledge of it by their act of naming. In effect, the poets are the first theologians, and the first name they assign, like Adam in the Garden of Eden, is that of "divinità," a generalized deity, while later they impart names to the other gods. The belief in the theological origin of poetry leads Boccaccio to assert that the nature of poetry is not significantly different from the methods of representation employed in scripture, which "quando con figura d'alcuna istoria quando col senso d'alcuna visione quando con l'intendimento d'alcuno lamento e in altre maniere assai mostranci l'alto misterio dell'incarnazione del verbo divino" (at times through the figure of some story, at times through the sense of some vision, at times through the understanding of some laments and in many other manners they show us the high mystery of the incarnation of the divine word).[8] Theology, he concludes with a statement that has the force of an aphorism, "niuna altra cosa è che una poesia di Dio" (is nothing else but God's poetry).[9]

This view of allegory as a common mode of significance for both poetry and theology elides the sharp distinction that Dante himself draws between the two in *Convivio* and the *Epistle to Cangrande*, where he explicitly claims that the *Divine Comedy* is patterned on the paradigm of Exodus, the account of the Jews' exile and return from Egypt to the Promised Land. But it recalls, as shown in chapter 2 above, Dante's reflection on the figurative language of the Bible in *Paradiso* IV. The relationship Boccaccio perceives between theology and poetry stops short, however, of Dante's insight about the link joining theology and poetry with exile.

I shall not be concerned here, then, with an inventory or articulation of the theme of exile, which would be quite a legitimate topic of inquiry. Let me simply say that it is well known that Dante has thorough awareness of himself as "exul immeritus" (an undeserving exile), that in the *Divine Comedy* there are specific references to all varieties of the experience of exile. Political exile is countered by exile as a mode of man's being on earth, as an alien here and a "peregrino" to heaven.[10] Exile is a term designating the spiritual condition of individual souls, as, for instance, in the line which tells of Boethius's redemption, "e da esilio venne a questa pace" (*Par.* X, 129) (from exile he came to this peace).[11] One can also add that "eterno essilio" (eternal exile) has the fixity of a formula to describe the state of the damned in hell. But a theme, however accurate, tends always to be of questionable value because it arbitrarily restricts and isolates what by virtue of metaphor transgresses all bounds and cannot be hedged within boundaries of literal definitions. The statement is not an abstract caveat against thematic criticism. Rather, it suggests the presence of a contradiction between the implication of exile—and we shall soon see its technical definition as that which is outside—and the critical mode of thematizing, which is a reduction of the text to the paradigms explicitly articulated in it. For Dante the language of exile is the language of poetry, which, almost to prove his point, philosophers and theologians who preceded him had banished from the region of rational discourse to the unreliable shadows of simulation or mere delightful ornamentation. To state it differently: Isidore of Seville understood exile, etymologically, as that which is outside.[12] A philosopher such as Boethius (and from this standpoint, as we have seen earlier, he marks the continuity of Plato in the Middle Ages) dismissed poetry as meretricious and unfaithful because it offers itself to many.[13] At the same time Aquinas entertained a theological suspicion of the knowledge poetry yields.[14] But like Boethius, Aquinas was a poet, or, to be more precise, he was a poet who abandoned poetry in favor of a rational univocal language that would lead fallen man along the path of the knowledge of God. Yet he never really ceased paying attention to the rift and complicity between theology and poetry—if one is to trust his remark, reported by his secretary Reginaldus of Piperno, that the theological work he had done could be easily interrupted, much as poetry had been interrupted earlier, for "it was all straw."[15] Dante, the "theologus nullius dogmatis expers" (theologian ignorant of no dogma), as we read in Boccaccio's *Trattatello*,[16] moves exactly within the problematic space where the discourse between poetry and theology is carried out and asks of theology and philosophy the very question he asks of poetry.

There is no doubt that in the *Divine Comedy* the writing of poetry is tied to the experience of exile. In *Paradiso* XVII the pilgrim asks his ancestor Cacciaguida to gloss for him the "parole gravi" (23) (heavy words) he has heard about his own future. Cacciaguida replies at first in "chiare parole e con preciso / latin" (34–35) (clear words and with precise discourse), predicting the future course of the pilgrim's life.

> Tu lascerai ogne cosa diletta
> più caramente; e questo è quello strale
> che l'arco de lo essilio pria saetta.
> Tu proverai sì come sa di sale

lo pane altrui, e come è duro calle
lo scender e 'l salir per l'altrui scale.

(55–60)

(You shall leave everything loved more dearly, and this is the shaft that the
bow of exile shoots first. You shall prove how salt is the taste of another man's
bread and how hard is the way down and up another man's stairs.)

Then Cacciaguida exhorts the pilgrim to deliver the truth of all he has
seen.

... Coscienza fusca.
o della propria o del'altrui vergogna
pur sentirà la tua parola brusca.
Ma nondimen, rimossa ogni menzogna,
tutta tua vision fa manifesta;
e lascia pur grattar dov'è la rogna.
Che se la voce tua sarà molesta
nel primo gusto, vital nodrimento
lascerà poi, quando sarà digesta.

(124–32)

(Conscience dark with its own or another's shame will indeed feel your words
to be harsh; but nonetheless put away falsehood and make plain all your vision, and then let them scratch where is the itch. For if your voice is grievous
at first taste, it will afterwards leave vital nourishment when it is digested.)

The poet's sense of his mission could hardly be overstated. Exile is the
condition from which his voice rises, but the displacement does not entail
a complacent isolation within a world largely indifferent to the private
truth the poet witnesses. Actually the references to his own words as a
palpable and edible substance place the poem within the tradition of the
public utterances of biblical prophets.[17] Like the prophets, Dante makes of
exile a virtue and a necessary perspective from which to speak to the world
and from which he can challenge its expectations and assumptions; like the
prophets, he also acknowledges that the truth he communicates is,
paradoxically, what further alienates him from the world he has already
lost.

The distance and confrontation between poet and world as the constitutive region of poetry is a persistent feature of Dante's moral imagination.
Yet the poet's dwelling in a condition of exile contradicts, on the face of it,
the statements repeated in a number of Dante's texts that his desire is to
return to Florence. Such, quite clearly, is the case in the celebrated song of
exile, "Tre donne intorno al cor mi son venute"[18] (Three women have
come round my heart), to which I now turn.

The status of the song in Dante's canon is made uncertain both by the additions that the poet is thought to have made later in his life and by the reasonable belief scholars generally profess that Dante intended it as the last poetic text to be commented on in the fourteen books he had originally planned for *Convivio*. Since as is well known this treatise on ethics was interrupted with the fourth book, it is impossible to determine the sort of philosophical thinking Dante would have drawn from the song. Taken by itself, the canzone is a transparent political-moral allegory of justice.[19] As one of the virtues of the soul and an abstract subject of ethical speculation, justice both affords and accounts for the double perspective of autobiography and allegory on which the movement of the poem hinges. The encounter between Self and the allegorical personification of Justice is staged at the outset of the first stanza with the three women who come to the poet's heart, where Love sits enthroned. One of them will identify herself later as "Drittura," but this is not Justice wielding the scepter and other accoutrements of might, such as sword or crown. Actually, the vexed countenance of "Drittura" and her two attendant offspring (generally interpreted as natural and positive law) tell a story of sorrow: children of God and reigning once in the Garden of Eden, they are now despised outcasts who roam the world. By a powerful move, this exile of Justice is revealed in the poet's own personal exile:

> E io, che ascolto nel parlar divino
> consolarsi e dolersi
> così alti dispersi,
> l'essilio che m' è dato, onor mi tegno:
> che, se giudizio o forza di destino
> vuol pur che il mondo versi
> i bianchi fior in persi,
> cader coi buoni è pur di lode degno.
>
> (73–80)

For all the proud distinction that the poet, made bold by the presence of the three lofty figures, sees in his exile, the reference to Justice's own consolation hints that the poet's claim may be another such attempt to be comforted, though consolation is not exactly what he seeks. The burden of the canzone is, in effect, an appeal that Mercy, the other daughter of God, may be shown to the poet, that the poem itself may generate desire for the flower of justice, as the first *conge*, picking up the metaphor of the white flower turned into a dark one, concludes: "e 'l fior, ch'è bel di fori / fa disiar ne li amorosi cori" (99–100).

From this perspective, "Tre donne intorno al cor" brings to a head what has been anticipated in the first book of *Convivio*:

Poi che fu piacere de li cittadini de la bellissima e famosissima figlia di Roma, Fiorenza, di gittarmi fuori del suo dolce seno—nel quale nato e nutrito fui in fino al colmo de la vita mia, con buona pace di quella, desidero con tutto lo cuore di riposare l'animo stancato e terminare lo tempo che m'è dato—per le parti quasi tutte a le quali questa lingua si stende, peregrino, quasi mendicando, sono andato, mostrando contro mia voglia la piaga de la fortuna, che suole ingiustamente al piagato molte volte essere imputata. (I, iii, 4–5)

(After it was the pleasure of the citizens of the fairest and most famous daughter of Rome, Florence, to cast me out of her dearest bosom (wherein I was born and nourished up to the summit of my life, and wherein with their good leave I desire with all my heart to rest my weary mind, and to end my allotted span), I have wandered through almost every region to which this tongue of ours extends, a stranger, almost a beggar, exposing to view against my will the stroke of fortune which is often wont unjustly to be charged to the account of the stricken.)[20]

There is in the passage the prayer that the punishment of exile may be repealed. Yet the context also suggests that there may be a special value to the pilgrim's homelessness. In the preceding chapter, as we saw earlier in the third chapter of this study, Dante records the admonition that to no man is it allowed to speak of oneself. Let me briefly restate the point of Dante's meditation. The convention, Dante says, has been violated by Boethius and St. Augustine, who have deployed an autobiographical focus in *The Consolation of Philosophy* and the *Confessions*, respectively, in order for Boethius to remove the suspicion of infamy from his own exile and, in the case of St. Augustine, to set a useful example that others might emulate. For Dante the immediate context for referring to his own experience of exile is to justify what could seem to be a lack of propriety and intellectual rigor in the philosophical commentaries he undertakes on his own poetry. But just as for Boethius consolation was a pretext to excuse "la perpetuale infamia de suo essilio, mostrando quello essere ingiusto, poi che alro escusatore non si levava"[21] (the lasting disgrace of his exile by showing that it was unjust, since no one else came forward as his apologist), for Dante, too, philosophical thinking offers no lasting consolation but is itself at one with exile; or, more precisely, exile is the metaphor for his ongoing philosophical self-interrogation.

Even in "Tre donne intorno al cor" consolation has a provisional but ultimately illusory and shallow value, which the poet must discard just as he discards other forms of self-deception. The reference to the heart where Love dwells and reigns is in a way a conceit meant to imply the poet's moral integrity and lack of treachery; the three women come to the heart both to speak frankly of what is near to the heart's desire and because they "sanno ben che dentro e quel che dico" (18). Their guileless conversation, as if between friends, is in turn a way of asserting the naked and open truth the poem will deliver to whatever friend of virtue it may find. There is, however, another doctrinal reason for the conceit: in reality, Dante raises the philosophical definition of justice here. Consistent with the views that have been commonplace since Plato, he understands justice not merely as an intellectual virtue, subject of and directed to speculative knowledge. Rather, justice is the transcendent truth of the cosmos as well as a moral habit of the will, and the heart is the place of its dwelling. This doctrinal element governs other aspects of the poem.

In a way, since justice is both transcendent and the internal ordering of man's will (as well as the mark of social harmony), it is appropriately represented as a dramatis persona outside of the self and as the friend of Love residing in the heart. At the same time, since Justice, in the guise of Astraea, is related to Good Venus ("Son suora a la tua madre," as she says to Love), the song appeals to the hearts in love to establish peace in the city. The poem's second *conge* begs precisely for the gift of peace:

> Canzone, uccella con le bianche penne;
> canzone, caccia con li neri veltri
> che fuggir mi convenne,
> ma far mi poterian di pace dono.
> Però nol fan che non san quel che sono:
> camera di perdon savio uom non serra,
> che 'l perdonare è bel vincer di guerra.

(101–7)

The stanza faintly echoes a passage from St. Augustine's *City of God*:

> Any man who has examined history and human nature will agree with me that there is no such a thing as a human heart that does not crave for joy and peace. One has only to think of men who are bent on war. What they want is to win, that is to say, their battles are but bridges to glory and peace. The whole point of victory is to bring opponents to their knees—this done, peace ensues. Peace, then, is the purpose of waging war.[22]

For St. Augustine the point is that "the peace of the irrational soul in the harmonious repose of the appetites, domestic peace and civic peace"[23] all prefigure the peace God promises in the heavenly Jerusalem. But Dante harbors no illusions, any more than St. Augustine ultimately does, about the advent of peace in the actuality of history. As we are told that "larghezza and temperanza" as well as the other virtues themselves go begging (63–64), the song voices Dante's tragic insight—fully deployed in the *Divine Comedy*, where the breakdown of justice is so complete as to make this a satanic world—about the unfeasibility of his heart's desire.

There are other elements in the poem that give weight to this darkening of Dante's vision. The antithesis in the first stanza between "di fore," where the three women coming round the poet's heart sit, and "dentro" (2–3), where Love sits, suggests that for all their nearness there is still a distance between these members of the same family. More important, as Justice proclaims that the virtues, though wounded now, will live on, the statement is at odds with Dante's presentiment of his own mortality, "che Morte al petto m'ha posto la chiave" (87). This sense of death is the point in the poem that marks the break between the hope that the poet may return to his city and the possible return of Justice. But Justice herself is involved in a tragic predicament. As she begins her lament she is pictured resting her head on her hand, "come succisa rosa" (21). The pathos that this image of fragility and short-lived splendor conveys is intensified by its textual resonance. Derived as it is from the *Aeneid* (IX, 435), the allusion evokes the deepest night of death in the whole of the Vergilian epic. It describes the death of Euryalus, who, having waited in vain to rescue his friend Nisus, tumbles to the avenging fury of the Latins. The celebration of friendship and the elegy for the two youths overwhelmed by the rage of war barely, if at all, mitigate Vergil's representation of a relentlessly broken world, where plunder and slaughter are the law and of which the Arcadian world of book VIII is the ironic setting. There is no doubt that this Vergilian echo is meant to put a tragic perspective on Dante's allegory of Justice.

In *De vulgari eloquentia* Dante refers to the three *magnalia*—*salus, virtus*, and *venus*—as the worthiest subjects to be treated by poets, and then he adds that the *cantio* is the most adequate form for the tragic style, appropriate to the treatment of those lofty themes.[24] In the canzone "Tre donne attorno al cor," the voice is that of Melpomene, the Muse that wears the tragic mask: this is the tragedy of Justice, who, born in the Garden of Eden where she dwelled virginal, now roams corrupt and unrecognized through the world; who has reproduced herself in the guises of natural and positive law but goes disfigured and naked among men. Through the crisis of Justice, the poem also tells the tragedy of the poet himself, who acknowledges his estrangement from the world, who begs forgiveness but can speak only to hearts that know only strife. However, we are not to dismiss the call for a return from exile as a mere rhetorical gesture. The pathos of the poem comes precisely from the fact that there is a genuine desire for peace. The desire is accompanied by the poet's clear tragic knowledge of the futility of his efforts.

If in the first envoi of the song there is the implication of a truth available at the surface of the allegory (let no man touch the dress, let the uncovered parts suffice), in the second envoi the harder and darker truth emerges. Here there is an extraordinary deployment of rhetorical resources: the apostrophe to the canzone, metaphorized as a dove, the bird of Venus; an antithesis between "bianche" and "neri"; extended alliteration (*canzone, bianche, caccia, uccella, convenne, pace,* etc.); a *captatio benevolentiae*; a moral aphorism (107). The presence of these figures contrasts with the "parlar divino" (73), the unadorned language and appearance of Justice, as if the poet meant to dramatize his own best effort at rhetorical persuasion—the effort, that is, of inducing feelings of peace not harbored by his readers. At the core of the stanza, however, there is the acknowledgment that the gift of peace will not be made, because his readers "non san quel che sono" (they don't know what I am) (105) The line reverses the knowledge that at the end of the first stanza the three women are said to have "ben sanno che dentro è quel ch'io dico" (know well that he of whom I speak is here). The reversal seals the poet's awareness of the misunderstanding of his voice, as well as the failure of his rhetoric to persuade.

The perception of the tragic disintegration of justice in the world of reality is carried over into the *Divine Comedy*. If the poem overtly enacts the unfolding of "infallibile giustizia" (infallible justice) as the "ministra / de l'alto Sire" (*Inf.* XXIX, 55–56) (ministress of the High Lord) in the system of punishments and rewards of the beyond; if it impatiently calls for the return of Astraea to the earth so that its original purity may be restored; if it privileges the epic of Roman history as nothing less than a providential instrument in the rule of law; and finally, if it singles out the justice and mercy of the emperor Trajan, the poem also dramatizes the harsh lawlessness dominant in the actuality of political practice. "Lo mondo è ben così tutto diserto / d'ogni virtute come tu mi sone, / e di malizia gravido e coperto" (*Purg.* XVI, 58–60) (The world is indeed as utterly deserted by every virtue as you declare to me, and pregnant and overspread with iniquity), Dante says to Marco Lombardo, who goes on to point out to the pilgrim the causes of the existing chaos. The blindness of the world, Marco states, is due to the eclipse of the two lights of Rome, and just as the light of the free will can relieve us of the burden and deceptions of sin, so an emperor who had some inkling of justice could discern at least the tower of the true city.

Since the moral crisis of the world seems to depend on a contingent crisis of authority, it would be possible to extrapolate a message of political optimism from Marco Lombardo's speech. But Dante knows that fallen man is denied the harmony of the Garden of Eden, and he also knows, as can be seen from the encounter with Justinian, the emperor who codified Roman law, that the history of Rome can appear as a story of a lust for power and violence against which the myth of its mission of universal justice crumbles. At stake in these remarks is the value of political history, punctuated, as it is in the *Divine Comedy*, by an awareness of the persistent madness of civil war, an experience by which every man is a stranger in his own home. The *Divine Comedy* is, in a real sense, the tragic text of the civil war. From this perspective, Lucan's vision and polemic against Vergil's ostensible celebration of the empire become Dante's own, not as a strategy to dismiss altogether the myth of political order but as a signal of its unavoidable precariousness.[25]

In this formulation we are far removed from any simple notion of a contrast between the order that the justice of the empire embodies and the provisional disorder of the times. The search for order in the community of man is a steady concern for Dante at the very moment in which he envisions, with a clarity that is hardly to be found anywhere outside of the *Divine Comedy*, exile not just as a punishment inflicted by the power of a man on another man but as the truth of man's being in history. From this radical sense of exile all forms of power and all accomodations to power are denounced as satanic; this exilic perspective, furthermore, inolves both the language of poetry and that of theology. There is, in fact, a theology of exile, which Dante brings to focus, quite appropriately, in the examination of the three theological virtues, faith, hope, and charity, to which the pilgrim is subjected respectively in *Paradiso* XXIV, XXV, and XXVI.[26]

Critics who have discussed the cantos conventionally have stressed the extent to which Dante's treatment of the three virtues moves within the canonical theological tradition. What is generally neglected, however, is the conspicuous pattern in the cantos of both direct and oblique references to exile—a pattern so clear as to indicate that exile, I submit, is the textual horizon within which Dante is engaged in a powerful rethinking of the theological virtues and, beyond that, in testing the nature of theological language.

The opening lines of *Paradiso* XXV, 1-9, dramatize the pilgrim's exile from his native city and express the hope that he may be allowed to return to Florence and be granted the laurel crown. Later in the same canto Beatrice anticipates the pilgrim's reply to St. James's question on hope by glossing Dante's journey to God in terms of the biblical Exodus:

> La chiesa militante alcun figliuolo
> non ha con più speranza, com' è scritto
> nel sol che raggia tutto nostro stuolo:
> però li è conceduto che d'Egitto
> vegna in Ierusalemme per vedere,
> anzi che 'l militar li sia prescritto.
>
> (52–57)

(The Church Militant has not any child possessed of more hope, as is written in the Sun that irradiates all our host; therefore is it granted him to come from Egypt to Jerusalem, that he may see, before his term of warfare is completed.)

The lines overtly reveal the poet's exile and mission as the reenactment of Exodus, the epic of the return of the Jews from their captivity in Egypt to the peace of Jerusalem. The epithet "militante" for the church echoes the pilgrim's "militare" and designates it not as the Church Triumphant but as the Exodus Church, "in via," and makes of Exodus the paradigm of salvation history.

Paradiso XXVI is almost equally divided between the examination on love by St. John and the pilgrim's exchange with Adam, who recounts his creation in the Garden of Eden, his fall, and his redemption through Christ's Harrowing of Hell. The loss of the Garden is presented as an exile into an alien land: "Or, figliuol mio, non il gustar del legno / fu per sè la cagion di tanto essilio, / ma solamente il trapassar del segno" (115–17) (Now know, my son, that the tasting of the tree was not in itself the cause of so long an exile, but solely the overpassing of the bound). Later Adam relates what could be called the diaspora of tongues, as he evokes the loss of the original unity and the construction of the Tower of Babel (124–38).

Paradiso XXIV, the canto of faith, bears only an oblique reference to exile, but it is framed by an explicit allusion to it. The final lines of canto XXIII dramatize the pilgrim's astonishment and delight at the vision of the triumph of Mary and of the Church Triumphant:

> Oh quanta è l'ubertà che si soffolce
> in quelle arche ricchissime che fuoro
> a seminar qua giù buone bobolce.
> Quivi si vive e gode del tesoro
> che s'acquistò piangendo nello essilio
> di Babillon, ove si lasciò l'oro.
>
> (*Par.* XXIII, 130–35)

(Oh how great is the abundance that is heaped up in those rich coffers, who were good sowers here below. Here they live and rejoice in the treasure which was gained with tears in the exile of Babylon, where gold was spurned.)

The thrust of the passage is the typological opposition, made familiar by St. Augustine's *City of God*, between the idolatry of gold at Babylon and the spiritual treasure of the heavenly Jerusalem.[27] The word "ubertà," etymologically from *ubera*, the mother's breast, describes the generosity and fruitfulness of this place in terms of a garden of milk and honey, and as such is the central metaphor throughout the *Paradiso*. The opposition between Babylon and the heavenly Jerusalem cannot be taken as absolute, for as the joy of paradise comes forth as a recompense for the anguish suffered at Babylon, Dante casts exile as an ascetic and redemptive experience. More to our concern, within the typological context that immediately precedes it, the opening apostrophe of *Paradiso* XXIV, 1–3, "O sodalizio eletto alla gran cena / del benedetto Agnello, il qual vi ciba / sì, che la vostra voglia è sempre piena" (O fellowship elect to the great supper of the blessed Lamb, who feeds you so that your desire is ever satisfied), echoes the account of Exodus. For the convivial world of heaven, which experiences God's bounty in its immediacy in fellowship, is the anagogical fulfillment of what appeared at the Last Supper in figure, the bread of affliction of Passover, which our fathers ate when they came out of Egypt.

But the emphasis on the paschal sacrament is of great moment because it provides a context in which we are brought up against the question of faith, the first of the three theological virtues. In contrast to the plenitude of the eschatological banquet, faith, like hope, is a virtue that belongs to the sphere of time. The emblem that describes the eternal dance of the souls who are revolving "come cerchi in tempra d'orioli si giran," (*Par.* XXIV, 13–14) (as wheels within the fittings of clocks revolve) hints that we, as readers, are bound to the domain of time as much as the pilgrim is. The metaphor of food eaten at this mystical banquet, moreover, gives a crucial twist to the understanding of faith. The canto is organized primarily as a confession of faith, as a statement of how faith reaches self-understanding. By combining tenets of Aristotelean-Thomistic philosophy with the gospel teachings, the pilgrim confesses an essential faith both in one eternal God, who unmoved, moves all heaven with love, and in the unity and trinity of the Godhead. Yet the object of faith is a faith in the event of the kerygma, the word of God recorded by the prophetic and apostolic texts. The definition of faith the pilgrim gives to St. Peter draws from and acknowledges the authority of St. Paul's epistle:

E seguitai: "Come 'l verace stilo
ne scrisse, padre, del tuo caro frate
che mise teco Roma nel buon filo,
fede è sustanza di cose sperate,
ed argomento de le non parventi;
e questa pare a me sua quiditate."

(*Par.* XXIV, 61–66)

(And I went on: "As the truthful pen of your dear brother wrote of it, who with you, father, put Rome on the good path, faith is the substance of things hoped for and the evidence of things not seen; and this I take to be its quiddity.")

One singular element of Dante's vision should be pointed out here: the harmonization of Pauline and Petrine theologies, the fraternal bonding of preacher and bishop, of institutional church and kerygmatic church, or, to put it at its most general, of prophecy and history both making up his sense of tradition. More to our textual concerns, the pilgrim's faith, he goes on

to say, comes to him from the plenteous rain of the Holy Spirit on the old
and new parchments, and by believing the truth

> ... che quinci piove
> per Moisè, per profeti e per salmi,
> per l'Evangelio e per voi che scriveste.
> poi che l'ardente Spirto vi fe almi;
>
> (*Par.* XXIV, 135–38)

(which rains through Moses and the Prophets and the Psalms, through the
Gospel and through you who wrote after the burning spirit made you holy.)

Retrospectively we can grasp the importance of the sacramental fullness
that opens the canto. In a sense, as hinted above, Dante would not accept
the distinction between the Church of the Word and the Church of the
Sacraments that arose from the theological debates that eventually would
split European Christendom. Faith to him is faith in the historical tradition of the prophetic word, in its power to transform and contain reality
and make the Revelation of the Word at one with history.

From one point of view, the acknowledgment of the authority of tradition hints that faith is primarily assent to the credibility of scriptures.[28]
This acknowledgment frees the profession of faith from the domain of
subjectivity and gives it a value that transcends the possibly arbitrary utterances of the individual self. Nonetheless, faith is exactly the virtue that
cannot be separated from selfhood, and in St. Peter's summons to the pilgrim, "Dì, buon cristiano, fatti manifesto: / fede che è?" (52–43) (Speak,
good Christian, and declare yourself: faith, what is it?), the phrase "fatti
manifesto" projects faith as a challenge to man to be seen and, by the same
token, implies that faith reveals the very foundations of one's being.

What the Pauline definition of faith, which Dante quotes, reveals is first
of all the temporality of one's life, for faith is the substance of hope and
thus places man in a world of time, where he can see only through a glass
darkly, beset by temptations and doubts. Faith is the ground of absolute
certainties, but there are degrees of it, and there are times when the light
of faith is eclipsed. This much is suggested in the canto by the brief speech
in which Beatrice asks St. Peter to test ("tenta") the pilgrim "intorno della
fede, / per la qual tu su per lo mare andavi" (*Par.* XXIV, 37–39) (regarding
the faith by which you walked the sea). The allusion is to Matthew 14:29,
where it is said that Peter walked on water to go to Jesus. Read in its entirety, however, the gospel story tells of St. Peter, who, while walking on
the water, grows afraid of the wind and begins to sink but is caught by the
hand of Jesus, who reproaches him, "O man of little faith, why did you
doubt?" The scene is so crucial that Thomas Aquinas in the *Summa* employs it as a text to argue for degrees of faith, in which fear and doubt are

never quite suppressed and which require the exercise of another virtue, that of courage.[29]

It is within the context of fortitude that we can understand why Dante always envisions the experience of faith in terms of an epic, with St. Dominic as the hero whose strength is tested in the daring warfare with the hydra of obstinate unbelief. Though without the legendary overtones that characterize the knightly adventures of St. Dominic, the pilgrim is also involved in a show of courage. Thus, he responds to St. Peter's test like a "baccellier" (46) (bachelor) who arms himself for what amounts to an intellectual *certamen* with the chief centurion. This conjunction of metaphors drawn from the practice of university examination and armed combat anticipates the formulation in *Paradiso* XXV of the Church Militant and the pilgrim's own "militar." More specifically, it depicts faith not just as a shield against error but as a heroic virtue that withstands fear and is inseparable from risk. Finally, the evocation of the the university milieu as the dramatic context for the determination of the question of faith suggests that Dante is addressing the issue of the relationship between knowledge and faith.

That faith is itself a form of knowledge is a tenet common to Bonaventure's theory of knowledge as illumination as well as to Albert the Great and Aquinas.[30] The differences among theologians largely consist in their different ideas about the role played by reason in arriving at the truth of faith. Dante, who steadily opposes in the poem the self-contradictory theory of "double truth," is here closer to the formulations of both Franciscan and Dominican masters, as an analysis of the text will show.

There is, to begin with, an ironic counterpoint between the rhetoric and the statement on faith. The impression of the reasonableness of faith, conveyed by the series of questions and answers between St. Peter and the pilgrim, is undermined by the fact that the content of faith can neither be captured in analytical statements nor submitted to the rigor of philosophical investigation. Philosophy can provide proofs, which faith mobilizes to make its case, yet the extensive presence of the vocabulary of philosophy throughout the canto openly parodies, as Bonaventure would, philosophy's tacit assumption of reason's sovereignty. Thus, the rain the Holy Ghost poured over the Bible is a "syllogism" that establishes the truth in such a way that in comparison to it every demonstration is dull. More important, faith appears as the substance of things hoped for and the "argomento" (65 and 78) of things not seen. The pains Dante takes in defining, first, "sustanza" (69 and 75) as the ground that underlies and sustains hope and, second, "argomento" (69 and 78) as the point of departure for reasoning into the realm of the unseen (76–78) make faith—which in itself is blind—a mode of vision, the condition whereby worlds are revealed, for indeed one sees what one believes. The term "argomento" also suggests

Dante's awareness of the complex theological reflections elicited by St. Paul's use of the term "argumentus."[31] At stake for Dante, I submit, is the *very nature of theological discourse and, to put it most simply, the place of reason in the understanding of faith.*

Theologians such as William of Auxerre, Albert the Great, and Thomas Aquinas agree that whereas in philosophy "argumentus" designates the rational process of persuasion with reason as the first principle, in theology its meaning is radically reversed. To the theologians "argumentus" describes the accountability of faith, the legitimacy in moving, when theological speculations are involved, from faith to those reasons that make faith credible. Fully conscious of the contradictory and double sense the word has in philosophy and theology, they explain the contradiction as a mark of the essential heterogeneity of the aims of the two disciplines.[32]

Dante subscribes to this rationale, and in *Paradiso* XXIV he turns around the *modus argumentativus* of faith in order to expose the limits inherent in the sophist's wit ("ingegno di sofista," 81). To him, and in this he follows the whole theological tradition, a faith that is fully rational has no merit. But Dante also gives a radical twist to St. Thomas's elaboration of the symbolic theology of the pseudo-Dyonisius. Aquinas argues that there is no room for "argumentus," which belongs to scientific discourse, in the treatment of the metaphoric language of the Bible, because metaphor by definition forbids the possibility of direct and precise knowledge. This insight is central to *Paradiso* XXIV, where, in effect, there is not a proper but a metaphorical definition of faith.[33]

St. Peter refers to faith obliquely as the "moneta," the alloy and weight of which have been examined, and then asks the pilgrim whether he has it in his purse. Dante replies: "Si, ho, lucida e si tonda, / che nel suo conio nulla mi s'inforsa" (*Par.* XXIV, 86–87) ("Yes, I have indeed, so bright and *so round that of its mintage I am in no doubt*). The etymological implication of "moneta," from "moneo," is a warning about the authenticity and preciousness of the imprint.[34] If one were to take the metaphor literally, however, there is an oddness to it, for money is a value that belongs to the kingdom of darkness, a worldly idol that counters St. Peter's and the poet's own indictment. From this point of view it would appear that the tenor of the metaphor is to show how faith displaces and subverts what the world holds dear. More important, the coin, as a metaphor of exchange, makes faith, which is the bedrock of all other virtues, a metaphor with a power to redefine or dismiss the values of the world, but which itself lies beyond any proper definition. At the same time, if "argumentus" refers to a modality of theological speculation, "substantia" refers faith to another virtue, that of hope.

As in the discussion on faith, the examination by St. James on hope reveals Dante's hope for the resurrection of the dead as the general expectation of the fulfillment promised by the prophetic writings. The specific definition given, "attender certo / de la gloria futura" (*Par.* XXV, 67–68) (sure expectation of future glory) discloses the nature of faith retrospectively; like faith, hope is a virtue of time, and, more precisely, it announces a belief in the future. In a sense, here lies the profound realism of hope, for it rejects as illusory the tendency to consider every experience as finite, or even to view the past as a closed and irretrievable experience. For the children of the promise, on the contrary, it is despair which is illusory; mistaking what is partial for the whole reality, despair prematurely decides that everything is over and that the future itself is empty. To have hope actually means that nothing is ever final, that the future may have possibilities that may alter the contours of what in the present one perceives as past and dead. If for the Greeks, who had no inkling of this sense of hope, hope was a cheat, a self-willed blindness to the unbearable pressures of life, for Dante hope is a form of desire that announces man's dislocation in the world of a future-oriented time, where a necessary rupture exists between experience and the assessment of its value and the present is the spot for man's waiting.[35]

What a man waits for, Dante says in *Paradiso* XXVI, is to live the virtue of charity, the greatest gift of the Spirit and the foundation of all creation. After all, love is the crown of all the theological virtues, for, in the words of St. Paul, love "bears all things, believes all things, hopes all things, endures all things" (I Cor. 13:4). In *Paradiso* XXVI, however, there is not even an attempt to define the crown of the virtues, both because the pilgrim's experiences in the beyond, as well as the whole of *Paradiso*, witness the reality of love and because love remains a persistent mystery. The pilgrim has been blind throughout the examination on charity conducted by St. John, the sharp-eyed eagle of love, and when Dante's sight is restored as St. Paul's was by the virtue of Ananias's hand he meets Adam, the first poet who named the world of the Garden and who now relates, first, his fall from the Garden into exile and, second, gives a brief history of the languages of man.

It is possible to account for this shift from the virtue of charity to Adam's original sin; the product of God's original act of love has been redeemed by the loving sacrifice of the second Adam. More than that, this is the point where we can grasp the profound reasons why exile systematically punctuates this stretch of the text. In effect, the occurrence of the fall from the Garden is not given merely as a theme but is metaphorically rendered as an exile into language. The prelapsarian tongue he used at creation, Adam states, was extinct before the building of the Tower of Babel. This explanation, as has often been remarked, substantially revises the theory Dante put forth in his *De vulgari eloquentia*, where he writes that "a certain form of speech was created by God along with the first soul. . . . In this form of speech Adam spoke, and in this form also all his descendants spoke, until the building of the tower of Babel, which is by interpretation the tower of Confusion, and this form of speech was inherited by the sons of Heber, who, after him are called Hebrews. The language remained with them long after the Confusion, in order that our Redeemer (who was, as to His humanity, to spring from them) might use not the language of confusion, but of grace."[36] In the economy of the treatise the continuity of the language of grace allows Dante to envision grammar as the tool by which to forge and order from the forest of multiple dialects one national language.

In *Paradiso* XXVI there is a drastic deviation from the myth of a persistent prelapsarian language. The Tower of Babel, Nimrod's unaccomplishable work, is now a sign of the lonely foreignness of every voice. This instability involves the names of God, who was first called on earth "I" and "El" (134–36). If in his discussion of the three theological virtues Dante clung to and deployed the truths of the theological language of the Bible, now, in the encounter with the original poet who has given a name to the Deity, which is the founding act of theological poetry, he probes the nature of the language of theology.

The classical views on the question of the names of God are well known. For the pseudo-Dionysius, as he argues in *De divinis nominibus*, there can be no naming or opinion of God, for the "inscrutable one is out of the reach of every rational process," beyond all theological representations and all categories of being.[37] Alan of Lille writes in his *Regulae theologicae* that "no name properly belongs to God" and that the names of God are ineffable because they signify the ineffable.[38] From this premise Alan argues, as Evans rightly points out, that theological language cannot simply be measured by the standards of the demands of the *artes*. Finally, for Aquinas the word "God" is justified because it is used analogically.[39] "He who is"—the name that God applies to Himself in Exodus in response to Moses' question—is the most appropriate name for God because it implies a pure existence outside of any temporal sequence. "Even more appropriate," Aquinas writes, "is the *Tetragrammaton* which is used to signify the incommunicable and, if we can say such a thing, individual substance of God." Aquinas, realistically, is forced to straddle between both agreeing and disagreeing with Dionysius. What we assert of God is loose "because no word used of him is appropriate to him in the way of signifying." It is also loose because "neither the Catholic nor the pagan understands the nature of God as he is in himself" and because "the words we use reflect the unavoidably composite way of understanding that our minds are capable of."[40]

In *Paradiso* XXVI grammar, whose focus is the variations of time and words, can never reach God. In the changes that occur in the names we use to call God, we confront the lack of any appropriate names available to us. If anything, the words we use for God reveal our yearning for and our distance from him. From this perspective poetry and theology, as Boccaccio intuited, are linked both by a longing for the absolute and by the cloud of unknowing hovering over them. Poetry, in short, as Alan of Lille intuited when, paradoxically, he found theology's imaginative speculations more exciting than secular studies,[41] is for Dante the necessary language of theology, for theology itself, when it moves to the threshold of thought, is a form of poetry. Radicalizing the insights of theologians such as St. Thomas, Dante, in fact, invests poetry with what he calls a "divina virtù." In the protasis to *Paradiso* the poet begs to be filled, as if he were a passive vacant vessel, with Apollo's power and adds:

> O divina virtù, se mi ti presti
> tanto che l'ombra del beato regno
> segnata nel mio capo io manifesti,
> vedra' mi al piè del tuo dilette legno
> venire, e coronarmi de le foglie
> che la materia e tu mi farai degno.

> (I, 22–27)

(O divine Power, if you do so lend yourself to me that I may show forth the image of the blessed realm which is imprinted in my mind, you shall see me come to your beloved tree and crown me with those leaves of which the matter and you shall make me worthy.)

So overt seems Dante's desire to receive the laurel in this invocation that it is small wonder that Boccaccio campaigned for his posthumous celebration. But we cannot be blind to the ambiguous, complex metaphors with which the poet's activity is cast in the initial cantos of *Paradiso*, which the next chapter will explore from a somewhat different angle of vision. For now, let me point out some aspects of Dante's poetic language present here. The first flagrant poetic ambiguity consists in the mixture of pagan mythology (Apollo presides) and Christian experience. The procedure is hardly unusual in this poem, where theology and poetic metaphor are systematically woven together on the principle that poetic fiction is a figure of Christian truth. Nonetheless, the harmonization of poetic myth and theological belief, however conventional a practice it is in the *Divine Comedy* and its Christian antecedents, hides in this context a number of moral and aesthetic tensions.

The poet prays Apollo that he be made into a "vaso" (*Par.* I, 14) (vessel), the repository of the god's power, just as St. Paul was a vessel of the Holy Spirit. The prayer for Apollo's poetic power shifts to a language of violence. *Paradiso* is referred to as an "aringo" (18) (arena), which, technically, is part of the Roman amphitheater where gladiator contests and shows were fought out. The agonistic-ludic metaphor introduces the myth of

Marsyas who, having challenged Apollo, the god of music, to a musical contest, was defeated and flayed by him (9–21). Since Marsyas's challenge was a usurpation of the god's powers, the simile in Dante's text plays out—and checks—the poet's awareness of presumption in his endeavor, the fear that his poetry is a violation of the boundaries the gods set upon man. This muffled suggestion of fear, which could more adequately be called awe, echoes the explicit and literal "paura" (fear) that scans the opening lines of *Inferno* I (6, 15, 19, 44, 53). There is a significant difference between the fear experienced in hell and the awe felt in paradise. The fear in hell carries with it a moral overtone and is a sign of the pilgrim's spiritual confusion as well as of the beginning of wisdom. The intimation of fear at the beginning of paradise belongs to the sphere of an esthetic experience. In either case, however, fear and awe mark the beginning of knowledge.

In *Paradiso*, more precisely, fear and awe are the underpinning of Dante's sense of the sublime or, as he refers to it, *admiratio*. There is in this stretch of the text a paronomasia—a repetition of words derived from the same root—which one can put under the overall heading of *admiratio*. The pilgrim's imagination is overwhelmed by the novelty of the sound and light, and he feels, he says, "ammirazion" (98) (wonder); he is also amazed at the speed with which he moves through the region of air and fire (98). Beatrice expounds the order of the heavens and urges Dante to wonder no more—"non dei più ammirar" (136)—and she adds that it would be a "maraviglia" (139) (wonder) if he did not move in the heavens as fast as he did. The paronomasia of the word for wonder occurs again in *Paradiso* II as the text evokes the Argonauts' amazement at seeing Jason drawing a plow (16–18); the image, as we have seen in chapter 8, reappears in *Paradiso* XXXIII, 96, where Neptune is said to "ammirar" (wonder) at the shadow cast by Jason's ship.[42]

What does *admiratio* mean for the poetics of *Paradiso*? Philosophical and theological speculations derive their origins from the experience of *admiratio*. As Aristotle says in his *Metaphysics*, men begin to philosophize because of wonder: they wondered in their original encounter with a reality they could not comprehend, and then they made some advances about questions such as the origin of the universe. Knowledge, in short, arises out of astonishment for what one fails to grasp. St. Thomas Aquinas glosses Aristotle's insight into *admiratio* as the description of the state of mind in the presence of the fearsome grandeur of reality.[43] "Admiratio," Aquinas says in a different context, depicts what exceeds cognition and is itself a "species timoris." Dante fully understands wonder's cognitive status and makes it into an esthetic category. A trace of his awareness is available in the *Epistle to Cangrande*. A good exordium, the *Epistle* says in the wake of Cicero's *De inventione*, aims at making the listener well disposed, attentive, and docile; the author, the *Epistle* continues, "touches on the source of amazement when he promises to tell things as remote as they are sublime, namely the condition of the kingdom of heaven" (admirabilitatem tangit, cum promittit se tam ardua tam sublimia dicere, scilicet conditiones regni celestis).

In *Paradiso* this form of amazement does not lead either pilgrim or poet into the reveries of silence. The amazement, which later in the history of literature will come to be known as the sublime, designates a rhetorical construction—a strategy whereby the pilgrim's own amazement can be renewed for the reader. But the sublime certainly describes also the pilgrim's response to the unfathomable mysteries of the *mirabilia Dei*: the perception of the design of infinity and of the mystery in which the holy is wrapped does not leave the poet speechless. On the contrary, the mystery generates discourse and impels him to embark on a venture that will bring him and us into the nearness of God's presence, which, paradoxically, is also a place farther away from him. From this viewpoint, Dante is the very antithesis of St. Paul. The allusion to St. Paul's rapture to the Third Heaven (*Par.* I, 73–75) signals Dante's departure from him: whereas Paul keeps as inviolable the secret of his vision, Dante makes his journey to God the very subject matter of the poem.

In effect, the domain of theological discourse is made vaster by Dante's decision to push back the limits of Pauline silence. There are specific structural elements in Dante's poetry that would show how deliberately he seeks to push ever further back the temptations of silence and to articulate the infinite voices of desire. From a purely formal standpoint, to mention the most prominent aspect of the poem, the unfolding of the narrative can be said to hinge on a series of questions and interrogative sentences which are triggered in the pilgrim by a mixture of astonishment, awe, fear, and pity variously aroused by the souls in the beyond. To every question, Vergil or Beatrice provides an answer which, in turn, is superseded by other questions and by other doubts in an ever widening spiral of discourses, and all together they figure the pilgrim's ongoing itinerary of knowledge as a process of language.

This digression on the rhetoric of the sublime Dante deploys in *Paradiso* intends to suggest that it would be inaccurate to believe that *Paradiso* is merely a version of apophatic mysticism, the *via negativa* that calls for silence in the encounter with God's dark light. The language of *Paradiso* records the vanishing traces, written on water, of a quest for the divinity; it also registers the poet's prayer that this desire to see God may be fulfilled. We ought to recall a comment on prayer by Alan of Lille.[44] Grammarians, Alan says, understand *oratio* as a fitting ordering of words. Theologians consider *oratio* a disposition of the mind, "which is often stirred by words when it is sluggish." For Dante grammar and theology are constitutive of his poetry as it traces language's distance, theological language included, from God. As a trace, the poet's language—and from Adam's speech we can infer all language—is an allegory of exile, a figure of man's displacement into an alien world. This sublime dimension of Dante's poetry shows the ultimate irreducibility of the poem to the parameters of history.

Chapter 10

ORDER AND TRANSGRESSION

THE PREVIOUS chapter ended with a brief analysis of the beginning of *Paradiso*. I suggested there that as Dante is about to venture over the uncharted domain of the blessed, he casts his new and last experience in a language that suggests both his awe at the spectacle he beholds as well as his sense of transgression. The awe, I said there, is conveyed by the language of *admiratio* punctuating the exordium of *Paradiso*, while the transgression is suggested by the poet's prayer that Apollo breathe in him, "sì come quando Marsia traesti / de la vagina de le membra sue" (*Par.* I, 20–21) (as when when you drew Marsyas from the sheath of his limbs). The reference is to the Ovidian story of the satyr who challenges Apollo to a musical contest on the reed pipes but is defeated and punished by the god.

In this chapter, which also has a recapitulative function, I would like to explore further the kind of transgression that is meant by such mythical recall in *Paradiso* I. Is it an ethical transgression? And in what way can one talk of transgression, given the providential, God-willed nature of the pilgrim's journey in the beyond? Perhaps the parallel myth of transgression evoked in *Purgatorio* I can shed some light on the sense of the invocation to Apollo in the opening canto of *Paradiso*. In *Purgatorio* I there is a poetic invocation to Calliope, the muse of epic poetry (10–12). As the pilgrim starts in humility his purgatorial ascent, the poet reflects obliquely on the presumption of the nine daughters of Pierus, who challenged the muses to a singing contest and were metamorphosed into magpies in punishment for their *hybris*. The feared transgression of the boundaries of the divinity has another extension later in the same canto. On seeing the pilgrim cross alive the barrier of death Cato wonders whether the laws of the abyss were broken (*Purg.* I, 43–48). Vergil's reply is clear: the pilgrim and his guide have not violated the eternal edicts; a lady from heaven moves and directs them.

Such is the sense of extraordinary grace granted to the pilgrim, and so forcefully is it voiced by the poet that even to ask about transgression in *Paradiso* is likely to appear to be a willful blindness, a way of troping Cato's narrow vision and, in the process, missing the most decisive challenge the poet mounts to our commonplace world of moral constraints. What to Cato, and to us, may seem a transgression is for the poet, in fact, a way of underlining the scandalous difference between worldly experience and the extraordinary spiritual experience that is central to his visionary purposes.

Because the pilgrim is undergoing an ethical education in order to have a full revelation of his mission, he is no Ulysses or Adam trespassing in pride the boundaries of what is allowed to men. Yet the poet's own visionariness has by necessity an incongruous edge. In the spacious construction of the poet's mind there is figured a direct encounter with the divinity, and the encounter is perilous for man, who traditionally is overwhelmed, as Marsyas is, by the energy of the god. But the encounter between man and god is equally dangerous for the divinity, for its purity is likely to be defiled in the contact with the human world of time and language.

This concern figures prominently in *Paradiso* I. The poetic memory of Marsyas's transgression (which the poet transcends by propitiating and not challenging Apollo) overlaps with the poet's awareness of being at the edge of theological transgression and of undertaking a unique linguistic challenge. He does not know, only God knows, he says, whether he has traveled over the heavens in the body or outside of the body:

> S'i' era sol di me quel che creasti
> novellamente, amor che 'l ciel governi,
> tu 'l sai, che col tuo lume mi levasti.

(Par. I, 73–75)

(Whether I was that part of me which Thou didst create last, O Love that rulest the heavens, Thou knowest, who with Thy light didst lift me.)

The lines echo, as I have repeatedly pointed out in earlier chapters, St. Paul's account of his own rapture to the Third Heaven: "And I know that this man was caught up in Paradise—whether in the body or out of the body I do not know, God knows—and he heard things that cannot be told, which man may not utter" (II Cor. 12:2–4). Unlike St. Paul, who observes silence as a way of safeguarding the secrets of the divinity, the poet violates the principle that the sacred be shrouded in mystical secrecy. He acknowledges that "trasumanar significar per verba / non si poria" (*Par.* I, 70–71) (the passing beyond humanity may not be set forth in words), but he is steady in his pursuit of vision, even if memory cannot bring back from forgetfulness the "oltraggio" (*Par.* XXXIII, 57), as he defines the visionary experience of God.

The Ovidian and Pauline rhetoric of transgression in *Paradiso* I is in stark contrast, however, to the vast scheme of metaphysical order Dante begins to describe a few lines down in the same canto. Undoubtedly, order is the guiding principle of Dante's vision as well as the focal point upon which the tensions of his thought converge. In the light of this vision of order, one is compelled to ask what the point is in the language of transgression Dante conjures up. Transgression logically presupposes order: Is transgression subversive of order? Is it ultimately absorbed into the pattern of order? Or is there an alternative? And what exactly is the model of order in the poem? I would like to begin by examining Dante's model of order.

Since the term "order" is so general as to appear vague, it must be recorded at the outset that no exhaustive definition of the word is given by the *Thesaurus linguae latinae*, where the entry for *ordo* necessarily avoids a rigid and absolute explanation.[1] We are told, instead, that etymologically *ordo* has a material origin: it derives from the work of weaving, and it denotes a texture or the interlaced threads of a fabric. Such an activity, which properly describes the movement of the woof around the warp, engenders the added sense of a regular file, series, or catalog, that which the Greeks call *taxis*. From its material, concrete beginnings the word *ordo* came to refer with Cicero to an ordered state of reality, or to the divine order of nature and cosmos. In grammar *ordo*, and its equivalent *dispositio*, is a technical term for the syntactical arrangement of words in a sentence. This grammatical resonance accounts for the kinship between *ordo* and a number of concepts that have moral or esthetic values, such as *proportio, decentia, and pulchritudo*. The semantic range of *ordo* extends to cover the description—and this is certainly true for Dante—of the angelic hierarchy, of social degree, or of political-military rank (*ordo* and *gradus*).[2]

A lexical analysis of the word, however useful, will never reveal the complex imaginative interactions Dante hinges on the notion of order. A quick glance at the concordances of Dante's Latin or Italian works[3] will show that all these levels of meaning enumerated by the *Thesaurus* are available in Dante, but an organic, synoptic summary of the conceptual extension of "order" that would be significant for the *Divine Comedy* is rather to be found in St. Augustine's *City of God* (XIX, 13). After discussing the notion of *confusio* (Babylon) as evil, St. Augustine reflects on peace as moral order which the law of nature preserves through all disturbances.

> The peace of the body, then, consists in the duly proportional arrangement of its parts. The peace of the irrational soul is the harmonious repose of the appetites, and that of the rational soul the harmony of knowledge and action. The peace of the body and soul is the well-ordered and harmonious life and health of the living creatures. Peace between man and God is the well-ordered obedience of faith to eternal law. Peace between man and man is well-ordered concord. Domestic peace is the well-ordered concord between those of the family who rule and those who obey. Civil peace is a similar concord among the citizens. The peace of the celestial city is the perfectly ordered and harmonious enjoyment of God and one another in God. The peace of all things is the tranquillity of order. Order is the distribution which allots things equal and unequal, each to its own place. And hence, though the miserable, in so far as they are such, do certainly not enjoy peace but are severed from that tranquillity of order in which there is no disturbance, nevertheless, inasmuch as

they are deservedly and justly miserable, they are by their very misery connected with order.

This extraordinary passage encapsulates the essence of St. Augustine's all-
inclusive vision of order.[4] His manifest claim is that an intelligible coherence penetrates the diverse forms of reality. Even evil, or that which denies
order, is subsumed by a dialectics of contraries within the overarching harmony of the whole. The satanic transgression, the fall of man, every sin in
hell—the central events of the radical disorder in creation—all are part and
parcel of a preordained harmony. St. Augustine restates this principle that
everything converges in the totality of order, whose foundation is God, in
De ordine. In this abstract, metaphysical musing on order we are explicitly
told that nothing exists without reason and outside of God's order, that
there is a preestablished harmony, to use Leibniz's formula, an "occultis-
simus ordo" underneath the undeniable imperfections of the physical
world.[5]

Clearly, the principle of sufficient reason and its attendant optimism
presides over St. Augustine's conceptualization of order. The implications
of such a principle are far-reaching. It implies, first of all, that all things,
good and bad, proceed from a most perfectly ordered plan (*De ordine* II, vii,
24). By the same reason for which God wills that good things exist, he also
wills that evil things should exist. Within this perspective, evil is ultimately
illusory, or it has what can be called an ethical and aesthetic justification.
Evil is necessary, it is believed, for without it there would be no good and
no understanding of the good; it is thought of as necessary, though by itself
insubstantial, as a means to the good or, and this is the aesthetic rationale
for evil, as a way of highlighting the harmony of the whole, "for as a picture
is often more beautiful and worthy of commendation if some colors in
themselves ugly are included in it, than it would be if it were uniform and
of a single order, so from an admixture of evils the universe is rendered
more beautiful and worthy of commendation."[6]

Such a view, in which everything is in its necessary place, leaves no room
for individual choice; it leads instead to the idea (heretical) of determinism.
Dante's representation of the metaphysical construction of the cosmos in
Paradiso I carries evidence of his consciousness of this problematic dimension of the doctrine. The general outline of the canto is the following. The
pilgrim has just entered paradise. Signaling the marvels he witnesses are
the sound of the harmony of the spheres as well as the emanation of great
light—day, he says, seems added to day (*Par.* I, 61). As the pilgrim beholds,
bewildered, the sublime scene, he wants to learn from Beatrice how it can
be that he should pass through the light bodies. Beatrice explains:

> . . . Le cose tutte quante
> hanno ordine tra loro, e questa è forma

che l'universo a Dio fa simigliante.
Qui veggion l'alte creature l'orma
de l'etterno valore, il quale è fine
al quale è fatta la toccata norma.
Ne l'ordine ch'io dico sono accline
tutte nature, per diverse sorti,
più al principio loro e men vicine;
monde si muovono a diversi porti
per lo gran mar de l'essere, e ciascuna
con istinto a lei dato che la porti.
Questi ne porta il foco inver' la luna;
questi ne' cor mortali è permotore;
questi la terra in sè stringe e aduna;
nè pur le creature che son fore
d'intelligenza quest'arco saetta,
ma quelle ch'hanno intelletto e amore.
La provedenza, che cotanto assetta,
del suo lume fa 'l ciel sempre quieto
nel qual si volge quel c'ha maggior fretta; . . .
Vero è che, come forma non s'accorda
molte fiate a l'intenzion de l'arte,
perch' a risponder la materia è sorda,
così da questo corso si diparte
talor la creatura, c'ha podere
di piegar, così pinta, in altra parte.

(Par. I, 103–22; 127–32)

(All things have order among themselves, and this is the form that makes the universe like God. Herein the high creatures behold the imprint of the eternal Power, which is the end whereof the aforesaid ordinance is made. In the order whereof I speak, all natures are inclined by different lots, nearer and less near unto their principle; whereof they move to different ports over the great sea of being, each with an instinct given it to bear it on: this bears fire upwards toward the moon; this is the motive force in mortal creatures; this binds together and unites the earth. And not only does this bow shoot creatures that lack intelligence, but also those that have intellect and love. The Providence which ordains all this, with its light makes ever quiet the heaven within which revolves the sphere that has the greatest speed. . . . To be sure, even as a shape often does not accord with the intention of the art, because the material is deaf to respond, so the creature sometimes does depart from this course, having the power, thus impelled, to swerve toward some other part.")

This cosmological vision of order whereby all entities of creation cohere in a pattern or design of scaled values—the hierarchical principle of more and less—depends on the belief that God's providence has imparted every conceivable perfection to things. Providence is to be understood as the *ratio ordinis*, as St. Thomas Aquinas defines it in the *Summa theologiae*.[7] The assertion of a providential order in the *Divine Comedy* is not unwarranted. As a matter of fact, Beatrice's speech on the unity and variety of the cosmos recapitulates views Dante has shared with us and staunchly upheld all along.

When the pilgrim is in Limbo, he lists Democritus as the philosopher who "il mondo a caso pone" (*Inf.* IV, 136) (ascribes the world to chance). Democritus's philosophical conceit, which is traditionally coupled to the dark imaginings of both Lucretius and Epicurus, that the universe is made of atoms whirling by chance in a vacuum, forever on the verge of colliding, is acknowledged by Dante and quickly dismissed. Even the representation of the blind, random rotation of Fortune (*Inf.* VII, 70–96), which triggers a perception of the tragic fall of man into the inescapable cycles of time, discloses the principle that the wheel of fortune does not turn haphazardly but according to God's providential plan.

What is unusual in Beatrice's speech is that the universe is shaped according to a criterion of aesthetic and ethical order. "Ordine" and "forma" are two words to be understood in their technical sense as, respectively, *ordo*, a standard of beauty, and *forma*, beauty itself.[8] At the same time, this order of creation, as Beatrice says, is based on the principle of similitude ("this is the form that makes the universe like God"). In a way, the statement echoes the Neoplatonic doctrine of man as the microcosm reflecting the macrocosm. But Dante, who is always aware that resemblance can be an occasion for error, makes resemblance a fundamental category in the perception and knowledge of order. The created world is connected to its Creator by the laws of analogy of relations. This means that there is no univocal identity between creatures and Creator. The resemblance is a vestige, an "orma," God has impressed on the degrees of creation. In this sense, the order of the universe is embodied by the Platonic idea of the Great Chain of Being, the virtual bond that stretches continuously from the clarity of the realm of unity to the dimness of multiplicity. This Platonic sequence of beings, distributed according to a hierarchy of values, implies that things participate by analogy in the divine essence.

More to the point, Beatrice's spatial representation of the material universe is not a frozen, static image of order. On the contrary, the chief feature of her exposition is the insertion of a dynamics within the diversity and gradations of the scheme of creation. All natures, we are told, move to different ports over the great sea of being, as naturally as fire goes upward. The model for this ordered universal motion is undoubtedly St. Augustine's. In the *Confessions* (XIII) he explains the doctrine of the so-called *pondus amoris*, or weight of love. By this doctrine the Platonic Great Chain of Being turns into the Great Chain of Love, into the law of spiritual gravity, according to which all things, pulled by their own weight, return to their proper place.

> Our rest, St. Augustine writes, is our place. Love lifts us up to it, and your good spirit raises our lowness *from the gates of death*. In your *good pleasure is our peace*. A body tends to go by its own weight to its own place, not necessarily downward toward the bottom, but to its own place. Fire tends to rise upward: a stone falls downward. Things are moved by their own weights and go toward their proper places. . . . When at all out of their place, they become restless; put these back in order and they will be at rest. My weight is my love: wherever I am carried, it is my love that carries me there. By your gift we are set on fire and are carried upward. (XIII, 9)

St. Augustine's spiritual universe maps the displacement of the heart striving to regain its place in the ladder of love. The restless movement of all creatures, which St. Augustine describes through the motion of natural entities (stone, fire), cannot be taken in a literal sense, as if a place or the inclination to a place by each finite being were naturally predetermined. For St. Augustine, his Platonism notwithstanding, the motions of natural things are metaphors for the spiritual pull of the soul. More overtly than St. Augustine, Dante, who is aware of the implications of optimism and predetermination in the principle of plenitude he sees operating in the cosmos, tempers his own metaphysical optimism. The tempering occurs by the image of the possible reversal in the natural trajectory of fire as well as by his stressing the individual's moral freedom. The image he employs for man's moral freedom is the image of art: "even as a shape often does not accord with the intention of the art, because the material is deaf to respond, so the creature sometimes departs from this course, having the power, thus impelled, to swerve towards some other part: and even as the fire from a cloud may be seen to fall downwards, so the primal impulse, diverted by false pleasure, is turned toward the earth."

Dante, then, combines the notion of an eternal, objective preestablished order of creation, independent of the human will, with the sense of the man's immanent ethical autonomy. The paradox this structure of necessity and moral freedom entails is self-apparent, for in a harmonious metaphysical scheme, such as Dante's, ethical autonomy means the possibility only of man's transgression. A classical solution to this predicament consists in absorbing the notion of autonomy within a larger metaphysics of universal harmony. The solution has the clear advantage of eliminating the rupture, the radical contradiction, represented by human freedom, which inherently distorts and obscures the claim of constitutive order in the cosmos.

How does Dante avoid the contradiction? He avoids it by redefining the understanding of order. In his effort to preserve the common acknowledgment of man's uniqueness, of man's potential disharmony, and of the freedom of the imagination, Dante envisions order as dynamic and not static. The dynamics, represented in the guise of an ongoing unfolding of creation, recognizes the dialectical interaction between the exact boundaries and clarity of closed forms and the as yet incomplete role and perfectibility of finite man ready to transgress all bounds.

From the standpoint of an ongoing process of creation and redemption of man, this understanding of order clearly echoes the classical conception put forth by the Chartrians, such as Bernard Sylvester and Alan of Lille. Bernard, in the wake of Ovid's myth of creation, describes the shaping of primordial, formless Silva; Alan presents in his *De planctu naturae* the disfiguration of the natural order yet groaning for the restoration of harmony.[9] Yet for all the indebtedness to his two twelfth-century predecessors, Dante's idea of the dynamic order of creation goes beyond their representations. There is in Dante a theology of power or force systematically deployed. The very first line of *Paradiso* does not name God directly; it announces, rather, the manifestation of God as the light of his glory. The motion of this light dramatizes the power of God and casts God, more precisely, as the Aristotelian Prime Mover: "La gloria di colui che tutto move" (The glory of the All-Mover); he is acknowledged, again in *Paradiso* I, both as "etterno valore" (107) and "divina virtù" (22), which denote God's power. The term "valore" reappears as an attribute of Apollo in the prayer the poet addresses to the god: "O buon Apollo, a l'ultimo lavoro /fammi del tuo valor sì fatto vaso" (13–14) (O good Apollo, for this last labor make me such a vessel of your power).

It could be remarked that the term "lavoro," used for the poet's work, is practically a metathesis of the word "valor" (power), as if to suggest that the poetic work is the locus where God's power is transfigured and, so to speak, reelaborated. By this detail we are given a hint of a central concern of the poem. The language of canto I of *Paradiso*, as I have shown in previous chapters, suggests the modality of the poet's passivity; he listens and waits, as if he were an empty vessel to be filled with the gifts of poetic inspiration. Passivity seems to be the privileged state favoring or inducing contemplation, dream-visions, and prayer, which are the metaphoric sinews of Dante's spirituality and poetics. But the pun on *lavoro/valor* affords us with a complementary perspective on Dante's conviction that work, as both will and action, is the unavoidable other side of the various forms of contemplation. Force, however, is not merely a subjective problem. Throughout canto I of *Paradiso* Dante suggests the presence of the force operative in the order of creation by the parallel deployment of the Pythagorean theory of the harmonics of the spheres and the metaphysics of light.

The Pythagorean and Platonic account of the planetary orchestration caused by the whirling motion of the heavenly spheres according to mathematical ratios is explicitly mentioned in *Paradiso* I: "Quando la rota, che tu sempiterni / desiderato, a sè mi fece atteso / con l'armonia che temperi e discerni" (76–79) (When the revolution which thou, by being desired, makest eternal, turned my attention unto itself by the harmony which thou dost temper and distinguish). The metaphysics of light, on the other hand, is evoked in the very exordium of *Paradiso*. The periphrasitc construction for God (1–3) ("the glory of him who moves all and penetrates and shines throughout the universe more in one part and less elsewhere") joins, as has been suggested above, the Aristotelean conception of God as the Prime Mover with the Neoplatonic motif of the hierarchical order of the universe according to varying degrees of light and darkness. From the luminosity of the empyrean to the obscure materiality of the earth, all bodies are ordered according to their degree of participation in the common form of light. The Neoplatonic view of the continuous gradation of light suggests that light is an activity; it is the principle of action and motion in all things because it is forever capable of propagating itself on all sides. Consistent with this, Dante's poem distinguishes between *lux* ("luce" which is inseparable from matter) and *lumen* ("lume" as the energy radiated from *lux*).

This elaborate figuration of a cosmological, overarching order, which by its very flexibility makes room for the principle of contingency and process and which contains the plurality of beings, is logically translated by Dante into two further questions. One is the question of ethical order. The other is an epistemological problem that can be formulated as the question of the knowledge of order, in the double sense of the phrase: How is knowledge ordered, and what kind of knowledge do we have of order? I should like to examine these two issues by starting with the question of knowledge.

A good place to investigate Dante's conceptual representation of order is the Heaven of the Sun (*Par.* X–XII), which for Dante is also the Heaven of Arithmetic. In *Convivio* (II, xiii, 15–19) he draws a comparison between the sun and the luminous science of numbers:

E lo cielo del Sole si può comparare a l'Arismetrica per due proprietadi: l'una si è che del suo lume tutte l'altre stelle s'informano; l'altra si è che l'occhio nol può mirare. E queste due proprietadi sono ne l'Arismetrica; chè del suo lume tutte si illuminano le scienze, però che li loro subietti sono tutti sotto alcuno numero considerati, e ne le considerazioni di quelli sempre con numero si procede. Sì come ne la scienza naturale è subietto lo corpo mobile, lo quale corpo mobile ha in sè ragione di continuitade, e questa ha in sè ragione di numero infinito; e la sua considerazione principalissima è considerare li principii de le cose naturali, li quali sono tre, cioè materia, privazione e forma, ne li quali si vede questo numero. Non solamente in tutti insieme, ma ancora in

ciascuno è numero, chi ben considera sottilmente; per che Pittagora, secondo
che dice Aristotile nel primo de la Fisica, poneva li principii de le cose naturali
lo pari e lo dispari, considerando tutte le cose esser numero. L'altra proprie-
tade del Sole ancor si vede nel numero, del quale è l'Arismetrica: che l'occhio
delo 'ntelletto nol può mirare; però che 'l numero, quant'è in sè considerato,
è infinito, e questo non potemo noi intendere.

(And the Heaven of the Sun may be compared to Arithmetic on account of
two properties: the first is that with its light all the other stars are informed;
the second is that the eye cannot behold it. And these two properties are in
Arithmetic, for with its light all the sciences are illuminated, since their subjects are all considered under some number, and in the consideration thereof,
we always proceed with numbers; as in natural science the subject is the movable body, which movable body has in it ratio of continuity, and this has in it
ratio of infinite number. Its foremost object, however, is to research the principles of natural entities, which are three, that is, matter, privation and form,
in which one sees the presence of numbers. . . . Therefore Pythagoras, according to Aristotle in the first book of his *Physics*, gives the odd and even as
the principles of natural things, considering all things to be number, to which
Arithmetic belongs, for the eye of the intellect cannot behold it, for number
considered in itself is infinite, and this we cannot comprehend.)

The word "arithmetic" means, according to Hugh of St. Victor's *Didascalicon* (II, 7), the "power of number."[10] The passage from *Convivio* acknowledges the power of number as the foundation of knowledge, although Dante says nothing here of the traditional Pythagorean assumption
that number inheres in the fabric and very depths of the cosmos. The
phrase from the Wisdom of Solomon (11:21) that God has arranged all
things according to number, measure, and weight, as well as the Pythagorean statement "tolle numerum omnibus et omnia pereunt," came to crys-
tallize the belief that numbers have mystical values and that the *ordo* of the
cosmos is embodied by arithmetic.[11] Nonetheless, in this very Heaven of
the Sun and Arithmetic, Dante reconsitutes the order of the universe and
asserts the sovereign rationality of the cosmos. This order is, above all,
conceptual, in the sense that the order of the cosmos can be known with
mathematical clarity.[12]

Appropriately enough, Dante meets the wise spirits who have knowledge of God. Prominent among them are St. Thomas and St. Bonaventure, who give a eulogy of, respectively, St. Francis (*Par.* XI) and St. Dominic (*Par.* XII) and who between them reconcile love and knowledge (12).
But to see how arithmetic, which is a branch of theoretical knowledge,
figures in and shapes the abstract idea of order in the Heaven of the Sun,
one should look at some thematic and metaphoric concerns that run

through these cantos. *Paradiso* X, for instance, begins with the contemplation of the Trinity:

> Guardando nel suo Figlio con l'Amore
> che l'uno e l'altro etternalmente spira
> lo primo e inefffabile Valore
> quanto per mente e per loco si gira
> con tant'ordine fè ch'esser non puote
> sanza gustar di lui chi ciò rimira.
>
> (*Par.* X, 1–6)

(Looking upon his Son with the love that the One and the Other eternally breathe forth, the primal and ineffable Power made with such order all that revolves in the mind or space that he who contemplates it cannot but taste of Him.)

By the end of canto X, the harmony in the dance and song of the twelve blessed (and enumeration, it can be added, is the principle of composition in this area where the wise spirits triumph) is compared to the revolution of the spheres in a clock:

> Indi, come orologio che ne chiami
> ne l'ora che la sposa di Dio surge
> a mattinar lo sposo perchè l'ami,
> che l'una parte e l'altra tira e urge,
> tin tin sonando con sì dolce nota,
> che 'l ben disposto spirto d'amor turge;
> così vid'io la gloriosa rota
> muoversi e render voce a voce in tempra
> e in dolcezza ch'esser non pò nota
> se non colà dove gioir s'insempra.
>
> (*Par.* X, 139–48)

(Then, like a clock which calls us at the hour when the Bride of God rises to sing her matins to the Bridegroom, that he may love her, in which the one part draws or drives the other, sounding *ting! ting!* with notes so sweet that the well-disposed spirit swells with love, so did I see the glorious wheel move and render voice to voice with harmony and sweetness that cannot be known except there where joy is everlasting.)

The representation of harmony in this passage is conveyed through the notion of sweetness (*dulcedo* is a musical metaphor, as any reader of *De vulgari eloquentia* and *Convivio* recalls)[13] and, directly, through the word "tempra" (146), which denotes, as has been seen in chapter 8, the cardinal virtue of temperance as well as the measure of time. More precisely: the symbolic harmony figured by the clock in the Heaven of Arithmetic plays out Plato's doctrine in the *Timaeus* that harmony depends on rhythm, on the power of numbers or arithmetical relationships arranged by temporal intervals within the sequence of sounds.

If the clock metaphor signals explicitly the mathematical-musical correspondence between microcosm and macrocosm, it is equally clear why Dante should discuss the doctrine of the Trinity in the Heaven of Arithmetic. Traditionally, theologians such as Boethius and Alan of Lille had made extensive use of mathematical language to reflect on the inner relation of the Trinity. God is described as the *sphaera infinita*, the infinite, intelligible sphere whose center is everywhere and whose circumference nowhere.[14] He is unity and has no plurality, so that, as one reads in the *Regulae theologicae*, multiplied by itself he is one. "In the Father is unity," says Alan, "in the Son equality, and in the Holy Spirit a concord of unity and equality; and all these three qualities are all one because of the Father, all equal because of the Son, and all unities because of the Holy Spirit."[15] But the central reason why arithmetic, which deals with the infinity of numbers and with abstract quantity, is yoked to theological discourse depends on the fact that arithmetic is the rigorous science working by its own principles (*iuxta propria principia*). By pulling together theology and arithmetic, Dante seems to draw theology within the confines of scientific discourse.

The desire to invest theology with the appearance of scientific rigor was, as has been hinted, fairly common. From Boethius to Alan to Aquinas there is in the discourse of theology a systematic adoption of the Euclidean vocabulary of axioms, *regulae*, and demonstrations designed to make theology appear as a self-evident science, a *theologia rationalis*, as Evans refers to it, which would exceed the contingent rules of the other *artes*. The grammar of theology Alan of Lille seeks to devise transcends all secular arts, for the language of theology deals with the absolute realm of God.[16] But Dante's procedure in the Heaven of the Sun is somewhat different, for here he wills to represent as a living totality the various branches of all knowledge. This totality, as a matter of fact, is given as the harmonious correlation of traditionally contradictory views. In canto X the polymaths around St. Thomas range from the encyclopedist Isidore to Boethius (who authored books on arithmetic and music as well the classic *Consolation of Philosophy*) to Peter Lombard; from Solomon, whose books are traditionally seen as the embodiment of the whole range of *humana doctrina*, to Bede, who authored the *Nature of Things*, to the mystics such as Richard of St. Victor and Dionysius the Areopagite to the canonist Gratian to Orosius, Albert the Great, and Siger of Brabant. Among the spirits around St. Bonaventure in canto XII are the grammarian Donatus, the prophet Nathan, the logician Peter of Spain, the historian Peter Comestor, Rabanus, who in his encyclopedia, *De rerum naturis*, revises in an allegorical key Isidore's still classical arrangement of knowledge, a visionary such as Joachim of Flora, Chrysostom, Hugh of St. Victor, and Anselm. More than that, Dante wills to show the unity of intellect and will (and the interdependence of Dominicans and Franciscans exemplifies his plan) and to harmonize intellectual positions which on earth had appeared antagonistic (that of Bonaventure and the "heresy" of Joachim of Flora or that of Aquinas and the "heresy" of Siger).[17]

In the representation of the wise spirits we witness another version of Dante's figuration of the circle of knowledge.[18] These two garlands of spirits now dance around the Sun, as the apostles danced around Christ. The dance, like the chants of all the blessed, is the dance of knowledge and love, of knowledge as lightness and joy, that has reached the essence of beatitude.[19] From a formal viewpoint, this harmonization of contradictory doctrinal positions, the blurring of boundaries between the transgressions of heresy and orthodoxy, points to and revises the model of epistemological order operative in Dante, and partly treated in chapter 1. In the Middle Ages, beside the Bible, which is literally a *bibliotheca*, there were two formal structures organizing the diverse domains of knowledge into a systematic unity. One was the encyclopedia, such as Isidore's, Hugh of St. Victor's, or St. Bonaventure's. The encyclopedia was a symbolic compilation, a selective totality, to use an oxymoron, of the heterogeneous disciplines. The other modality was the *Summa*, such as Albertus the Great's or Aquinas's, which was a logical compendium of arguments and counterarguments aiming to define the cosmos as an ordered and intelligible totality, from metaphysics to the Trinity, angelology, ethics, and politics.

The relationship between these two modalities of representation of the unity and totality of knowledge was not without its strains. In a way, they stood for the classical opposition between erudition and speculation. The theologians, such as St. Thomas, who upheld principles of rational knowledge, effectively sought to dismiss the encyclopedists' version of knowledge as if it were an immobile anachronism, a hodgepodge of precision and whim. To the calcified fossils of science available in the encyclopedias, to the pseudototality of their representations barely concealing lacunas and omissions, to their overt antiquarianism disguised as a cultivation of the slow deposits of wisdom in time, the *Summae* countered with an idea of knowledge which was understood not as an aggregate of agreed-on, immutable topics but as the purity of intellectual speculation, as the mind's supreme quest for logical and systematic coherence. We have seen in earlier chapters how thorough is Dante's critique of Scholasticism because of what he perceived as its downplaying of the power and value of aesthetics and of history. Here we must stress his endorsement of this central strain of the Scholastics' style of thought, aware, as he no doubt was, that his was a time when Scholasticism's totalizing projects, embodied by the *Summae*, were hegemonic. But this was also a time when the encyclopedic mode came to full flower with the likes of Vincent of Beauvais, Brunetto Latini, Thomas of Cantimprè, and Bartholomeus Anglicus.

It is no surprise, then, that Dante should collapse in the *Divine Comedy* the historical opposition between the two modes, as he mixes in his representation biblical exegesis, Scholasticism, history, encyclopedic and mythographic lore, Plato and Aristotle, concrete Florentine politics, orthodox theological doctrines, and daring personal innovations. A precedent for this type of imaginative construction was certainly the Homeric encyclopedia, which Dante did not know but which induced Vico to link together under the common rubric of foundational poetry the two sublime poets of the past. Closer to Dante's own intellectual and experiential world were the cathedrals with their truly encyclopedic structures, texts such as *L'Ymage du monde* or the *Roman de la rose*, which Dante knew all too well in its broad range of moral, political, and doctrinal issues. And he was certainly mindful, as the multiple borrowings from Albert the Great's reelaborations of all the sciences show, that there need not be a disjunction between the erudite and speculative forms of knowledge.

As Dante puts forth his vision of the marriage of love and wisdom in these cantos, he lays out an ordered, formal outline of the method by which one arrives at the truth. He never explicitly distinguishes, as, say, Hugh of St. Victor does in his *Didascalicon*, between *order* and *method*. In the *Didascalicon* (III, 8–9) Hugh jots down the varieties of order, such as the order of the disciplines (from grammar through dialectics to arithmetic and music); the order of narration (which is described, in a fairly conventional manner, as natural and artificial); and the order, finally, in the exposition of a text (letter, sense, and inner meaning). To know the order of an entity, Dante says in *Convivio*, quoting St. Thomas, is a sovereign act of reason.[20] The method of expounding a text, on the other hand, is said to consist in analysis, moving from things which are finite and defined to things which are infinite and undefined. But we also learn by descending from universals to particulars.

Hugh's methodological self-reflexiveness, which is quite legitimate in this treatise on reading, cannot be said to be endorsed by Dante. The method or route of the *Divine Comedy* is certainly Exodus; but in cultural terms it resembles the model of education envisioned by another Victorine, Honorius of Autun, in that it maps the journey of knowledge through exile to the heavenly fatherland. *Paradiso* X–XII, more specifically, in the mathematical context of relational quantity and mobile magnitude, sketches the circle of knowledge as jurists and historiographers, grammarians and logicians, mystics and encyclopedists are brought together in the conviction that genuine knowledge is never an act of exclusion, limited computation, and measurement. The quantifiable order of knowledge is a relation which connects and entails all the disciplines of the curriculum in a circular movement which is embodied by the two dancing wheels of spirits.

How are the heterogeneous, discrete disciplines joined together? Isidore of Seville joins them through the systematic application of the grammatical principle of etymology. His underlying belief is that the origin of words, whether arbitrary or not, gives a privileged access to their sense. For Dante, on the other hand, what animates the totality of knowledge into an ordered whole made of discrete parts and, at the same time, rescues it from being a mere repository of dated, isolated fragments arranged through the fiction of alphabetical order is the power of metaphor and poetry to uncover hidden resemblances underneath ostensibly unrelated disciplines.

Paradiso XII reveals Dante's sense of the complications which arise in the constitution of order. In the canto the Franciscan Bonaventure tells the life of St. Dominic, the preacher who believes in the primacy of the intellect in moral choices.[21] Dominic embodies for Dante the conjunction of faith and knowledge, and this conjunction is dramatized by his mystical marriage to faith (61–63). This bond, which appears also as a union of doctrine and will (97) makes Dominic the champion of doctrinal orthodoxy: he is, as matter of fact, the "gran dottore" (85) in the midst of the heretics, who are those who choose to interpret faith according to their own subjective perspective. The description of Dominic as "the husbandman whom Christ chose to help him in his garden" prepares the account of his preaching to the heretics: his force, we are told, strikes on the heretical stocks ("li sterpi eretici percosse / l'impeto suo," 100–101). Order, it seems, is not the total harmony of existing viewpoints; rather, it is gained at the cost of excluding those who transgress the unity of order.

To be sure, Dante's idea of the heretics—sinners who transgress canonical norms by privileging subjective choices—is fairly complex. The heretics, whom in a philosophical sense he designates summarily as the Epicureans of *Inferno* X, are philosophical libertines and despotic warmongers: *Inferno* X, appropriately, is the canto of civil war and Frederick II. The Epicureans are traditionally linked to the atomists, such as Democritus, condemned for cutting the world to size. They simplify, in effect, the world of choice, for, ironically enough, they abolish choices in their upholding the hegemony of undifferentiated pleasure as the aim of life. Cicero's classical critique of the paradoxical ethics of the Epicureans, which I am here restating, holds good for Dante. Nonetheless, in the Heaven of the Sun Dante finds room for dissenters, as has been discussed earlier in this book, such as Joachim of Flora and Siger of Brabant: philosophical or doctrinal dissent is understood as a contingent, provisional experience which the canonical version of opinion has the power to absorb and legitimize. In the canto of St. Dominic, however, there is a less optimistic, less univocal representation of order. Dominic's force seeks to uproot the Cathars' heresy of love, and, consequently, his idea of order depends on what denies order most: violence. At the same time, the metaphoric language of the canto also suggests that order is to be understood not as an acceptance of the divisive subjectivism of heresy or diversified plurality but as mutuality of consent, which finds its epitome in the metaphor of marriage.

The order St. Dominic establishes is also represented in terms of grammar. At the level of its rhetorical structure, the canto is organized through what is called a *figura etymologica*: Dominic's own name is taken to mean that he is possessed by the Lord—"e perchè fosse qual'era in costrutto, / quinci si mosse spirito a nomarlo / del possessivo di cui era tutto. / Domenico fu detto" (*Par.* XII, 67–70) (And, that he might in very construing be what he was, a spirit from up here went forth to name him by the possessive of Him whose he wholly was. Dominic he was named). His father, Felice, we are told, was "veramente Felice" (79), and his mother was truly Giovanna, if the noun, being interpreted, means as is said (80–81).

The adoption of this grammatical principle in the Heaven of Arithmetic has some notable consequences. Grammar, or the prescriptive science of correct articulation, of the proper sequence and arrangement of words, appears as the artifice controlling the possible drift of language, the contrivance which guarantees a possible linguistic order. Relevant to the present conceptualization of knowledge is the fact that the order of grammar unveils the harmony inherent in any linguistic utterance. Harmony, in effect, comes forth through the necessary mutuality connecting the various parts of a sentence, when the sentence has to make sense. By the same token, the use of etymologies announces the existence of a substantial kinship, a mutuality, between words and their referents. A version of this kinship is made manifest in both cantos X and XII of *Paradiso* through the technique of *nomination*, which Dante deploys extensively. The wise spirits, in fact, are all duly named. The procedure of recording the names of the characters is all too frequent in the *Divine Comedy*: in Limbo, for instance, the catalog of names from the the world of classical antiquity (*Inf.* IV, 121–44) dramatizes the "onrata nominanza" (76) (honored fame) that is those spirits' reward. More than that, the proper names give their bearers an unequivocal designation and reflect their historical identity. It can be said that the proper name of a thinker is the point at which the contingency and history of the self converge with the history of thought. The grammatical order, then, is all encompassing: it establishes nominal identities and differences for the tabulation of knowledge; it extends into language the abstract order of arithmetic; it provides the ground for casting Dominic's prophetic language as the unity of words and reality.

The mingling of grammar and theology, so prominent in *Paradiso* X and XII, as it is in so many other places of the poem we have examined earlier, forces on us the unavoidable suspicion that the divine order is reducible to a question of linguistic propositions. A brief history of the relationship between the two disciplines will shed light on the implications of the problem. Theologians, from Boethius to Anselm and Alan of Lille, had long reflected on the epistemology of grammar and its relation to theology.[22] Boethius, for instance, complained about the *inopia verborum* in Latin theological speculations, while Anselm pondered whether or not words for God could be used in a proper sense, and whether or not words are unavoidably transgressive in theology. Alan of Lille, on the other hand, remarks in the preface to his *Distinctiones* that the language of the Bible cannot be measured in the light of rules codified by the *artes sermocinales*. The word of God, says Alan in the wake of Gregory the Great and Peter Damian, cannot be subjected to the laws of grammar—a phrase that had become, because of its lapidary quality, an emblem and recurrent perspective in the history of theology.[23] In the *Incarnation of Christ and the Seven Liberal Arts*, moreover, Alan focuses on the breakdown of both grammar and logic to account for the wondrous paradox of the Incarnation.

The event of the Incarnation shatters the possibility of logical and grammatical order, for Christ, the *verbum* and the *copula* between contingency and permanence, is outside of all rules. In God there is a beginning without a beginning and an end without an end; the Virgin is mother; God becomes man. Confronted with these radical paradoxes, grammar, which deals with rules of passivity and activity, cannot explain how action begets passions; arithmetic finds unity turning into something other than itself; logic discovers its fallacies. In short, "In hac verbi copula / Stupet omnis regula" (In the copula of the verb every rule is confounded). The liberal arts' quandary figures also in the *Anticlaudianus*, where the virginity of Mary dramatizes the rationally inexplicable event whereby nature falls silent, the force of logic is banished, rhetoric's judgment is destroyed, and reason wavers.

This sequence of paradoxes, which stand at the center of Alan's vision, punctuates the prayer St. Bernard directs to the Virgin in the last canto of the poem. Much like Alan, who in his *Anticlaudianus* describes Mary as the woman who is now like her own mother Eve before the Fall, Dante draws a picture whereby the pattern of theological order is a transgression of the order of the sciences; the Virgin is both the mother and a daughter of her own son; the circle of the geometers cannot be squared.[24] All this means that the discourse of theology, upon which the immanent paradigms of order are predicated, is itself a supreme transgression of the rules of grammar. Incarnational theology, in which the poem is rooted and from which the poem takes its imaginative energy, turns around all conventions and is the point of origin for Dante's representation of order.

In *Paradiso* I Dante calls up Marsyas's myth of transgression against Apollo. The shadow of the poet's own possible transgression looms at the start of *Paradiso* II as he claims the novelty, daring, and epic quality of his venture: "L'acqua ch'io prendo già mai non si corse" (7) (The water which I take was never coursed before). He proceeds, he adds, with the favorable breeze of Minerva behind his boat of poetry, with the guidance of Apollo, and with the assistance of the Muses, who uncover for him the map of the heavens. The gods are here duly propitiated. Yet the invocation of the pagan gods, for all the harmonization between poetic myth and Christian revelation effected over the last cantos of *Purgatorio*, forces on us the suspicion of a lingering tension between theology and myth. More precisely, the model for Dante's poetic enterprise in *Paradiso* is Jason's quest. From a moral standpoint, Jason, as a deceiver of women during the expedition of the Argonauts, is lodged among the flatterers and seducers in *Inferno* XVIII (85 ff.). His heroic quest, nonetheless, is recalled both in *Paradiso* II (16–18) and in *Paradiso* XXXIII (94–96), where the shadow cast by the *Argo* is said to trigger Neptune's *admiratio*. What is powerful and unique about this mythic configuration of Dante's visionary quest is its uncompromising, absolute quality. The pilgrim, who occasionally looks away from the horror of hell or covers his eyes when confronting danger, does not do so as he approaches the divinity.

In effect, the memory of Marsyas and the myth of the Argonauts stand for the Dantesque vision of poetry as simultaneously order and transgression. It is order in the measure in which it reflects the order of the cosmos, and in that it is governed by rules of grammar or the demands of the pilgrim's ethical education. It is transgression, not merely because metaphor in its various forms, such as *translatio*, catachresis or *abusio*, *usurpatio*, and so on, is intrinsically a violation of the literal, or because the artificial order of the narrative alters and violates the natural order of experience. Rather, and more fundamentally, poetry is transgression in the measure in which it unveils the poetic foundation of the world. It is transgression, finally, in that poetry—as the myths punctuating *Paradiso* tell us—is a form of audacious thought, the unavoidably dangerous path poets tread as they push the frontiers of vision beyond the turns of the common day.

In Ovid's poetry, say, transgression is, paradoxically, the norm, for it best captures the unpredictable, wondrous operations of nature or the equally unpredictable transactions between whimsical, cruel gods and men. In Dante's poetry, by contrast, order is paramount. Inseparable from it, however, are both the perception of a theological transgression at the heart of human constructions of reality and the idea that poetry, which gives shapes to that reality, is an imaginative foray beyond the barriers of ordinary knowledge. The poem scours all the imaginable and unimaginable violations of the special trust of love; it indicts all confusions of the secular and the sacred; it laments over history's darkest hours when all norms of nature and authority are flouted. But the poem brings us to the farthest limit of the human and also beyond the human. As it does so, it probes the depths of our historical memories; forges the language of our future; maps the path of our vision; shows us our divine goal; challenges us to it; extends the reach of the soul.

I began this chapter by sketching the presence of an option between transgression and order. The question was whether transgression is to be subsumed into a paradigm of order or whether order is subverted by transgression. I have reached the point where order and transgression no longer appear as merely antagonistic terms within the poetic and theological universe Dante forges. Each of them—order and transgression—ceaselessly entails the other in Dante's visionary poetry. I will conclude the argument by referring briefly to the ethical resonance this scheme of mutuality between order and transgression has in the *Divine Comedy*.

As is known, the system of punishment in hell depends on categories drawn from Aristotle's *Ethics*. This means that the regulative principle of conduct acknowledges the principles of nature and natural justice. The symmetrical balance of vices and virtues in *Purgatorio*, on the other hand, reflects the dependence of social bonds and values on the doctrine of love, which is not a libertine or epicurean doctrine (since this type of love a priori excludes freedom and the order of the polity) but is one of mutuality. The ethical core of the purgatorial doctrine complements the Aristotelian system, and both are certainly applicable to life on earth; together they constitute, as a matter of fact, the centerpiece of Dante's vision of world order. But there are other extensions in the poem to Dante's moral idea of order—questions of justice, peace, courtesy, and exile—which are available in the Heaven of Mars, which is also the Heaven of Music (*Par.* XV–XVII).

That Dante is a poet of justice hardly needs belaboring. But he is also a peace poet, and this needs a gloss. The tradition of peace poetry in Western literature is, to be sure, fairly skimpy. Poets—think of Bertran de Born, of Ezra Pound, of Dante himself in his *De vulgari eloquentia*—would rather write of a call to arms and theorize a poetics of war. (In our age think of Hemingway; at most they write of a farewell to arms.) More often than not, they celebrate victories or they dream of peace as an escape from the savagery of war. They rarely write of peace as the condition for life and the aim of life, and almost never, if one excepts Tolstoy, Isaiah, and the Gospels, of peace as a scandalous reproach to the ways of the world. Dante belongs to this tradition of scandal.

In *Paradiso* XV–XVII Dante encounters his grandfather, Cacciaguida, who had been a crusader at Jerusalem, which means *visio pacis*.[25] The strands of war and peace are entangled together: Cacciaguida has fought a war for peace, and yet Dante, who knows, as few poets do, the strife and the grief of the heart, entertains no illusion that the horror of violence, the tragedy of the civil war, the power of evil, will soon end. As he exposes and denounces all forms of violence—the violence of political interests, of desire, history, and even the violence involved in hermeneutical projects such as his own—Dante keeps his sight fixed on the hope for peace. From the perspective of this hope, a virtue that understands time as futurity, one grasps the depth, passion, and temper of Dante's vision of a world order, for hope is the reproachful theological virtue informing his belief in a providential empire that would unify and order the appetites of all men.

This hope appears in the cantos of the Heaven of Mars as a memory of the communal virtues of peace, humble and patient poverty, continence, the education of children; it also appears as courtesy and hospitality to be extended to the poet in exile: "Lo primo tuo refugio e 'l primo ostello / sarà la cortesia del gran Lombardo" (*Par.* XVII, 70–71) (Your first refuge and first inn shall be the courtesy of the great Lombard). Courtesy and exile, I submit, are more than mere facts of the poet's sorrowful future. Because they figure a life of need and of gratitude, while everyone else becomes ungrateful, angry and malevolent against the pilgrim-poet (64–66), courtesy and exile come forth as ethical virtues.[26]

Courtesy is to be understood in this area of *Paradiso*, where the pilgrim's future is foretold, as magnificence (85) and liberality (88–90)—sparks of virtue, as Dante says (83), which can be subsumed together under the general heading of what Aristotle and Aquinas call *eutrapelia*. *Convivio* (II, x, 8) records that the word *cortesia* resonates with a memory of the beautiful manners of the ancient courts, which now have become places of wickedness. Various cantos of *Inferno* have staged this moral concern of the poet. *Inferno* V, to recall the most blatant example, is the canto where the libertine pleasures of courtly love are represented. Through Paolo and Francesca we are enabled to grasp the world of the court as Chretien de Troye saw it in his *Chevalier de la charrette*: a dim world where heroism has become self-complacency, where heroes are no longer up to the new challenges and to their own fame as heroes, where great deeds have become remote legends, where desire is politics, for it is desire for the queen, and where adultery ratifies the sovereignty of pleasure. Canto V of *Inferno*, the most erotic canto of the *Divine Comedy*, is also the canto where desire and politics converge (the most prominent among the sinners, aptly, are queens whose sin entails the detruction of their cities).

In *Inferno* XIII, to mention another well-known canto, the court, the locus of the admnistration of justice and where the compiler of the *Book of*

Justice, Pier delle Vigne, worked, is a place of injustice, while, ironically, Pier delle Vigne's suicide is a violation of the very principles of natural justice which shape his legal thought.[27] In *Paradiso* XVII courtesy cannot be thought of as equal to the nettling evils of the age, and it is even less a seed for a new spiritual order. Most simply, courtesy is a ceremony of kindness, in its primary etymological sense, a gift of comfort extended to the discomfited mind of the exile.

Dante, Poet of the Desert focused on history as the locus of exile. I will add here that there is an ethics of exile, which rescues it from being exclusively a harsh punishment inflicted by warring factions on the presumed innocent. The imaginative model for this understanding of exile is Vergil's *Aeneid*. It is probably not well known that the book of the *Aeneid* Dante draws from with insistence is the third book, which deals with the Trojan hero's quest for a homeland and with the deluded hopes, which are quickly shattered, that Aeneas's intolerable experiences may soon be over. Book III of the *Aeneid*, in short, wraps the hero in the pathos of his great suffering. Ironically, it is later, after Aeneas has reached his promised land, that he turns into the epic warrior, with all the ominous shadows of destructiveness and violence the definition carries along. By contrast to this diminution of the hero's moral greatness in the war against the Italians, book III of the *Aeneid* casts his exile as the condition of moral life.

Dante compounds the autobiographical, personal experience of exile with the Vergilian poetics of exile, but he utterly transfigures the existential and poetic dimensions by his radical recognition that exile is the central experience of the religious imagination. The recognition that one is not where (and what) one should be is a most economical way to describe the unquiet heart rankled by its very being out of place. The dislocation, however, is not only theological; it is an existential experience, and in this sense it is part of an existential theology, for it involves the poet's own irreducible contingency, our history and our understanding of history. It comes from the memory of the Fall, and yet it does not concern the mere past at all; if anything, it concerns the future. The religious imagination looks forward to the future in the belief that there lies the promised new heaven and new earth. While it expects the apocalyptic future, it abides in the present with the clear-eyed and realistic awareness that patterns of order are necessary and yet fragile; that one is called to belong to the structure of the city and, at the same time, that one is to live like a stranger in that city; that one is in time and, in every sense of the phrase, out of time. The simultaneity of history and utopia is the heart of Dante's exilic poetry.

As the poet ventures into the unbounded space of exile, he calls for courtesy, hospitality, and comfort. These virtues constitute, plainly, an affective morality, in the sense that they show that harmony rests upon a mutuality of love, upon man's will to share in and create a world where the pieces of the broken present are pieced together. As always, Dante, who sees poetry as ethics, returns us to the riddle of history, to the burdens of time, to the truths of facts and not merely to the truths of reason. He returns us to the tangle and shimmer of private and public memories, longings, and promises. Here, in history and against history, he drafts his dazzling vision of our historical existence and bestows it on us: by his gift he asks us, in a metaphor that recalls and transcends the spinning of the Fates, to put the woof into the web of which he has set the warp.

Chapter 11

THEOLOGIA LUDENS

IN THE *Summa theologiae* St. Thomas Aquinas asks whether or not play can ever be a moral virtue ("utrum in ludis possit esse aliqua virtus"). He proceeds to probe the issue by reviewing, first, the position of St. Ambrose, who, on the authority of the biblical verse "woe to you who laugh now, for you shall weep" denies that any virtue can lie in playing games. St. Ambrose's position is confirmed by Chrysostom's belief that the devil, not God, sends us to sport. It is further supported by the opinion of Aristotle, who states in the *Ethics* (X, 6) that playful acts are not directed to any purpose beyond themselves and, therefore, no virtue is engaged in play. Thomas's response is that pleasure ("delectatio"), which is the aim of play, is a remedy for weariness of the soul. But as he allows for this kind of solace, Aquinas sounds some warnings. The first is to avoid jokes which are shameful or obscene. Just as we do not give children complete liberty to play, so the light of a sound mind should be cast on our very fun. This sense of propriety, good manners, and reasonableness is what Aristotle calls *eutrapelia*, a playful disposition which must always be consistent with the dignity of the subject. Since theology is about matters of the greatest moment, St. Thomas follows St. Ambrose in banishing jocularity ("iocum") from theology, though not from social converse: "Although sometimes decent and pleasant, jokes are abhorrent to the Church's doctrine and discipline, for how can we adopt practices not found in the Scriptures?"[1]

Eutrapelia is listed in *Convivio*, which is a text admittedly in the tradition of Aristotle's *Ethics*, as one of the eleven moral virtues Dante would probably have discussed had the treatise been completed. In *Convivio*, more precisely, *eutrapelia* is called a virtue which moderates us in our solaces.[2] But in the *Divine Comedy* there is hardly any room, predictably enough, for playful or humorous words or deeds to which to turn in order to soften the edge of attention. A small vestige of the virtue of *eutrapelia*, and of its spiritual limits, is possibly to be found in Limbo, the playground of classical wisdom, where Dante meets "la bella scola" (the fair school) of poets—Homer, Horace, Ovid, Lucan, and Vergil himself (*Inf.* IV, 94). The Latin "schola," from the Greek *schole*, retains what the etymology designates: the time and space of leisure and pleasant conversation. In this shadowed *locus amoenus* the pagan spirits' pastime is dignified and proper. The aesthetic principle of decorous discrimination as to what is or is not proper is announced by Dante's own lines: the poets, we are told, spoke together of things which were fitting for that place and of which it is now fitting to be silent ("parlando cose che 'l tacere è bello, / sì com'era 'l parlar colà dov'era," *Inf.* IV, 104–5) (talking of things it is well to pass in silence, even as it was well to speak of them there). The leisure of "humana conversatio," as Aquinas would call it, is the soul's provisional solace for the pilgrim, but for the poet it is a spiritual trap.[3]

Another humorous interlude occurs, in deliberate symmetry to the scene in Limbo, in *Purgatorio* IV, where Belacqua's ease, his unwillingness to undertake promptly the purgatorial ascent, moves the pilgrim "un poco a riso" (122) (a little to smile). Ease is definitely out of place in this metaphoric land of longing and unquiet hearts, just as good manners would have been incongruous in the harsh confrontations betwen pilgrim and sinners in hell. All in all *eutrapelia*, which as a social-moral virtue Dante finds important, is by itself spiritually inadequate in the beyond.

There is, however, in the *Divine Comedy* a pattern of figurations and concerns which dramatize how far beyond St. Thomas's prudence or constraint about play Dante's vision stretches. I shall argue in this chapter, as a matter of fact, that Dante takes to task the too literal terms in which Aristotle, St. Thomas Aquinas, or St. Ambrose discussed and bracketed the question of play. Play, for Dante, *is* the domain of pleasure, but it is, above all, the realm of aesthetics. The relationship I am positing between play and esthetics goes beyond the common aim of pleasure the two activities engender. Dante deploys the language of play for a large range of questions, and this chapter starts with an inventory of the significance play has in the *Divine Comedy*. We shall see, for instance, imaginative bonds between play and exile in classical, biblical, and patristic traditions; we shall focus, to anticipate, on play as a metaphoric and critical perspective on war and violence, as the embodiment of a comical vision, as a deluded image of triumph, and, finally, as an imaginative context for the beauty of divine creation. I shall leave out the question of Dante's linguistic playfulness, the creative inventiveness he displays above all in *Paradiso*, for the very good reason that this aspect has received considerable critical attention in recent years.[4] There is a necessary link between play and aesthetics, for the language of play—and this is the core of my argument—invests the world of poetry, and in general of aesthetics, with the values and attributes reserved for playful activities. Because play and art are tied together in Dante's understanding of the divinity, it follows that play for him cannot be taken apart from theology; more than that, in a radical departure from the opinions of classical theologians, such as Aquinas, play and theology are unthinkable except in their imaginative interaction.[5]

It must be stressed at the outset that nowhere in the critical corpus on the *Divine Comedy* do we find an extended, systematic exploration of what

I call *theologia ludens*. The reason for so striking a gap, it is fair to say, lies in the common perception of Dante as a stern moralist, as a poet of stark moods who subordinates the pleasure play entails to the majesty of moral ends. Such a perception is not entirely wrong. Dante's condemnation of impersonators, falsifiers of words and deeds, mimes, and actors in *Inferno* resembles the attack against spectacles, mimics, buffoons, jesters, and jugglers unleashed by Christian apologists such as Tertullian, Cyprian, and John of Salisbury.[6]

One may even recall, in this context, the harsh judgment of St. Augustine, who rejects all images as shadow figures of the Platonic cave and for whom the imagination is but a *fabrica idolorum*.[7] On the stage of reason, St. Augustine argues, there can be no place for the figments of the theater, for the fabulous theologies of a Varro or the integuments of ancient myth.[8] Accordingly, games are a spiritually dangerous activity: for this sense of danger one may remember, for instance, St. Augustine's dramatization of the Roman *ludi circenses*, where murder turns into a spectacle that entices his friend Alypius; one may even remember the robbery of the pear tree, also in the *Confessions*, which is at first cast as a mere boys' prank.[9] These games, far from being innocent diversions, are a steady focus of fascination for St. Augustine, for they trigger a moral crisis. It ought to be mentioned, however, that this banishment of the world of deceptive images and spectacles is not the whole of Augustinianism, for in fact there is an Augustinian theological aesthetics: the conviction, articulated in his *De musica*, that the realm of beauty is coextensive with the divinity.[10]

For all the complexity at the core of St. Augustine's thought, his perspective is in substantial agreement with the rigorism of the apologists such as Cyprian and Tertullian. A genuinely novel viewpoint vis-à-vis the apologetic tradition is that of St. Thomas Aquinas, who retrieves Aristotle's classification of *eutrapelia* as a moral virtue and thereby tempers the excesses of the earlier church fathers. The brunt of Aquinas's ethics of play, in truth, was made available by figures such as Guillaume de Conches and Hugh of St. Victor. In his *Didascalicon* Hugh devotes a passage to theatrics, which he lists as one of the seven mechanical arts along with commerce, agriculture, medicine, hunting, and so on. Theatrics, which is the science of entertainment, encompasses for Hugh acting, recitals, dancing, choral processions, wrestling in the gymnasia, racing on foot or by horse or chariot, songs and music at banquets, playing dice, and singing the praises of the gods in the temple. These entertainments are numbered among legitimate activities, for "by enjoyment the mind is refreshed; or, as is more likely, seeing that people necessarily gather together for occasional amusement, they desired that places for such amusement might be established to forestall the people's coming together at public houses, where they commit lewd or criminal acts."[11]

Hugh of St. Victor's broad definition of play as a therapy for social-moral ills and as an activity investing the sundry manifestations of art and diversion certainly stands behind Aquinas's understanding of the moral dignity of play. Such a definition, as will be shown, only partly shapes Dante's own insight into play. In fact, by itself it is but a reductive containment of Dante's perception of the centrality of play. Dante, for instance, is only too aware of Vergil's representation of the games played by the Trojans in Sicily on the anniversary of Anchises' death. In *Convivio* (IV, xxvi, 14), while giving a conventional allegorization of the *Aeneid* in the Neoplatonic tradition of Bernard Sylvester and John of Salisbury, he refers to the "giuochi in Cicilia" (Sicilian games) as the occurrence in which Aeneas loyally kept the promises he had pledged to his companions. In *Il fiore*, as the entry for "gioco" in the *Enciclopedia dantesca* records, the same word is variously used to mean a game, competition, or even deception and simulation. What I am suggesting is that Dante's vision of play certainly pulls together patristic, philosophical, and theological threads. This means that play for Dante entails physical games, social converse, issues of simulation and appearances, and, more centrally, questions of theology and aesthetics (creation as a work of art, music, beauty, etc.). In terms of the traditions of play, it must be added that Dante's vision transcends the above-mentioned strands in thinking about play, for he is aware of and absorbs the insights made available by the poets of more recent literary history.

As a poet, in fact, Dante wills to reverse the role *jongleurs* played as truants, as itinerant performers of troubadouric songs in the courts of Provence and Italy. This is not to suggest, however, that Dante's concern with play signals a lapse or escape into intellectual frivolity. On the contrary, his figuration of the world *sub specie ludi* stems from his vision that play, as an esthetic manifestation, is the activity that best uncovers God's deepest being. This vision is made possible by a poetic tradition which resonates with the voices of jugglers, the "sonatori, trovatori e belli favellatori" (players, troubadours and fine fablers) housed at the *Magna Curia* of Frederick II, as the *Novellino* reports;[12] with the monologues of the *giullari*, who are the descendants of the Roman mimes and who shape texts such as the *Ritmo laurenziano*, the *Ritmo cassinese*, the *Rime dei memoriali bolognesi*, and even the *Contrasto* of Cielo d'Alcamo; and with the language of the *poeti giocosi*, whose themes of the tavern, of gluttony (*gula*, from which the term "goliard" possibly derives), of boasts, games of dice, and so on, make them the counterparts of figures such as Primas, the archpoet of Cologne, Gautier de Chatillon, and of the poets who compose the *carmina burana*.[13] The opposition between Paris and Orléans, between philosophy and poetry, comes to the fore in their texts. It is their practice of poetry as play, albeit in a blasphemous vein, which is both the background of and the perspective for Dante's radical theological imaginings. The socially and morally marginal utterances of these poets, who are generally dismissed as buffoons, hangers-on, and vagrants, are crucial to the elaboration of Dante's own *Comedy*, and they foreshadow for him the Games of God.

The language of play in the *Divine Comedy* is not always so heavily charged, though it appears with high frequency throughout the poem and, with deliberate symmetry, in cantos XV and XVI of each canticle.[14] Why exactly these cantos should be textured by play metaphors will be evident later. For the time being, let me point out their figurative parallels.[15] In *Inferno* XV, to recall the most prominent instance, Brunetto Latini races to rejoin his fellow sinners, and in his footrace he looks like a winner, though, ironically, he is, like the rest of them, a loser. The scene is imaged by a reference to the annual running game held in Verona: "Poi si rivolse, e parve di coloro / che corrono a Verona il drappo verde / per la campagna; e parve di costoro / quelli che vince, non colui che perde" (121–24) (Then he turned about and seemed like one of those that run for the green cloth in the field at Verona, and he seemed not the loser among them, but the winner).

The play metaphor, no doubt, conveys Brunetto's delusive triumph and, beyond that, the deluded sense he has of himself as the precursor. It also turns around, I would like to suggest, St. Paul's figuration of his life an an athletic contest. In II Timothy 4, while false teachers, teachers who suit their likings, are exposed, St. Paul summarizes his life's work: "The time of my dissolution," St. Paul writes, "is near. I have fought the good fight. I have run the full distance, and I have kept the faith. And now there is waiting for me the prize of victory awarded for a righteous life." If the Pauline gloss ironizes the claim of Dante's own teacher, there is another ironic contrast to Brunetto, which is also articulated through a play image. In *Paradiso* XVI, Cacciaguida, the athlete of Christ, mentions the last ward reached during the Florentine "annuale gioco" (42) (annual game) to evoke his own birthplace. Unlike Brunetto, Cacciaguida mentions the spot not as the triumphant finish line for his race but as a point of departure to go with the crusaders to Jerusalem.

The oblique link in *Paradiso* XVI between games and war (Cacciaguida is in the Heaven of Mars and was a martyr at the crusade) is found also in *Inferno* XVI. The pilgrim has just left Brunetto, and, while he is still in the ditch of the sodomites, three Florentines recognize him as a fellow citizen. The first of the three sinners is Guido Guerra—and his name could hardly have been more emblematic of his life lived "col senno assai e con la spada" (39) (with much counsel and with the sword). The line, one might add, crystallizes the traditional attributes of the hero, *fortitudo et sapientia*, and it announces the theme of "cortesia e valor" (67) (courtesy and valor) as aristocratic virtues which have been tragically superseded, Dante goes on to say, by the bourgeois, mercantile ethos of sudden gains (73ff.). The other two sinners are Tegghiaio Aldobrandini, who was involved in the defeat of Montaperti, and Iacopo Rusticucci, and all three of them are embodiments of civic values. As the three sinners approach the pilgrim, they make a wheel of themselves, "qual sogliono i campion far nudi e unti" (22) (as champions are used to do, naked and oiled).

The epic simile, which Boccaccio and Benvenuto da Imola explain respectively as the ancient "lutta" and public wrestling taking place in country feasts, recalls the wrestling bout Vergil describes in *Aeneid* III, 279–82.[16] The Trojans, so Aeneas tells Dido, have been journeying over the distant lands of Thracia, Crete, Delos, and the land of the Strophades, and have now reached Leucata. In Leucata they give offerings to the gods and hold ritual games. "My comrades strip naked: sleek with oil, they try their strength in Ilian wrestling matches, glad to have slipped past so many Argive towns." The games the weary Trojans play are certainly an interlude to the ordeals of their exile; through them, just as in the games held on the anniversary of the death of Anchises in book V of the *Aeneid*, they figure their nostalgia and hope for a life of ease. In the games of book V, to be sure, violence disrupts the illusion of tranquillity and of persistent heroics the Trojans' exercises are meant to dramatize. Their women, as a matter of fact, burn the ships while the soldiers are busy reenacting the gymnastics and bouts they were wont to practice on the plains of Troy and still look forward to deploying in future heroic confrontations.

The games for these heroes are a symbol of their nostalgia for the past as well as a spiritual preparation for battles that lie ahead. But for the women the games signify a different reality. By burning the ships they resist and renounce the violence and death they see lurking in their future as they quest for their promised land. The games on the anniversary of Anchises' death tempt the women into the illusion that the joyful experience of play can become a concrete, lasting reality in which men and women will abide and from which they will not escape. There is a grandeur, no doubt, in the women's desire for a peaceful existence, in their desire to change play into reality. But Vergil also allows us to see how deluded the women are in their wish. The games the men play signal for their women their desire to forget death; or, to say it differently, they wish to commemorate death, Anchises' death, but as if death were an event of the past, so that they can go on with the business of ordinary living. By their act of violence, which is meant to stop the men's dreams of war, the women come forth as impatient utopists, for they yield to the equally alluring dream of the idyllic world of play. The actions of the women and men in book V of the *Aeneid*, then, dramatize two opposed versions of history and utopia. The men view their present as an interlude between a heroic past in Troy and a promised golden future in Italy; the women want to live in an eternal present, but, by that very choice, they foreclose time. What has to be stressed from the viewpoint of the present concerns, however, is that play in the *Aeneid* is simultaneously a mark of exile and utopia.

An oblique gloss on the imaginative link between war and games in the *Aeneid* and in *Inferno* XVI is available in Isidore of Seville. Book XVIII of his *Etymologies* is devoted to the question of "de bello et ludis" (war and games). The two activities are joined by their common competitive aim, yet they do not belong to the same moral space. After reviewing various types of war (just and unjust wars, civil war, battles, etc.), Isidore examines the etymology of *ludus*. The games ("ludi") originated, he says, from Lydian refugees who reached Tuscany guided by Tyrrenus when the civil war with his brother was over.[17] But in *Inferno* XVI the civil war has not ended. The athletic metaphor for these sinners, thus, announces as illusory their belief that theirs is still the heroic age, that theirs is the epic world of the *Aeneid*. The metaphor also hints that, as in the *Aeneid*, play is a provisional mask hiding the violence of war.

Play metaphors do not simply figure, however, in such a fragmentary way as symbolic, discrete counters to various moral experiences or as emblems of agonic contests. In *Purgatorio* XV, in a language resembling Hyginus's *Poetica astronomia*, the yearly revolution of the sun across the sky, which dodges now to one side now to the other of the equator, is called the circle that plays like a child—"che sempre a guisa di fanciullo scherza" (5). The metaphorical bond between astronomy and play indicates that play is more than a moral question whose value is to be determined (though it certainly is also that); it is the essence of the workings of the cosmos and of God's creation. This same insight into the metaphysical value of play is dramatized again in *Paradiso* X. The stars, as indicated in the previous chapter, dance around the sun the way the apostles, according to the apocryphal Acts of John, danced around the Savior.

The play activity of God emerges explicitly in *Purgatorio* XVI, where Marco Lombardo explains to the pilgrim the origin of evil. Evil does not originate in the stars but in man's own moral conduct. At the moment of creation, Marco says, the soul issues forth from her Maker's hand like a child who is later led astray by false pleasures:

> Esce di man a lui che la vagheggia
> prima che sia, a guisa di fanciulla
> che piangendo e ridendo pargoleggia,
> l'anima semplicetta che sa nulla,
> salvo che, mossa da lieto fattore,
> volontier torna a ciò che la trastulla.
>
> (*Purg.* XVI, 85–90)

(From His hands, who fondly loves it before it exists, comes forth after the fashion of a child that sports, now weeping, now laughing, the simple little

soul, which knows nothing, save that, proceeding from a glad Maker, it turns
eagerly to what delights it.)

In the economy of the narrative, this idyllic picture of the soul's creation,
which in *Purgatorio* XXV is represented in terms of the creation of art, is in
sharp contrast to the confusion of the world Marco Lombardo goes on to
evoke. More to the point, the harmonious playfulness binding the Creator
to his creatures is a miniature representation of what is called *theologia
ludens*, the view of God as a playmaker waiting for the soul to return home
to play.[18] The return of the soul, which is a transparent allusion to the
Platonic motif of the *reditus animae*, has the delight of play as the reward
God grants. To think of play as constitutive of the divinity implies some
historical questions as well as a number of theological corollaries, to which
I now turn.

In historical terms the play metaphor, as has just been implied, is Platonic as well as mythical, while its biblical components are less evident but
no less important. The myth of the feast of the gods—the gala of pleasures,
conviviality, and laughter on Olympus—is certainly a strain in the imagination of *theologia ludens*.[19] And although the feast is a radically Christian
experience, in that every day is a holy day, there is very little play (but songs
and dances are less infrequent) in the Bible. It is as if play and exile, unlike
in the *Aeneid*, were mutually exclusive in biblical history. The Jews, we are
in fact told, hung up their lyres on the willows, for how could they sing the
Lord's song while dwelling in a foreign land? The story was even told in
the Middle Ages about the musings of a theologian, Petrus Cantor, as to
whether Christ ever laughed.[20] There are, nonetheless, sporadic passages
in the Bible that disrupt or shed light on what seems to be the uniformly
high seriousness of the Judaic ethos. Isaac, whose name is etymologized as
laughter, was seen playing with Rebecca; there are, as I said, occasional
joyous dances and songs; and at least two passages are the ground in which
the idea of *theologia ludens* is rooted. The first is from Proverbs 8:27–31:

> When he established the heavens, I was there,
> when he drew a circle on the face of the deep,
> when he made firm the skies above,
> when he established the fountains of the deep,
> when he assigned to the sea its limit,
> so that the waters might not transgress his command,
> when he marked out the foundations of the earth,
> then I was beside him, like a master workman;
> and I was daily his delight,
> rejoicing before him always,
> rejoicing in his inhabited world
> and delighting in the sons of men.

The second passage, which inspires one of Dante's examples of humility in *Purgatorio* X, is from II Samuel 6:5, which tells of David dancing before the ark: "And David and all the house of Israel were making merry before the Lord with all their might, with songs and lyres and harps and tambourines and castanets and cymbals."

These two biblical passages were pulled together by both Greek and Latin church fathers to convey an insight into divine creation as an aesthetic construction shaped by a playful God. Tertullian, who, as was pointed out earlier in this chapter, judged harshly man's indulgences in theatrics, still proclaimed the principle of the Games of God. His *Liber de spectaculis*, which became also the title for Cyprian's own opuscule, is a systematic synopsis of Roman *ludi*, theater (*res scenicas*), pagan literature, and all forms of idolatry to which he opposes the truth of the *spectaculum domini*. Divine Wisdom, Tertullian says, "orders the world with him," and the word he uses is "modulare." Gregory Nazianzen crystallizes the aesthetic-theological speculations as he writes that "the Logos on high plays, stirring the whole cosmos back and forth, as he wills, into shapes of every kind."[21] More precisely, a mystic of Clairvaux, whose thinking is in the mold of St. Bernard, casts Jesus as a harlequin, as the Lord of the Dance, and writes of Jesus as the "dancers' master," who has a great skill in the dance—"he turns to the right and turns to the left"—and all must follow the deftness of his teaching.[22]

From a substantial point of view, barely hidden in Dante's metaphor of play is the metaphysical conviction that the creation of man and of the universe is not an act of necessity, the consequence of inexorable Tyche, but one of free, spontaneous choice. This point is also borne out by the textual fact that *Purgatorio* XVI is the context in which Marco Lombardo unequivocally asserts man's free will. At the same time, the view of *Deus ludens* makes play a *sacer ludus*, a sacred activity, which, as such, puts work in a different perspective from the conventional one. From the perspective of God as Playmaker, it can be said that work is no longer the telos of life; play, rather, is both the foundation and the aim of life. Further, as the creation of the soul is grounded in God's play activity, this view of God means that to play is to accept rules established by God; it also means that man is not to play God, but to be content with God's play as he lets the soul play.

It is well known that Plato refers to man as the "plaything" of God. The definition signals that man's nobility, indeed the highest perfection within a creature's grasp, is available to man when he is engaged in play. The human soul is truly successful in its process of *paideia* when it grasps the state of freedom, which is the essence of the experience of play as well as of the education of the spirit. But this is not to say that human beings are mere marionettes, as the aging Plato would come to believe in the *Nomoi*.

For Dante, more to the point, the soul of man is neither a toy in the hands of the gods nor is it a spectator in the divine game of the Logos, whom many call chance, with no part to play in a scheme of things that transcends him.

The epithet Marco Lombardo uses in his speech to qualify the soul, "semplicetta" (*Purg.* XVI, 88) (little simple), allows us to perceive a somewhat different story. A thick moral darkness, Marco says, has descended on the world, although an inner light of judgment is given by God to human beings. It is in this darkness that the simple soul comes to be. The word "simple" designates the soul primarily as an entity without guile or deceit. In strictly theological terms, however, simplicity is the attribute of the divinity, in that God is the Good, which alone is simple and (therefore) unchangeable. Only those things which are truly divine are called simple, because in them quality and substance are one and the same. In short, the epithet of the soul's simplicity suggests the substantial likeness between the soul and God. The sense of this identity is explained by St. Augustine, among others, who in the *City of God* writes that "the immaterial soul is illumined with the immaterial light of the simple wisdom of God, as the material air is irradiated with material light."[23] He also adds that just as the air, when it is deprived of this light, grows dark, so the soul, deprived of the light of wisdom, grows dark. For St. Augustine as well as for Dante, the original likeness can dim into dissimilitude, or, to say it differently, man can choose to be like the angels or to be God's antagonist, which puts him in touch with the devil. The metaphysical world of play in the *Divine Comedy*, as will be seen now, is primarily the space of performance for demons and angelic intelligences.

The place where the joy of divine play is experienced, predictably enough, is *Paradiso*, which is thoroughly organized and represented through play metaphors. The domain of play, as has been suggested earlier, is vast, and it involves the most disparate aesthetic manifestations. The symbolic representation of God's cosmos occurs through esthetic phenomena: the music of the spheres, accordingly, is heard in paradise; the heavenly city is a garden of delights as well as an amphitheater; the blessed sing and dance; the universe laughs; the heavens themselves rhythmically whirl around the divine being; stars dance and woo each other with a weight of love that keeps the universe from falling asunder. These play activities are a sign of the pleasures of beatitude; they are also the various dimensions of aesthetic beauty, whose aim, like that of play, is pleasure. Against a theological tradition, such as that of St. Thomas Aquinas, which banishes play and aesthetics from the sovereign discourse of theology, Dante shows that the essence of the divinity, as we now are going to see, can be grasped through art.

That aesthetics, as the disinterested, playful activity which makes available the beauty and pleasure of creation, is the structuring principle of

Paradiso is suggested at the very outset of the text. The very first words of *Paradiso* I, "La gloria di colui che tutto move" (The glory of the All-Mover), draw attention to what Hans Urs von Balthasar has called *The Glory of the Lord*, to the idea that the epiphany of the Lord, the revelation of the depth of God's being, is an aesthetics of God's light and splendor. As a way of gauging the implications of these aesthetic claims for theology, a preliminary question is in order. Can one speak of aesthetics in the Middle Ages? Because in the Middle Ages, as is by now known, one cannot find sustained treatises on the autonomy of beauty, on subjective aesthetic judgments and taste, it has been repeatedly said that the period did not produce a genuine theory of aesthetics. It has been increasingly clear, however, that at no time was philosophical thinking more permeated by aesthetic concerns than it was then. The universe—for the theologians and the church fathers alike—is an implicit aesthetic construction built with mathematical rigor. Its symmetrical arrangement and harmonious relations are conveyed by the verses from the *Book of Wisdom* which I explored in a different context earlier in this book: "You have made everything in measure, in weight and number." More to the point, the fathers speak of the aesthetics of the human body,[24] while Chalcidius speaks of the incomparable beauty of the world and Honorius of Autun finds that the world is constructed like a lyre.[25] These examples can be multiplied, yet they are tangential and give only a glimpse of the question at hand. The thought of the Victorines, however, with their focus on light, sound, and color, as well as the complex speculations on beauty by Albert the Great, St. Thomas Aquinas, and St. Bonaventure decisively display how large the aesthetic faculty looms in metaphysical and ethical questions.[26]

Aquinas's assertions on beauty, its threefold properties of *claritas* (radiance), *consonantia* (which is proportion and order), and *integritas* (the perfection of being), are too well known to be detailed here.[27] And equally well known is his understanding of form (the *splendor formae*), the inner essence that shines through and gives an intelligible shape to the phenomenal materiality of objects. What is probably less well known is that St. Thomas can sound remarkably like Plato or Plotinus when he reflects on beauty. "Without beauty, what would become of being?" wonders Plotinus. For St. Thomas, beauty—as a definition, he says "pulchra enim dicuntur quae visa placent" (those things are called beautiful which please us when they are seen)—is a transcendental category;[28] it is the formal perfection of being and the quality that makes an essence appear for immediate perception and pleasure.

In the *Commentary on the Divine Names*, a text by the pseudo-Dionysius that became the focus of extended meditations for Scotus Eriugena and Albertus Magnus as well as a Victorine such as Hugh, beauty is the attribute of the person of the Son and, along with *bonum* and *verum*, it is one the names of God.[29] For Aquinas this transcendental notion of beauty,

whereby God finds all things beautiful, makes problematical any talk about
aesthetic beauty, which deals with contingent, subjective perceptions.
Dante's poetic thinking, on the other hand, claims the preeminence of the
cognitive value of *aisthesis*, as he makes available in the space of his representation both the bewitchment of beauty, in *Inferno* and in *Purgatorio*, and
the *paideia* of beauty, the goodness of beauty, or *kalokagathia* in *Paradiso*.

At a doctrinal level this doubleness of beauty is kept rigorously distinct
in the *Divine Comedy*, especially as Dante represents angels and devils. In
Inferno XXXI the pilgrim encounters the giants, who are the offspring of
fallen angels copulating with daughters of men. In this topsy-turvy world
that parodies the hierarchical order of Paradise, the giants are intermediate
beings in a scale of evil that finds in Lucifer its epitome. There is no trace
now in Lucifer of his original beauty and splendor, and the line that describes him, "La creatura ch'ebbe il bel sembiante" (*Inf.* XXXIV, 17) (The
creature who had the fair look), seals the loss of Lucifer's pristine beauty.
The emphasis on the lost beauty of Lucifer is also present in the description of the giants in *Inferno* XXXI. Dante compares, in fact, the face of
Nimrod, the proud builder of the Tower of Babel, to the huge bronze
pinecone that stood in Rome, and he adds that his other bones were "a sua
proporzion" (60) (in proportion to the face). The word "proporzion" is to
be taken in its specific aesthetic sense, since proportion, as Aquinas has it,
is one of the three requisites of beauty.[30]

This oblique allusion to the beauty of Nimrod is not, in and of itself,
Dante's own innovation. As a matter of fact St. Augustine in *The City of God*
remarks exactly on the beautiful appearance of the giants: "And it pleased
the Creator to produce them, that it might thus be demonstrated that neither beauty, nor yet size and strength, are of too much moment to the wise
man, whose blessedness lies in spiritual and immortal blessings, in far better and more enduring gifts, in the good things which are the peculiar
properties of the good, and are not shared by good and bad alike. It is this
which another prophet confirms when he says "These were the giants,
famous from the beginning, that were of so great stature, and so expert in
war."[31] In the *Divine Comedy*, however, Nimrod's is a grotesque beauty, an
extinct art of Nature: "Natura certo, quando lascio' l'arte / di sì fatti ani-
mali, assai fè bene / per torre tali essecutori a Marte" (*Inf.* XXXI, 49–51)
(Nature assuredly, when she gave up the art of making creatures such as
these, did right well to deprive Mars of such executors). The giants' gro-
tesqueness is a case of what can be called the medieval sublime, for it engenders horror and fear in the pilgrim (39, 44), just as in the past the giants
frightened the gods (95).

By contrast, *Paradiso* XXVIII and XXIX, which focus on angelology,
feature a world of order and play created and established by God for the
spirits. The "ordine," which Dante emphasizes in *Paradiso* XXIX, 31,

translates "ordo," which is a term for beauty, as the previous chapter has made clear. The word designates both an aesthetic *and* a theological-moral conception, and Dante binds the two—aesthetics and theology—together. Before discussing, however, the radical implications of this conjunction, we must look at the doctrinal aspects of Dante's speculations on the angels.

The poet's speculations, as a matter of fact, are placed within the Neoplatonic theory of the plenitude and continuity of God's creation, the so-called Great Chain of Being, which translates rank into value and which posits the necessary presence of intermediate hierarchical grades between the oneness and simplicity of God and the materiality of contingent forms. The mettle for these ideas is the pseudo-Dionysus's *Celestial Hierarchy*, in the light of which, as is well known, Dante corrects the views on angels held by St. Gregory the Great and Dante himself in *Convivio*.[32] As a followup to this doctrinal self-correction Beatrice proceeds to discuss in *Paradiso* XXIX the nature and function of the angelic intelligences. Her exposition is punctuated by the language of play and dance, which is not merely a technique; it is the perspective from which Dante mounts a critique of the major theological and philosophical conjectures on angelology.

The essence of the divine act of creation is restated by Beatrice in terms of God's pleasure, not necessity. Time, we are told, began with the creation of the material universe, when the eternal love, "come i' piacque" (*Par.* XXIX, 17) (as he pleased), opened in "nuovi amor" (18) (new loves). The opposition in the same line 18 between "nuovi amor" and "etterno amore" (eternal love) reflects on itself, and thus effectively discards the Averroistic doctrine of the eternity of the world, which Averroes accepts on the authority of Aristotle's *Physics*. The opinion that the world is eternal and the concomitant belief that there never was a first man were condemned as heretical by Bishop Tempier in 1270. This proposition, it can be added, saw the two major exponents of thirteenth-century theology on opposite sides of the question. St. Thomas Aquinas knew that the eternity of the world, asserted by Averroes, could not be philosophically demonstrated. Although he allowed that such may indeed be the case, he chose to follow Albert the Great's belief in creation ex nihilo. St. Bonaventure, on the other hand, took Averroes' position head-on. Against Averroes, Bonaventure believed that the creation of the world could be rationally demonstrated, while the notion of an eternal world (*productio ex nihilo*) is self-contradictory and absurd: since the number of souls is finite, St. Bonaventure argued, it follows that the universe must have had a beginning.[33]

These doctrinal disagreements over the eternity of the world extend to the debate on the nature of angels. The debate, actually, is the watershed between Christian philosophy and pagan conceptions because the assumptions of an intelligible universe hinge on it. Philo Judaeus speaks of pure spirits peopling the air, who are called demons by the philosphers and angels by Moses. Porphiry and Iamblichus count angels among the demons, while the pseudo-Dionysius holds to the total incorporeity of the angels. Dante upholds here the view of immaterial angels, whom he calls "puro atto" (*Par.* XXIX, 33) (pure act), whereas matter, which for Dante is pure potentiality (34), lies at the foot of the ladder of creation.

The theory of the angels' absolute transcendence, which to Petrus Olivi seemed to make pagan deities out of these separate substances, is Aristotle's and Averroes'.[34] My point is that the conviction, predominant among scholars, that Dante is steadily and systematically engaged in the *Divine Comedy* in repudiating Averroistic principles of philosophy certainly needs correction. At times, as here, he does endorse Averroistic ideas. In this context Dante's major agreement with Averroes comes to the fore, let me add, as he identifies the angels with the intelligences that move the spheres. The angels' perfection, in fact, lies in the performance of such an operation: "non concederebbe che 'motori / sanza sua perfezion fosser cotanto" (*Par.* XXIX, 44–45) (It would not admit that the movers could be so long without their perfection). Finally, at a doctrinal level Dante departs from both Philo's and Porphiry's identification of angels with demons.[35] Consistently with church teachings he distinguishes between rebellious, fallen, and faithful angels (52–55).

This configuration of textual strains in Dante's discussion of the angels is a mark of his intellectual syncretism, of the prodigious, multiple vibrations in his magisterial voice. Much is at stake in this style of fabulation. In a primary way, it is as if he peeks into the stubborn contradictions housed by divisive philosophies and juggles them into his own master version of the angelic myth. The assertion of his authority is, effectively, a function of his bold manipulation of available sources and texts. But the harmonization Dante produces is not a mechanical and, finally, reductive compendium of heterogeneous fragments. Rather, he inserts within his borrowings from disparate philosophical speculations that which his sources bypass or never acknowledge: the fact that their systematic, mutually exclusive philosophical broodings are not and cannot be construed as the truth. They are polemical, partial glimmers of the total light, or, at best, resilient imaginative constructions akin to an aesthetic vision which only a poet such as Dante is empowered to deliver. The aesthetic turns into a genuine source of knowledge and is the perspective from which to put to the test the claims of knowledge advanced by philosophical discourses.

Dante's awareness that the aesthetic imagination is close to understanding the mode of angelic existence is shown by his deployment of the language of play (dance, music, and song) in his dramatic rendition of the angels. In *Paradiso* XXXI the angels, like a swarm of bees at work (7–9), sing God's glory. The hint that in the white rose of heaven work is play is fully articulated in *Paradiso* XXIX. The faithful angels, called by Dante "sustanze gioconde" (76) (jocund substances), are said to experience delight in their "arte . . . da circuire" (52–54), their contemplation and dancing around God to the implicit tune of the spheres, the melodious sound which is caused, in the language of Macrobius, by the rapid motion of the spheres themselves. In short, the Neoplatonic myth of the harmony of the universe, known as *musica mundana*, is the imaginative point of convergence between theological order and aesthetic order in *Paradiso*.

In and of itself the heavenly music of the angelic songs and dances echoes the motif of the harmony of the spheres announced in *Paradiso* I: "Quando la rota che tu sempiterni / desiderato, a sè mi fece atteso / con l'armonia che temperi e discerni . . ."(75–78) (When the revolution which Thou, by being desired, makest eternal turned my attention unto itself by the harmony which Thou dost temper and distinguish . . .). This Pythagorean theme of the musical construction of the universe, which Martianus Capella, Boethius, and Cassiodorus elaborate for the Middle Ages, provides the intellectual frame within which to account for the ludic metaphors Dante deploys in the cantos. He speaks, in fact, of "angelici ludi" (*Par*. XXVIII, 126) (angelic sports), and later in *Paradiso* XXX their feast is "il triunfo che lude" (10) (the triumph that sports). The word "triunfo," further, calls for a special gloss. The Greek *thriambos*, which stands behind "triunfo," designates a hymn to Bacchus sung in festal procession. In Latin the word came to signify a procession to celebrate the victorious return of a Roman general or a poet's coronation. Dante certainly uses the word "triunfar" (*Par*. I, 29) exactly that way to describe the victories of the poet and of Caesar. In *Purgatorio* XXIX, 107, the appearance of the triumphal chariot ("un carro . . . triunfal") in the middle of the allegorical representation of universal history marks the transformation of history into a theatrical performance with standard-bearers, sweet sounds, the slow motion of the twenty-four elders crowned with lilies, and voices singing hosanna, which is the song of cosmic worship of God.

The representation of paradisaic reality in aesthetic terms does not mean that ethics is excluded from it. On the contrary, there is an ethos to music. The Greek *harmonia*, which is an agreement and accord of disparate parts, aims at producing in the individual soul a moral order, which is figured by music. This principle of the ethical character of music is central to Plato's theory of education, and Macrobius reaffirms Plato's insight:

> Every soul in the world is allured by musical sounds so that not only those who are more refined in their habits, but all the barbarous people as well, have adopted songs by which they are inflamed with courage or wooed to pleasure;

for the soul carries with it into the body a memory of the music which it knew in the sky, and is so captivated by its charms that there is no breast so cruel or savage as not to be gripped by the spell of such an appeal.[36]

Macrobius's mixture of ethics and music is the ground of Dante's *theologia ludens*. To be sure, music, which for Dante, as we have seen in the introductory remarks to this study, is the essence of poetry, has its own ravishing power on the mind. Casella's song, which is a *musica humana*, engenders in the pilgrim a spiritual state which can best be uderstood by Dante's own gloss on music in *Convivio* II: "Music draws to itself the human spirits which are, as it were, mainly vapors of the heart, so that they almost cease from action of their own, so undivided is the soul when it listens to music; and the virtue of all the spirits is, as it were, concentrated in the spirit of sense which receives the sound."[37] But the moral ambiguities of music, dramatized by the song of Casella, are muted in *Paradiso*. Music, the art through which we hear the tacit motion of time, is translated into a vibration of God's light.

By endorsing the traditional coupling of ethics and music, and more generally ethics and beauty, Dante, in effect, makes aesthetics, by virtue of its inherent link with ethics, a supreme theory of value. Because aesthetics is the faculty that transforms essences into images, it consistently shapes the common perception of reality. More than that, as is the case in several medieval representations of biblical and Christian stories, aesthetics forces those stories within its won criteria of symmetry and order. The recognition of the power of aesthetics to shape the mind is not without consequences. The claim of power, in effect, is inseparable from an awareness of aesthetics' problematic status. It is in this very claim that the radical, potentially subversive threat of aesthetic beauty lies. As if by its own magic spell, beauty transforms appearance into apparition, for as beauty translates, as it must, an essence into an appearance, it actually displaces the essence into the imaginary. There can be little doubt that the philosophers' effort to contain or circumvent aesthetics and play signals their perception of beauty's compulsions. But few poets have understood, as Dante has understood, how bewitching beauty can be: it is bewitching because it can never be perceived if not as a ravishing image.

Readers of the *Vita nuova* hardly need be reminded of the power of an image of beauty to mesmerize, to engender a vanishing epiphany in the haze of the daylight world, and, simply, to disorient the lover by inducing delirious states, reveries, and nightmares in which the consistency of commonplace reality dissolves. In the *Divine Comedy* the dream of the Siren, as we have seen in chapter 7, is a version of this sorcery of beauty. In *Paradiso* XXX, as Beatrice leaves the pilgrim, the poet's art is said to have been a lifelong pursuit of her elusive beauty, from which he must now desist.

Beatrice's beauty is a function of the pilgrim's vision, but there is no sense in this portion of the poem of the dangerousness of her appearance. Nonetheless, Beatrice warns against appearances in *Paradiso* XXIX. Let us recall the context of her warning. In an angry counterpoint to the play of the angels, Beatrice makes a doctrinal point. The angels, she says, have no memory: they have no need to remember the past, since they see the eternal present in God's eye. She then attacks those who philosophize on earth and who are attracted by the love of appearances:

> sì che là giù, non dormendo si sogna,
> credendo e non credendo dicer vero;
> ma ne l'uno è più colpa e più vergogna.
> Voi non andate giù per un sentiero
> filosofando: tanto vi trasporta
> l'amor de l'apparenza e 'l suo pensiero.
>
> (*Par.* XXIX, 82–87)

(Thus down there men dream while awake, believing or not believing that they speak truth—but in the one case is the greater blame and shame. You mortals do not proceed along one same path in philosophizing, so much does the love of show and the thought of it carry you away.)

The love of appearances, which here mean false appearances, leads away from the path of truth; the same love of show, as the text reemphasizes a few lines down in the same canto ("Per apparer ciascun s'ingegna e face /sue invenzioni," 94–95—each tries for display, making his own inventions), makes the philosophers neglect and pervert scripture (88–90), while they concoct improbable reasons for the solar eclipse at Christ's passion. The burden of Beatrice's attack is the sleep of reason—how rationality edges toward the insubstantiality of dreams—as well as the eclipse of faith in the schools (70), which never probe beneath but actually wallow in appearances and forget what is essential. At the same time, Beatrice's attack projects the world of appearance as a derealization of the solid, substantial density of the real: appearances and images replicate the world and reveal the underlying reality. As they double the world of reality, however, images have the power to obscure and elide the very substantiality they represent.

In *Paradiso* XXIX Dante views appearances as illusory, as simulations of the truth, but he does not quite confront here the radical inconsistency of appearances, the way appearances hollow out substances. It is in the area of fraud in *Inferno*, however, that we encounter the diabolical caricature of angelic play and, more generally, the representation of hoaxes and counterfeits as threats to the hard core of reality. In *Inferno* XXI and XXII, where barrators are punished, Dante features the grotesque activity of demons, the so-called *commedia dei diavoli*: the devils' "nuovo ludo" (*Inf.* XXII, 118) (new sport); their mode of leaping, which is a parodic dance; their tricks ("buffa," 133); the scuffles in a boiling pond; scatological sounds (which are a *musica diabuli*)—these are the wares of comic laughter as well as the devils' play.

That this is the exact context within which the two cantos have to be read is made manifest by Dante's reference to "la mia comedia" (*Inf.* XXI, 2) (my comedy). It is also stressed by the extended images of tournaments and jousting opening *Inferno* XXII: "Io vidi già cavalier muover campo, / e cominciare stormo e far lor mostra, / e talvolta partir per loro scampo; / corridor vidi per la terra vostra, / o Aretini, e vidi gir gualdane, / fedir tornamenti e correr giostra") (1–6) (Ere now have I seen before now horsemen moving camp, and beginning an assault and making their muster, and sometimes retiring to escape; I have seen coursers over your land, O Aretines; and I have seen the starting of raids, the onset of tournaments, and the running of jousts). This grotesque mixturte of horror, play, and laughter (the sinners are tortured, the devils roar with laughter, the pilgrim is scared of being thrown down) is punctuated by the low, comic style. The images of *Inferno* XXII, more precisely, recall the trivialities of the *carmina potatoria* and *lusoria*, "ma ne la chiesa / coi santi, e in taverna coi ghiottoni" (14–15) (but in church with saints and with guzzlers in the tavern). This tradition of the *carmina burana* is yoked to the rhetoric of the *sermo jocosus* that the *poeti giocosi*, such as Cecco, Folgore, Meo dei Tolomei, Forese, and Dante himself, have deployed.

From one point of view, Dante rejects the profanities of that comic style, and its implicit moral abjection, as he assigns them to this place of evil. By deploying the stylisitc register of the *sermo jocosus* in the area of barratry, he also suggests that sports and laughter are experiences of moral degradation, literally the effect of man's fall from the Garden of Eden, which, as such, stand in sharp juxtaposition to the upward movement of the pilgrim's *commedia*. In this sense, it can be said that Dante appropriates the attacks unleashed against the immorality of spectacles and theater by the early church apologists, such as Tertullian, Cyprian, and John of Salisbury, whom I have referred to earlier in this chapter. Spectacles, in their view, are immoral because they trap the mind in illusion and sham and because they hold it back from its spiritual *askesis*. From another point of view, however, these blasphemous, vulgar sports show forth a reality that escapes those who are caught in the ordinary domain of nature: the sports reveal the magic, illusory constitution of the world; they reveal, in addition, the persistent presence of a supernatural reality, albeit in its demonic shape. Dante's ethical judgment of these aesthetic forms is unequivocally firm, but his poetry rescues them from his own judgment.

There was in the twelfth century a bold defense of the ugly and horrid which may stand behind Dante's imaginative retrieval of the demonic. In general, the medieval aesthetics of the ugly is rooted in the principle of the divine redemption of the low, sinful state of mankind. More specifically, Hugh of St. Victor actually believed that God may be discovered more easily in ugly forms than in externally beautiful ones. The pure appearing of beauty, one can say, chains the mind to the sensible world, but what one experiences as ugly forces one away from the contemplation of itself and urges one to transcend it. Hugh writes:

> Quando per pulchras formas laudatur Deus, secundum speciem huius mundi laudatur. . . . Quando vero per dissimiles et a se alienas formationes laudatur, supermundane laudatur, quoniam (tunc) nec idem esse dicitur nec secundum id, sed supra id totum aliud per quod laudatur. [38]

> (When God is praised through beautiful forms, he is praised according to the beauty of this world. . . . When, however, he is praised through forms which are dissimilar and alien from him, he is praised supernaturally, because (then) he is not said to be the same as or according to that, but above all that through which he is praised.)

Hugh's Neoplatonic aesthetics is confirmed by other medieval aestheticians, such as Alexander of Hales, who in his *De pulchritudine universi* acknowledges the aesthetic necessity of contrasts in order to highlight beauty: just as the beauty of a picture may be enhanced by a dark color in the proper place, so the beauty of the universe, it is often said, is enhanced by moral errors. We have seen in the preceding chapter the broader moral implications of such a doctrine. For now, it is sufficient to stress that it exactly captures the paradox dramatized in the representation of the "comedy of the devils": Dante's ethical stance rejects the universe of shams and hoaxes as morally wrong, but they remain essential both to this spiritual ascent and to his writing of it.

Dante's moral judgment of these illusory forms depends, no doubt, on his insight into the dangerousness of aesthetics, and I would like to look briefly at two instances in *Inferno*, where the play metaphors are again used. The first case, to which I have referred from a different angle in chapter 8, occurs in *Inferno* XX where the pilgrim meets Michael Scot, "che veramente / de le magiche frode seppe il gioco" (116–17) (who truly knew the game of magic frauds). The other case occurs in *Inferno* XXIX, the canto of alchemists and impersonators, where Griffolino, "parlando a gioco" (112) (speaking in jest), who promised to teach Albero da Siena the art of flying, to be a Daedalus (116), is burned for failing to keep his promise.

The reference to Daedalus, which commentators on this canto generally neglect, may shed considerable light on the issues at hand. The story of Daedalus, the artificer who escapes from the labyrinth he built for Minos, is the mythical Neoplatonic paradigm of the flight of the soul and its final deliverance from the world of matter. As such, for all its transparent jocular force, the recalling of Daedalus hints at the eerie bond between alchemy and Neoplatonism. The alchemists, who believe that there is a secret, valuable core beneath the world of deceptive appearances, are like the Neoplatonists, who seek to transcend the illusions of nature. But these alchemists, just as the magician Michael Scot, never penetrate the veil of appearances and abide in coverings and disguises. Griffolino and Michael Scot are both masters of illusion: their "gioco" is, quite literally, the illusory doubling and counterfeiting of being. Like actors on the stage and hypocrites (who, for Isidore of Seville, are actors), they violate the principle of identity. To say it in the Neoplatonic language the text overtly evokes, their art is "di natura buona scimia" (*Inf.* XXIX, 139) (a good ape of nature), for it is an artifice of sterile simulation. From this standpoint, all the sinners who deal in fraud—the falsifiers of words and deeds, counterfeiters, hypocrites, impersonators (who suffer a disfiguration of skin in an overtly parodic reversal of the etymological meaning of *pulcher* from *cutis*)—are players for whom reality is an optical illusion.[39] Daedalus, the artisan for whom the illusion of art is his own trap, is their archetype.

In a way, the fraudulent sinners tread the same path the mystics do (and the angels, that of the devils), although they move toward opposite destinations. The mystics, as shown in chapter 8, are convinced that the image is unreal and yet unavoidable, and, therefore, they seek to pierce through the insubstantial image in order to experience direct vision, which means that they end up blinded by the light. The fraudulent sinners, equally convinced that images are illusory and that, in addition, there is nothing behind them, plunge into them, manipulate them at will, and in the glare of their alchemies and other simulations they unveil the illusoriness of matter, if only to discover, at the same time, the resistance of matter. One thing is nonetheless certain: as the fraudulent sinners attempt to hollow out the solidity of the real world, they effectively signal how to them substances are dissolved into pure emptiness. In short, these evildoers are aesthetes whose sparkling simulations destroy the natural order of work and production. Against them, Dante asserts that theirs are lurid imitations of the prodigious art of Nature.

As is often the case in the *Divine Comedy*, talking about an issue inevitably leads one to its polar opposite: the pastoral to history, utopia to exile, ethics to aesthetics and then back to ethics, play to work. In the metaphoric reversal from play to the morality of work, it appears that one is playing a losing game. More precisely, I have argued that aesthetics, which is God's activity, is the ground of ethics and of all knowledge, but, paradoxically, it is subordinated to ethics in the unfolding of the poem. Freed from any moral constraints, aesthetics becomes aestheticism; coupled with ethics, aesthetics has the power to displace ethics. One is forced to the inescapable conclusion that whereas God plays, man is enjoined to work and that there yawns a tragic gap between God's being and man's life. It could be answered, as a way of accounting for this gap, that aesthetics has a double value, that its value (and this is overtly the language of ethics) lies exactly in this problematical doubleness, to be indistinguishable from ethics but, for this very reason, to be capable of effacing ethics.

The predicament the above formulation entails is not final in the *Divine Comedy*, for Dante still explores, as St. Thomas Aquinas does, possible continuities between the playing of God and the playing of man. The Garden of Eden, the original realm of play and ease, the golden age dreamed by poets, is imaginatively recalled as the fixed time and place of play with binding laws, which are, nonetheless, breached by man's sin. In this Garden pleasure holds sway ("lo tuo piacer omai prendi per duce," (*Purg.* XXVII, 131—henceforth take your pleasure for guide). Matelda is seen singing, picking flowers, laughing, and moving with dancelike steps (*Purg.* XXVIII, 40–54). The reference to Psalm 91, *Delectasti* (80), a psalm of tranquillity and time off, heightens the quality of the place as a playland where a song of joy and praise is given to God's name, his constancy, and his love. The pleasure the pilgrim experiences in the Garden is what Aristotle in his *Ethics* calls the crown of an activity, that which comes to man once the work is completed.

In the world of history the virtue of *cortesia*, whose range of meaning ever since Cicero, Quintilian, the Provençal poets, and Dante himself has encompassed *urbanitas, curialitas, iocunditas, facetiae* (modesty, polite manners, affability of speech, generosity), among other virtues, stands as the central value of both city and court.[40] In effect, Dante's *cortesia* is a version of the virtue of *eutrapelia*, and its importance and crisis was highlighted in the preceding chapter. In cantos XV and XVI of each canticle of Dante's poem, let us now stress, the civic-moral category of *cortesia* has been eclipsed by the present corruption. Yet Dante's hope that the "cortesia del gran lombardo" (*Par.* XVII, 71) (courtesy of the great Lombard) will comfort his exile marks his ongoing commitment to the ethical values put forth by Aristotle and Aquinas.

Side by side with this social virtue, the experience of play is available to the Christian in the liturgy of the church.[41] More than that, Franciscan spirituality, the practice of the *ioculatores Domini*, as the Franciscans are called, embodies the theology of play in action. The model for this theology is Jesus himself, whose Roman mantle and crown of thorns is a parodic caricature of the regal *insignia* of the world.[42] But the Franciscans, the "friars of the cornet," as Salimbene speaks of them, are the best mimes of the Lord of the Dance. Their reputation as troubadours of poverty and as *jongleurs* of God springs from the legend of St. Francis himself, who, as one reads in the second *Vita* by Celano, "when the sweetest melody of spirit would bubble up in him . . . he would burst in songs of joy in French which express the breath of the divine whispers his ear perceived. . . . He would make, out of the stick he would pick up from the ground, a violin, and pretending he would pluck unseen strings in French."[43]

The singing in French is, no doubt, a pun on the saint's name, but it also alludes to the bond between friars and troubadours and trouvères. Dante dismisses the poet-tumblers of Provence; he dismisses, and Cacciaguida's prophecy in *Paradiso* XVII certainly alludes to it, the idea of the poet as an idle parasite-courtier picking crumbs at the dining table of power; but he gives his assent to poets such as Sordello and Arnaut Daniel, and he also gives his assent to Francis's theology of play, which is the spiritual extension of the poetic practice of the *jongleurs*. Among the Franciscans, it may be added, St. Bonaventure fully grasps St. Francis's insight into the playfulness of God.

In *Paradiso* XI, the canto of St. Francis, Dante represents the essence of that insight. What St. Francis conveys in *Paradiso* XI through his exuberant jests, his miming of Christ, his parody of family institutions, of rituals of courtly love for Lady Poverty—a widow despised and neglected by all for over a thousand years (64–66)—of the ceremony of marriage, of the rhetoric of war, of the values of wealth, and of clothing as status symbol, is a *playful* and *comical* vision.[44] It is the vision, at the same time militant and prophetic, of the religious imagination capable of crossing all boundaries of commonplace values, of peering in delight at the things of the world that have equal standing with one another in God's eye. St. Francis's play, most simply, is a yielding to God's summons to a radical homelessness. Play, which is said to have begun with the Lydian refugees, turns into a metaphor that reverses, as David's dance does in *Purgatorio* X, the shape of the world, and it is, as the *Aeneid* suggests, simultaneously a sign of exile and utopia.

Dante's own comic text, which captures the "comic" essence of God, fuses together work and play, and it stems from such exilic and utopian vision. Never before and never after has poetry played such a visionary task in encompassing the most diverse contradictions and experiences—what St. Bonaventure calls *aequalits numerosa*—in man's life. The *Divine Comedy* witnesses the breakdown of human projects and bonds and justice, and it overwhelms us with its chronicles of man's inhumanity to man. But the poet knows what his comic vision means. He knows, through his musings on play and his own imaginative effort, that tragedy, with its all too solid horrors, may not be real, no more real, at any rate, than the night is real for the mystic, who knows all along that the dark is no dark, and that the night is the fugitive shadow of the blazing light. Play to Dante evokes the feast of thinking by which man plays and meets the Playmaker. Through play the poet asks of old men to dream dreams and of the young to see visions, as he once did and he now does. Through play, finally, the poet knows that play can be the shakiest of illusions—the bottomless dream of man's long night. In the space of this knowledge, which is both playful and without softness, lie the vast compass and the frugal beauty of Dante's vision.

NOTES

INTRODUCTION

1. The bibliography on medieval encyclopedias is vast. I shall mention here Fontaine 1959; the excellent studies by Michaud-Quantin 1966; de Gandillac 1966 on premedieval and medieval encyclopedias; and Fumagalli and Parodi 1985, who describe very well the organization of knowledge by both Neckham and Bartolomeus Anglicus, as does Bouard 1930. An important study by Marigo 1916 focuses on the literary components in *specula* and *tresors* of the thirteenth century. For the teaching of the "artes" in Bologna see Vecchi 1951. Of larger theoretical interest is Viarre 1975; for historically more recent efforts to unify knowledge see Tega 1983. More generally see Foucault 1970 and Gonzalez 1990 for an excellent reconstruction of the "archive," which Gonzalez construes as the radical emblem of Latin American imagination. That the encyclopedic literary structure has not faded in our time is shown by Santi 1990, pp. 61–94, who inscribes Pablo Neruda's *Canto general* within the tradition of cosmological poetry.

2. The question of education—which is at the heart of the encyclopedia—has been studied by Jaeger 1949 for classical antiquity. For the Middle Ages see the crucial works of Alverny 1946; Courcelle 1948; Marrou 1958 and 1982; and Leclercq 1962. Of great interest are also Paré, Brunet, and Tremblay 1933; Potter 1936; McGarry 1948; and Kevane 1964. For a historical view of education in Italy see Wieruszowski 1967. A modern, general philosophical rationale of aesthetic education is provided by Schiller 1954.

3. Rajna 1928 has studied the denomination of *trivium* and *quadrivium*. The history of the seven liberal arts has been periodically examined. See Abelson 1906; Paetow 1910; Simone 1949, who relates the seven liberal arts to theology; Stahl 1971; and, Wagner 1983 and Hadot 1984, who in recent years have submitted the liberal arts to an intensive scrutiny. See also Lutz 1956 and Weisheipl 1964 and 1965 for the classification of the arts. A particularly successful volume is *Arts libéraux et philosophie au moyen age* 1969. It is difficult to stress how important all the contributions to that volume have been to shaping my thinking in this study. I would like to mention, however, some items I have found to be particularly valuable: Marrou (pp. 5ff.); O'Donnel (pp. 127ff.); Delhaye (pp. 161ff.); Kibre (pp. 175ff.), who writes a stimulating account of the *quadrivium* in thirteenth-century universities (mainly Paris); Verdier (pp. 305ff.) on the iconography of the liberal arts; Baker (pp. 469ff.) on the *artes liberales* in St. Augustine's *De magistro*; Gomez Nogales (pp. 493ff.) on the liberal arts in Spanish-Moslem thought; Crouse (pp. 531ff.) on Honorius of Autun's idea of the arts as stations on the way to the *patria*; and Toccafondi (pp. 639ff.) on Aquinas.

4. The phrase is by Fontaine 1959. See also the thematic treatment of grammar in encyclopedias by Feltrin 1985.

5. Curtius 1963, pp. 221–25. Curtius, who argues for the "cognitional function" of Dante's poetry, correctly places the debate within the general classification of the sciences. Is theology a science or not? He refers to Alexander of Hales's view of the proximity of concepts such as *ars* and *scientia* (p. 222). Poetic representation ("modus poeticus") does not pertain to science, and this means that divine wisdom stands beyond the rules of human reason (p. 223). Albert the Great (*Summae theologiae* I, q. 5, m. 5) does not classify the Bible according to the *modus poeticus*. Aquinas, as Curtius correctly reports, uses the phrase that poetry is the lowest of all sciences in his *Summa theologiae* I, 1, 9, objection.

6. See the excellent studies by Wetherbee 1969 and 1972; see also Michel 1980.

7. The classic study that reports the terms of the controversy is Hissette 1977. For a discussion of the value of *fabula* in the Middle Ages see Dronke 1974. For the place of theology among the arts see Cuervo 1932; Chenu 1935 and 1968; and Benoit 1989. Wippel 1977 gives a reliable overview of the condemnations of 1270 and 1277.

8. Leff 1968 gives a solid account of the debate; see also Little 1926, Paré 1947, and Nemetz 1956. The magisterial studies by van Steenberghen 1955, 1966, and 1974 are indispensable. See also Maurer 1981.

9. See, for instance, Ghisalberti 1932.

10. Herman 1979.

11. A sense of the crisis of the times is embodied by the polemics—which take place at the pastoral-ecclesial, theological, and political levels—at the University of Paris. See Glorieux 1925, Thouzellier 1927, Douie 1954, Tierney 1964, Leff 1968, Mandonnet 1976, van Steenberghen 1977, Thillet 1978, Poirion 1980, and Szittya 1986.

12. The question of Greek, Arabic, Jewish, and Christian speculations on imagination, poetry, and prophecy has been variously studied by Wolfson 1935, Walzer 1962, Hardison 1968, Portelli 1982, Watson 1986, and Black 1989. Menocal 1987 has confronted the deeper causes of the ideological constructions—a mixture of misrepresentation and erasures—of Arabic culture in medieval scholarship.

CHAPTER 1

1. It is appropriate that an encyclopedic form of scholarship should flourish around an encyclopedic poem par excellence such as the *Divine Comedy*. The *Enciclopedia dantesca*, thus, recapitulates many earlier efforts to give a totalizing picture of the contents of the poem. One could mention the "dictionaries" of the *Divine Comedy*, such as Toynbee 1914, Scartazzini 1905, and, more recently, the *Divine Comedy and the Encyclopedia of Arts and Sciences* 1988, edited by Di Scipio and Scaglione. Scholars who deliberately work within the encyclopedic mode and seek to explain or account for "everything" in the poem include Sarolli 1971, who seeks to retrieve the symbolic universe of the poem (from the symbolism of lapidaries to number symbolism), and, recently, Boyde 1981, who also seeks to define the scientific and "pan-logic" universe of Dante. Neither raises the issue of poetry as the medium holding the symbolic totality of the poem together.

2. The idea of poetry as encyclopedic (reasserted, as far as Dante goes, by his commentators) was explicitly formulated for the Middle Ages by Bernard of

Chartres. In *The Metalogicon* (I, 24), after illustrating how grammar is the foundation of philosophy and virtue (I, 23), John of Salisbury describes the analytical method followed by his great teacher, Bernard, who used to teach his students in the awareness that *fabule* "image all the arts"—from rhetoric to logic and ethics. Cf. *The Metalogicon* I, 23–24, pp. 65–71. The texts by the earlier Dante commentators are available in Mazzotta 1991, especially p. 36.

3. What can be called the dreamy knowledge drafted in the *Vita nuova*—the links between intellect and love, prose and poetry, etc.—has been increasingly at the forefront of recent criticism. The complex relation between poetry and prose has been the subject of a suggestive and impressive study by Stillinger 1992; Harrison 1988 rightly begins his study by stressing "Dante's dream." Menocal 1991, in a rather radical vein, invokes the cabala as the master text of the *Vita nuova*, and by these terms she means the "magic" of poetry as well as other imaginative extensions of poetry, such as the act of "the writing of the universe," the concept of synchronicity, and the elusive issue of Dante's secret knowledge.

4. "Sì come dice lo Filosofo nel principio de la prima Filosofia, tutti li uomini naturalmente desiderano di sapere. La ragione di che puote essere ed è che ciascuna cosa, da providenza di prima natura impinta, è inclinabile a la sua propria perfezione; onde, acciò che la scienza è ultima perfezione de la nostra anima, ne la quale sta la nostra ultima felicitade, tutti naturalmente al suo desiderio semo subietti" (*Conv.* I, I, 1–2). See the general sketch of Dante's theory of knowledge ("La conoscenza umana") by Nardi 1985, pp. 135–72. See also Corti 1983.

5. The definition of philosophy takes place in the context of a critique of a fragmentary, dismembered understanding of knowledge and in the assertion of the interdependence of all the sciences: "E così, acciò che sia filosofo, conviene essere l'amore a la sapienza, che fa l'una de le parti benivolente; . . . Per che sanza amore e sanza studio non si può dire filosofo, . . . sì come sono molti che si dilettano in intendere canzoni ed istudiare in quelle, e che si dilettano studiare in Rettorica o in Musica, e l'altre scienze fuggono e abbandonano, che sono tutte membra di sapienza. Nè si dee chiamare vero filosofo colui che è amico di sapienza per utilitade, sì come sono li legisti, li medici e quasi tutti li religiosi, che non per sapere studiano ma per acquistare moneta o dignitate" (*Conv.* III, xi, 8–10). The passage is commonplace enough. Cf., for instance, Hugh of St. Victor's *Didascalicon*: "Philosophy, then, is the love and pursuit of Wisdom" (I, 2, p. 48).

6. This is the opening sentence of Hugh's *Didascalicon*, and I mention it because it is a deliberate echo of the *Summum bonum* of Plato's *Timaeus* and of Boethius's Platonic *De consolatione philosophiae*, bk. III, metre ix. Trovato 1990 has sensitively restudied the problem.

7. This book does not attempt to investigate the occurrence of all these themes. In fact, questions such as Dante's concern with the seven mechanical arts—fabric making, armament, commerce, agriculture, hunting, medicine, and theatrics—figure very little. (The last chapter will discuss theatrics.) I have sought to describe the mechanical arts in Boccaccio's *Decameron* (see Mazzotta 1986). For a general idea of these problems, which would deserve fuller treatment, see Ovitt 1983. For the overview of Dante's themes see Sarolli 1971 and, more recently, Boyde 1984. Many of these thematic contents of the *Divine Comedy* have received adequate treatment by both scholars and technical compendia such as the *Enciclopedia dantesca*. The

didactic tradition—at least in the area of the Latin Middle Ages—has been investigated by Jaeger 1939, Marrou 1948, and Courcelle 1948.

8. Marcia Colish 1968 has written an exemplary account of Dante's treatise. See also Mengaldo 1978. Cf. Nardi 1985, pp. 173ff.

9. The translation is by Dods, p. 527.

10. Corti 1981. Her views have been challenged by Pagani 1982, Mengaldo, 1978, and, recently, by Scaglione 1988, pp. 34–41. See also the bibliography and the assessment of the the whole question by Ascoli 1990.

11. The idea of poetry as involving all the arts, which goes back to Homer's poetic encyclopedia, has been given a solid theoretical—and exclusively Aristotelian—foundation by Trimpi 1983. See also Havelock 1963; cf. Barilli's 1984 probings into the interaction between rhetoric and poetry across various periods of intellectual history.

12. Petrocchi 1961.

13. For a traditional understanding of the definition see Schiaffini 1958 and Buck 1965. My argument stresses Dante's sense of poetry as the dynamic locus of interaction of many different arts. In this sense poetry responds to his dynamic idea of knowledge. More precisely, I would see in Dante's frequent uses of synesthesia, especially in the *Divine Comedy*—e.g. "ove 'l sol tace" (*Inf.* I, 60); "d'ogne luce muto" (*Inf.* V, 28), to mention the most glaring examples—a dramatization of different but interpenetrating sensory experiences. On the whole issue of synesthesia see the remarks by Cambon 1970.

14. The canto has been analyzed with great care by Marti 1962. Cf. also Freccero 1986, "Casella's Song" (*Purg.* II, 112), pp. 186ff.

15. The relevant passages in the description by Hugh of St. Victor reads: "The varieties of music are three: that belonging to the universe, that belonging to man, and that which is instrumental. Of the music of the universe, some is characteristic of the elements, some of the planets, some of the seasons. . . . Of the music of man, some is characteristic of the body, some of the soul, and some of the bond between the two. . . . Music is characteristic of the soul partly in its virtues, like justice, piety, and temperance; and partly in its powers, like reason, wrath, and concupiscence" (Taylor, p. 69). The definition echoes Plato's *Republic* X; see also Boethius, *De institutione musica* I, 2, as well as Isidore's *Etymologies* and Cassiodorus's *Institutiones*. More generally see Spitzer 1963, Pirrotta 1968, Monterosso 1965, and Pestalozza 1988.

16. Yates 1972 analyzes the psychological-philosophical debates on memory. See also Carruther 1990. Cf. the suggestive critical readings by MacDonald 1987.

17. The locus classicus for this idea of memory is St. Augustine, who in the *Confessions* writes: "I shall pass on, then, beyond this faculty in my nature as I ascend by degrees toward Him who made me. And I come to the fields and special palaces of memory, where lie the treasures of innumerable images of all kinds of things that have been brought in by the senses. There too are our thoughts stored up. . . . When I am in this treasure house, I ask for whatever I like to be brought out to me, and then some things are produced at once, some things take longer and have, as it were, to be fetched up from a more remote part of the store . . . Here are kept distinct and in their proper classification all sensations which come to us, each by its own route."

18. Boccaccio's commentary on *Inferno* IV (especially the "esposizione litterale," pp. 170ff.) stresses throughout Dante's interest in the encyclopedic tradition. Boccaccio glosses the line "O tu ch'onori scienza e arte" (*Inf.* IV, 73) by recalling Albert the Great's and Aquinas's division of knowledge as *sapienza*, *scienza*, and *arte* (respectively for divine things, the natural, and the human worlds). He then explains that Vergil's poems make use of "l'artificio di qualunque liberale arte, secondo che le oportunità hanno richiesto" (p. 190). In the allegorical exposition he identifies the seven gates "le sette arti liberali," and he explains the liberal arts as follows: "E chiamansi 'liberali' per ciò che in esse non osava, al tempo che i Romani signoreggiavano il mondo, studiare altri che liberi uomini; o vogliam dire che liberali si chiamano per ciò che elle rendono liberi molti uomini da molti e vari dubbi, ne' quali sanza esse intrigati sarebbono. . . . E nondimeno da sapere non esser di necessità, a colui che odierno filosofo vuol divenire, sapere perfettamente e del tutto oportuno, sì come al filosofo la gramatica e la dialettica, al poeta e all'oratore la gramatica e la retorica; poi sapere dell'altre i principi, e sapergli bene, e assai a ciascuno" (p. 277). See also L'Ottimo where the gloss to the "nobile castello" reads: "Qui descrive sotto forma di un castello, cosí situato per lo quale vuole che s'intenda la Filosofia comuna, la quale è cerchiata delle sette liberali arti, Grammatica, Dialettica, Rettorica, Geometria, e Aritmetica, ed Astro [the rest of the word for Astrologia, as the editor points out, is missing, and so is Music], cioè mondana dilettazione, o vero la disposizione, o vero abito dello intelletto umano; il quale fiumicello passò lievemente, e per questo vuol mostrare che scienziati erano, e che entrarono per tutte e sette liberali arti" (p. 43). For a thorough account of the canto see Mazzoni 1965; see also the reading by Iannucci 1985 in terms of Dante's tragic insight into pagan knowledge. For Dante's Vergil and the tradition of the seven liberal arts, see Nolan 1988; more generally see Mazzoni for further bibliography.

19. Freccero's critical work (1986) hinges on the notion of *conversion*, which he is at pains to clarify in the light of Jaeger's understanding of *paideia* (pp. 180ff.) The motif of education of self is also a crucial concern of Charity's 1966.

20. See Green 1967, Wetherbee 1969, Stock 1972, and Poirion 1980. See also Wetherbee's 1973 introduction to his translation of the *Cosmographia*.

21. See Quilligan 1977.

22. See Poirion 1973.

23. See Fleming 1984, Poirion 1980, Gunn 1952, and Paré 1947.

24. The translation is taken from Wetherbee 1973, p. 76.

25. Wetherbee 1973, especially pp. 34–62 of the introduction to *Cosmographia*.

26. Delhaye 1963. For a more general treatment of the theme of the seven liberal arts see Delhaye 1969. More to the point see Trout 1979 and Michel 1980.

27. Mazzotta 1979, especially pp. 138–41. Of great value are also additional remarks in a typological-political vein by Elio Costa 1989. Fredi Chiappelli 1989 sheds extraordinary light on the whole canto.

28. The concrete history of education—libraries, teachers, texts—in Dante's Florence has been well delineated by Davis 1984 in at least two important chapters: "Education in Dante's Florence" and "Brunetto Latini and Dante," pp. 137–97. Cf. also the excellent article by Wieruzsowski 1967.

29. Delius 1887.

30. The links between Brunetto and the Chartrian idea of nature has been treated by, among others, Pezard 1950. For a general study of the theme of nature see Economou 1972. On the canto of Brunetto see also the richly textured argument by Mussetter 1984.

31. This classification ought to be related to the one Brunetto offers in his *Rettorica* 17, 6, ed. Maggini, where there is a science of language (the *trivium*), a mathematical science (the *quadrivium*), a logic, a theology, and a physics, which comprise the theoretical sciences. The "scienza pratica" contains ethics, economics, and politics (pp. 41ff.). See also Aquinas's *Super librum Boethii de trinitate* q. 5, a. 1, ad 3.

CHAPTER 2

1. Lourdaux and Verhelst 1979; and Riche and Lobrichon 1984. See also Danielou and Devoto 1962; Smalley 1984; De Lubac 1959–64; and Chenu 1969.

2. Grabois 1975 describes in some detail the intellectual relations previous to Nicholas of Lyra. See also Blumenkranz 1951 and Grabois 1984.

3. Of great importance are Chenu 1968 and Chatillon 1984.

4. For the consciousness of history elaborated by the Victorines see Chenu 1968 and De Lubac 1959–61. The locus classicus is the history of medieval aesthetics by Edgar de Bruyne 1946, especially chapter 5 of volume 3. See also Hugh of St. Victor, *De tribus diebus*, edited by Vincenzo Liccaro. For a general account of the artistic thought of the Victorines see Assunto 1975.

5. I refer here to the debates aiming at establishing those biblical passages that were to be considered history, allegory, or tropology, or all of these exegetical categories combined. For the discrepancy between letter and allegorical interpretation which lies at the center of patristic reflection, it suffices to mention Hugh of St. Victor, *Didascalicon* VI, c. 10: "Some sense is fitting, other unfitting. Of unfitting sense, some is incredible, some impossible, some absurd, some false. You find many things of this kind in the Scriptures, like the following: 'They have devoured Jacor.' And the following: 'Under whom they stoop that bear up the world.' And the following: 'My soul hath chosen hanging.' And there are many others." Bacon's sense of how much the *ordo allegoriae* differs from the *ordo historiae*, and of the necessity to know the languages, is formulated in his *Compendium studii theologiae*, c. 8.

6. Peter Abelard, *Opera* I, 680.

7. It may be of interest to mention the definition of free will from *Monarchia* I, xii, 6: "maximum donum humane nature a deo collatum . . . sicut in Paradiso *Comedie* dixi." See also chapter 6 below for a further discussion of the *liberum arbitrium*.

8. *Summa theologiae* IIa, IIae, 88, 1, 2. St. Thomas also discusses the vow of Jephthah—whom St. Paul includes in his list of saints, Hebrews 11:32—in article 2 of question 88.

9. The *topos* of Jephthah's daughter is studied by Alexion and Dronke 1971.

10. Prudentius, *Liber peristefanon* II, 257–77. St. Ambrose deals briefly with the figure of Lawrence in his *De officiis*, bk. II, c. 28.

11. Nardi 1944, "Il libero arbitrio e la storiella dell'asino di Buridano," pp. 287–303.

12. See also the *De doctrina christiana* III, 5, and III, 10, on sacrifice.

13. Quintilian (III) defines a figure as a *mutatio*, p. 301. Dante uses the word metaphor in terms of *transumptio* in the *Epistle* III, 2–4. Alan of Lille's sense of metaphor as *translatio* has been studied by Evans 1983, pp. 29–33.

14. *Summa theologiae* Ia, q. I, art. 10, ad 3, writes: "Non enim cum scriptura nominat Dei brachium, est literalis sensus quod in deo sit membrum huiusmodi corporale: sed id quod per hoc membrum significatur, scilicet virtus operativa."

15. Isidore, *Etymologiarum.*, I, xxxvii, 22. For a general rationale of the biblical tropes see Evans 1984.

16. For a general overview of the thrust of John of Salisbury's polemics see Tacchella 1980. See also Wilks 1984 and Brasa 1980. For the problem of grammar one should consult Hunt 1980; *Arts liberaux et philosophie au moyen age* 1969, pp. 753–949, contains a full range of grammar's associations with the *artes* of the *trivium*, including its connection with ethics, logic, and theology. See also Delhaye 1958; Leclerq 1943–45 and 1948b; and de Lubac 1960. For a briefer description of the importance of grammar in the context the seven liberal arts cf. Huntsman 1983. For Dante studies see Scaglione 1988.

17. Wetherbee 1972 and, more recently, Leupin 1989 have explored the issue in a considerable range of medieval texts. Cf. also Pezard 1950.

18. Ziolkowski 1985; Chenu 1935.

19. Evans 1983, pp. 21–41 and 64–85.

20. Varro (VI, 77): "Potest enim aliquid facere et non agere, ut poeta facit fabulam et non agit . . . et sic a poeta fabula fit." For a scholastic description of art as an activity that belongs to the practical order of making (as opposed to the order of doing, where prudence, *recta ratio agibilium*, belongs) see Maritain 1962, pp. 7–22.

21. The information is available in the *Liber Nimorod*. See the discussion on the astronomical lore of the book in Livesey and Rouse 1981. The Nimrod of *Inferno* XXXI has been studied by Lemay 1963.

22. Peter of Spain in his *Tractatus appellationum* from the *Summulae* writes: "Appellatio est acceptio termini pro re existente . . . Differt autem appellatio a significatione et suppositione, quia appellatio est tantum de re existente sed suppositio et significatio sunt tam pro re existente quam pro re non existente." (p. 44).

23. The phrase "consequentia nomina rebus esse" occurs in Justinian's *Institutiones*, as Nardi 1985, pp. 173–78, points out.

24. The randomness of sacrificial violence is powerfully treated by Girard 1972. Girard's analysis lacks a linguistic theory, which Dante's text—and this at least is my contention here—provides. It should be added that throughout the *Divine Comedy* Dante relies heavily on etymology as a vehicle of knowledge. The *foundation* of the etymological category, as I argue above in this chapter, is not, however, Cratylism. Cf. Jolivet 1975.

25. "Mea grammatica Christus est," announces Peter Damian as he contrasts the Rule of Benedict to the rules of Donatus (*PL* 145:306C). Damian's rigorism is not an isolated occurrence. Cf. Leclerq 1948 on Smaragdus; De Lubac 1960 on Gregory; and Delhaye 1958.

26. This is the principle discussed and illustrated by Auerbach 1959.

27. De Lubac 1959, vol. I.

28. The phrase, which highlights the novelty of the messianic event, occurs in the commentary on the Gospel of John (*PL* 122:320B).

CHAPTER 3

1. "A li sette primi [cieli] rispondono le sette scienze del Trivio e del Quadrivio, cioè Grammatica, Dialettica, Rettorica, Arismetrica, Musica, Geometria e Astrologia. A l'ottava spera, cioè a la stellata, risponde la scienza naturale, che Fisica si chiama, e la prima scienza, che si chiama Metafisica; a la nona spera risponde la Scienza morale; ed al cielo quieto risponde la scienza divina, che è Teologia appellata." The passage occurs in the *Convivio* II, xiii, 7–8.

2. Brunetto Latini, *La rettorica*, defines rhetoric as follows: "Rettorica èe scienzia di due maniere: una la quale insegna dire, e di questa tratta Tulio nel suo libro; l'altra insegna dittare, e di questa, perciò che esso non ne trattò così del tutto apertamente, si nne tratterà lo sponitore nel processo del libro, in suo luogo e suo tempo come si converrà" (3). General studies on rhetoric include still valuable contributions by Baldwin 1928 and Murphy 1974. On the *ars dictaminis* see Kristeller 1961; Wieruszowski 1971, pp. 359–77; and Haskins 1927, pp. 138–50, which surveys the revival of 'oratio' in the Roman political and judicial fields as well as the renewed importance of the epistolary style in the Middle Ages. This art of drafting official letters and documents, identified in the Bolognese *dictatores*, finds its authority in Alberic of Monte Cassino, *Breviarium de dictamine*, and Boncompagno of Signa, *Antiqua rhetorica*. Excellent work has been done by Haskins 1929, pp. 170–92; also Benson 1977, pp. 31–48, and Witt 1982.

3. Brunetto Latini writes (4): "Et ee rettorica una scienza di bene dire, ciò è rettorica quella scienza per la quale noi sapemo ornatamente dire e dittare." The quote echoes the conventional definition of rhetoric. Cf. Isidore of Seville, "Rhetorica est bene dicendi scientia in civilibus quaestionibus, ad persuadendum iusta et bona" (*Etym.* II, i, 1), and Martianus Capella, *De nuptiis Philologiae et Mercurii*, V. The theory of the *ornatus* in Dante is tied to the principle of linguistic *convenientia*. Cf. *De vulgari eloquentia* II, i, 2–10. See Tateo 1960, pp. 209–11. For the *ornatus* and the various degrees of style see Geoffrey of Vinsauf, *Poetria nova*, pp. 830ff. Cf. Matthew of Vendome, *Ars versificatoria* II, 9–10. For the *colores rhetorici* see Brunetto Latini, *Li livres dou tresor* III, x, 3. Cf. *Vita nuova* XXV, 7 and 10. The remarks by C. Grayson 1963 and Schiaffini 1969 are useful.

4. "Ad pulchritudinem tria requiruntur. Primo quidem *integritas* sive perfectio: quae enim diminuta sunt, hoc ipso turpia sunt. Et debita *proportio* sive consonantia. Et iterum *claritas*; unde quae habent colorem nitidum, pulchra esse dicuntur." (*Summa theologiae* I, 39, 8). Cf. the classic work by De Bruyne 1946.

5. *Convivio* II, xii, 9.

6. "Quella cosa dice l'uomo essere bella cui le parti debitamente si rispondono, per che de la loro armonia resulta piacimento. Onde pare l'uomo essere bello, quando le sue membra debitamente si rispondono; e dicemo bello lo canto, quando le voci di quello, secondo debito de l'arte, sono intra sè rispondenti. Dunque quello sermone è più bello, ne lo quale più debitamente si rispondono [le parole]" (*Conv.* I, v, 13).

7. *De vulgari eloquentia* II, iv, 1–3. The same disapproval of those who compose without awareness of rules is expressed in *Vita nuova* XXV, 5 and 10.

8. *Ars versificatoria* IV, 5.

9. The definition occurs, as was widely discussed in chapter 1 above, in *De vulgari eloquentia* II, iv, 2–3. For other, compelling views on Dante's understanding of poetry see Schiaffini 1958 and Buck 1965. More generally see McKeon 1953, "Poetry and Philosophy in the Twelfth Century: The Renaissance of Rhetoric," pp. 297–318, and Barberi-Squarotti 1959.

10. "Rettorica è scienza d'usare piena e perfetta eloquenzia nelle pubbliche cause e nelle private." Brunetto Latini, *Rettorica* IV. Cf. also *Li livres dou tresor* III, 1–2, and Cicero's *De inventione* I, 1–2, for the power of eloquence in the city. More generally see Galletti 1938. Cf. *De vulgari eloquentia* I, xvii, 1, for the complex senses in which language is envisioned as "illustre, cardinale, aulicum et curiale."

11. Paparelli 1975 views allegorical poetry in rhetorical terms. For a review of the theological understanding of allegory see Pepin 1970.

12. The tension between the liberal arts—and rhetoric chief among them—has been neglected by Dante studies, although medieval scholarship has probed the issue. See, for instance, Delhaye 1958, de Lubac 1960, and Weisheipl 1965.

13. A convenient summary is available in the *Enciclopedia dantesca* 4:892–93.

14. *Conv.* I, i, 1.

15. "Philosophiae species tripartita est: una naturalis, quae Graece Physica appellatur ... altera moralis, quae Graece Ethica dicitur, in qua de moribus agitur: tertia rationalis, quae Graece vocabulo Logica appellatur.... In Physica igitur causa quaerendi, in Ethica ordo vivendi, in Logica ratio intellegendi versatur.... Ethicam Socrates primus ad corrigendos conponendosque mores instituit, atque omne studium eius ad bene vivendi disputationem perduxit" (*Etym.* II, xxiv, 3–5).

16. Cf. *Conv.* IV, iv.

17. "Onde, sì come dice lo Filosofo nel primo de la Fisica, la natura vuole che ordinatamente si proceda ne la nostra conoscenza, cioè procedendo da quello che conoscemo meglio in quello che conoscemo non così bene: dico che la natura vuole, in quanto questa via di conoscere è in noi naturalmente innata.... Io adunque, per queste ragioni, tuttavia sopra ciascuna canzone ragionerò prima la litterale sentenza, e appresso di quello ragionerò la sua allegoria, cioè la nascosa veritade" (*Conv.* II, i, 13–15). The passage is the conclusion of Dante's treatment of the allegory of poets.

18. Gilson 1963, "Philosophy in the *Banquet*," pp. 83–161. But see the sharply critical review by Nardi 1944, "Dante e la filosofia," pp. 209–45.

19. "Aristoteles autem ... tribus in generibus rerum versari, rhetoris officium putavit, demonstrativo, deliberativo, iudiciali. Demonstrativum est quod tribuitur in alicuius certae personae laudem aut vituperationem; deliberativum, quod positum in disceptatione civili habet in se sententiae dictionem; iudiciale, quod positum in iudicio habet in se accusationem et defensionem aut petitionem et recusationem" (*De inventione* I, v, 7).

20. Quoted from the *Vita nuova* XXVIII, 2.

21. In chapter XXVIII, 2, Dante writes: "E avvegna che forse piacerebbe a presente trattare alquanto de la sua partita da noi, non è lo mio intendimento di trat-

tarne qui per tre ragioni: la prima è che ciò non è del presente proposito, se volemo guardare nel proemio che precede questo libello." De Robertis in his glosses to this passage from the *Vita nuova* rightly refers to the *Epistle to Cangrande* (xiii, 44) for the sense of proem: "proemium est principium in oratione rhetorica sicut prologus in poetica et preludium in fistulatione." The quotation, which is from Aristotle's *Rhetoric* (III, 14), introduces Dante's own distinction between rhetoric and poetry which is central to our discussion: "Est etiam prenotandum, quod prenuntiatio ista, que comuniter exordium dici potest, aliter fit a poetis, aliter fit a rhetoribus. Rhetores enim concessere prelibare dicenda ut animum comparent auditoris; sed poete non solum hoc faciunt, quin ymo post hec invocationem quandam emittunt. Et hoc est eis conveniens, quia multa invocatione opus est eis, cum aliquid contra comunem modum hominum a superioribus substantiis petendum est, quasi divinum quoddam munus." The quotation from the *Epistle to Cangrande* is taken from *The Letters of Dante* 13:44–48, ed. Paget Toynbee.

22. See the pithy remarks by Contini 1960, in *Poeti del duecento*, 2:522–23.

23. Here are some of the main bibliographical items on Cavalcanti's poem: Casella 1944; Shaw 1949; and Nardi 1983, "Filosofia dell'amore nei rimatori italiani del duecento e in Dante," pp. 9–79, and "L'averroismo del 'primo amico' di Dante," pp. 81–107. See also Nardi 1966, "Dante e Guido Cavalcanti," pp. 190–219, and "L'amore e i medici medievali," pp. 238–67. See also Corti 1983, "Guido Cavalcanti e una diagnosi dell'amore," pp. 3–37.

24. 24 *De inventione* I, vii, 9.

25. The reference is to the first sonnet of the *Vita nuova* ("A ciascun'alma presa e gentil core"), which produced poetic responses by Cavalcanti, Cino da Pistoia ("Naturalmente chere ogni amadore"), and Dante da Maiano ("Da ciò che stato sei dimandatore"). Cf. Mazzotta 1983 for the interplay between past and future in the *Vita nuova*.

26. "Audite quanto Amor le fece orranza, / ch'io 'l vidi lamentare in forma vera / sovra la morta imagine avvenente; / e riguarda ver lo ciel sovente, / ove l'alma gentil già locata era, / che donna fu di sì gaia sembianza" (*Vita nuova* VIII, vi).

27. The divinity and/or rhetoricity of the god of love is a commonplace of love poetry. Cf. Cavalcanti's jocular pose: "Per man mi prese, d'amorosa voglia, / e disse che donato m'avea il core; / menommi sott'una freschetta foglia, / là dov'e' vidi fior' d'ogni colore; / e tanto vi sentiò gioia e dolzore, / che 'l die d'amore—mi parea vedere." On this problem see Hyde 1986.

28. *Vita nuova* XXV, i-ii.

29. *Rettorica* VIII.

30. Singleton 1977.

31. G. Salvadori, *Sulla vita giovanile di Dante* (Rome 1906), pp. 113–14, remarks that the comparison derives from St. Thomas Aquinas (*Summa contra gentiles* II, 43), who quotes Aristotle. St. Thomas actually gets it from Averroes' commentary on the *Metaphysics*.

32. "I miei sospiri, / che nascon della mente ov'è Amore / e vanno sol ragionando dolore / e non trovan persona che li miri, / giriano agli occhi con tanta vertute, / che 'l forte e 'l duro lagrimar che fanno / ritornebbe in allegrezza e 'n gioia."

33. "La sentenzia d'Aristotile fece cotale, che rettorica è arte, ma rea, per ciò che per eloquenzia parea che fosse avenuto più male che bene a' communi e a' divisi. Onde Tullio ... conclude che noi dovemo studiare in rettorica, recando a cciò molte argomenti, li quali muovono d'onesto e d'utile e possibile e necessario" (*Rettorica* VII); cf. also p. 16 on how the eloquent and wise man establishes cities and justice. More generally see Mazzotta 1979, 66–106.

34. "Philosophia est divinárum humanarumque rerum, in quantum homini possibile est, probabilis scientia. Aliter: Philosophia est ars artium et disciplina disciplinarum. Rursus: Philosophia est meditatio mortis, quod magis convenit Christianis qui, saeculi ambitione calcata, conversatione disciplinabili, similitudine futurae patriae vivunt" (*Etym.* II, xxiv, 9).

35. *Etymologiarum* II, 24, 5.

36. "E io adunque, che non seggio a la beata mensa ... intendo fare un generale convivio ... vegna qua qualunque è [per cura familiare o civile] ne la umana fame rimaso, e ad una mensa con li altri simili impediti s'assetti ... e quelli e questi prendono la mia vivando col pane, che la farà loro e gustare e patire" (*Conv.* I, i, 10–14).

37. Wieruszowski 1943; Davis 1984, pp. 137–65. Cf. also Vecchi 1951.

38. Leo 1951; Nardi 1966, pp. 220–37.

39. See Mazzotta 1979, pp. 157–58.

40. *Rettorica* V. On Brunetto cf. Wieruszowski 1971, pp. 589–627; cf. also Alessio 1979. More generally see Davis 1984, pp. 166–97. For Pier della Vigna see Paratore 1968, pp. 178–220, and Stephany 1982.

41. Cf. Truscott 1973; Rossi 1965 focuses on the logical argument of the canto.

42. "Deinde in hiis que dicenda occurrunt debemus discretione potiri, utrum tragice, sive comice, sive elegiace sint canenda. Per tragediam superiorem stilum inducimus, per comediam inferiorem, per elegiam stilum intelligimus miserorum. Si tragice canenda videntur, tunc assumendum est vulgare illustrem, et per consequens cantionem ligare. Si vero comice, tunc quandoque mediocre quandoque humilem vulgare sumatur; et huius discretionem in quarto huius reservamus ostendere. Si autem elegiace, solum humile oportet nos sumere" (*De vulgari eloquentia* II, iv, 5–6). Cf. also *Rhetorica ad Herennium* IV, viii, and *Ars versificatoria* II, 5–8.

43. *Ars versificatoria* II, ix.

44. See Mazzotta 1979, pp. 66–106, for this question and for additional bibliography.

45. An extensive bibliography of the canto is available in Berardi 1975.

46. "E poi ridisse: 'Tuo cuor non sospetti; / finor t'assolvo, e tu m'insegna fare / si come Penestrino in terra getti'" (*Inf.* XXVII, 100–102).

47. The whole passage reads: "Di questa parola [sc. fede] intendo che coloro ànno fede che non ingannano altrui e che non vogliono che lite nè discordia sia nella cittadi, e se vi fosse si la mettono in pace. Et fede, sì come dice un savio, è lla speranza della cosa promessa; e dice la legge che fede è quella che promette l'uno e l'altro l'attende. Ma Tulio medesimo dice in un altro libro *delli offici* che fede è fondamento di giustizia, veritade in parlare e fermezza delle promesse; e questa èe quella virtude ch'è appellata lealtade" (*Rettorica* XIX).

48. Cf. Mazzotta 1979, pp. 78–81.

49. "E queste due proprietadi sono ne la Dialettica: chè la Dialettica è minore in suo corpo che null'altra scienza, chè perfettamente è compilata e terminata in quello tanto testo che ne l'Arte vecchia e ne la Nuove si trova; e va più velata che nulla scienza, in quanto procede con più sofistici e probabili argomenti più che altra" (*Conv.* II, XIII, 12).

50. "There are, moreover, many false conclusions of the reasoning process called sophisms, and frequently they so imitate true conclusions that they mislead not only those who are slow but also the ingenious when they do not pay close attention" (St. Augustine, *On Christian Doctrine* II, xxxi).

51. The link is made by St. Bonaventure, *Legenda duae de vita S. Francisci seraphici* III, 21–22. Cf. also Thomas of Celano, *Vita prima*, chap. 9, par. 22. Celano writes that, while preaching, St. Francis spoke with such "fervor" (an overt metaphor of fiery spirituality) that he "made a tongue of his whole body." Guido da Montefeltro, a Franciscan, is now, ironically, trapped in a tongue of fire. Cf. *Vita prima* I, 27, 73. The importance of Franciscan prophecy and the Joachistic extension of it in Dante has been magisterially illustrated by Kaske 1961. More generally see Reeves 1969, pp. 135–228.

52. The phrase is from Revelations 7:12. The scriptural phrase is used by St. Bonaventure, *Legenda maior*, preface, *Opera omnia*, p. 632.

53. "L'un fu tutto serafico in ardore; / l'altro per sapienza in terra fue / di cherubica luce uno splendore" (*Par.* XI, 37–39); "Cherubin interpretatur plenitudo scientiae" (*Summa theologiae* I, 63, 7).

54. The debate has been much examined. See Perrot 1895, Thouzellier 1927, Douie 1954, and Congar 1961. For a brilliant literary understanding of the question see Szittya 1986.

55. See Paetow 1910, Glorieux 1946, Haskins 1957, Le Goff 1957, and Leff 1968.

56. I am indebted to Lecoy de la Marche 1886, Owst 1961, Zwart 1927, and Fleming 1977.

57. "Tale qual è, tal è; non ci è relione. / Mal vedemo Parisi, che ane destrutt' Asisi: / co la lor lettoria messo l'ò en mala via" (Iacopone da Todi, *Laude*, p. 293).

58. "Just as the Egyptians had not only idols and grave burdens which the people of Israel detested and avoided, so also they had vases and ornaments of gold and silver and clothing which the Israelites took with them secretly when they fled. . . . In the same way all the teachings of the pagans contain not only simulated and superstitious imaginings . . . but also liberal disciplines. . . . These are, as it were, their gold and silver. . . . When the Christian separates himself in spirit from their miserable society, he should take this treasure with him for the just use of teaching the gospel" (*On Christian Doctrine* II, xl).

59. An eloquent opposition to the use of logic in theological discourse is voiced by St. Bonaventure, *In hexaemeron* VI, 2–4, V, 360–61.

60. The attack against the Pharisees depends on the authority of Matthew 23:15, "Vae vobis scribae et pharisaei." For the attack against the Franciscans see William of St. Amour, *De periculis* II, 18–41. Cf. also *Le roman de la rose* 11605–36. Cf. also Rutebeuf, "Du *Pharisien* ou c'est d'hypocrisie," in *Oeuvres complètes de Rutebeuf*, pp. 391–402.

61. Congar 1961.

62. The ecclesiastical-legal texts of Boniface VIII are in *Decretalium collectiones* II, cols. 937–1124. Cf. especially col. 1053. See also Stickler 1977.

63. The medieval recurrence of the *topos* has been investigated by Kaske 1958 in his classic article. Cf. also Curtius 1963, pp. 178ff.

64. For the *topos* of the fox see St. Gregory, *Expositio super Cantica Canticorum* in *PL* 79:500; see also *PL* 114:283, 168:870, and 191:773; cf. *The Exempla of Jacques de Vitry*, ed. T. F. Crane (London, 1890), p. 125, and *Roman du renart* IV, 125–461. More generally see Glorieux 1925, pp. 480–81; cf. also Rutebeuf, *Poèmes concernant l'université de Paris*.

65. *Le roman de la rose* 11200. Dante echoes the word which refers to the Franciscans as Guido da Montefeltro describes himself, "Io fui uom d'arme, e poi fui cordigliero" (*Inf.* XXVII, 67).

66. The whole passage reads: "Il font un argument au monde / Ou conclusion a honteuse: / Cist a robe religieuse, / Donques est il religieuse / . . . La robe ne fait pas le moine" (*Le roman de la rose* 11052–59).

67. The passage reads: "Car Protheiis, qui se soulait / Muer en tout quanqu'il voulait, / Ne sot one tant barat ne guile / Con Je faz . . . / Or sui chevaliers, or sui moines, / Or sui prelaz, or sui chanoines, / Or sui clers, autre eure sui prestres, / E sai par cueur trestouz langages, / . . . Or cordeliers, or Jacobins" (*Le roman de la rose* 11181–200). This is the passage that Dante will echo in *Il fiore* (see note 68).

68. This is sonnet 101 from *Il fiore*, ed. E. G. Parodi, in the *Enciclopedia dantesca*. Cf. also sonnet 92 for references to William of St. Amour (and Siger of Brabant) and links between preachers and False Seeming.

69. "O insensata cura de' mortali, / quanto son difettivi sillogismi / quei che ti fanno in basso batter l'ali" (*Par.* XI, 1–3).

70. The sense of how unstable is the definition of each art is conveyed by Paul Abelson 1906, an early study of the liberal arts. Cf. also the definition of dialectics given by Isidore of Seville: "Dialectica est disciplina ad discernendas rerum causas inventa. Ipsa est philosophiae species, quae Logica dicitur, id est rationalis, definiendi, quaerendi et disserendi potens. Docet enim in pluribus generibus quaestionum quemadmodum disputando vera et falso diiudicentur" (*Etym.* II, xxii, 1); Cf. also John of Salisbury, *Metalogicon* II, xxiv, and Hugh of St. Victor, *Didascalicon* I, xi.

CHAPTER 4

1. Gilbert 1925, p. vi. Gilbert's monograph is still valuable in that it brings together the materials for Dante's treatise on justice, such as Aristotle's *Ethics* V, which Gilbert rightly considers the main source for Dante's thought; St. Thomas's commentary on *Ethics*, to which Dante alludes in *Conv.* II, xiv, 14–15 ("chè Morale Filosofia, secondo che dice Tommaso sopra lo secondo de l'Etica, ordina noi a l'altre scienze"), and IV, viii, 1 ("Lo più bello ramo che de la radice razionale consurga si è la discrezione. Chè, sì come dice Tommaso sopra lo prologo dell'Etica, 'conoscere l'ordine di una cosa ad altra è proprio atto di ragione,' e è questa discrezione"); and Cicero's *De officiis*. Of course, Reade 1909 remains of great interest for Dante's moral system. For a speculative study of Plato's, Aristotle's and Aquinas's idea of justice see MacIntyre 1988.

2. "Lo cielo cristallino, che per Primo Mobile dinanzi è contato, ha comparazione assai manifesta a la Morale Filosofia; chè Morale Filosofia, secondo che dice Tommaso sopra lo secondo de l'Etica, ordina noi a l'altre scienze. Chè come dice lo Filosofo nel quinto de l'Etica, 'la giustizia legale ordina le scienze ad apprendere, e comanda, perchè non siano abbandonate, quelle essere apprese e ammaestrate'" (*Conv.* II, xiv, 14). See Vasoli's commentary for the meaning of "giustizia legale."

3. Lottin 1931. Lottin sketches the development of the idea of natural law from Gratian and the Decretalists through the pre-Scholastics and the Dominican masters at Paris (Roland of Cremona and Hugh of St. Cher to Aquinas in the commentaries on Peter Lombard's *Sentences*, on Aristotle's *Nichomachean Ethics*, and in the *Summa theologiae*). See also *The Cambridge History of Later Medieval Philosophy*, ed. Kretzmann, 1982, pp. 705–19, where the sources of the medieval concept of natural law (Cicero, Seneca, St. Paul, the *Digest*, Isidore, down to Albert the Great's commentary on Aristotle's *Ethics* V and to Aquinas's *Summa theologiae* Ia Iae, q. 94, a. 1–4) are discussed. I stress the fifth book of Aristotle's *Ethics* because it is there that he establishes the distinction between legal justice and natural justice.

4. Aquinas, *Commentary on the Nicomachean Ethics* V, lecture XII, 1019: "We must consider that that justice is natural to which nature inclines men. But a twofold nature is observed in man. One is that which is common to him and other animals. The other nature belongs to man properly inasmuch as he is a man, as he distinguishes the disgraceful from the honorable by reason. However, jurists call only that right natural which follows the inclination of nature common to man and other animals, as the union of male and female, the education of offspring, and so forth. But the right which follows the inclination proper to the nature of man, i.e. precisely as he is a rational animal, the jurists call the right of the peoples (*jus gentium*)." On the traditions of natural law see Lottin 1931; see also H. Johnson 1987.

5. Reade 1909. For a general history of the reception and interpretation of Aristotle's *Ethics* see *The Cambridge History of Later Medieval Philosophy*, ed. Kretzmann, 1982, pp. 657–72.

6. *Commentary on Ethics* V, lecture XII, 1016: "He (Aristotle) says first that there is a twofold division of political justice: natural justice and political justice. This is the same as the division that the jurists make, namely that one kind of right is natural and the other positive. They call right the very thing that Aristotle calls the just object. Isidore too says in *Libri etymologiarum* (Bk V, Ch III) that right is as it were what is just." In the *Summa theologiae* (IIa IIae, 57, 1) St. Thomas inquires into "de jure" and quotes Celsus, who says that "jus est ars boni et aequi." He continues by acknowledging St. Augustine's definition of justice as "love serving God alone." In the response to the question Aquinas concludes that justice implies "aequalitatem quamdam." We shall see later the importance of this notion of adequation and equality for Dante.

7. Maritain 1962.

8. I have drawn the above account from *The Cambridge History of Later Medieval Philosophy*, ed. Kretzmann, 1982, pp. 657–86.

9. Ghisalberti 1932; Allen 1982.

10. See *Epistle to Cangrande* (*Epistola* X, par. 7). The lines in the text are discussed by de Lubac 1959, 1:23. De Lubac attributes this popular definition of the fourfold levels of exegesis to Nicholas of Lyra.

11. A useful summary of the *contrapasso* and an excellent bibliography by Silvio Pasquazi are in the *Enciclopedia dantesca*, s.v. See also Vazzana 1959. There have recently been a few revisionary studies on the notion of the *contrapasso*. See, above all, Abrams 1984; see also, for a different focus, Gross 1983.

12. *Ethics* (B. 1132 b 21): "Some philosophers seem to think that, generally speaking, justice is reciprocation, as the Pythagoreans held; in this way they defined justice without reciprocation." Aristotle rejects this view, for "Such justice is at variance with true justice in many situations, for example, if a prince strikes another it is not required that the prince be struck, but if another strikes the prince such a man should not only be struck but also punished in addition. Moreover, it makes a great deal of difference whether the offender acts voluntarily or involuntarily." In the *Commentary on the Nicomachean Ethics* (V, lecture VIII, 971) Aquinas focuses on the ways in which the statement that reciprocation is justice is true. See also *Summa theologiae* IIa IIae, 61, 4: "The term *contrapassum*, literally 'counter-suffered,' spells an exact concordance of a reaction with the antecedent action."

13. *Summa theologiae* IIa IIae, 61, 4, resp. For the bibliography on the "contraposso" see Pasquazi 1961; cf. the recent musings by Abrams 1984.

14. Kantorowicz 1957. More recently Durling 1981 has studied the poetics of the body in the context of heresy and schism.

15. "Schisma ab scissura animorum vocata. Eodem enim cultu, eodem ritu credit ut ceteri; solo congregationis delectatur discidio" (*Etym.* VIII, iii, 5).

16. The phrase by Macrobius, who is actually describing the medical order of the human body, occurs in his *Commentary on the Dream of Scipio* I, VI, p. 116.

17. Kantorowicz 1957, pp. 390ff.

18. *Commentary on the Nicomachean Ethics* (V, Lecture IV) focuses on distributive and commutative justice. In section 934 Aquinas adds: "He (Aristotle) explains that the just thing is a mean according to a certain relationship of proportions. To prove this he takes for granted that the equal consists in at least two things between which an equality is considered. Therefore, since the just thing is both a mean and an equal, inasmuch as it is just, it is necessarily a relation to something, . . . but inasmuch as it is an equal it pertains to certain matters in which equality between two persons is taken into account." Cf. also *Summa theologiae* IIa IIae, 61, which is devoted to an analysis of commutative and distributive justice.

19. *Summa theologiae* IIa IIae 61, 2, resp.

20. *Commentary on the Dream of Scipio*, trans. Stahl, I, v, pp. 98–99.

21. Del Lungo 1898 (pp. 105–28) understands the lines and the scene in a fairly standard manner. This idea of revenge can be best understood in the light of Brunetto Latini's *Tesoretto* (2121–2134): "S'afeso t'è di fatto, / dicoti a ogne patto / che tu non sie musorno, / ma di notte e di giorno / pensa de la vendetta, /e non aver tal fretta / che tu ne peggior' onta, / chè 'l maestro ne conta / che fretta porta inganno, / e 'ndugio è par di danno; / e tu così disgrada: / ma pur, come che vada / la cosa, lenta o ratta, / sia la vendetta fatta." Cf. Dante's own *Rime* (103:83): "Chè bell'onor s'acquista in far vendetta." See also *Purgatorio* VI, 17–18, for the idea of forgiveness. In the gloss to lines 31–36 of *Inf.* XXIX Ottimo writes: "Qui l'Autore discuopre la cagione, per la quale il detto Geri del Bello minacciava; ciò era, perch'elli era stato morto a Ghiado, e non era la sua morte ancora vendicata per alcuno delli Alighieri, i quali dell'onta e ingiuria sono consorti, cioè a una sorte e a una parte tenuti insieme. E qui riprende la cattività sua, e degli altri suoi consorti,

e infama tacitamente il pestilenzioso animo de' Fiorentini, che mai non dimenticano la ingiuria, nè perdonano senza vendetta l'offesa" (p. 498). See also Francesco da Buti: "che bench'io avesse in cuore di non farne vendetta, ora l'ho molto in più" (1:742). Natalino Sapegno in Getto 1964 (1: 572) sees Dante as oscillating between human passion for revenge and Christian transcendence of the impulse.

22. "And the law of nature is something which is implanted in us not by opinion, but by a kind of innate instinct; it includes religion, duty, gratitude, revenge, reverence, and truth. Religion is the term applied to the fear and worship of the gods. . . . Revenge is the act through which by defending or avenging we repel violence and insult from ourselves and from those who ought to be dear to us, and by which we punish offences" (Cicero, De inventione II, xxii, 65–66).

23. The "paradox of justice and mercy" in Anselm and Peter Damian is treated magisterially by Pelikan 1978, 4:108–18.

24. Lactantius, "De ira Dei," takes to task stoic characterizations of a remote and indifferent divinity. For an extended study of divine vengeance see Mroz 1941, especially pp. 11ff.

25. Sarolli 1971 (pp. 337ff.) interprets, in the light of the encyclopedic principle, the emblem of justice (the lily) in Paradiso XVIII.

26. See Trovato 1991.

27. "Dico che la loro [of riches] imperfezione primamente si può notare ne la indiscrezione del loro avvenimento, nel quale nulla distributiva giustizia risplende. . . . E cui non è ancora nel cuore Alessandro per li suoi reali benefici? Cui non è ancora lo buono re di castella, o il saladino, o il buon Marchese di Monferrato, o il buono Conte di Tolosa, o Beltramio dal Bornio" (Conv. IV, xi, 6–14).

28. The reference is to Ethics V, 11. The passge by St. Thomas is in Summa theologiae IIa IIae, 58, 3, contra.

29. "E quest'è l'una ineffabilitade di quello che io per tema ho preso; e consequentemente narro l'altra, quando dico: Lo suo parlare. E dico che li miei pensieri—che sono parlare d'Amore—'sonan sì dolci' che la mia anima, cioè lo mio affetto, arde di potere ciò con la lingua narrare; e perchè dire nol posso, dico che l'anima se ne lamenta dicendo. . . . E questa è l'altra ineffabilitade; cioè che la lingua non è di quello che lo 'ntelletto vede compiutamente seguace . . . e dico che se difetto fia ne le mie rime, cioè ne le mie parole che a trattare di costei sono ordinate, di ciò è da biasimare la debilitade de lo 'ntelletto e la cortezza del nostro parlare" (Conv. III, iii, 14–iv, 4).

30. "Aequus est secundum naturam iustus dictus, ab aequitate, hoc est ab eo quod sit aequalis; unde et aequitas appellata, ab aequalitate, quadam scilicet" (Etym. X, 7). For the problem of metaphor and legal equity in the Aristotelian tradition see Eden 1986, especially pp. 25–61.

31. "Deinde considerandum est be vitiis oppositis pacio pertinentibus ad opus: quae sunt schisma, rixa, seditio et bellum." The statement introduces Summa theologiae IIa IIae, 3a, where St. Thomas takes up the discussion of the vices against charity. Schism and war are extensively retreated in Summa theologiae IIa IIae, 39 and 40. In Dante's vision—poetic, moral, and epistemological—the divisions of schism and war (both experiences do not make what is partial into a totality) are obviously fundamental errors, as they are in Aquinas.

32. The source of information for Fra Dolcino is Villani, Cronica VIII, 84. For

the historical context on Fra Dolcino see Merlo 1989. More specifically, Nardi 1966, pp. 355–66.

33. I draw this information from the excellent pieces by D'Alverny 1950 and Kritzeck 1964. For Bernard and Peter the Venerable see Leclercq 1975.

34. On Bertran see Boyers 1926–27, Shapiro 1974, Barolini 1979, and Picone 1979. For the biblical-political typology between Bertran and Achitophel see Sarolli 1971, p. 321.

35. Sarolli 1971, p. 385. See also the fine theoretical musings by Pietropaolo 1989.

CHAPTER 5

1. Most useful for this chapter has been the bibliographical compilation by Ashworth 1978. More specifically see Nemetz 1956, Vasoli 1968, Evans 1984, Colish 1985, and Vance 1987. Of interest for the thought of John of Salisbury are Brasa 1960 and Tacchella 1980. For the treatment of dialectics within the liberal arts see Herman 1979, and Stump, "Dialectics," in Wagner 1983, pp. 125–46.

2. "Dialectica est disciplina ad disserendas rerum causas inventa. Ipsa est philosophiae species, quae Logica dicitur, id est rationalis definiendi, quaerendi et disserendi potens. Docet enim in pluribus generibus quaestionum quemadmodum disputando vera et falsa diiudicentur" (Isidore of Seville, *Etym.* II, xxii). See also Rabanus Maurus, *De clericorum institutione*, in *PL* 107:397. For Rabanus logic has the power to unveil the errors of heretics and their fallacious syllogisms. See also Alcuin, *De fide sanctae Trinitatis*, in *PL* 101:9ff., where logic is tied to metaphysics. Cf. also Scotus Eriugena, *De divisione naturae* I, in *PL* 122:469ff.

3. I depend here on Ebbesen 1981.

4. But see Gustavo Costa 1988 for an interesting discussion of this art. Cf. Ryan 1958 for a view of the *trivium* in John of Salisbury.

5. Wieruszowski 1946. See also Rabuse 1966 and 1973.

6. "Ideo et Hermes Graece, quod sermo, vel interpretatio, quae ad sermonem utique pertinet, hermeneia dicitur" (*Etym.* VIII, xi, 45). See also Martianus Capella, *De nuptiis* II, 136.

7. "According to the lesson of the allegory, as soon as he reached adolescence, Mercury, the god of eloquence, in accordance with the exhortation of his mother, wed Philology" (*Metalogicon*, trans. McGarry, pp. 245–46).

8. Michaud-Quantin 1970, "L'emploi des termes *logica* et *dialectica* au moyen age," pp. 59–72; Weisheipl 1964 and 1965.

9. See notes to *Convivio* II, xiii, 12, 99, 225–26.

10. *De nuptiis*, IV, 327–34.

11. "Only when it is associated with other studies does logic shine" (*Metalogicon* IV, 28).

12. The *quaestio*, as the structure of logical arguments, has been variously studied. See, above all, Bertola 1961 and 1964; see also Vanni Roirghi 1967, pp. 179–92, and Chenu 1969, pp. 13–32.

13. The semantics of the Modistae, accompanied by abundant bibliography, is treated by Pinborg in *The Cambridge History of Later Medieval Philosophy* 1982, especially pp. 254–69.

14. Corti 1981.

15. In the *Summa theologiae* III, 2, 1–3—which are questions devoted to the mode of union of the incarnate Word—St. Thomas comments on the monophysitism of Eutyches, as presented by Boethius, and on Nestorianism. See, for instance: "A second type of union is of complete things, that however, are transmuted, as when a compound is made up from elements. Some have asserted [Eutyches] that the union of the Incarnation was accomplished in the manner of such a composition" (art. 1, resp.).

16. Firelli 1987; more generally see Ullmann 1975 and Kelly 1984 on the traditions of law, politics, and logic. For the history of medieval jurisprudence see the concise and well-documented studies by Radding 1988 and Kantorowicz 1970, pp. 93–110. The bibliography by Alford 1984 is extremely valuable. Less cogent, but of sure interest to what I take to be Dante's concerns here, is Adams 1969.

17. There is a voluminous literature on the importance of the duel in medieval judicial arguments. See Kantorowicz 1970.

18. Nardi 1967, "Il concetto dell'Impero nello svolgimento del pensiero dantesco," pp. 239–305, and "Tre pretese fasi del pensiero politico di Dante," pp. 306–45, argues for the Averroistic side. Gilson 1963, "Philosophy in the *Monarchy*," pp. 162–224, counters Nardi's views. He stresses rightly the limits of Dante's Thomism and reads *Monarchia* in terms of Dante's "ideal of a universal Empire" (p. 224). See also Sarolli 1971, pp. 215–25.

19. Most interesting is the essay by Durling 1981; see also the richly suggestive piece by Brown 1982. On general issues of war cf. Contamine 1984.

20. Gilson 1963, especially pp. 206–24; Nardi 1944, pp. 209–45, where there is a lengthy discussion of Gilson's volume.

21. The bibliography on this controversial issue is vast. See Mandonnet 1976, especially the last chapter, "Siger de Brabant, Thomas d'Aquin et Dante," pp. 293–318; Gilson 1963, pp. 257–81 and 308–27, where he considers claims of Siger's "Averroism" and "Thomism" by Mandonnet and van Steenberghen respectively; Nardi 1967; and Corti 1981, especially pp. 77–101.

22. Weber 1970; van Steenberghen 1977; Hissette 1980.

23. Mengaldo in *Enciclopedia dantesca* 1970–78, 2:490–91, gives a broad synopsis of Dante's understanding of *discretio*. One sense of the term is formulated by Dante by quoting St. Thomas Aquinas's own definition: "Lo più bello ramo che de la radice razionale consurga si è la discrezione. Chè, sì come dice Tommaso sopra lo prologo dell'Etica. 'Conoscere l'ordine d'una cosa ad altra è proprio atto di ragione,' e è questa discrezione" (*Conv.* IV, viii, 1). In *De vulgari eloquentia* I, i, i, and I, iii, 1, *discretio* is a principle of order and is tied to *electio*.

24. See Black 1989.

25. Maurer 1981. See also Hissette 1977 and 1980.

CHAPTER 6

1. The motif of memory as the eye of the imagination has been studied by Yates 1972. On the role of the poetic imagination in medieval literature see Wetherbee 1976.

2. In *Convivio* II, xiii, 24, Dante acknowledges the power of music to draw to itself man's minds, "che quasi sono principalmente vapori del cuore, sì che quasi

cessano da ogni operazione: sì e l'anima intera, quando l'ode, e la virtù di tutti quasi corre a lo spirito sensibile che riceve lo suono." Elsewhere Dante wills to probe the sense of the word "mente," and he writes: "Dico adunque che lo Filosofo nel secondo de l'Anima, partendo le potenze di quella, dice che l'anima principalmente hae tre potenze, cioè vivere, sentire e ragionare: e dice anche muovere; ma questa si può col sentire fare una, però che ogni anima che sente, o con tutti i sensi o con alcuno solo, si muove; sì che muovere è una potenza congiunta col sentire. E secondo che esso dice, è manifestissimo che queste potenze sono intra sè per modo che l'una è fondamento de l'altra; e quella che è fondamento puote per sè essere partita, ma l'altra, che si fonda sopra essa, non può da quella essere partita. Onde la potenza vegetativa, per la quale si vive, è fondamento sopra 'l quale si sente, cioè vede, ode, gusta, odora e tocca; e questa vegetativa potenza per sè puote essere anima, sì come vedemo ne le piante tutte. La sensitiva sanza quella essere non puote, e non si trova in alcuna cosa che non viva; e questa sensitiva potenza è fondamento de la intellettiva, cioè de la ragione: . . . E quella anima che tutte queste potenza comprende, e perfettissima di tutte l' altre, è l'anima umana, la quale con la nobilitade de la potenza ultima, cioè ragione, participa de la divina natura a guisa di sempiterna intelligenza; . . . e però è l'uomo divino animale da li filosofi chiamato" (*Conv.* III, ii, 11–15). "Mente" is defined as that power of the soul capable of "virtù ragionativa, o vero consigliativa."

3. In *Convivio* II, ix, 4, Dante briefly discusses optics and modes of visions, and he writes: "E qui si vuol sapere che avvegna che più cose ne l'occhio a un'ora possano venire, veramente quella che viene per retta linea ne la punta de la pupilla, quella veramente si vede, e ne la imaginativa si suggella solamente. E questo è però che 'l nervo per lo quale corre lo spirito visivo, è diritto a quella parte, e però veramente l'occhio l'altro occhio non può guardare, sì che esso non sia veduto da lui." The editors of *Convivio* gloss the passage by quoting Aristotle's *De anima* (III, 7, 431a, 16–17; 8, 432a, 8–9), where the "imaginativa" or "fantasia"—from which the intellect draws the material for its knowledge—is discussed. For Aristotle's theory of mind and imagination see Wedin 1988. More generally see Watson 1986 and the brilliant study by Wolfson 1935. Of great interest for the link between Avicenna's idea of imagination and Aristotle is Portelli 1982. See also Hoorn 1972; cf. also Blaustein 1984.

4. Newman 1967 applies convincingly to Dante's text the Augustinian paradigm suggested by Bundy 1927.

5. Hissette 1977, pp. 239–41.

6. In addition to the texts mentioned by Hissette (note 5 above) see Blaustein 1984. Cf. St. Augustine, *City of God* V, 1–8, on free will and the influence of the stars.

7. It is possible to suggest, given the political context of the discussion on free will and determination, that astrology is to Dante a suspect science because it can be used to legitimize the political authority of tyrants, who, having no dynastic or popular source of legitimacy, would avail themselves of the justifications provided by astrologers such as Guido Bonatti at the court of Ezzelino da Romano (1237–56) at Padua.

8. An excellent review of the range of meanings of *intenzione* is by Gregory in *Enciclopedia dantesca* 1970–78, 3:480–82. See also Nardi 1985, "La conoscenza umana," especially pp. 138–41. In *Convivio* III, ix, 7, Dante writes: "Queste cose

visibili, sì le proprie come le comuni in quanto sono visibili, vengono dentro a l'occhio—non dico le cose, ma le forme loro—per lo mezzo diafano, non realmente ma intenzionalmente, sì quasi come in vetro transparente." The passage echoes Aristotle's *De anima* III, 8, 431b. Averroes in his commentary on *De anima* II, 4, t. c. 49, understands "intentio" as the material representation of an object. See also Aquinas's *Summa contra Gentiles* I, 53, quoted by Singleton in his notes to *Purgatorio* XVIII, 23. I found the study of Pegis 1983 compelling.

9. Cf. *Paradiso* IV, 41–42: "però che solo da sensato apprende / ciò che fa poscia d'intelletto degno." The tenet must be complemented by Beatrice's warning that "dietro ai sensi / vedi che la ragione ha corte l'ali" (*Par.* II, 56–57). In *Convivio* II, iv, 17, Dante asserts that it is from sense that "comincia la nostra conoscenza." Yet he knows that there is an intellectual knowledge that transcends the senses: "pure risplende nel nostro intelletto alcuno lume de la vivacissima loro [separate substances] essenza." In *Convivio* III, iv, 9, the limit of the intellect's power to grasp separate substances lies in the "fantasia."

10. I have slightly altered Toynbee's translation (p. 201) to fit the grammar of my sentence.

11. On Epicurean *voluptas* see Brown 1982. Cf. also St. Augustine, *City Of God* V, 9, for a critique of Cicero's understanding of free will.

12. *Monarchia* I, xii, 2. Cf. Murari 1905, pp. 318–20, for the links between Dante and Boethius.

13. I am translating from Nardi 1944, "Il libero arbitrio e la storiella dell'asino di Buridano," p. 302. Cf.: "Si ergo iudicium moveat omnino appetitum et nullo modo preveniatur ab eo, liberum est; si vero ab appetitu quocunque modo preveniente iudicium moveatur, liberum esse non potest, quia non a se, sed ab alio captivum trahitur" (*Monarchia* I, xi, 4–5).

14. Hissette 1977, pp. 241–51. Cf. Lottin 1942–49, 1:274–77.

15. *Summa theologiae* I, 83, 8; cf. also I-II, 13, 1; *De veritate* XXII, 15. On the whole issue see Lottin 1942–49, "Nature du libre arbitre," 1:207–16; Cf. also Gilson 1956, pp. 252–56.

16. Cf. the account by Leff 1968, especially pp. 225–28.

17. Of great interest on the problem of the soul in the thirteenth century is Pegis 1963. Cf. also on the question of the soul and its faculties, the possible intellect (and the polemic against Averroes' interpretation of Aristotle's *De anima*), Aquinas, *Summa contra Gentiles*, chaps. 58–65.

18. Aquinas, *On the Unity of the Intellect against the Averroists*, trans. Zedler, chap. IV, par. 89, pp. 60–61. Cf. also Albert the Great, *De unitate intellectus contra Averroem*, in *Opera omnia* 10:437–76. The relation of Siger's writings to St. Thomas's treatises is far from clear. Mandonnet 1976 believed that St. Thomas attacked Siger's *De anima intellectiva*, but Van Steenberghen 1977 has refuted him. It may be that Aquinas's polemic was directed against the *Quaestiones in tertium de anima*. Cf. the remarks in the translation of the the the *De unitate* by Nardi 1947; cf. Gilson 1955, pp. 396–97

19. *On the Unity of the Intellect against the Averroists*, trans. Zedler, chap. IV, par. 105, p. 61.

20. Stillinger 1992 has studied the tradition and function of the commentary in the *Vita nuova*; cf. also D'Andrea 1980; Singleton 1977, and Shaw 1976.

21. Cf. Corti 1983; see also the introduction to the translation of Cavalcanti's poetry by Nelson 1986, especially pp. xxxvi–liii.

22. *De anima* I, 5 (5 rb); IV, 1 (17 va). Avicenna's topography of the mind is referred to and opposed to St. Augustine's three modes of vision by Aquinas, *Summa theologiae* I, 78, 4. Cf. Albert the Great, *De apprehensione* and *Sum. de Creat.*, in *Opera omnia* 3 and 2, respectively. See also Bundy 1927, pp. 177ff.

23. Richard of St. Victor, *The Twelve Patriarchs*; for Benjamin Minor see chaps. V and VI, pp. 58–59.

24. Richard of St. Victor, *The Twelve Patriarchs*, chap. XVI, p. 68.

25. "Un secondo accenno all'*immaginativa* si ha nel *Purgatorio*, là dove si dice, che essa compie un lavorio nel quale non è soccorsa dalle impressioni dei sensi esterni, ma da 'lume che nel ciel s'informa,' cioè dall'influenza naturale delle sfere celesti e non, come pensano erroneamente alcuni, da specie intelligibili partecipate per grazia" (Nardi 1984, "La conoscenza umana," p. 140). Nardi goes on to stress that Dante's sense of the mind's visionary experiences (cf. *Purg.* IX, 16–18: "la mente nostra, peregrina / più da la carne e men da' pensier presa, / a le sue vision quasi è divina") is Platonic and not Aristotelian in origin. Cf. Singleton's commentary on *Purgatorio* XVII, 13–18.

26. St. Thomas Aquinas gives an extended analysis of wrath, both as a virtue (righteous indignation) and as a vice against the order of reason in the *Summa theologiae* IIa IIae, 158, 1–8. Cf. Aristotle's *Ethics* II, 5, cited by Aquinas.

27. *Summa theologiae* IIa IIae, 158, 1, r., quotes Gregory's *Moralia* V, 45 (*PL* 75:727). In article 4 Aquinas cites Chrysostom.

28. Wack 1990, especially pp. 74ff.; cf. Ciavolella 1976 and, above all, the magisterial study on medieval physicians by Nardi 1959.

CHAPTER 7

1. "Hic homo singularis intelligit," writes Aquinas in his *De unitate intellectus contra Averroistas*, chap. III, par. 62. Cf. notes 18 and 19 in the previous chapter. Cf. also Nardi 1960, "Individualità e immortalità nell'averroismo e nel tomismo," pp. 209–20.

2. Rosen 1988. The debate has received fresh attention from Spariosu 1991, pp. 141–93. Cf. also Havelock 1961.

3. The bibliography on *Purgatorio* XIX is vast. I shall refer to items that touch on my argument. Hollander 1969, pp. 136ff., connects the dream of the Siren with the preceding cantos of *Purgatorio* and the vision of Beatrice in *Purgatorio* XXX (p. 144). The typology of dreams in Dante has recently been drafted by Cervigni 1986. For the earlier tradition of dreams, visions, and prophecy see the special issue on "Sogni, visioni e profezie nell'antico cristianesimo," in *Augustinianum* 29 (1989), particularly the noteworthy articles by M. Dulaye, E. Giannarelli, and G. M. Vian.

4. "We shall read today in the book of experience. Turn your minds inward upon yourselves, and let each of you examine his own conscience in regard to those things that are to be mentioned." Thus writes St. Bernard in *Canticles* III, 1, 1. St. Bonaventure, in the same vein, believes that by entering "our own self, that is, our own mind," one can see reflected God's image (*Itinerarium* III, 1, Quaracchi V, 303).

5. For the sin of *acedia* see Wenzel 1967. For the deadly sins see Bloomfield 1952.

6. "Aenigma est quaestio obscura, quae difficile intellegitur, nisi aperiatur, ut est illud (*Iudic.* 14, 14): 'De comedente exivit cibus, et de forte egressa est dulcedo' significans ex ore leonis favum extractum. Inter allegoriam autem et aenigma hoc interest'" (*Etym.* I, xxxvii, 26). Cf. Pepin 1976, Dronke 1974, and above all Chenu 1955.

7. Iacopo della Lana, *Purgatorio* XIX, p. 209, writes: "Or l'autore fittivamente nella sua visione introduce una femmina così inordinata ne' suoi membri, come lo testo palesa, poi in processo di tempo ella si rifà e diventa piacevile, e nel parlare faconda; le quali diversitadi hanno per allegoria a significare la avarizia, . . . L'altra diversità, che appare nella sua piacevolezza e facundia, hae a significare per allegoria lo parere dell'animo perverso e inviluppoto nelle sue dillettazioni, il quale ha tutto lo suo intendimento in possedere ricchezza temporale." In the Ottimo Commento, on the other hand, one reads: "Sicchè altro non vuole dire la detta femmina, se non che io sono donna di dilettazione libidinosa circa le temporali dilettazioni" (*Purg.* XIX, p. 341).

8. Mazzeo 1960; Grandgent 1975, p. 165.

9. Mazzotta 1979, pp. 66–106; Nardi 1985, pp. 125–34 and 135–72.

10. This passage is quoted by Antin 1961.

11. Pierre de Beauvais, *Le bestiaire*, art. XI, p. 68.

12. Wilpert 1929; Cumont 1942; Courcelle 1944.

13. Shaw 1938; Nardi 1944, pp. 23–40; Corti 1983.

14. Doignon 1986; Antin 1961; Courcelle 1974, 2:415–22.

15. Cf. Paolini 1982 for fuller bibliography. For a different understanding of autobiographical confession see De Man 1979; cf. Freccero 1986, passim, and Dronke 1970.

16. Harrison 1988 has grasped the poetic questions of Beatrice's body and temporality. For Beatrice's role in the *Divine Comedy*, however, von Balthasar 1973 is indispensable. See also the elegant musings by Pelikan 1990, whose title, *Eternal Feminines*, deliberately alludes to and splendidly complements von Balthasar's "The Eternal Feminine," in *The Glory of the Lord*, 3:101ff. For a suggestive idea of the value of chastity, cf. Foucault 1982.

17. Mazzotta 1983; Stillinger 1988; Harrison 1988.

18. D'Andrea 1988.

19. *Contra academicos*, I, 6, 16, and I, 8, 23, where St. Augustine distinguishes between the wisdom of God and man's wisdom as the effort to reach the knowledge of God. St. Thomas Aquinas, in *Summa theologiae* IIa IIae, q. 19, a. 7, resp., writes "cum autem sapientia sit cognitio divinorum." For an exhaustive study of man's knowledge in relation to God's see Javelet 1967.

20. The phrase comes from Job 28:28. It is used by St. Jerome, *PL* 29:95. For its occurence in St. Augustine see Marrou 1958, pp. 366–67. See also Lactantius, *Institutiones divinae* IV, 3. For Vico see his conclusion to the *New Science*.

21. *Commentary on the Sentences* 3 d 35, I, 2, i. Cf. Pieper 1958, pp. 68–72. Pieper here quotes the suggestive phrase "sans l'amour la contemplation n'existerait pas" (p. 120) by H. A. Montagne. Cf. also Pieper 1952.

22. For a rich and persuasive account of this "visione" see Gilson 1974; cf. Nolan 1970.

CHAPTER 8

1. "Et postquam dixit quod fuit in loco illo Paradisi per suam circumlocutionem, prosequitur dicens se vidisse aliqua que recitare non potest qui descendit. Et reddit causam dicens 'quod intellectus in tantum profundat se' in ipsum 'desiderium suum,' quod est Deus, 'quod memoria sequi non potest.' Ad que intelligenda sciendum est quod intellectus humanus in hac vita, propter connaturalitatem et affinitatem quam habet ad substantiam intellectualem separatam, quando elevatur, in tantum elevatur, ut memoria post reditum deficiat propter transcendisse humanum modum. Et hoc insinuatur nobis per Apostoalum ad Corinthios loquentem, ubi dicit: 'Scio hominem, sive in corpore sive extra corpus nescio, Deux scit, raptum usquae ad tertium celum, et vidit arcana Dei, que non licet homini loqui.' Ecce, postquam humanam rationem intellectus ascensione transierat, quid extra se ageretur non recordabatur. Et hoc est insinuatum nobis in Matheo, ubi tres discipuli cediderunt in faciem suam, nichil postea recitantes, quasi obliti. Et in Ezechiele scribitur: 'Vidi, et cecidi in faciem meam.' Et ubi ista invidis non sufficiant, legant Richardum de Sancto Victore in libro De Contemplatione, legant Bernardum in libro De Consideratione, legant Augustinum in libro De Quantitate Anime, et non invidebunt. Si vero in dispositionem elevationis tante propter peccatum loquentis oblatrarent, legant Danielem, ubi et Nabuchodonosor invenient contra peccatores aliqua vidisse divinitus, oblivionique mandasse. Nam 'qui oriri solem suum facit super bonos et malos, et pluit super iustor et iniustos,' aliquando misericorditer ad conversionem, aliquando severe ad punitionem, plus et minus, ut vult, gloriam suam quantumcunque male viventibus manifestat" (*Epistle to the Cangrande*, in (*Epistola* XIII, par. 28, pp. 638–40).

2. The view of Dante as a prophet has become a commonplace in criticism. See Nardi 1985, "Dante profeta," pp. 265–326. See also Sarolli 1971, "Dante, *Scriba Dei*," pp. 381–419. It falls outside of the orbit of their interests to consider the tension between vision and language or contemplation as ecstasy. I have found useful in this regard historical works by Zarb 1938, Reeves 1964, and more recently Torrell 1974a and 1974b. See also the speculative essay by Bori 1989.

3. Richard of St. Victor, *The Mystical Ark*, I, 4, p. 157. I select a few passages from Richard's definition: "Contemplation is the free, more penetrating gaze of a mind, suspended with wonder concerning manifestations of wisdom; or certainly as it was determined by a distinguished theologian of our time who defined it in these words: Contemplation is a penetrating and free gaze of a soul extended everywhere in perceiving things; but meditation is a zealous atttention of the mind, earnestly pursuing an investigation concerning something. Or thus: Meditation is the careful gaze of the soul employed ardently in a search for truth; thinking, however, is the careless looking about of a soul inclined to wandering. . . . And so, it is the property of contemplation to cling with wonder to the manifestation of its joy. And in this, assuredly, it seems to differ as much from meditation as from thinking. For thinking, as has already been said, always turns aside here and there with a rambling

walk, while meditation always aims, with fixed advancement, toward further things." On the question of Richard's definition see Chatillon 1940. Cf. Dante's pithy definition of contemplation: "e così la contemplazione è più piena di luce spirituale che altra cosa che qua giù sia" (*Conv.* IV, xxii, 17).

4. The passage, which I deploy as a gloss on Rachel's mirror (*Purg.* XXVII, 104–9) is taken from Richard's *The Twelve Patriarchs*, chap. 72, p. 130. Of great interest to my argument is also Richard's distinction of the six degrees of contemplation (*The Mystical Ark*, I, 6, pp. 161–64). The first kind of contemplation is engaged in imagination; the second involves imagination and reason; the third is formed in reason according to the imagination; the fourth is formed in reason according to reason; the fifth is above reason; the sixth is that which "is engaged with those things which are above reason and seem to be beyond or even against reason. In this highest and most worthy watchtower of all contemplations the rational soul especially rejoices and dances when from the irradiation of divine light it learns and considers those things against which all human reason cries out" (163). Cf. Leclercq 1953.

5. The bibliography on Bernard and on Bernard and Dante is very rich. I shall point out either some essential items or items that contain substantial and recent bibliographical information. Gilson 1940, Englert 1987, Aversano 1990, and Botterill 1991. Leclercq's work on Bernard is fundamental to my understanding of contemplation as the source of culture; I refer to his work in note 9 below.

6. Chadwick 1968.

7. The links between Gregory and Bernard are well established, but see the entry 'contemplation' in *Dictionnaire de la spiritualité*, s.v.

8. What I am describing here is the brunt of Bonaventure's *Itinerary of the Mind to God*. On Bonaventure's spirituality and epistemology see Dady 1939, Kleinz 1944, Bougerol 1963, Bettoni 1964, and Gilson 1984. For the question of *askesis* see also Hugh of St. Victor's *De contemplatione et eius speciebus* as well as *Six opuscules spirituels*.

9. Leclercq's insights into contemplation as the foundation of culture—a theme that extends to and binds together Petrarch and Cusanus—are pivotal to my discussion. Leclercq, as is known, has devoted several works to Benedictine and Cistercian humanism and their medieval extensions. See Leclercq 1948a, 1962, and 1963. The monastic motif of *otia* has been given a suggestive philosophical rationale in the study on leisure and contemplation by Peiper 1952 and 1958. See also Mazzotta 1988.

10. The issues that I shall raise here have been shaped by Chenu 1948a, 1962, and 1963.

11. On the Ovidian echo see Brownlee 1986.

12. *De fato*, a. 4. There is an excellent discussion of Albert's concept of astrology by Betsey Barker Price, "The Physical Astronomy and Astrology of Albertus Magnus," in *Albertus Magnus and the Sciences* 1983, pp. 155–85. See also the rich survey by Zambelli 1982 and, in a larger medieval context, Wedel 1920. The themes of astrology and astronomy in Dante have been summarily discussed by Kay 1988. There are textually detailed references to astrology in Dante's *Petrose* in Durling and Martinez 1990, especially pp. 79–107. For the questions of astronomy see Gizzi 1974 as well as the classical study by Orr 1913. More generally, see Bouche-

Leclerq 1963. For a recent overview of Albert the Great's thought see De Libera 1990; more generally see D'Alverny 1970.

13. See Thorndike 1923, 2: 319ff., for Bonatti's writings on astronomy. See more generally Garin 1983.

14. See the classical study of Klibansky, Panofsky, and Saxl 1979. See also Rabuse 1972 and 1973. For the dramatic importance of the celestial bodies in Dante's imagination see again Rabuse 1966. For the mythography of Saturn and its symbolic associations (e.g. horoscope) see the rich documentation in Durling and Martinez 1990.

15. In the *Laus eremiticae vitae* Peter Damian writes: "Eremus namque est paradisus deliciarum, ubi tamquam redolentium species pigmentorum vel rutilantes flores aromatum, sic fragantia spirant odoramenta virtutum" (*PL* 145:246–51). This monastic motif has been studied by Leclercq 1948.

16. VII, 6–10. "In terris dictum templum locus augurii aut auspicii causa quibusdam conceptis verbis finitus. . . . In hoc templo faciundo arbores contitui fines apparet et intra eas regiones qua oculi conspiciant, id est tueamur, a quo templum dictum, et contemplare, ut apud Ennium in Medea: Contempla et templum Cereris ad laevam aspice. Contempla et conspicare id[em] esse apparet, ideo dicere tum, cum te[m]plum facit" (VII, 8–9).

17. Benedict, *Regula* I, 10–11; cf. also LXI.

18. See the suggestive piece on liturgy and time in Dante by Rigo 1980; more generally see Guardini 1935. On monastic singing of scripture see Dubois 1984.

19. Iacopo della Lana, *Par.* XXI, pp. 316–17. The quotation is from Firmici Materni, *Matheseos libri VIII*, bk. III, 2, pp. 97. Cf. Klibansky, Panofsky, and Saxl 1979, pp. 149–50.

20. In the discussion of the steps of the soul's descent from the sky to the regions of this life, Macrobius says: "By the impulse of the first weight the soul, having started on its downward course form the intersection of the zodiac and the Milky Way to the successive spheres lying beneath, as it passes through these spheres, not only takes on the aforementioned envelopment in each sphere by approaching a luminous body, but also acquires each of the attributes which it will exercise later. In the sphere of Saturn it obtains reason and understanding, called *logistikon* and *theoretikon*; in Jupiter's sphere, the power to act, called *praktikon*; in Mars' sphere, a bold spirit or *thymikon*; in the sun's sphere, sense-perception and imagination, *aisthetikon* and *phantastikon*; in Venus' sphere, the impulse of passion, *epithymetikon*; in Mercury's sphere, the ability to speak and interpret, *hermeneutikon*; and in the lunar sphere, the function of molding and increasing bodies, *phytikon*" (chap. XII, 13–14).

21. For Damian's spiritualty see Gonsette 1956. For his idea of contemplation as a quest for wisdom and the tension between wisdom and knowledge see Benedetti 1975. For an insightful account of holiness see Pasquini 1987.

22. *The Mystical Ark* V, iv, p. 315.

23. "Quos gentilitas vates appellant, hos nostri prophetas vocant, quasi praefatores, quia porro fantur et de futuris vera praedicunt. Qui autem [a] nobis prophetae, in Veteri Testamento videntes appellabantur, quia videbant ea quae ceteri non videbant, et praespiciebant quae in mysterio abscondita sunt" (Isidore, *Etym.* VII, viii, 1–2). Cf. the rich studies by Torrell (1974a and 1974b).

24. "It is clear to me that what Moses experienced at the revelation on Mount Sinai was different from that which was experienced by all other Israelites, for Moses alone was addressed by God, and for this reason the second person singular is used in the ten Commandments; Moses then went down to the foot of the mount and told his fellow-men what he had heard" (*The Guide for the Perplexed* II, xxxiii, p. 221).

25. "On the other hand on the verse, *I said in my consternation, Men are all a vain hope* [Psalm 30: 2], the *Gloss* says: 'Ecstasy is meant here, when the mind is not moved by fear, but by some inspiration of revelation is drawn upward'" (*Summa theologiae* IIa IIae, 175, 2, c). The refrence is to the *Gloss* of Augustine, *PL* 36:230, as the editors of the *Summa* point out.

26. "The human mind is rapt up to God to contemplate divine truth in three ways. First, to contemplate it by certain imaginative comparisons. This was the sort of trance that came upon Peter. Second, to contemplate it by its effects upon the intellect. This was the ecstasy of David who said, *In my consternation, All men are a vain hope*. Third, to contemplate the divine truth in its essence. Such was the ecstasy of Paul and even of Moses. Fittingly enough, for as Moses was the first doctor of the Jews, so Paul was the first Doctor of the Gentiles. The divine essence cannot be seen by created intellect except through the light of glory, of which the psalm speaks, *in thy light we shall see the light*. There are two ways in which a man can participate in this light. First, by an immanent form. Thus with saints made blessed in heaven. Secondly, by a sort of transient affection, as was said of the light of prophecy. In this way was the light in St. Paul when he was rapt up. And so from such a vision he was not simply blessed (so that the blessedness would redound upon his body), but only in a degree. Being rapt up in this way relates in some sense to prophecy" (*Summa theologiae* IIa IIae, 175, 3, resp).

27. *The Mystical Ark* V, xvii, pp. 339–40. Cf. also Aquinas, who ponders whether or not prophecy is a steady disposition, a *habitus*, as he says, quoting Averroes' *De anima*. St. Thomas refers to Elisha (II Kings 5:15) and to St. Gregory's gloss on the harp that would be played so that "the spirit of prophecy might come down upon him and fill his mind with future realities" (*Summa theologiae* IIa IIae, 171, 2, contra). For Richard's theology see Roques 1962. See also Javelet 1962a and 1963. For Richard's mysticism see Dumeige 1952.

28. For a study of the figure in medieval literature see Wetherbee 1976. Trovato 1987 has convincingly shown how Dante's sense of "ingegno" recalls the *Metalogicon*.

29. "You should interpret Mercury sometimes as a star and sometimes as eloquence: he is a star in that fable in which Venus commits adultery with Mercury, by which you understand those stars in the ascendant joining their forces; Mercury is eloquence when he seeks marriage with Philology. For eloquence without wisdom is of little help, and indeed it is often harmful. . . . He is said to carry a wand with which he divides . . . the purveyors of poisonous words" (Bernard Silvestris, *Commentary on the First Six Books of Virgil's Aeneid*, p. 26).

30. *Institutio oratoria* VIII, vi, 51. Cf. *Rhetorica ad Herennium* IV, 43; *Poetica nova*, 226–40.

31. These motifs are to be found throughout the work of Damian. See, for instance, *De perfectione monachorum*, in *PL* 145:306; and *De sancta simplicitate scien-*

tiae inflanti anteponenda, in *PL* 145:695 and 702. *De perfectione* is above all an attack against the spiritual decay of the monastic order, and there are traces of the attack in Dante's figuration of Peter Damian. It is in *De divina omnipotentia* that Peter Damian writes: "Veniant dialectici, sive potius, ut putantur, haeretici: ipsi viderint; veniant, inquam, verba trutinantes, quaestiones suas buccis concrepantibus ventilantes, 'prponentes,' 'assumentes,' et, ut illis videtur, 'inevitabilia concludentes,' ac dicant" (xi, p. 110, Brezzi).

32. I draw the information on the debates on the beatific vision from Dondaine 1952. Cf. also Contenson 1959 and Dinzelbacher 1981.

33. The works of Davy 1954 and Dechanet 1942 are essential to an understanding of Guillaume. In the *Epistola ad Fratres de Monte Dei* (par. 112, p. 232) Guillaume presents the scheme of *lectio, meditatio*, and *oratio*. See on this the fascinating analysis by Baudelet 1985, pp. 223ff.

34. For the question of Dante's beatific vision see Brandeis 1962 and the poignant article by Pasquini 1987. On the mystics' theology of love see Jacoff 1984. More generally see Hyde 1986 and Colombo 1987, especially pp. 60–71 and the excellent bibliography.

35. For an entirely different interpretation of grief see Englert 1987.

36. A still valid survey of mystical writing is by Butler 1923. I found very useful—and I found the comments always lucid—Zolla 1978. The essays by De Certau 1964 and 1986 are remarkable. Within the scholarship on the *Divine Comedy* see Gardner 1913; Colombo 1987, which focuses on the links between Dante and Richard of St. Victor, is technically impeccable; see also Hawkins 1984a. Recently Carugati 1991 has given a splendid and thoughtful reassessment of poetry and mysticism. A view complementary to the magisterial study by Giuliana Carugati is being elaborated by Ginny Jewiss in her doctoral dissertation. "Dante: The Body and the Soul of Love" (New Haven, Conn.: Yale University, forthcoming in 1993).

37. *The Divine Names* IV, 5–13, pp. 77–82. See Dondaine 1953 and Roques 1954 and 1958.

38. Gilson 1940.

39. For the relation between intellect and love in the mystical tradition see Javelet 1961 and 1962 and Dechanet 1945. But it is Baudelet 1985 who draws in his richly documented study the wide coordinates of Guillaume's understanding of the *affectus amoris* in *De natura et dignitate amoris*; of the *amplexus caritatis* in the *Expositio altera super Cantica Canticorum*, where one also finds the maxim that *quod enim amandum est, intelligendum est* (par. 122). For the phrase *intellectus amoris* see the *Expositio*, pars. 21 and 105. See "Amour-Connaissance-Experience" in Baudelet 1985, pp. 236–70.

40. The links between Bonaventure and the mystical tradition treated in this chapter are studied by Bougerol 1971a and 1971b. See also Bougerol 1963.

41. It is of interest to recall Dante's understanding of perspective in terms of vision: "Sì che secondo lui, secondo quello che si tiene in astrologia ed in filosofia poi che quelli movimenti furon veduti, sono nove ciele mobili; lo sito de li quali è manifesto e diterminato, secondo che per un'arte che se chiama perspettiva, e [per] arismetrica e geometria, sensibilmente e ragionevolmente è veduto, e per altre esperienze sensibili: sì come ne lo eclipsi del sole appare sensibilmente la luna essere sotto lo sole, e sì come per testimonianza d'Aristotile, che vide con li occhi

(secondo che dice nel secondo De Celo et Mundo) la luna, essendo nuova, entrare sotto a Marte da la parte non lucente, e Marte stare celato tanto che rapparve da l'altra parte lucente de la luna, ch'era verso occidente (*Conv.* II, iii, 6–7). For a historical view of perspective see Federici Vescovini 1968. Cf. also Parronchi 1959.

CHAPTER 9

1. Boli 1988.

2. Isidore of Seville, *Quaestiones in Vetus Testamentum*, in *PL* 83:246A-B; Gregory, *Moralia in Job*, in *PL* 750B; more generally, cf. the definition "Sodoma interpretatur caecitas" in *PL* 113:131B. I have dealt more extensively with these metaphors in *Inf.* XV in Mazzotta 1979, pp. 138–41. Cf. E. Costa 1989. See also chapter 1 above.

3. *Inferno* XV, 119–20.

4. "Ciò che narrate di mio corso scrivo, / e serbolo a chiosar con altro testo / a donna che saprà, s'a lei arrivo" (*Inf.* XV, 88–90). It may be added that Dante uses the word "chiosar" in a technical sense, as if to show his teacher his grasp of techniques of reading. Hugh of St. Victor defines two words—commentary and gloss— which are part of Dante's hermeneutical lexicon as follows: "Commentaries (*commentaria*) are so named as from *cum mente* (with the mind) or from *comminiscor* (call to mind); for they are interpretations, as, for example, commentaries on the Law or on the Gospel. Certain persons say that the word 'comments' should be restricted to books of the pagans, while 'expositions' should be kept for the Sacred Books. The word 'gloss' is Greek, and it means tongue (*lingua*), because, in a way, it bespeaks (*loquitur*) the meaning of the word under it" (*Didascalicon* IV, xvi).

5. *Trattatello*, p. 461.

6. *Trattatello*, p. 443.

7. For the passages in the *Genealogy of the Gentile Gods* see Boccaccio, *Boccaccio, on Poetry*, pp. 35–39.

8. *Trattatello*, p. 472.

9. *Trattatello*, p. 475.

10. "O frate mio, ciascuna e cittadina / d'una vera citta; ma tu vuo' dire / che vivesse in Italia peregrina" (*Purg.* XIII, 94–96) (O my brother, each one here is a citizen of a true city: but you mean one that lived in Italy while a pilgrim).

11. The line on redemption as a dialectics between exile and peace (which is the etymology of Jerusalem) finds a direct correspondence with Cacciaguida's salvation. Cf. "e venni dal martirio a questa pace" (*Par.* XV, 148) (and I came from martyrdom to this peace). For the typological resonance of "peace" in these two lines see Mazzotta 1979, p. 126.

12. "Exilium dictum quasi extra solum. Nam exul dicitur qui extra solum est" (*Etym.* V, xxvii, 28).

13. *De consolatione philosophiae*, I, prose 1. See chapter 7 above for a detailed discussion of the problem.

14. "Poetry employs metaphors for the sake of representation, in which we are born to take delight. Holy teaching, on the other hand, adopts them for their indispensable usefulness, as just explained" (*Summa theologiae* 1, q. 1, art. 9, resp.).

15. For the full account of this radical change of mind see Josef Pieper 1957, pp. 89ff. Cf. Gilson 1956.

16. *Trattatello*, p. 459.

17. "Thy words were found, and I ate them; and Thy words became a joy to me, and the rejoicing of my heart" (Jeremiah 15:16). See also the similes in Isaiah 55:10–11.

18. The text that follows is taken from Dante's *Rime* (1–107).

> Tre donne intorno al cor mi son venute,
> e seggonsi di fore;
> che dentro siede Amore,
> lo quale è in segnoria de la mia vita.
>
>   Tanto son belle e di tanta vertute,
> che 'l possente segnore,
> dico quel ch'è nel core,
> a pena del parlar di lor s'aita.
>
>   Ciascuna par dolente e sbigottita,
> come persona discacciata e stanca,
> cui tutta gente manca
> e cui vertute nè belta non vale.
> Tempo fu già nel quale,
> secondo il lor parlar, furon dilette;
> or sono a tutti in ira ed in non cale.
> Queste così solette
> venute son come a casa d'amico;
> che sanno ben che dentro è quel ch'io dico.
>
> Dolesi l'una con parole molto, e 'n su la man si posa
> come succisa rosa:
> il nudo braccio, di dolor colonna,
>   sente l'oraggio che cade dal volto;
> l'altra man tiene ascosa
> la faccia lagrimosa:
> discinta e scalza, e sol di sè par donna.
>
>   Come Amor prima per la rotta gonna
> la vide in parte che il tacere è bello,
> egli, pietoso e fello,
> di lei e del dolor fece dimanda.
> "Oh di pochi vivanda,"
> rispose in voce con sospiri mista,
> "nostra natura qui a te ci manda;
> io, che son la più trista,
> son suora a la tua madre, e son Drittura;
> povera, vedi, a panni ed a cintura."
>
>   Poi che fatta si fu palese e conta,
> doglia e vergogna prese

lo mio segnore, e chiese
chi fosser l'altre due ch'eran con lei.
   E questa, ch'era sì di pianger pronta,
tosto che lui intese,
più nel dolor s'accese,
dicendo: "A te non duol de gli occhi miei?"
   Poi cominciò: "Si come saper dei,
di fonte nasce il Nilo picciol fiume
quivi dove 'l gran lume
toglie a la terra del vinco la fronda:
sovra la vergin onda
generai io costei che me'è da lato
e che s'asciuga con la treccia bionda.
Questo mio bel portato,
mirando sè ne la chiara fontana,
generò questa che m'è più lontana."
   Fenno i sospiri Amore un poco tardo;
e poi con gli occhi molli,
che prima furon folli,
salutò le germane sconsolate.
   E poi che prese l'uno e l'altro dardo,
disse: "Drizzate i colli:
ecco l'armi ch'io volli;
per non usar, vedete, son turbate.
   Larghezza a Temperanza e l'altre nate
del nostro sangue mendicando vanno.
Però, se questo è danno,
piangano gli occhi e dolgasi la bocca
de li uomini a cui tocca,
che sono a' raggi di cotal ciel giunti;
non noi, che semo de l'etterna rocca:
che, se noi siamo or punti,
noi pur saremo, e pur tornerà gente
che questo dardo farà star lucente."

   E io, che ascolto nel parlar divino
consolarsi e dolersi
così alti dispersi
l'essilio che m'è dato, onor mi tegno:
   che, se giudizio o forza di destino
vuol pur che il mondo versi
i bianchi fiori in persi,
cader co'buoni è pur di lode degno.
   E se non che de gli occhi miei 'l bel segno
per lontananza m'è tolto dal viso,
che m'have in foco miso,
lieve mi conterei ciò che m'è grave.

Ma questo foco m'have
già consumato sì l'ossa e la polpa
che Morte al petto m'ha posto la chiave.
Onde, s'io ebbi colpa,
più lune ha volto il sol poi che fu spenta,
se colpa muore perchè l'uom si penta.

  Canzone, a' panni tuoi non ponga uom mano,
per veder quel che bella donna chiude:
bastin le parti nude;
lo dolce pome a tutta gente niega,
per cui ciascun man piega.
Ma s'elli avvien che tu alcun mai truovi
amico di virtù, ed e' ti priega,
fatti di color novi,
poi li ti mostra; e 'l fior, ch'è bel di fori,
fa' disiar ne li amorosi cori.

  Canzone, uccella con le bianche penne;
canzone, caccia con li neri veltri,
che fuggir mi convenne,
ma far mi poterian di pace dono.
Però nol fan che non san quel che sono:
camera di perdon savio uom non serra,
che 'l perdonare è bel vincer di guerra.

Three women have come round my heart, and sit outside it, for within sits Love who holds sway over my life. They are so beautiful and of such dignity that the mighty Lord, I mean him in my heart, almost shrinks from speech with them. They each seem sorrowful and dismayed, like those driven from home and weary, abandoned by all, their virtue and beauty being of no avail. There was a time, to judge from their account, when they were loved: now all regard them with hostility or indifference. All alone, then, they have come as to the house of a friend, for they know well that he of whom I speak is here.

One of them begins to lament bitterly, resting her head on her hand like a clipped rose: her bare arm, a column for grief, feels the rain that falls from her eyes; her other hand conceals the tear-stained face: ungirt and barefoot, only in her person does she reveal herself a lady. When Love first saw, through the torn dress, that part of her which it is decent not to name, in pity and anger he asked about her and her grief. "O food of the few," she replied, her voice mingled with sighs, "it is our kinship that makes us come to you; I, who am the saddest, am sister to your mother; I am Justice—poor, as you see, in dress and girdle."

When she had revealed herself and made herself known, sorrow and shame seized my lord, and he asked who were the other two with her. And she, who had wept so readily, no sooner heard him than she kindled with yet more grief and said: "Have you no pity on my eyes?" Then she began: "As you surely know, the Nile springs, as a little stream, from its source there where the great light takes the osier-leaf from the earth: by the virgin wave I brought forth her who is at my side and who dries her tears with her yellow hair. She, my fair child, gazing at herself in the clear spring, brought forth her who is further from me."

His sighs made Love falter a little: then, with eyes moist that before had been heedless, he greeted his unhappy kinsfolk. And then, seizing both his arrows, he said: "Lift up your heads: here are the weapons I have chosen—weapons, you see, that are tarnished from disuse. Generosity and Temperance and the others born of our blood go begging: and yet, though this is a disaster, let the eyes that weep and the moths that wail be those of mankind whom it concerns, having fallen under the rays of such a heaven; not ours, who are of the eternal citadel. For though we are wounded now, we shall yet live on, and a people will return that will keep this arrow bright."

And I who listen to such noble exiles taking comfort and telling their grief in divine speech. I count as an honour the exile imposed on me; for if judgement or force of destiny does indeed desire that the world turn the white flowers into dark, it is still praiseworthy to fall with the good. And were it not that the fair goal of my eyes is removed by distance from my sight—and this has set me on fire—I would count as light that which weighs on me. But that fire has already so consumed by bones and flesh that Death has put his key to my breast. Even if I was to blame for it, the sun has now circled for several moons since that was cancelled, if blame dies through repentance.

Congedo (1). Song, let no man touch your dress to see what a fair woman hides; let the uncovered parts suffice; deny to all the sweet fruit for which all stretch out their hands. But should it ever happen that you find someone who's a friend of virtue, and he should ask you, put on fresh colours and then show yourself to him; and make the flower that has outward beauty be desired by hearts in love.

Congedo (2). Song, go hawking with the white wings; song, go hunting with the black hounds—which I have had to flee, though they could still make me the gift of peace. It is because they don't know what I am that they don't do so: a wise man will not lock the chamber of forgiveness; for to forgive is fine victory in war.

19. For a bibliography and the canonical understanding of the poem see the entry by Pazzaglia in *Enciclopedia dantesca* 1970–78, 5:709–11.

20. *Convivio* I, iii, 4–5. *The Banquet*, p. 38.

21. *Convivio* I, ii, 13–14. The passage in its entirety reads: "This necessity moved Boethius to speak of himself in order that, under the pretext of finding consolation, he might palliate the lasting disgrace of his exile by showing that it was unjust, since no one else came forward as his apologist" (*The Banquet*, pp. 36–37).

22. St. Augustine, *The City of God* XIX, 12.

23. *The City of God* XIX, 13. The passage, which unfolds as an exposition of the motif of order and peace, will be studied in chapter 10 below.

24. *De vulgari eloquentia* II, ii, 8–9. For the tragic style of the song see II, vi, 6.

25. See for an extended exploration of the issue Mazzotta 1979, especially pp. 3–65.

26. The traditional readings of the three cantos are best exemplified by the views put forth by Jenni, Rodolico and Donadoni, respectively, on *Paradiso* XXIV, XXV, and XXVI in Getto, ed., *Letture dantesche, Paradiso*, pp. 483–548.

27. *The City of God* XVI, 4, and XX, 17, for Babylon and Jerusalem, respectively.

28. The importance of this element in Albert the Great's thought—as is clear from his commentary on the *Sentences* of Peter Lombard (in III *Sent.* dist. 24, a. 8)—has been highlighted by Gossman 1974, pp. 158–70.

29. *Summa theologiae* IIa IIae, q. 5, art. 4, as opposed to IIa IIae, q. 7. Aquinas discusses whether "timor" is an effect of faith.

30. Gilson 1943, pp. 84–91; more generally Bettoni 1950.

31. Hebrews 11:1. Cf. Mohrmann 1951.

32. The range of the debate is carefully examined by Chenu 1969, especially pp. 32–52 and 58–68; cf. Benoit 1989 and Bandoux 1937.

33. "Fede è sustanza di cose sperate / e argomento delle non parventi; / e questa pare a me sua quiditate" (Faith is the substance of things not seen; and this I take to be its quiddity) (*Par.* XXIV, 64–66). Faith is clearly defined in terms of another theological virtue, hope. Later in the canto faith is referred to in terms of the metaphor of a "coin." On this metaphor, and its extension in the poem see Shoaf 1983, especially pp. 10–13 and 39ff. That the "proper" definition of faith is doubtless a theological problem of some moment is made evident by St. Thomas's remarks in the *Summa theologiae* IIa IIae, q. 4, art. 1.

34. "Moneta appellata est quia monet ne qua fraus in metallo vel in pondere fiat" (Isidore of Seville, *Etym.* XVI, xvi, 8).

35. I have much benefited from Pinckaers 1958 and, more recently, from Bougerol 1985.

36. *De vulgari eloquentia* I, vi, 4.

37. The quotation is from *The Divine Names*, chap. 1. For the importance of the text see *Summa theologiae* I, q. 13, art. 1, obj.

38. "Cun enim nullum nomen Deo proprie conveniat," rule 19, *PL* 210, col. 630C; see also rule 21, col. 631. For Alan's links to *De tropis loquendi* and the question of figurative language in the Bible see Evans 1983, pp. 23–31. A survey of the problem in terms of its grammatical and theological implications is given by Chenu 1935.

39. *Summa theologiae* I, q. 13, art. 10, resp.

40. *Summa theologiae* I, q. 13, art. 11, resp.; and art. 12, resp.

41. Evans 1983, p. 170.

42. Dante's "sublime" has been magisterially studied by Boitani 1989, pp. 250–78.

43. I rely heavily on the excellent article by Godin 1961.

44. N. M. Haring, "A Commentary on Our Father by Alan of Lille," *Analecta Cistercensia* 31 (1975): 149–77. Evans 1983, p. 171.

CHAPTER 10

1. The article on *ordo* will be published in the *Thesaurus*; it is currently available in *Ordo* 1979, pp. 13–22. The entry is by Ursula Keudel.

2. See *The Celestial Hierarchy* and *The Ecclesiastical Hierarchy* for a pervasive understanding of order. Hierarchy itself is defined by the pseudo-Dionysius as a "sacred order" (chap. 3) of *The Celestial Hierarchy*. *The Ecclesiastical Hierarchy*, on the other hand, is a guidance into the degrees of mysteries or secretly revealed truths.

3. A. Duro, "Ordine, *ordo* e loro derivati nelle opere di Dante," in *Ordo* 1979, pp. 185–233.

4. In *The City of God* VIII, 4, St. Augustine also refers to the *ordo vivendi* as the moral domain of philosophy. This concept reappears in St. Bonaventure's *De reductione artium ad theologiam* IV, 11. On St. Bonaventure's ideas of *ordo* see Jacqueline Hamesse, "Le concept *Ordo* dans quelques oeuvres de Saint Bonaventure," in *Ordo* 1979, pp. 27–57. See also Roberto Busa, "*Ordo* dans les oeuvres de St. Thomas d'Aquin," in the same *Acta*, pp. 59–184.

5. See on this Lovejoy 1960, to which I refer in subsequent pages of this chapter. Of great interest is the critique of Lovejoy by Mahoney 1987. In *De ordine* St. Augustine writes that "nihil omnino sine causa fieri" (I, iv, 10) and that everything converges in the idea of order (I, ii, 4).

6. The passage is from Abelard, who is quoting st. Augustine's *De ordine*. Abelard, *Epitome theologiae christianae*, in *PL* 182, col. 1052. See also Lovejoy 1960, pp. 67–86.

7. "Ipsa igitur ratio ordinis rerum in finem, providentia in Deo nominatur. Unde Boethius dicit quod *providentia est ipsa divina ratio in summo omnium principe constituta, quae cuncta disponit.* Dispositio autem potest dici tam ratio ordinis rerum in finem, quam" (*Summa theologiae* Ia, 22, 1). Cf. also Boethius, *De consolatione philosophiae* IV, 6.

8. In *Convivio* III, xv, 11 (but see also IV, xxv, 12), Dante links beauty (which is traditionally understood as *integritas*, proportion, and clarity) with order: "chè così come la bellezza del corpo resulta da le membra in quanto sono debitamente ordinate, così la bellezza de la sapienza, che è corpo di filosofia come detto è, rsulta da l'ordine de le virtù morali."

9. These themes are treated by Stock 1972 and Wetherbee in his introduction to Bernard's *Cosmographia*; see also Wetherbee 1969.

10. Hugh's passage reads in its entirety: "The Greek word *ares* means *virtus*, or power, in Latin; and *rithmus* means *numerus*, or number, so that 'arithmetic' means 'the power of number.' And the power of number is this—that all things have been formed in its likeness" (*Didascalicon* II, 7, p. 67). For the metaphoric bond between wisdom and arithmetic, which is the focus of these cantos of *Paradiso*, it is appropriate to look at the following passage in the *Discalicon* I, 2: "Pythagoras was the first to call the pursuit of wisdom philosophy. . . . Pythagoras . . . established philosophy as the discipline of those things which truly exist and are of themselves endowed with unchangeable substance." Cf. also Boethius, *De arithmetica* I, ii: "Whatever things were constructed by the primeval Nature of things were formed according to the pattern of numbers. For this was the principal element in the Mind of the Creator." More generally see Kibre, "The *quadrivium* in the Thir-

teenth-Century Universities," in *Arts liberaux et philosophie au moyen age* 1969, pp. 175–91. For excellent bibliography on arithmetic, its iconography and its place in the scheme of the liberal arts see Michael Masi, "Arithmetic," in Wagner 1983, pp. 147–68.

11. In *De nuptiis Philologiae et Mercurii* arithmetic is the Pythagorean art of discovering the mystical significance of numbers. Cf. also Bede, *De temporum ratione*, in *PL* 90, cols. 293–578, and Rabanus Maurus, *Liber de computo*, in *PL* 107, cols. 669–728.

12. Foster 1972.

13. Two citations from *Convivio* will suffice to show that "dolcezza" is coupled with harmony by Dante: "Li versi del Salterio sono sanza dolcezza di musica e d'armonia"; "Nulla cosa si può de la sua loquela in altra trasmutare, sanza rompere tutta sua dolcezza e armonia," respectively from *Convivio* I, vii, 15, and I, vii, 14.

14. This is the seventh rule of Alan's *Regulae theologicae*, in *Textes*, p. 164; also in *PL* 210:624C. Evans 1983 discusses the importance of the mathematical sciences in Boethius's *De hebdomadibus*, pp. 67–73.

15. *Regulae theologicae*, in *PL* 210:624c. This is the fourth rule and is taken from St. Augustine, *De doctrina christiana* I, 5.

16. De Lubac 1960, pp. 185–226, treats the history of the formula that the Bible cannot be subjected to the laws of Donatus. "Ubi constructio non subiacet legibus Donati" is Alan's formulation. Evans 1983, p. 38, rightly suggests that the importance traditionally assigned to Donatus over Priscian, as Dante also does, derives from Gregory the Great's dictum.

17. The history of the early medieval debate on Solomon's *sapientia* (with special reference to Origen's exegesis) has been treated by Leanza 1974. Within Dante studies the salvation of Solomon, who is the emblem of love and wisdom, has been glossed by Sarolli 1974, pp. 210–15. For the question of heresy as a problem of *reading* see Mazzotta 1979, pp. 279ff.

18. The other two explicit figurations, as shown in chapter 1 above, occur in Limbo and *Inf.* XV. It is only too well known that Dante defines philosophy as "amoroso uso di sapienza, lo quale massimamente è in Dio, però che in lui è somma sapienza e sommo amore e sommo atto" (*Conv.* III, xii, 12). On the theme of "sapienza" in Dante's *Convivio* see Corti 1983, pp. 78–155. I would stress that the dance of the wise spirits dramatizes the joyful, harmonious mingling of knowledge and love. This is not the case in Limbo and in the punishment of the sodomites.

19. On the problem of dance as an esthetic issue see the suggestive and brilliant essay by Leeuw 1963. For a historical reconstruction of the "dance of the stars" see Freccero 1986, pp. 221–44, where one can find a passage from the apocryphal Acts of John describing Jesus as the Lord of the Dance, ordering his apostles to make a ring around him and dance. The image is crucial to what I call *theologia ludens*, which I explore fully in the next and final chapter. The passage reads: "So He commanded us to make as it were a ring, holding one another's hands and Himself standing in the middle. He said, 'Respond "Amen" to me.' He began, then, to sing a hymn and to say: 'Glory to Thee, Father!' And we, going about in a ring, said: 'Amen.' Glory to Thee, Word! Glory to Thee, Grace! Amen. . . . I would wash myself and would wash. Amen. Grace is dancing. I would pipe, dance all of you! Amen. I would mourn, lament all of you! Amen. . . . The twelfth number is dancing

above. Amen. And the Whole that can dance. Amen" (*The Apocryphal Acts*, trans. B. Pick, p. 181).

20. "Lo più bello ramo che de la radice razionale consurga si è la discrezione. Chè, sì come dice Tommaso sopra lo prologo dell'Etica, 'conoscere l'ordine d'una cosa ad altra è proprio atto di ragione,' e è questa discrezione" (*Conv.* IV, viii, 1). Cf. St. Thomas's commentary on *Ethics* I, I, lect. i, n. 1: "Sicut dicit Philosophus in principio Metaphysicae, sapientis est ordinare. Cuius ratio est, quia sapientia est potissima perfectio rationis, cuius proprium est cognoscere ordinem. Nam etsi vires sensitivae cognoscant res aliqua absolute, ordinem tamen unius rei ad aliam cognoscere est solius intellectus aut rationis."

21. For a general reading of this canto and a bibliography see Mazzotta 1979, pp. 295–305.

22. The problem was confronted, as has been argued throughout this study, by St. Augustine, who in *De doctrina christiana* III, xxix, 40–41, insists on the importance of a knowledge of the rhetorical tropes for the preacher. He also felt, as he makes clear in the *Confessions* I, 18, that excessive attention to barbarisms and solecisms can distract from the importance of the referents of words. See on this chapter 1 above; see also the extended discussion by Leupin 1989; Ziolkowski 1985, especially pp. 110ff.; and de Lubac 1959–61.

23. The phrase used by Boethius in his *Contra Eutychen* III, p. 88, is "verborum inops," as is applied to the Greeks as not being short of words. Anselm—see Evans 1983, p. 34—reflects on the meaning of *proprie* as applied to scripture. For Alan the *artes* take us to the "limen theologiae" (Evans, 1983, pp. 46–48).

24. Jacoff 1988 has elegantly treated the dialectics between transgression and transcendence in the figuration of Mary.

25. Schnapp 1986, especially pp. 36–69.

26. The next chapter will return to the virtue of *cortesia*. For the time being let me mention a passage from *Convivio* II, x, 8: "Cortesia e onestade è tutt'uno; e però che ne le corti anticamente le vertudi e li belli costumi s'usavano, sì come oggi s'usa lo contrario, si tolse quello vocabulo da le corti, e fu tanto a dire cortesia quanto uso di corte. Lo quale vocabulo se oggi si togliesse da le corti, massimamente d'Italia, non sarebbe altro a dire che turpezza." The virtue of courtesy had been stressed by, among others, Bonvesin de La Riva; the *Novellino*, and the *Tesoretto* XV, 139–49. For a history of *cortesia* see Jaeger 1985.

27. The core of Dante's thought on Pier delle Vigne is condensed in the words the suicide secretary speaks: "L' animo mio, per disdegnoso gusto, / credendo col morir fuggir disdegno / ingiusto fece me contra me giusto" (*Inf.* XIII, 70–72). The knotty idea of justice stated by a figure who claims an almost stoical rationality and logic and who, ironically, is the victim of passions that obfuscate his judgment acquires dramatic sharpness when seen in the context of the chaotic natural world the soul inhabits as well as the pledges and oaths (and, generally, the forensic rhetoric deployed for his representation). It is of interest to point out that one reads in the *Liber Augustalis* calls for the "observation of justice" (p. 97), and references to Frederick as "the fountain of justice"—"a Curia, velut a fonte rivuli, per regnum undique norma iustitiae derivetur" (p. 98). Cf. Kantorowicz 1957, pp. 97–143. For the tradition of stoic logic and ethics in the Middle Ages see, respectively, the excellent Colish 1985 and Verbeke 1983.

CHAPTER 11

1. *Summa theologiae* IIa IIae, 168, art. 2. The line from scripture Ambrose quotes, as the notes to Aquinas stress, is from Luke 6:25. Ambrose's own comments are to be found in his *De officiis* I, 23 (*PL* 16, col. 59). Aquinas is well aware of St. Augustine's counsel (*De musica* II, 14) that "ludicra verba et facta" can at times provide relief from the pressures of life. Cicero in his *De officiis* I, 29, objects to the "genus jocandi . . . petulans, flagitiosum, obscoenum." The *eutrapelos* for Aquinas is "a pleasant person with a happy cast of mind who gives his words and deeds a cheerful turn." See also Aquinas's further considerations in *Summa theologiae* IIa IIae, 168, art. 3 and 4.

2. *Convivio* IV, xvii, 4–6, lists the Aristotelian virtues from Fortitude, to Temperance, Magnanimity, Truth, etc. "La decima si chiama Eutrapelia, la quale modera noi ne li sollazzi, facendo quelli e usando debitamente."

3. *Summa theologiae* IIa IIae, 168, 3, r. "Ad tertium dicendum quod, sicut dictum est, ludus est necessarius ad conversationem humane vitae. Ad omnia autem quae sunt utilia conversationi humanae deputari possunt aliqua officia licita."

4. Many studies have been devoted to Dante's neologisms as expressions of his linguistic playfulness and creativity. Ghino Ghinassi, "Neologismi," in *Enciclopedia dantesca* 4:37–38, is very thorough. But he does not explore the link between the two concepts. Even less does he try to come to terms with Dante's *utopian* imagination, of which the neologisms are signs—his reaching out into the untapped possibilities of language and the mind. Closer to these concerns is the suggestive piece by Schildgen 1989.

5. The most sustained and original exploration of aesthetics and theology is by Balthasar 1982, whose point of departure is the philosophical thought of Schiller 1954. Of historical interest remains the theory put forth by Huizinga 1955. For a critique of Huizinga see Mazzotta 1986 and Spariosu 1989.

6. Tertullian opposes to the lies of the pagan theater the marvels of natural spectacles—of the sun, moon—and of God's history as it is played out in the mighty act of the Last Judgment. For Tertullian and Cyprian see *De spectaculis* (*CCSL*) 1:225ff. and *De spectaculis liber*, in *PL* 4, cols. 809–18, respectively. John of Salisbury articulates a much more nuanced position about music and theater than either of his predecessors does. In the *Policraticus* (I, 6) John writes about music as the liberal art that embraces the universe; he adds that the fathers of the church have always praised music because of its power to control the violence of the evil spirits. He concludes, however, that music is also related to voluptuousness and to the evil of feasting, what the Latins call *convivium* (pp. 30–34.) In I, 8 (pp. 36–39), John turns his attention to actors, mimics, and jugglers. He admits that the actor's profession is honorable. In his age, however, spectacles are linked to idleness: mimics, buffoons, wrestlers, sorcerers, jugglers, and magicians are in great vogue, he contends. Reasonable mirth, he concludes in anticipation of Aquinas, is not unbecoming; yet excessive indulgence in it is viewed as disgraceful because it triggers incontinence of mind and lewdness.

7. The idea and the phrasing of the imagination's shadow figures occur in *De vera religione* 40. Cf. von Balthasar 1984, 2:124.

8. St. Augustine's attack against Varro is available in *The City of God* VI, 2–7.

See, for instance, the following passage: "That theology, therefore, which is fabulous, theatrical, scenic, and full of all baseness and unseemliness, is taken up into the civil theology; and part of that theology, which in its totality is deservedly judged to be worthy of reprobation and rejection, is pronounced worthy to be cultivated and observed" (p. 194).

9. St. Augustine relates the experience of Alypius in the *Confessions* V, 8. Alypius, who had a fatal passion for the circus, as is related in chapter 7, goes to the arena, which was "seething with savage enthusiasm" (p. 123). When in the course of the fight a man falls, the roar from the mass of spectators overwhelms Alypius's intended resistance to the bloody show. The account of the robbery of the pear tree is in *Confessions* II, 3.

10. *De musica* VI, 38. Cf. Svoboda 1933, pp. 37ff.

11. *Didascalicon* II, 27, p. 79. See the important studies by Olson 1982 and 1986 on the question of literature as time off and of theatrics respectively. See also the sensitive musings on the idea of feast by Takada 1988.

12. "Lo 'mperadore Federigo fue nobilissimo signore; e lla gente ch'avea bontade venia a llui di tutte le parti, però che l'uomo donava volentieri e mostrava belli sembianti a chi avesse alcuna speziale bontà. A llui veniano sonatori, trovatori e belli favellatori, uomini d'arti, giostratori, schermidori, e d'ogni maniera gente" (*Novellino* XIX, 21, p. 173).

13. The early Italian texts are available in *Poeti del duecento* 1:3–28, 765–88, etc. Muratori delineates the tradition of *ludi* and *joci* up to the Commedia dell'Arte. Very useful are the pieces by Faral 1910, Menendez Pidal [1924] 1957, Curtius 1939, and Battaglia 1958. See the brilliant essay by Leclercq 1975. The opposition between Paris and Orléans, the poetic world of the archpoet and the *ordo vagorum*, is masterfully treated by Waddell 1989, especially pp. 161–242. Recently Picone 1989 has drawn a stylistic map of "giulleria" in the *Commedia*. Cf. the magisterial study by Martì 1953. See also Toschi 1978.

14. A baffling play metaphor occurs in *Purgatorio* VI, 1–9: "Quando si parte il gioco de la zara, / colui che perde si riman dolente, / repetendo le volte, e tristo impara; / con l'altro se ne va tutta la gente; / qual va dinanzi, e qual di dietro il prende, / e qual dallato li si reca a mente; / el non s'arresta, e questo e quello intende; / a cui porge la man, più non fa pressa; / e così da la calca si difende." What makes the simile baffling is both the reference to the game of hazard and the fact that the pilgrim appears as the winner and Vergil as the loser, as if by chance. Commentators usually refer to the glosses on the canto by Iacopo della Lana and Ottimo to explain the mechanics of the game. The metaphor of the pilgrim as the winner is undercut in the unfolding of canto VI as the poet evokes the morass of Italian politics. More fundamentally, nothing for Dante happens by chance. There is a rhetoric of humility deployed here as if to downplay, as it were, the fact of the pilgrim's providential election. On the weighty question of contingency in medieval philosophy and science, which really has no direct bearing at all on Dante's metaphor, see Maier 1984, pp. 341–82.

15. Since I do not discuss *Paradiso* XV, it may be well to point out the presence of the play metaphor in this canto: "L'una vegghiava a studio de la culla, / e consolando, usava l'idioma / che prima i padri e le madri trastulla; / l'altra, traendo a la rocca la chioma, favoleggiava con la sua famiglia / d'i Troiani, di Fiesole e di

Roma" (121–26). The delight procured by one's language and by the mythic accounts of origins suggests a specifically *literary* delight.

16. In his comment on this canto Boccaccio writes: "Usavano gli antichi, e massimamente i Greci, olti giuochi e di diverse maniere, e questi quasi tutti facecano nelli lor teatri . . . e tra gli altri giuochi, usavano il fare alle braccia, e questo giuoco si chiamava *lutta*. E a questi giuochi non venivano altri che giovani molto in ciò esperti, e ancora forti e atanti delle persone, e chiamavansi *atlete*, li quali noi chiamamo oggi *campioni*; e, per potere più espeditamente questo giuoco fare, si spogliavano ignudi" (*Esposizioni*, p. 689). Benvenuto adds: "Ad cuius [of the scene] intelligentiam est sciendum quod antiquitus in magnis solemnitatibus deorum, maxime in Grecia apud Montem Olympum, fiebant varia et diversa spectacula, ad quae videnda concurrebant maximae turbae hominum; . . . sicut etiam a simili videmus hodie, ad festa maxime quae fiunt in villis" (*Comentum* 1:534–35). I would further suggest that this infernal spectacle is the inverted image of the heavenly dance, such as the one of *Paradiso* X, referred to in chapter 10. On *Inferno* XVI cf. Pasquazi 1961; see also Vallone 1965.

17. *Etymologiarum* XVIII, xvi, 1–15: "Spectacula, ut opinor, generaliter nominantur voluptates quae non per semetipsa inquinant, sed per ea quae illic geruntur. . . . Ludorum origo sic traditur: Lydios ex Asia transvenas in Etruria consedisse duce Tyrreno, qui fratri suo casserat regni contentione. . . . Varro autem dicit ludos a luso vocatos, quos iuvenes per dies festos solebant ludi exultatione populorum delectare. . . . Ludus autem aut gymnicus est, aut circensis, aut gladiatorius, aut scenicus."

18. The most probing speculations into the question of *theologia ludens* have been advanced by Rahner 1972 and Miller 1970. I have found most useful the ground-breaking essay by Guardini 1935; the impressive little book by Pieper 1952; the rich philosophical musings by Fink 1960; Caillois 1961; the study of religious anthropology by Cox 1969; and the excellent, radical essays by Spariosu 1989 and 1991. For further bibliography see Mazzotta 1986, pp. 7–8.

19. Cf. Wind 1948 for a history of the tradition.

20. Petrus Cantor, in *PL* 205:203CD.

21. Rahner 1972, pp. 11ff., gives a number of citations about the "Playing of God"—from Plato's *Laws* to Plotinus's *Enneads* III, 2, 15, to the Bible, etc. The phrases by Tertullian and Gregory Nazianzen are from *Adversus Hermogenem* 18, 4 (*PL* 2, col. 236c), and *Carmina* I, 2, 2 (Rahner 1972, pp. 22–23.)

22. The passage is quoted by van der Leeuw 1963, p. 30. Cf. also Cox 1969, "A Dance before the Lord," pp. 48–55.

23. *City of God* XI, 10, pp. 354–55.

24. The notion can be found in Cicero's *Tusculans* IV, 31: "et ut corporis est quaedam apta figura membrorum cum coloris quadam suavitate eaque dicitur pulchritudo." The conviction is repeated in texts such as Ambrose's *Hexameron* VI, 9; St. Augustine's *De ordine* I, 2, 14; 18; Lactantius's *De opificio Dei*. Cf. De Bruyne 1946; cf. also Svoboda 1933; more recently Gregory 1955, pp. 55ff. For Dante's aesthetics see "Dante's Conception of Love and Beauty" by Mazzeo 1958, pp. 50–83; see also Took 1984. Cf. more generally Michel 1982; Phelan 1932.

25. The idea reflects Plato's *Timaeus*—that the world is formed according to the principles of grandeur, goodness, beauty, and perfection. The broad history of the

problems and theories of the harmony of the cosmos has been delineated by Duhem 1954–59. See Gregory 1955 for the Chartrian understanding of the beauty of the cosmos. This same idea was repeated by Quintilian, *Institutio oratoria* I, x, 9–33. Honorius of Autun writes: "the universe is ordered like a lyre, in which there is a consonace of many things, like chords" (*PL* 172:1179, chap. 2).

26. The subject has been so thoroughly investigated that I can list here some of the most notable bibliographical items: Santayana 1955 and De Bruyne 1975, respectively, for a philosophical and historical treatment of beauty. Of great value I also found Phelan 1932, Pouillon 1946, Spargo 1953, Maritain 1961 and 1962, and Eco 1970 and 1986. Leeuw 1963 is very suggestive.

27. *Summa theologiae* I, 5, 4, ad 1: "Three things are necessary for beauty: first, integrity or perfection, for things which are lacking in something are for this reason ugly; also due proportion or consonance; and again, clarity, for we call things beautiful when they are brightly colored."

28. The passage occurs in *Summa theologiae* I, 5, 4, ad 1.

29. In *The Divine Names* IV, pp. 71–85, pseudo-Dionysius goes from the name "Good" for the divine subsistence to "light" and to beauty. "The Beautiful is therefore the same as the Good, for everything looks to the Beautiful and the Good as the cause of being, and there is nothing in the world without a share of the the Beautiful and the Good. . . . This—the One, the Good, the Beautiful—is in its uniqueness the Cause of the multitudes of the good and the beautiful" (p. 77). For the importance of the pseudo-Dionysius for John Scotus, for the twelfth century (Hugh of St. Victor), and for Scholasticism (Albert, Aquinas, and Bonaventure) see the remarks by Leclercq in Dionysius [pseud.], *Complete Works*, pp. 25–32. See also Eco 1970, p. 50.

30. See also *Convivio* I, v, 13, and IV, xxv, 12, where Dante writes: "Quella cosa dice l'uomo essere bella, cui le parti debitamente si rispondono, per che de la loro armonia resulta piacimento"; "E quanto elli [il corpo] è bene ordinato e disposto, allora è bello per tutto e per le parti; chè l'ordine debito de le nostre membra rende uno piacere non so di che armonia mirabile, e la sua disposizione, cioè la sanitate, getta sopra quelle uno colore dolce a riguardare."

31. *The City of God* XV, 24, p. 514. On the lore of giants the encyclopedic work by Stephens 1984 is indispensable.

32. The correction, and excellent bibliography on the problem, is admirably treated by A. Mellone in the *Enciclopedia dantesca* 1:268–69, under "angelo," and 3:123, under "gerarchia angelica." Cf. also *Convivio* II, v, 6–8. Of interest are Cicchitto 1940, pp. 380–89, and Fallani 1965, 3:107–22.

33. A recent and rich history of the controversy, which saw Siger of Brabant, Boethius of Dacia, Aquinas, Bonaventure, Egidio Romano, etc. involved, is by Bianchi 1984. The implications of the controversy for Dante are variously treated by Morghen 1979 and Corti 1981; cf. also Foster 1977.

34. Mellone 1974, p. 195. Cf. also Duhem 1917, 5:365–66. Cf. also Nardi 1956, Boyde 1981, pp. 172–201, and Cornish 1990.

35. I take the information on Philo, Iamblichus, and Porphiry from Gilson 1956, pp. 160–73.

36. *Commentary on the Dream of Scipio*, p. 195. Cf. Pirrotta 1966 and 1968.

37. "Ancora, la Musica trae a sè li spiriti umani, che quasi sono principalmente vapori del cuore, sì che quasi cessano da ogni operazione: sì e l'anima intera, quando l'ode, e la virtù di tutti quasi corre a lo spirito sensibile che riceve lo suono" (*Conv.* II, xiii, 24). Cf. Hutton 1980.

38. *In hierarchiam coelestem*, in *PL* 175, col. 978. For the aesthetics of the ugly in Hugh, cf. De Bruyne 1975, 2:213ff. More generally, cf. Krestowsky 1947.

39. "Pulcer ab specie cutis dictus, quod est pellis; postea transiit hoc nomen in genus. Nam pulchritudo hominis aut in vultu est . . . aut in capillis . . . aut in oculis . . . aut in candore . . . aut in lineamentis" (Isidore, *Etym.* X, 203). For an idea of infernal farce see Spitzer 1944.

40. Jaeger 1985.

41. Guardini 1935 and Rahner 1972 ("The Playing of the Church"), pp. 46–64, have written excellent accounts of the deliberate playfulness of the liturgy.

42. The literary aspects of parody have been illustrated recently by Giannetto 1977 and, more extensively, by Lehmann 1963. Peck 1980 devotes a chapter of his study on Iacopone da Todi to illustrate the Franciscan theology of the "Fool of God," pp. 153–86. It may be added that at least one reason why Franciscans are the butt of satire in medieval literature has to do with the self-humbling, self-parodic thrust of their theology.

43. The passage by Celano is cited from *Francis of Assisi, Writings and Early Biographies*, ed. Habig 1973, II, xc, 127, p. 467. I have found most invaluable on Franciscan spirituality Fleming 1977, especially "The Jugglers of the Lord" and the pages on Franciscan lyricists, pp. 174–89. Equally rich in Franciscan exegetical practice is Fleming 1982. See also Petrocchi 1965 and Vona 1984.

44. On the idea of the "comical" in Dante see the sensible piece by Ferrucci 1980, "The Meeting with Geryon," pp. 66–102. See also Barolini 1984, pp. 214–22, for a consideration of the dialectics between comedy and tragedy. I found of interest a chapter in a manuscript by Massimo Verdicchio, "The Comedy of the *Commedia*," in "Allegories of Dante's *Commedia*," that I hope will soon be published. For a traditional account of the "comic" see Sannia 1909.

BIBLIOGRAPHY

SOURCES AND ANCIENT TEXTS

Acta Joannis. Ed. Theodore Zahn. Erlangen: Deichert, 1880.

——. Trans. B. Pick. In *The Apocryphal Acts of Paul, Peter, John, Andrew and Thomas*. Chicago: Open Court, 1909.

Alan of Lille. *Anticlaudianus*. Ed. R. Bossuat. Paris: J. Vrin, 1955.

——. *Anticlaudianus or the Good and Perfect Man*. Trans. with commentary by James J. Sheridan. Toronto: Pontifical Institute of Mediaeval Studies, 1973.

——. *The Plaint of Nature*. Trans. with commentary by James J. Sheridan. Toronto: Pontifical Institute of Mediaeval Studies, 1980.

——. *Regulae theologicae*. In *Textes inedits d'Alain de Lille*. Ed. M. T. d'Alverny. Paris: Vrin, 1965. Also in *PL* 210:621–84.

——. *Rhythmus de incarnatione Christi*. In Migne, *Patrologia latina (PL)* 210:577A–580A.

Albert the Great. *B. Alberti Magni . . . Opera omnia*. Ed. Auguste and Emile Borgnet. Paris: Vives, 1890–99.

Alexander Neckham. *De natura rerum*. Ed. T. Wright. Rolls Series 34. London, 1863. Reprint. Nendeln: Liechtenstein, 1967.

Aquinas, St. Thomas. *Aristotle's De anima in the Version of William of Moerbeke and the Commentary of St. Thomas Aquinas*. Trans. Kenelm Foster and Silvester Humphries. New Haven, Conn.: Yale University Press, 1954.

——. *Commentary on the Nicomachean Ethics*. 2 vols. Library of Living Catholic Thought. Trans. C. I. Litzinger. Chicago: Regnery, 1964.

——. *De unitate intellectus contra Averroistas* (On the unity of the intellect against the Averroists). Trans. with an introduction by Beatrice H. Zedler. Milwaukee: Marquette University Press, 1968.

——. *In librum beati Dionysii de Nominibus expositio*. Ed. C. Pera. Turin: Marietti, 1950.

——. *Summa theologiae* (Latin text and English trans). Blackfrairs Edition. New York: McGraw-Hill, 1964.

Aristotle. *The Metaphysics*. Trans. Hugh Tredennick. Cambridge, Mass.: Harvard University Press, 1935–36.

——. *The Nicomachean Ethics*. The Loeb Classical Library. Ed. and trans. H. Rackham. Cambridge, Mass.: Harvard University Press, 1939.

——. *On Physics*. Trans. P. H. Wicksteed and F. Cornford. New York: Putnam, 1929–34.

——. *The Rhetoric and the Poetics of Aristotle*. Trans. W. Rhys Roberts and Ingram Bywater. A Modern Library Book. New York: Random House, 1954.

Augustine, St. *The City of God*. Trans. Marcus Dods. New York: The Modern Library, 1950.

——. *The Confessions of St. Augustine*. Trans. Rex Warner. New York and Toronto: New American Library, 1963.

Augustine, St. *De doctrina christiana.* See *Corpus christianorum* 28, 1970.

———. *De ordine.* See *Corpus christianorum* 29, 1970.

———. *De quantitate animae* (The greatness of the soul). Trans. Joseph Colleran. Westminster, Md.: The Newman Press, 1950.

———. *On Christian Doctrine.* Trans. D. W. Robertson, Jr. New York: Liberal Arts Press, 1958.

Averroes. *Commentarium magnum in Aristotelis De anima libros.* Ed. F. S. Crawford. Cambridge, Mass.: The Medieval Academy of America, 1953.

Bartholomeus Anglicus. *De proprietatibus rerum.* Frankfurt, 1601. Reprint (facs). Frankfurt, 1964.

———. *On the Properties of Things, John Trevisa's Translation of Bartholomeus Anglicus, De proprietatibus rerum: A Critical Text.* 2 vols. Ed. M. C. Seymour et al. Oxford, 1975.

Benedict, St. *Regola di San Benedetto volgarizzata nel buon secolo.* A cura di Emmanuele Lisi. Florence: Barbera, 1855.

Benvenuto de Rambaldis de Imola. *Comentum super Dantis Aldigherij Comoediam.* 5 vols. Ed. J. P. Lacaita, Florence: Barbera, 1887.

Bernard of Clairvaux, St. *On Consideration.* Trans. George Lewis. Oxford: Clarendon Press, 1908.

———. *The Steps of Humility.* Trans. George Bosworth Burch. Cambridge, Mass.: Harvard University Press, 1940.

Bernard Silvestris. *Commentary on the First Six Books of Virgil's Aeneid.* Ed. and trans. E. G. Schreiber and T. E. Maresca. Lincoln: University of Nebraska Press, 1979.

———. *The Cosmographia of Bernardus Silvestris.* Trans. Winthrop Wetherbee. New York: Columbia University Press, 1973.

———. *De mundi universitate libri duo sive megacosmus et microcosmus.* Ed. C. Barach and J. Wrobel. [Innsbruck, 1876]. Reprint. Frankfurt a. M., 1964.

Boccaccio, Giovanni. *Boccaccio on Poetry.* Ed. and trans. Charles S. Osgood. New York: The Library of Liberal Arts, 1956.

———. *Esposizione sopra la Comedia di Dante.* A cura di Giorgio Padoan. In *Tutte le opere di Giovanni Boccaccio,* a cura di Vittore Branca. Milan, 1965.

———. *Trattatello in laude di Dante.* Ed. Pier Giorgio Ricci. Vol. 3 of *Tutte le opere,* ed. Vittore Branca. Milan, 1974.

Boethius. *De institutione arithmetica. De institutione musica.* Ed. Friedlein. Leizig: Teubner, 1867.

———. *The Theological Tractates. The Consolation of Philosophy.* Ed. and trans. H. F. Stewart and E. K. Rand. Loeb Classical Library. London: Heinemann, 1946.

Boethius of Dacia. *De summo bono.* In *Boethii Daci opera. Topica. Opuscola,* ed. Nicholas G. Green-Pederson. Corpus philosophorum danicorum, vol. 6, part 2. Copenhagen, 1976.

Bonaventure, St. *Opera omnia.* Ed. PP. Collegii a san Bonaventura. In *De reductione artium ad theologiam* 5 (1891). Quaracchi. 1882–1902.

———. *The Soul's Journey into God. The Tree of Life. The Life of St. Francis.* Trans. Ewert Cousins. The Classics of Western Spirituality. New York: The Paulist Press, 1978.

Buti, Francesco da. *Commento di Francesco da Buti sopra la Divina commedia di Dante Alighieri*. Ed. Crescentino Giannini. Pisa: Nistri, 1858.

Cassiodorus. *De institutione divinarum litterarum. De artis et disciplinis liberalium litterarum*. In *PL* 70:1105–1220. *De schematibus, tropis, et quibusdam locis rhetoricis s. scripturae*. In *PL* 70:1269–80.

Cavalcanti, Guido. *The Poetry of Guido Cavalcanti*. Trans. Lowry Nelson, Jr. New York: Garland Press, 1986.

——. *Rime*. A cura di Domenico de Robertis. Turin: Einaudi, 1986.

Chretien de Troyes. *Arthurian Romances*. Ed. and trans. W. W. Comfort. Everyman's Library. New York: Dutton, 1967,

Cicero. *De finibus bonorum et malorum*. Ed. and trans. H. Backham. Loeb Classical Library. Cambridge, Mass.: Harvard University Press, 1967.

——. *De inventione. De optimo genere oratorum. Topica*. Trans. H. M. Hubbell. Loeb Classical Library. Cambridge, Mass.: Harvard University Press, 1976.

——. *De natura deorum*. Ed. and trans. A. S. Pease. Cambridge, Mass.: Harvard University Press, 1958.

——. *De republica. De legibus* (with an English translation by Clinton Walker Keys). New York: Putnam, 1928.

——. *De officiis*. Ed. Paolo Fedeli. Milan: Mondadori, 1965.

——. *Tusculanorum disputationum*. Ed. O. Plasberg. Leipzig: Teubner, 1917.

Corpus christianorum series latina (*CCSL*). Turnhout: Brepols.

Cyprian. *De spectaculis liber*. In *PL* 4:809–18.

Damian, Peter. *De divine omnipotentia*. Testo critico con introduzione a cura di P. Brezzi. Traduzione di Bruno Nardi. Edizione nazionale dei classici del pensiero italiano. Florence: Vallecchi, 1943.

——. *Opera omnia*. In *PL* 144–45.

Decretalium collectiones. In *Corpus iuris canonici*, 2 vols., ed. E. Friedberg. Leipzig: Tauchnitz, 1881–1922.

Dionysius [pseudo.] *The Complete Works* (*The Divine Names, The Mystical Theology, The Celestial Hierarchy, The Ecclesiatical Hierarchy*). Trans. Colm Luibheid. The Classics of Western Spirituality. New York: Paulist Press, 1987.

——. *De caelesti herarchia*. Trans. John Scotus (Eriugena). In *PL* 122:1035–70.

Du Cange, Charles Dufresne. *Glossarium mediae et infimae latinitatis*. 10 vols. in 5. Graz: Akademische Druck–V. Verag Sanstalt, 1954.

Faral, Edmund. *Les arts poetiques du XIIe et du XIIIe siecles: Recherches et documents sur la technique litteraire du moyen age*. Paris, 1924 (reprint 1962).

Firmici Materni, Iulius. *Matheseos libri VIII*. Eds. W. Kroll and F. Skutsch. 2 vols. Leipzig: Teubner, 1968.

Francis of Assisi, Writings and Early Biographies: English Omnibus of the Sources for the Life of St. Francis. Ed. Marion A. Habig. Chicago: Franciscan Herald Press, 1973.

Geoffrey of Vinsauf. *Poetria nova*. See Faral, pp. 194–262.

——. *Poetria nova of Geoffrey of Vinsauf*. Trans. Margaret F. Nims. Toronto: University of Toronto Press, 1967.

Guillaume de Lorris and Jean De Meun. *Le roman de la rose*. Ed. Daniel Poirion. Paris: Garnier-Flammarion, 1974.

Guillaume de Saint-Amour. *De periculis*. In Ortwin Gratius. *Fasciculum rerum expetendarum*. Ed. Edward Brown. London, 1690.

Guillaume de Saint-Thierry. *De contemplando Deo*. Ed. and trans. M.-M. Davy. In *Deux traites de l'amour de Dieu*. Paris: J. Vrin, 1953.

———. *De natura et dignitate amoris*. Ed. and trans. M.-M. Davy. In *Deux traites de l'amour de Dieu*. Paris, 1953.

———. *Expositio altera super Cantica Canticorum*. Ed. J.-M. Dechanet. Trans. M. Dumontier. In *Exposé sur le Cantique des cantiques*. Sources chretiennes 82. Paris, 1962.

Henri d'Andeli. *The Battle of the Seven Arts: A French Poem by Henry d'Andeli, Trouvere of the Thirteenth Century*. Ed. and trans. Louis John Paetow. Memoirs of the University of California 4, no. 1. Berkeley: University of California Press, 1914.

Honorius of Autun. *De anima exsilio et patria*. PL 172:1241–46.

———. *Imago mundi*. Ed. Valerie I. J. Flint. In "Honorius Augustodunensis: 'Imago mundi,'" *Archives d'histoire doctrinale et litteraire du moyen age* 49(1982): 7–153.

———. *Liber duodecim quaestionum*. PL 172:1177–86.

Hugh of St. Victor. *La contemplation et ses espèces* Ed. Roger Baron. Tournai. Paris: Desclée, 1955.

———. *Didascalicon*. Ed. and trans. with notes and commentary by Jerome Taylor. In *The 'Didascalicon' of Hugh of St. Victor*. New York: Columbia University Press, 1961.

———. *Six opuscules spirituels*. Ed. and trans. with notes and commentary by Roger Baron. Sources chretiennes 135. Paris: Editions du Cerf, 1969.

Hyginus, Gaius Iulius. *Fabulae. Poeticon astronomicon*. In August van Staveren, *Authores mythographi latini*. Amsterdam: Luchtmans, 1742.

Iacopo della Lana. *Commedia di Dante degli Allagherii*. 3 vols. Ed. Luciano Scarabelli. Bologna: Tipografia Regia, 1866.

Iacopone da Todi. *Laude*. Ed. F. Mancini. Bari: Laterza, 1980.

Isidore of Seville. *Etymologiarum sive originum libri XX*. 2 vols. Ed. W. M. Lindsay. Oxford: Clarendon Press, 1911.

John of Garland. *Integumenta Ovidii: Poemetto inedito del secolo XIII*. Ed. Fausto Ghisalberti. Testi inediti o rari 2. Messina, 1933.

———. *Parisiana poetria*. Ed. and trans. Traugott Lawler. New Haven, Conn.: Yale University Press, 1977.

John of Salisbury. *Metalogicon libri III*. Ed. C. J. Webb. Oxford: Clarendon Press, 1929.

———. *The Metalogicon of John of Salisbury: A Twelfth-Century defense of the Verbal and Logical Arts of the Trivium*. Trans. with an introduction by Daniel D. McGarry. Westport, Conn.: Greenwood Press, 1982.

———. *Policratici sive de nugis curalium et vestigiis philosophorum libri VIII*. 2 vols. Ed. C. J. Webb. Oxford: Oxford University Press, 1909.

———. *The Statesman's Book of John of Salisbury*. Trans. John Dickinson. New York: A. A. Knopf, 1927.

Lactantius. "De ira Dei." In *Divinarum institutionum libri VII*. Antwerp, 1532.

Latini, Brunetto. *Li livres dou tresor*. Ed. F. J. Carmody. Berkeley and Los Angeles: University of California Press, 1948.

———. *Tesoretto*. In G. Contini, *Poeti del duecento*, 2:169–284. Milan: Ricciardi, 1960.

———. *La rettorica*. Ed. Francesco Maggini. Florence: Le Monnier, 1968.

Macrobius. *Commentarii in somnium Scipionis.* Ed. Jacob Willis. Leipzig: Teubner, 1970.

———. *Commentary on the Dream of Scipio.* Ed. and trans. William Harris Stahl. Records of Civilization, Sources and Studies 48. New York: Columbia University Press, 1952.

———. *Saturnalia.* Ed. J. Willis. In *Opera*, vol. 1. Leipzig: Teubner, 1970.

Martianus Capella. *De nuptiis Philologiae et Mercurii.* Ed. Adolfus Dick, with additions by Jean Preaux. Stuttgart: Teubner, 1925.

Matthew of Vendome. *Ars versificatoria.* See Faral, pp. 109–93.

———. "Matthew of Vendome: Introductory Treatise on the Art of Poetry." Trans. Ernst Gallo. *Proceedings of the American Philosophical Society* 118 (1974): 51–92.

Moses Maimonides. *The Guide of the Perplexed.* 2d rev. ed. Trans. from the original Arabic text by M. Friedlander. New York: Dover Publications, 1962.

Muratori, L. *Antiquitates italicae medi aevi.* Vol. 2. De spectaculis et ludis publicis medi aevi 29. Milan, 1793.

Novellino. Testo critico, introduzione e note a cura di Guido Favati. Genoa: Bozzi, 1970.

On the Eternity of the World, by St. Thomas Aquinas, Siger of Brabant and St. Bonaventure. Trans. C. Vollert, L. Kendzierski, and P. Byrne. Milkwaukee: Marquette University Press, 1964.

Ottimo. *L'Ottimo commento della Divina commedia.* 3 vols. Ed. Accademia della Crusca. Pisa: Capurro, 1827–29.

Ovid. *Metamorphoses.* Ed. and trans. Frank Justus Miller. Loeb Classical Library. Cambridge, Mass.: Harvard University Press, 1977.

Patrologiae cursus completus (PL). Ed. J. P. Migne: Paris, 1844–64 (with later printings).

Peter of Spain. *The Summulae logicales.* Ed. and trans. Joseph P. Mullally. Publications in Medieval Studies 8. Notre Dane, Ind.: University of Notre Dame Press, 1945.

Petrus Cantor. *Verbum abbreviatum.* In *PL* 205:23–554.

Pierre de Beauvais. *Bestiaire.* Ed. critique per Guy R. Mermier. Paris: A. G. Nizet, 1977.

PL. See *Patrologiae cursus completus.*

Poeti del duecento. 2 vols. A cura di Gianfranco Contini. Milan-Naples: Ricciardi, 1960.

Prudentius. *Liber peristefanon.* See *Corpus christianorum* 126, 1966.

Quintilian. *Institutio oratoria.* 4 vols. Ed. and trans. H. E. Butler. Loeb Classical Library. Cambridge, Mass.: Harvard University Press, 1976.

Rabanus Maurus. *De rerum naturis (De universo).* PL. 111:9–614.

Richard of St. Victor. *Les quatre degres de la violente Charité.* Trans. with notes and introduction by Gervais Dumeige. Paris: J. Vrin, 1955.

———. *The Twelve Patriarchs, The Mystical Ark, Book Three of the Trinity.* Trans. Grover A. Zinn. The Classics of Western Spirituality. New York: Paulist Press, 1979.

Ristoro d'Arezzo. *La composizione del mondo colle sue cascioni.* Ed. Alberto Morino. Scrittori italiani e testi antichi. Florence: Accademia della Crusca, 1976.

Roman de renart. Ed. D. M. Meon. Paris: Treuttel et Würtz, 1826.

Rutebeuf. *Oeuvres completes de Rutebeuf.* Ed. Edmond Faral and Julia Bastin. In *Romance Philology* 17 (1963/64).

————. *Poemes concernant l'université de Paris.* Ed. H. H. Lucas. Manchester: 1952.

Siger de Brabant. *Quaestiones logicales. Impossibilia. Quaestiones naturales. Quaestiones in physicam.* In *Ecrits de logique, de morale et de physique,* critical ed., B. Bazan. Louvain: Publications universitaires, 1974.

————. *Tractatus de aeternitate mundi.* Ed. Bernardo Bazan. In Siger de Brabant, *'Quaestiones in tertium de anima,' 'De anima intellectiva,' 'De aeternitate mundi,'* critical ed., Philosophes medievaux 13. Louvain: Publications universitaires, 1972.

Tertullian. *De spectaculis.* See *Corpus christianorum* 1:225–53, 1954.

Thierry of Chartres. *Commentarius in Boethii librum contra Eutychen et Nestorium.* Ed. Nicholas M. Haring. In *Commentaries on Boethius by Thierry of Chartres and His School,* Studies and Texts 20. Toronto: Pontifical Institute of Medieval Studies, 1971.

Thomas of Cantimpré. *Liber de natura rerum.* Ed. H. Boese. Berlin, De Gruyter, 1973.

Thomas of Celano. *Vita prima.* Ed. M. Bihl. In *Analecta franciscana* 10 (1941).

Varro. *On the Latin Language.* 2 vols. With English trans. by Roland G. Kent. The Loeb Classical Library. Cambridge, Mass.: Harvard University Press, 1928.

Vincent of Beauvais. *Bibliotheca mundi Vincentii Burgundi, ex ordine Praedicatorum venerabilis episcopi Bellovacensis, speculum quadruplex, naturale, doctrinale, morale, historiale.* 4 vols. Douai: Belleri, 1624.

Wright, Thomas, ed. *Anglo-Latin Satirical Poets of the Twelfth Century.* 2 vols. [London, 1872.]. Reprint. New York: Kraus Reprint, 1964.

WORKS AND STUDIES ON DANTE

Abrams, Richard. 1984. "Against the *Contrapasso:* Dante's Heretics, Schismatics, and Others." *Italian Quarterly* 27:5–19.

Alessio, Giancarlo. 1979. "Brunetto Latini e Cicerone (e i dettatori)." *Italia medievale e umanistica* 22:123–69.

Alverny, Marie-Thérèse d'. 1970. "Dante et les astrologues de son temps." *Bulletin de la Société d'études dantesques du Centre universitaire mediterranéen* (Nice) 19:3–15.

Andrea, Antonio d'. 1980. "La struttura della *Vita nuova:* Le divisione della rime." *Yearbook of Italian Studies* 4:13–40.

Ascoli, Albert Russel. 1990. "'*Neminem ante nos*': Historicity and Authority in the *De vulgari eloquentia.*" Dante and Modern American Criticism, *Annali d'italianisca* ed. D. Cervigni, 8:186–231.

Assunto, Rosario. 1975. *Ipotesi e postille sull'estetica medievale con alcuni rilievi su Dante teorizzatore della poesia.* Milan: Marzorati.

Auerbach, E. 1959. "Figura." In *Scenes from the Drama of European Literature: Six Essays,* trans. R. Manheim. New York: Meridian Books.

Aversano, Mario. 1990. *San Bernardo e Dante: Teologia e poesia della conversione.* Salerno: Edisud.

Balthasar, Hans Urs von. 1973. "*Dante:* Viaggio attraverso la lingua, la storia, il pensiero della *Divina commedia*" (trans. from *Herrlickkeit* II), trans. G. Magagna. Brescia: Morcelliana.

Barberi Squarotti, G. 1959. "Le poetiche del Trecento in Italia." In *Momenti e problemi di storia dell'estetica* 1:255–91. Milan: Marzorati.

Barolini, Teodolinda. 1979. "Bertran de Born and Sordello: The Poetry of Politics in Dante's *Comedy*." *PMLA* 94 (3). 395–405.

———. 1984. *Dante's Poets: Textuality and Truth in the Comedy*. Princeton, N.J.: Princeton University Press.

Berardi, Gian Luigi. 1975. "Dante *Inferno* XIX." In *Letteratura e critica: Studi in onore di Natalino Sapegno* 2:93–147. Rome: Bulzoni.

Bertocchi, Cosimo. 1887. *Dante geometra: Note di geografia medioevale*. Turin: Istituto Fornaris-Marocco Editore.

Boli, Todd. 1988. "Boccaccio's *Trattatello in laude di Dante* or *Dante Resartus*." *Renaissance Quarterly* 41:389–412.

Botterill, Steven. 1991. "Bernard of Clairvaux in the Trecento Commentaries on Dante's *Commedia*." *Dante Studies* 109.

Boyde, Patrick. 1981. *Dante Philomythes and Philosopher: Man in the Cosmos*. Cambridge: Cambridge University Press.

Boyers, Hayden. 1926–27. "Cleavage in Bertran de Born and Dante." *Modern Philology* 24:1–3.

Brandeis, Irma. 1962. *The Ladder of Vision: A Study of Dante's Comedy*. Garden City, N.Y.: Doubleday.

Brownlee, Kevin. 1984. "Why the Angels Speak Italian: Dante as Vernacular *Poeta* in *Paradiso* XXV." *Poetics Today* 5:597–610.

———. 1986. "Ovid's Semele and Dante's Metamorphoses: *Paradiso* XXI–XXIII." *MLN* 101:147–56.

Buck, August. 1965. "Gli studi sulla poetica e sulla retorica di Dante e del suo tempo." In *Atti del Congresso internazionale di studi danteschi* 1:249–78. Florence: Sansoni.

Busnelli, Giovanni. 1907. *L'Etica Nicomachea e l'ordinamento morale dell'Inferno di Dante*. Bologna: Zanichelli.

Cambon, Glauco. 1970. "Synaesthesia in the *Divine Comedy*." *Dante Studies* 88:1–16.

Carugati, Giuliana. 1991. *Dalla menzogna al silenzio: La scrittura mistica della Commedia di Dante*. Bologna: Il Mulino.

Casella, Mario. 1944. "La canzone d'amore di Guido Cavalcanti." *Studi di filologia italiana* 7:97–160.

Cervigni, Dino C. 1986. *Dante's Poetry of Dreams*. Biblioteca dell' "Archivum romanicum" 198. Florence: Olschki.

Charity, A. C. 1966. *Events and Their Afterlife: Dialectics of Christian Typology in the Bible and Dante*. Cambridge: Cambridge University Press.

Chiappelli, Fredi. 1989. "Il colore della menzogna nell'*Inferno* dantesco." *Letture classensi* 18:115–28. Ravenna: Longo.

Cicchitto, Leone. 1940. *Postille bonaventuriano-dantesche*. Rome: Miscellanea francescana.

Colombo, Manuela. 1987. *Dai mistici a Dante: Il linguaggio dell'ineffabilita*. Pubblicazioni della Facoltá di Lettere e Filosofia dell'Universitá di Pavia 40. Florence: La Nuova Editrice.

Cornish, Alison. 1990. "Planets and Angels in *Paradiso* XXIX: The First Moment." *Dante Studies* 108:1–28.

Corti, Maria. 1981. *Dante a un nuovo crocevia.* Milan: Libreria Commissionaria Sansoni.

———. 1983. *La felicità mentale: Nuove prospettive per Cavalcanti e Dante.* Turin: Einaudi.

Costa, Elio. 1989. "From *locus amoris* to Infernal Pentecost: The Sin of Brunetto Latini." *Quaderni d'italianistica* 10 (1–2): 109–132.

Costa, Gustavo. 1988. "Dialectic and Mercury (Education, Magic, and Religion in Dante)." In *The "Divine Comedy" and the Encyclopedia of Arts and Sciences* (q.v.), 43–64.

Davis, Charles T. 1984. *Dante's Italy and Other Essays.* Philadelphia: University of Pennsylvania Press.

Del Lungo, Isidoro. 1898. *Dal secolo e dal poema di Dante: Altri ritratti e studi.* Bologna.

Delius, Nicolaus. 1887. "Dante's *Commedia* und Brunetto Latini's *Tesoretto.*" *Jahrbucher der deutschen Dantesgesellschaft* 4:12–13.

Di Pino, Guido. 1962. *La figurazione della luce nella Divina commedia.* 2d ed. Messina-Florence: D'Anna.

The 'Divine Comedy' and the Encyclopaedia of Arts and Sciences. 1988. Ed. Giuseppe di Scipio and Aldo Scaglione. Acta of the International Dante Symposium, 13–16 Nov. 1983, Hunter College, New York. Amsterdam and Philadelphia: John Benjamins.

Durling, Robert. 1981. "Farinata and the Body of Christ." *Stanford Italian Review* 2:5–35.

Durling, Robert M., and Martinez, Ronald L. 1990. *Time and the Crystal: Studies in Dante's 'Rime Petrose.'* Berkely and Los Angeles: University of California Press.

Enciclopedia dantesca. 1970–78. Ed. Umberto Bosco and Giorgio Petrocchi. 6 vols. Rome: Istituto dell'Enciclopedia italiana.

Fallani, Giovanni. 1965. *Poesia e teologia nella Divina Commedia.* Milan: Marzorati.

Ferrucci, Franco. 1980. *The Poetics of Disguise: The Autobiography of the Work in Homer, Dante, and Shakespeare.* Ithaca, N.Y.: Cornell University Press.

Firelli, Piero. 1987. "Sul senso del diritto nella *Monarchia.*" *Letture classensi* 16:79–87. Ravenna: Longo.

Forti, Fiorenzo. 1961. "Il limbo dantesco e i megalopsichoi dell'*Etica Nicomachea.*" *Giornale storico della letteratura italiana* 138:329–64.

Foster, Kenelm J. 1972. "The Celebration of Order: *Paradiso* X." *Dante Studies* 90:109–24.

———. 1977. *The Two Dantes and Other Studies.* London: Darton, Longman & Todd.

Freccero, John. 1986. *Dante: The Poetics of Conversion.* Ed. Rachel Jacoff. Cambridge, Mass.: Harvard University Press.

Gardner, Edmund G. 1913. *Dante and the Mystics.* New York: Dent.

Getto, Giovanni, ed. 1964. *Letture dantesche: Inferno, Purgatorio, Paradiso.* 3 vols. Florence: Sansoni.

Ghinassi, Ghino. 1973. "Neologismi." In *Enciclopedia dantesca* (q.v.) 4:37–38.

Gilbert, Allan H. 1925. *Dante's Conception of Justice.* Duke University Publications. Durham, N.C.: Duke University Press.

Gilson, Etienne. 1963. *Dante and Philosophy.* Trans. David Moore. New York: Harper & Row.

———. 1974. *Dante et Beatrice: Etudes dantesques.* Paris: J. Vrin.

Ginsburg, Warren. 1988 "Place and Dialectic in *Pearl* and Dante's *Paradiso.*" *A Journal of English Literary History* 55:731–53.

Gizzi, Corrado. 1974. *L'astronomia nel poema sacro.* Naples: Loffredo.

Grandgent, C. H. 1975. *Companion to the Divine Comedy.* Ed. C. S. Singleton. Cambridge, Mass.: Harvard University Press.

Grayson, C. 1963. "Dante e la prosa volgare." *Il verri* 9:6–26.

Gross, Kenneth. 1985. "Infernal Metamorphoses: An Interpretation of Dante's 'Counterpass.' *MLN* 100:42–69.

Hardie, Colin. 1965. "*Purgatorio* XIX: The Dream of the Siren." In *Letture del Purgatorio*, ed. V. Vettori, 217–49. Lectura dantis internazionale. Milan: Marzorati.

Hardt, Manfred. 1988. "Dante and Arithmetic." In *The "Divine Comedy" and the Encyclopedia of Arts and Sciences* (q.v.), 81–94.

Harrison, Robert P. 1988. *The Body of Beatrice.* Baltimore: The Johns Hopkins University Press.

Hart, Thomas Elwood. 1988. "Geometric Metaphor and Proportional Design in Dante's *Commedia.*" In *The "Divine Comedy" and the Encyclopedia of Arts and Sciences* (q.v.), 95–146.

Hawkins, P. S. 1984a. "Dante's *Paradiso* and the Dialectic of Ineffability." In *Ineffability: Naming the Unnameable from Dante to Beckett.* New York: AMS Press.

———. 1984b. "Resurrecting the Word: Dante and the Bible." *Religion and Literature* 16 (3): 59–71.

Hollander, Robert. 1969. *Allegory in Dante's Commedia.* Princeton, N.J.: Princeton University Press.

———. 1974. "*Vita nuova*: Dante's Perception of Beatrice." *Dante Studies* 92:1–18.

———. 1983. "*Purgatorio* XIX: Dante's Siren/Harpy." In *Dante, Petrarch, Boccaccio: Studies in the Italian Trecento in Honor of Charles S. Singleton*, ed. A. S. Bernardo and A.-L. Pellegrini, 77–88. Binghamton, N.Y.: SUNY Medieval and Renaissance Texts and Studies.

Holloway, Julia Bolton. 1985. "The *Vita nuova*: Paradigms of Pigrimage." *Dante Studies* 103:103–24.

Iannucci, Amilcare A. 1985. "Vergil and the Tragedy of the Virtuous Pagans in Dante's *Commedia.*" *Vergilius* 31:145–78.

Jacoff, Rachel. 1985. "Sacrifice and Empire: Thematic Analogies in San Vitale and the *Paradiso.*" In *Renaissance Studies in Honor of Craig Hugh Smyth*, ed. A. Morrogh, F. Superbi Gioffredi, P. Morselli, and E. Borsook. Florence: Giunti Barbera.

———. 1988. "Transgression and Transcendence: Figures of Female Desire in Dante's *Commedia.*" *Romanic Review* 79:129–42.

Jacomuzzi, Angelo. 1970. "Il *topos* dell'ineffabile nel *Paradiso* dantesco." In *Da Dante al Novecento: Studi critici offerti dagli scolari a Giovanni Getto nel suo ventesimo anno di insegnamento universitario*, 27–59. Milan: Mursia.

Kaske, R. E. 1961. "Dante's 'DXV' and 'Veltro.'" *Traditio* 17:185–254.

———. 1974. "Dante's *Purgatorio* XXXII and XXXIII: A Survey of Christian History." *University of Toronto Quarterly: A Canadian Journal of the Humanities* 43 (3): 193–214.

Kay, Richard. 1988. "Astrology and Astronomy." In *The "Divine Comedy" and the Encyclopedia of Arts and Sciences* (q.v.), 147–62.

Kibre, Pearl. 1988. "Dante and the Universities of Paris and Oxford." In *The "Divine Comedy" and the Encyclopedia of Arts and Sciences* (q.v.), 367–71.

Lemay, Richard. 1963. "Le Nimrod de l'*Enfer* de Dante et le *Liber Nemroth.*" *Studi danteschi* 40:57–128.

Leo, Ulrich. 1951. "The Unfinished *Convivio* and Dante's Rereading of the *Aeneid.*" *Medieval Studies* 13:41–64.

Marti, Mario. 1953. *Cultura e stile nei poeti giocosi del tempo di Dante*. Pisa: Nistri-Lischi.

Mazzeo, Joseph A. 1958. *Structure and Thought in the 'Paradiso.'* Ithaca, N.Y.: Cornell University Press.

———. 1960. *Medieval Cultural Tradition in Dante's 'Commedia.'* Ithaca, N.Y.: Cornell University Press.

Mazzocco, Angelo. 1987. "Dante's Notion of the 'Volgare Illustre': A Reappraisal." In *Papers in the History of Linguistics*, ed. Hans Aarsleff, Louis G. Kelly, and Hans-Josef Niederehe, 129–41. Proceedings of the Third International Conference on the History of the Language Sciences, Princeton, N.J., 19–23 Aug. 1984. Studies in the History of the Language Sciences 38. Amsterdam: John Benjamins.

Mazzoni, Francesco. 1965. "*Inferno* IV, saggio di un nuovo commento alla *Commedia*: Il canto IV dell'*Inferno.*" *Studi danteschi* 42:29–206.

Mazzotta, Giuseppe. 1979. *Dante, Poet of the Desert: History and Allegory in the* Divine Comedy. Princeton, N.J.: Princeton University Press.

———. 1983. "The Language of Poetry in the *Vita nuova.*" *Rivista di studi italiani* 1:3–14.

———. 1991. *Critical Essays on Dante*. Critical Essays on World Literature. Boston: G. K. Hall.

Mellone, A. 1974. "Il canto XXIX del *Paradiso.*" *Nuove letture dantesche*. Florence: Casa di Dante in Roma.

Mengaldo, P. V. 1978. *Linguistica e retorica di Dante*. Pisa: Nistri-Lischi.

Menocal, Maria Rosa. 1991. *Writing in Dante's Cult of Truth from Borges to Boaccaccio*. Durham, N.C., and London: Duke University Press.

Morghen, R. 1979. "Dante e Averroe." In *L'Averroismo in Italia* 49–62. Atti dei Convegni Lincei 40. Rome: Accademia nazionale dei Lincei.

Murari, R. 1905. *Dante e Boezio*. Bologna: Zanichelli.

Musseter, Sally. 1984. "*Ritornare a lo suo principio*: Dante and the Sin of Brunetto Latini." *Philological Quarterly* 63:431–48.

Nardi, Bruno. 1944. *Nel mondo di Dante*. 2d ed. Rome: Edizioni di storia e letteratura.

———. 1956. "Il canto XXIX del *Paradiso.*" *Convivium* 24:294–302.

———. 1966. *Saggi e note di critica dantesca*. Milan-Naples: Ricciardi.

———. 1967. *Saggi di filosofia dantesca*. 2d ed. Florence: La Nuova Italia.

―――. 1983. *Dante e la cultura medievale.* Nuova edizione a cura di Paolo Mazzatinti. Bari: Laterza.

Newman, F. X. 1967. "St. Augustine's Three Visions and the Structure of the *Commedia.*" *MLN* 82:56–78.

Nolan, Barbara. 1970. "The *Vita nuova:* Dante's Book of Revelation." *Dante Studies* 88:51–77.

―――. 1988. "Dante's Vergil, the Liberal Arts, and the Ascent to God." In *Allegoresis: The Craft of Allegory in Medieval Literature,* ed. J. Stephen Russell, 27–47. New York and London: Garland Publishing.

Orr, M. A. 1913. *Dante and the Early Astronomers.* London: Wingate.

Ovidio, Francesco d'. 1892. *Dante e la filosofia del linguaggio.* Naples: Tipografia della regia Università.

Padoan, Giorgio. 1977. *Il pio Enea, l'empio Ulisse.* Ravenna: Longo.

Pagani, Ileana. 1982. *La teoria linguistica di Dante. "De vulgari eloquentia": Discussioni, scelte, proposte.* Naples: Liguori Editore.

Paolini, Shirley J. 1982. *Confessions of Sin and Love in the Middle Ages: Dante's Commedia and St. Augustine's Confessions.* Washington, D.C.: The Catholic University Press of America.

Paparelli, G. 1975. "*Fictio:* La definizione dantesca della poesia." In *Ideologia e poesia di Dante,* 53–158. Florence: Olschki.

Paratore, Ettore. 1968. *Tradizione e struttura in Dante.* Florence: Sansoni.

Parronchi, A. 1959. "La perspettiva dantesca." *Studi danteschi.* 36:5–103.

Pasquazi, Silvio. 1961. "Il canto XVI dell'*Inferno.*" In *Lectura Dantis Scaligera,* 5–34. Florence: Le Monnier.

―――. 1970–79. "Contrapasso." In *Enciclopedia dantesca* (q.v.).

Pasquini, Emilio. 1987. "Le metafore della visione nella 'Commedia.'" In *Letture classensi* 16:129–51. Ravenna: Longo.

Pazzaglia, Mario. 1967. *Il verso e l'arte della canzone nel De Vulgari Eloquentia.* Florence: La Nuova Italia.

Pelikan, Jaroslav. 1990. *Eternal Feminines: Theological Allegories in Dante's 'Paradiso.'* New Brunswick, N.J., and London: Rutgers University Press.

Pepin, Jean. 1970. *Dante et la tradition de l'allegorie.* Montreal: Institut d'études mediévales.

Pestalozza, Luigi. 1988. *La musica nel tempo di Dante.* Atti del convegno tenuto a Ravenna, September 1986. Milan: Unicopli.

Petrocchi, Giorgio. 1961. *Il 'De vulgari eloquentia' di Dante.* Dispense del corso di storia della lingua. Messina: La Editrice Universitaria.

Pezard, André. 1950. *Dante sous la pluie de feu.* Etudes de philosophie medievale 40. Paris: J. Vrin.

Picone, Michelangelo. 1979. "I trovatori di Dante: Bertran de Born." *Studi e problemi di critica testuale* 19:71–84.

―――. 1989. "Giulleria e poesia nell a *Commedia:* Una lettura intertestuale di *Inferno* XXI–XXII." In *Letture classensi,* ed. Anthony Oldcorn, 18:11–30. Ravenna: Longo Editore.

Pietropaolo, Domenico. 1989. "Dante's Paradigms of Humility and the Structure of Reading." *Quaderni d'italianistica* 10 (1–2): 199–211.

Pirrotta, Nino. 1966. "*Ars nova* e *Stil novo.*" *Rivista italiana di musicologia* 1:3–19.

Pirrotta, Nino. 1968. "Dante *musicus:* Gothicism, Scholasticism, and Music." *Speculum* 43:245–57.

Rabuse, Georg. 1966. "I corpi celesti, centri di ordinamento dell' immaginazione poetica di Dante." *Annali dell'Istituto universitario orientale di Napoli* 8:215–44.

———. 1972. *Die goldene Leiter in Dantes Saturnhimmel.* Schriften und Vortrage des Petrarka-Instituts Koln 25. Cologne: Krefeld.

———. 1973. "Les paysages astrologiques de la 'Divine comedie.'" *Bulletin de la Société d'études dantesques du Centre universitaire mediterranéen* (Nice) 21:57–68.

Reade, W. H. V. 1909. *The Moral System of Dante's Inferno.* Oxford: Clarendon Press.

Renaudet, Augustin. 1952. *Dante humaniste.* Paris: Societé d'Edition "Les belles lettres."

Renucci, Paul. 1954. *Dante disciple et juge du monde greco-latin.* Clermond-Ferrand: G. de Bussac.

Rigo, Paola. 1980. "Tempo liturgico nell'epistola dantesca ai principi e ai popoli d'Italia." *Lettere italiane* 32:222–31.

Rossi, Louis R. 1965. "The Fox Outfoxed (*Inferno* XXVII)." *Cesare Barbieri Courier* 7:13–23.

Russo, Vittorio. 1970–78. "Arti liberali." In *Enciclopedia dantesca* (q.v.).

Sanctis, Francesco de. 1955. *Lezioni sulla Divina commedia.* Ed. Michele Manfredi. Scrittori d'Italia 214. Bari: Laterza.

———. 1970. *Storia della letteratura italiana.* Milan: Feltrinelli.

Sannia, Enrico. 1909. *Il comico, l'umorismo e la satira nella Divina commedia.* Milan: Hoepli.

Sarolli, Gian Roberto. 1971. *Prolegomena alla Divina commedia.* Florence: Olschki.

Scaglione, Aldo. 1988. "Dante and the *Ars grammatica.*" In *The "Divine Comedy" and the Encyclopedia of Arts and Sciences* (q.v.), 27–41.

Scartazzini, G. A. 1905. *Enciclopedia dantesca.* Continuata da A. Fiammazzo. Milan: Hoepli.

Scherillo, Michele. 1897. "Bertran dal Bornio e il Re Giovane." *Nuova antologia* 154:452–78.

Schiaffini, A. 1958. "'Poesis' e 'poeta' in Dante." In *Studia philologica et litteraria in honorem L. Spitzer,* 379–89. Bern: Francke Verlag.

———. 1969. *Tradizione e poesia nella prosa d'arte italiana dalla latinità medievale al Boccaccio.* Rome.

Schildgen, Brenda Deen. 1989. "Dante's Neologisms in *Paradiso* and the Latin Rhetorical Tradition." *Dante Studies* 107:101–19.

Schnapp, Jeffrey T. 1986. *The Transfiguration of History at the Center of Dante's Paradise.* Princeton, N.J.: Princeton University Press.

Shapiro, Marianne. 1974. "The Fictionalization of Bertran de Born (*Inferno* XXVIII)." *Dante Studies* 92:107–16.

Shaw, J. E. [1929] 1976. *Essay on the 'Vita nuova'* [Princeton, N.J.: Princeton University Press]. Reprint. Millwood, N.Y.: Kraus Reprint Company.

Shoaf, Richard A. 1983. *Dante, Chaucer, and the Currency of the Word.* Norman, Okla.: Pilgrim Books.

Singleton, Charles. [1949] 1977. *An Essay on the 'Vita nuova'* [Cambridge, Mass.:

Harvard University Press]. Reprint. Baltimore: The Johns Hopkins University Press.

———. 1967. *Dante Studies 2: Journey to Beatrice*. Cambridge, Mass.: Harvard University Press.

Spitzer, Leo. 1944. "The Farcical Elements in *Inferno*, Cantos XXI–XXII." *MLN* 59:83–88.

Stephany, William. 1982. "Pier della Vigna's Self-Fulfilling Prophecies: The 'Eulogy' of Frederick II and *Inferno* 13." *Traditio* 38:193–212.

Stump, Eleonore. 1986. "Dante's Hell, Aquinas' Moral Theory, and the Love of God." *Canadian Journal of Philosophy* 16:181–98.

Takada, Yasunau. 1988. "'Heavene' in Criseyde: Dante's 'Festa' and Chaucer's 'Festa.'" *Philologia anglica*, 299–305. Festschrift for Professor Y. Terasawa. Tokyo: Kenkyusha.

Took, J. F. 1984. *'L'Etterno Piacer': Aesthetic Ideas in Dante*. Oxford: Clarendon Press.

Toynbee, Paget. 1914. *Concise Edition of Proper Names and Notable Matters*. Oxford: Clarendon Press.

Trovato, Mario. 1987. "The Semantic Value of *Ingegno* and Dante's *Ulysses* in the Light of the *Metalogicon*." *Modern Philology* 84 (3) 258–66.

———. 1990. "Dante's Poetics of the Good." *Annali d'italianistica* (Dante and Modern American Criticism, ed. D. Cervigni) 8:232–56.

Truscott, James G. 1973. "Ulysses and Guido: *Inferno* XXVI and XXVII." *Dante Studies* 91:47–72.

Vallone, Aldo. 1965. "Il canto XVI dell'*Inferno*." In *Studi su Dante medievale*, 179–205. Florence: Olschki.

Vazzana, Steno. 1959. *Il contrapasso nella Divina commedia: Studio sull'unità del poema*. Roma: Ciranna.

Viscardi, Antonio. 1970–78. "Bertram dal Bornio." In *Enciclopedia dantesca* (q.v.).

Vona, Pietro di. 1984. "Dante filosofo e San Bonaventura." *Miscellanea francescana* 84:3–19.

Wieruszowski, H. 1946. "An Early Anticipation of Dante's 'Cieli' e 'Scienze.'" *MLN* 41:217–28.

Modern Works and Studies

Abelson, Paul. 1906. *The Seven Liberal Arts: A Study in Medieval Culture*. New York.

Adams, Jeremy Y. duQuesnay. 1969. "The Political Grammar of Isidore of Seville." In *Arts liberaux et philosophie au moyen age*. Actes du Quatrieme congres international de philosophie medievale, 27 Aug.–2 Sept. 1967. Montreal and Paris: J. Vrin.

Albertus Magnus and the Sciences: Commemorative Essays. 1983. Ed. J. A. Weisheipl, OP. Toronto: Pontifical Institute of Mediaeval Studies.

Alexion, Margaret, and Dronke, Peter. 1971. "The Lament of Jephtha's Daughter: Themes, Traditions, Originality." *Studi medievali*, serie terza 12:819–63.

Alford, John A., and Seniff, Denis P. 1984. *Literature and Law in the Middle Ages: A Bibliography of Scholarship*. New York and London: Garland Publishing.

Allen, Judson Boyce. 1976. "Hermann the German's Averroistic Aristotle and Medieval Poetic Theory." *Mosaic: A Journal for the Comparative Study of Literature and Ideas* 9:67–81.

———. 1982. *The Ethical Poetic of the Later Middle Ages: A Decorum of Convenient Distinction*. Toronto: University of Toronto Press.

Alverny, Maria-Thérèse d'. 1946. "La sagesse et ses sept filles: Recherches sur les allégories de la philosophie et des arts liberaux au IX et au XII siècle." In *Mélanges dédiées à la mémoire de Felix Grat* 1:245–78. Paris: Pecqueur-Grat.

———. 1950. "Pierre le Venerable et la légende de Mahomet." *A Cluny*. Congres . . . juillet 1949. Dijon: Bernigaud & Privat.

———. 1964a. "Alain de Lille et la 'Theologia.'" In *L'homme devant Dieu: Mélanges offerts au Père Henri de Lubac* 2: 111–28. Paris: Aubier.

———. 1964b. "Les muses et les sphères célestes." In *Classical, Medieval and Renaissance Studies in Honor of Berthold Ullman* 2:13–19. Rome: Edizioni di storia e letteratura.

Antin, Paul. 1961. "Les Sirènes et Ulysse dans l'oeuvre de S. Jérôme." *Revue des études latines* 39:232–41.

Arts liberaux et philosophie au moyen age. 1969. Actes du Quatrième congres international de philosophie médiévale, Université de Montréal, Canada. 27 Aug.–2 Sept. Montreal: Institut d'études médiévales.

Ashworth, E. J. 1978. *The Tradition of Medieval Logic and Speculative Grammar from Anselm to the End of the Seventeenth Century: A Bibliography from 1836 Onwards*. Toronto: Institue of Mediaeval Studies.

Augustinianum. 1989. Vol. 19. Rome, S-7 Maggio 1988.

Baker, Peter Harte. 1969. "Liberal Arts as Philosophical Liberation: St. Augustine's *De Magistro*." See *Arts Liberaux*: 469–79.

Baldwin, Charles S. *Medieval Rhetoric and Poetic to 1400*. Gloucester, Mass.: Peter Smith.

Balthasar, Hans Urs von. 1982. *The Glory of the Lord: A Theological Aesthetics*. 3 vols. (Trans. of *Herrlickkeit*), Ed. Joseph Fessio and John Riches. San Francisco: Ignatius Press.

Barberi Squarotti, G. 1959. "Le poetiche del Trecento in Italia." *Momenti e problemi di storia dell'estetica* 1:255–91. Milan: Marzorati.

Barilli, Renato. 1984. *Poetica e retorica*. Milano: Mursia.

Baron, Roger. 1957. *Science et sagesse chez Hugues de Saint-Victor*. Paris: P. Lethielleux.

Battaglia, Salvatore. 1958. "La trasmissione giullaresca." *Filologia Romanza* 5(3–4): 225–46.

Baudelet, Yves-Anselme. 1985. *L'expérience spirituelle selon Guillaume de Saint-Thierry*. Paris: Editions du Cerf.

Baudoux, B. 1937. "Philosophia 'Ancilla theologiae.'" *Antonianum* 12:293–326.

Benedetti, Angelo. 1975. *Contemplazione e poesia in Pier Damiano*. Brescia: Paideia.

Benoit, Paul. 1989. "La théologie au XIIIe siècle: Une science pas comme les autres." In *Elements d'histoire des sciences*, ed. Michel Serres, 177–95. Paris: Bordas.

Benson, Robert L. 1977. "Protohumanism and Narrative Technique in Early Thirteenth Century Italian 'Ars Dictaminis.'" In *Boccaccio: Secoli di vita*, ed. M.

Cottino Jones and E. F. Tuttle, 31–48. Atti del Congresso internazionale Boccaccio 1975. Ravenna: Longo.

Bertola, E. 1961. "I precedenti storici del metodo del *Sic et non* di Abelardo." *Rivista
di filosofia neo-scolastica* 53:255–80.

———. 1964. "La *quaestio* nella storia del pensiero medievale, secoli XI e XII.
Aquinas 28:51–75.

Bettoni, Efrem. 1964. *Saint Bonaventure*. Trans. Angelus Gambatese. Notre Dame,
Ind.: University of Notre Dame Press.

Bianchi, Luca. 1984. *L'errore di Aristotile: La polemica contro l'eternità del mondo nel
XIII secolo*. Pubblicazioni della facoltà di lettere e filosofia dell'Università di Milano 104. Florence: La Nuova Italia.

Black, Deborah L. 1989. "The 'Imaginative Syllogism' in Arabic Philosophy: A
Medieval Contribution to the Philosophical Study of Metaphor." *Medieval Studies* 51:241–67.

Blaustein, Michael. 1984. *Averroes on the Imagination and the Intellect*. Ann Arbor,
Mich.: University Microfilms.

Bloomfield, Morton. 1952. *The Seven Deadly Sins: An Introduction to the History of a
Religious Concept with Special Reference to Medieval English Literature*. East Lan-
sing, Mich.: Michigan State College Press.

Blumenkranz, B. 1951. *"Siliquae porcorum*: L'exégèse médiévale et les sciences pro-
fanes." In *Mélanges d'histoire du moyen âge dédiés a la mémoire de L. Halphen*. Paris:
Presses Universitaires de France.

Boitani, Piero. 1984. *Chaucer and the Imaginary World Of Fame*. Chaucer Studies
10. Cambridge: D. S. Brewer.

———. 1989. *The Tragic and the Sublime in Medieval Literature*. Cambridge: Cambridge University Press.

Bori, Pier Cesare. 1989. *L'estasi del profeta*. Bologna: Il Mulino.

Bouard, Michel de. 1930. "Encyclopedies médiévals sur la connaissance de la nature et du monde au Moyen Age." In *Revue des questions historiques*. 112: 258–304.

Bouche-Leclerq, Auguste. [1899] 1963. *L'Astrologie grecque*. [Paris]. Reprint. Brus-
sels: Culture et Civilisation.

Bougerol, J.-G. 1963. *Introduction to the Works of Bonaventure*. Trans. J. de Vinck.
Paterson, N.J: Franciscan Institute.

———. 1971a. "S. Bonaventure et S. Bernard." *Antonianum* 46:3–79.

———. 1971b. "S. Bonaventure et Guillaume de Saint-Thierry." *Antonianum*
46:268–71.

———. 1985. *La théologie de l'espérance aux XIIe et XIIIe siècles*. 2 vols. Paris: Etudes
augustiniennes.

Brasa, Mariano Diez. 1980. "Las artes del lenguaje en Juan de Salisbury." *La ciudad
de Dios* 193:19–45.

Broglie, Guy de. 1960. "La notion augustinienne du sacrifice 'invisible' et 'vrai.'"
Recherches de science religieuse 48:135–65.

Brown, Emerson. 1982. "Epicurus and *Voluptas* in Late Antiquity: The Curious
Testimony of Martianus Capella." *Traditio: Studies in Ancient and Medieval History, Thought and Religion* 38:75–106.

Bruyne, Edgar de. [1946] 1975. *Etudes d'esthétique médiévale*. 3 vols. Bruges: "De
Tempel." Reprint Geneva.

Bundy, Murray Wright. 1927. *The Theory of the Imagination in Classical and Medieval Thought*. Studies in Language and Literature 12. Urbana, Ill.: University of Illinois Press.

Butler, Cuthbert. 1923. *Western Mysticism: The Teaching of Saints Augustine, Gregory and Bernard on Contemplation and the Contemplative Life*. New York: Dutton.

Caillois, Roger. 1961. *Man, Play and Games*. Trans. Meyer Barash. New York: The Free Press of Glencoe.

The Cambridge History of Later Medieval Philosophy: From the Rediscovery of Aristotle to the Disintegration of Scholasticism 1100–1600. 1982. Ed. Norman Kretzmann, Anthony Kenny, and Jan Pinborg. Cambridge: Cambridge University Press.

Carruthers, Mary J. 1990. *The Book of Memory: A Study of Memory in Medieval Culture*. Cambridge: Cambridge University Press.

Certeau, Michel de. 1964. "'Mystique' au XVIIe siècle: Le problème du langage 'mystique.'" In *L'homme devant Dieu: Mélanges offerts au père Henri de Lubac* 2:267–91. Paris: Ed. Montaigne.

———. 1986. *Heterologies: Discourse on the Other*. Trans. Brian Massumi. Theory and History of Literature 17. Minneapolis: University of Minnesota Press.

Chadwick, O. 1968. *John Cassian: A Study in Primitive Monasticism*. 2d ed. Cambridge: Cambridge University Press.

Châtillon, Jean. 1940. "Les trois modes de la contemplation selon Richard de Saint-Victor," *Bulletin de littérature ecclésiastique* 1:3–26.

———. 1984. "La Bible dans les Ecoles du XIIe siècle." In *Le moyen age et la Bible*, 163–97. Bible de tous les temps. Sous la direction de Pierre Riche and Guy Lobrichon. Paris: Editions Beauchesne.

Chenu, M. D. 1935. "Grammaire et théologie au XIIe et XIIIe siècles." *Archives d'histoire doctrinale et littéraire du moyen âge* 10:5–28.

———. 1955. "*Involucrum*: Le mythe selon les théologiens mediévaux." *Archives d'histoire doctrinale et littéraire du moyen âge* 23:75–79.

———. 1968. *Nature, Man and Society in the Twelfth Century*. Trans. Jerome Taylor and Lester K. Little. Chicago: University of Chicago Press.

———. 1969. *La théologie comme science au XIII siècle*. Librairie philosophique J. Vrin. Paris: J. Vrin.

Ciavolella, Massimo. 1976. *La 'malattia d'amore' dall'antichità al medioevo*. Strumenti di ricerca, 12–13. Rome: Bulzoni.

Clark, Mary. 1964. "Platonic Justice in Aristotle and Augustine." *Downside Review* 82:25–35.

Colish, Marcia J. 1968. *The Mirror of Language: A Study in Medieval Theory of Knowledge*. New Haven, Conn.: Yale University Press.

———. 1985. *The Stoic Tradition from Antiquity to the Early Middle Ages*. 2 vols. Studies in the History of Christian Thought 25. Leiden: E. J. Brill.

Congar, Yves M.-J. 1961. "Aspects ecclésiologiques de la querelle entre mendiants et séculiers dans la seconde moitié du XIIIe siècle et le début du XIVe." *Archives d'histoire doctrinale et littéraire du moyen âge*. 36. 28:35–151.

Contamine, Philippe. 1984. *War in the Middle Ages*. Trans. Michael Jones. Oxford: Blackwell.

Contenson, P.-M. de. 1959. "Avicennisme latin et vision de Dieu au début du XIIIe siècle." *Archives d'histoire doctrinale et littéraire du moyen âge* 26:29–97.

Courcelle, Pierre. 1944. "Quelques symboles funéraires du neo-platonisme latin: Le vol de Dédale—Ulysse et les sirène." *Revue des études anciennes* 46:65–93.

———. 1948. *Les lettres grecques en occident, de Macrobe a Cassiodore.* 2d ed. Bibliothèque des Ecoles françaises d'Athènes et de Rome 159. Paris.

———. 1960. "Le thème du regret: *Sero te amavi, pulchritudo.* . . ." *Revue des études latines* 38:264–95.

———. 1967. *La consolation de philosophie dans la tradition littéraire: Antecedents et posterité de Boece.* Paris: Etudes augustiniennes.

———. 1974. *Connais-toi toi-meme de Socrate a Saint Bernard.* 3 vols. Paris: Etudes augustiniennes.

———. 1975. "L'interprétation évhémériste des Sirènes-courtisanes jusqu'au XIIe siècle." In *Gesellschaft-Kultur-Literatur*, 33–48. Rezeption Und Originalitat Im Wachsen Einer Europaischen Literatur Und Geistigkeit. Beitrage Luitpold Wallach Gewidmet. Stuttgart: Anton Hiersemann.

Cox, Harvey G. 1969. *The Feast of Fools: A Theological Essay on Festivity and Fantasy.* Cambridge, Mass.: Harvard University Press.

Crouse, Robert Darwin. 1969. "*Honorius Augustodunensis*: the Arts as *via ad patriam*." See *Arts Liberaux*: 531:39.

Cuervo, M. 1932. "La teologia como ciencia y la sistematizacion teologica segun S. Alberto Magno." *Ciencia tomista* 46:173–99.

Cumont, Franz. 1942. *Recherches sur le symbolisme funéraire des romains.* Paris: Geuthner.

Curtius, Ernst Robert. 1939. "Scherz un Ernst in mittelalterlicher Dichtung." *Romanische Forschungen* 53:1–26.

———. 1963. *European Literature and the Latin Middle Ages.* Trans. Willard R. Trask. Harper Torchbooks. The Bollingen Library. New York and Evanston, Ill.: Harper and Row.

Dady, Mary Rachel. 1939. *The Theory of Knowledge of Saint Bonaventure.* Philosophical Studies 52. Washington, D.C.: Catholic University of America Press.

Dahan, G. 1980. "Notes et textes sur la poetique au moyen âge." *Archives d'histoire doctrinale et littéraire du moyen âge* 47:171–239.

Danielou, Jean and Devoto, Giacomo, eds. 1963. *La Bibbia nell' alto medioevo.* Spoleto: Centro italiano di studi.

Davy, M.-M. 1954. *Théologie et mystique de Guillaume Saint-Thierry.* Etudes de théologie et d'histoire de la spiritualité 15. Paris: Vrin.

Dechanet, Jean-Marie. 1942. *Guillaume de St. Thierry, l'homme et son oeuvre.* Bibliothèque médiévale, spirituels prescolastiques, 1. Bruges and Paris: Editions C. Beyaert.

———. 1945. "*Amor ipse intellectus est*: La doctrine de l'amour-intellection chez Guillaume de Saint-Thierry. *Revue du moyen âge latin* 1:349–74.

Delhaye, Philippe. 1958. "'Grammatica' et 'Ethica' au XIIe siècle." *Recherches de théologie ancienne et médiévale* 25:59–110. Reprint. In *Enseignement et morale au XIIe siècle*, 83–134. Paris: Editions du Cerf, 1988.

———. 1963 "La vertu et les vertus dans les oeuvres d'Alain de Lille." *Cahiers de civilisation médiévale* 6:13–25.

Dictionnaire de spiritualité ascétique et mystique. 1932–. Ed. M. Viller et al. Paris: Beauchesne.

———. 1969. "La place des arts liberaux dans les programmes scolaires du XIII siècle." See *Arts liberaux 1969.*

Dinzelbacher, P. 1981. *Vision und Visionsliteratur im Mittelalter.* Stuttgart: Hiersemann.

Doignon, Jean. 1986. "Le symbolisme des Sirènes dans les premiers dialogues de Saint Augustin." In *La mythologie: Clef de lecture du monde classique,* 113–19. Hommage à R. Chevallier. Tours. Centre de recherches A. Piganiol.

Dondaine, H.-F. 1952. "La vision beatifique au XIIIe siècle" (followed by an assortment of 13th-century texts relating to the beatific vision). *Recherches de théologie ancienne et médiévale* 19: 60–130.

———. 1953. *Le corpus dionysien de l'Université de Paris au XIIIe siècle.* Rome: Edizioni di storia e letteratura.

Douie, Decima L. 1954. *The Conflict between the Seculars and the Mendicants at the University of Paris in the Thirteenth Century.* Aquinas paper 23. London: Blackfriars.

Dronke, Peter. 1970. *Poetic Individuality in the Middle Ages.* Oxford: Oxford University Press.

———. 1974. *Fabula: Explorations into the Uses of Myth in Medieval Platonism.* Leiden-Cologne: E. J. Brill.

Dubois, Jacques. 1984. "Comment les moines du moyen âge chantaient et goutaient les Saintes Ecritures." In *Le moyen age et la Bible,* 261–98. Bible de tous les temps. Sous la direction de Pierre Riche and Guy Lobrichon. Paris: Edition Beauchesne.

Duhem, P. 1954–59. *Le système du monde. Histoire des doctrines cosmologiques de platon a Copernic.* 10 vols. Paris: A. Hermann et Fils.

Dumeige, Gervais. 1952. *Richard de Saint-Victor et l'idée chrétienne de l'amour.* Paris: Presses universitares de France.

Dupré, Louis. 1989. "The Christian Experience of Mystical Union." *The Journal of Religion* 69:1–13.

Ebbesen, Sten. 1981. *Commentaries and Commentators on Aristotle's* Sophistici Elenchi: *A Study of Post-Aristotelian Ancient and Medieval Writings on Fallacies.* 3 vols. Corpus commentarium in aristotelem graecorum 7, pt 2. Leiden: Brill.

Eco, Umberto. 1970. *Il problema estetico in Tommaso d'Aquino.* Seconda edizione riveduta. Milan: Bompiani.

———. 1986. *Art and Beauty in the Middle Ages.* Trans. Hugh Bredin. New Haven, Conn., and London: Yale University Press.

Economou, George D. 1972. *The Goddess 'Natura' in Medieval Literature.* Cambridge, Mass.: Harvard University Press.

Eden, Kathy. 1986. *Poetic and Legal Fiction in the Aristotelean Tradition.* Princeton, N.J.: Princeton University Press.

Englert, R. W. 1987. "Bernard and Dante: Rituals of Grief." *American Benedictine Review* 38:1–13.

Evans, G. R. 1983. *Alain of Lille.* The Frontiers of Theology in the Later Twelfth Century. Cambridge: Cambridge University Press.

———. 1984. *The Language and Logic of the Bible: The Earlier Middle Ages.* Cambridge: Cambridge University Press.

Favati, Guido. 1975. *Inchiesta sul dolce stil nuovo.* Quaderni di letteratura e d'arte 26. Florence: Le Monnier.

Federici Vescovini, Graziella. 1968. "La 'perspectiva' nell'enciclopedia del sapere medievale." *Vivarium* 6:36–45.

Feltrin, Paola. 1985. "Il ruolo della grammatica nell'organizzazione medievale del sapere." *Rivista di storia della filosofia* 40:159–66.

Fink, Eugen. 1960. *Spiel Als Weltsymbol.* Stuttgart: W. Kohlnammer.

Fleming, John. 1977. *An Introduction to Franciscan Literature of the Middle Ages.* Chicago: University of Chicago Press.

———. 1982. *From Bonaventure to Bellini: An Essay in Franciscan Exegesis.* Princeton, N.J.: Princeton University Press.

———. 1984. *Reason and the Lover.* Princeton, N.J.: Princeton University Press.

Fontaine, J. 1959. *Isidore de Seville et la culture classique dans l'Espagne wisigothique.* Paris: Etudes augustiniennes.

Foucault, Michel. 1970. *The Order of Things: An Archeology of the Human Sciences* (a trans. of *Les mots et le choses*). New York: Pantheon.

———. 1982. "Le combat de la chastete." *Communications* 35:15–25.

Fredborg, K. M. 1974. "Petrus Helias on Rhetoric." *Cahiers de l'Institut du moyen age grec et latin, Universite de Copenhague* 13:31–41.

Fumagalli, Mariateresa, and Massimo Parodi. 1985. "Due enciclopedie dell'Occidente medievale: Alessandro Neckam e Bartolomeo Anglico." Momenti e modelli nella storia dell'enciclopedia. Il mondo musulmano, ebraico e latino a confronto sul tema dell'organizzazione del sapere. In *Rivista di storia della filosofia.* 40:51–90.

Gabriel, Astrik L. 1962. *The Educational Ideas of Vincent of Beauvais.* Notre Dame, Ind.: University of Notre Dame Press.

Galletti, A. 1938. *L'eloquenza (dalle origini al XVI secolo): Storia dei generi letterari.* Milan: Vallardi.

Gandillac, Maurice de. 1966. "Encyclopedies pre-médiévales et medievales," *Cahiers d'histoire mondiale* 9:483–518.

Garin, Eugenio. 1983. *Astrology in the Renaissance: The Zodiac of Life.* Trans. Carolyn Jackson and June Allen. London: Routledge & Kegan Paul.

Gellrich, Jesse. 1985. *The Idea of the Book in the Middle Ages: Language, Theory, Mythology and Fiction.* Ithaca, N.Y., and London: Cornell University Press.

Ghellinck, J. de. 1948. *Le mouvement théologique du XIIe siècle.* Bruges. Reprint Bruxelles: Culture et civilisation, 1969.

Ghisalberti, F. 1932. "Arnolfo d'Orleans, un cultore di Ovidio nel s. XII." *Memorie del Reale istituto lombardo di scienze e lettere* 24:157–234.

Giamatti, A. Bartlett. 1969. *The Earthly Paradise and the Renaissance Epic.* Princeton, N.J.: Princeton University Press.

Giannetto, Nella. 1977. "Rassegna sulla parodia in letteratura." *Lettere italiane* 29:461–81.

Gilson, Etienne. 1934. *La théologie mystique de Saint Bernard.* Paris: Vrin.

Gilson, Etienne. 1955. *History of Christian Philosophy in the Middle Ages*. New York: Random House.

————. 1956. *The Christian Philosophy of St. Thomas Aquinas*. Trans. L. K. Shook. New York: Random House.

————. 1965. *The Philosophy of Saint Bonaventure*. Trans. Illtyd Trethowan and Francis Joseph Sheed. Paterson, N.J.: St. Anthony Guild Press.

Girard, René. 1972. *La violence et le sacré*. Paris: Grasset.

Glorieux, P. 1925. "Prelats français contre religieux mendiants: Autour de la bulle *Ad fructus uberes*." *Revue de l'histoire de l'église de France* 11:309–31; 471–95.

————. 1933–34. *Repertoire des maitres en théologie de Paris au XIII siècle*. 2 vols. Paris: J. Vrin.

————. 1946. "La faculté de théologie de Paris et ses principaux docteurs au XIIIe siècle." *Revue d'histoire de l'église de France* 32:241–64.

Godin, Guy. 1961. "La notion d'admiration." *Laval théologique et philosophique* 17:35–75.

Goldstein, Catherine. 1989. "L'un et l'autre: Pour une histoire du cercle." In *Eléments d'histoire des sciences*, ed. Michel Serres, 129–50. Paris: Bordas.

Gomez Nogales, Salvador. 1964. "Las artes liberales y la filosofia hispano-musulmana." See *Arts Liberaux*: 493–508.

Gonsette, J. 1956. *Pierre Damien et la culture profane*. Essais philosophiques 7. Louvain and Paris: Publications universitaires de Louvain.

Gonzalez Echevarria, R. 1990. *Myth and Archive: A Theory of Latin American Narrative*. Cambridge: Cambridge University Press.

Gossman, Elisabeth. 1974. *Foi et connaissance de Dieu au moyen âge*. Traduit de l'allemand par Elisabeth Pfirrmann. Paris: Les Editions du Cerf.

Grabois, Aryeh. 1984. "L'exégèse rabbinique." In *Le moyen âge et la Bible*, 233–60. Bible de tous le temps. Sous la direction de Pierre Riche and Guy Lobrichon. Paris: Edition Beauchesne.

Green, Richard Hamilton. 1967. "Alan of Lille's *Anticlaudianus*: Ascensus mentis in deum." *Annuale médiévale* 8:3–16.

Gregory, Tullio. 1955. *Anima mundi: La filosofia di Guglielmo di Conches e la scuola di Chartres*. Florence: Sansoni.

————. 1985. "I sogni e gli astri." In *I sogni nel medioevo*. Seminario internazionale, Roma, 2–4 Oct. 1983. Lessico intellettuale europeo 25. Rome: Edizioni dell'Ateneo.

Guardini, Romano. 1935. *The Spirit of Liturgy*. Trans. Ada Lane. New York: Sheed and Ward.

Gunn, Alan M. F. 1952. *The Mirror of Love: A Reinterpretation of the "Romance of the Rose."* Lubbock, Tex.: Texas Tech Press.

Hadot, I. 1984. *Arts liberaux et philosophie dans la pensée antique*. Paris: Etudes augustiniennes.

Hardison, O. B. 1968. "The Place of Averroes' Commentary on the *Poetics* in the History of Medieval Criticism." *Medieval and Renaissance Studies* 4:57–81.

Harvey, E. Ruth. 1975. *The Inward Wits: Psychological Theory in the Middle Ages and the Renaissance*. London: Warburg Institute.

Haskins, C. H. 1927. *The Renaissance of the Twelfth Century*. Cambridge: Cambridge University Press.

————. 1929. "The Early *Artes Dictandi* in Italy." In *Studies in Medieval Culture*, 170–92. Oxford: Oxford University Press.

————. 1957. *The Rise of the Universities*. Ithaca, N.Y.: Cornell University Press.

Havelock, E. 1963. *Preface to Plato*. Cambridge, Mass.: Harvard University Press.

Herman, Gerard. 1979. "Henri d'Andeli's Epic Parody: *La bataille des sept arts.*" *Annuale medievale* 18:54–64.

Hissette, Roland. 1977. *Enquete sur les 219 articles condamnes a Paris le 7 mars 1277*. Philosophes medievaux 22. Louvain: Publications universitaires de Louvain.

————. 1980. "Etienne Tempier et ses condamnations." *Recherches de théologie ancienne et médiévale* 48:231–70.

Hoorn, Willem van. 1972. *As Images Unwind: Ancient and Modern Theories of Visual Perception*. Amsterdam: University Press.

Huizinga, Johan. 1955. *Homo Ludens: A Study of the Play Element in Culture*. Trans. R. F. C. Hull. Boston: Beacon Press.

Hunt, Richard William. 1941–43. "Studies on Priscian in the Eleventh and Twelfth Centuries. I: Petrus Helias and His Predecessors." *Medieval and Renaissance Studies* 1:194–231. Reprint. In Hunt 1980.

————. 1980. *The History of Grammar in the Middle Ages: Collected Papers*. Ed. G. L. Bursill-Hall. Amsterdam Studies in the Theory and History of Linguistic Science 3, Studies in the History of Linguistics 5. Amsterdam.

Huntsman, Jeffrey F. 1983. "Grammar." In *The Seven Liberal Arts in the Middle Ages*, ed. David L. Wagner, 58–95. Bloomington, Ind.: Indiana University Press.

Hutton, James. 1980. *Essays on Renaissance Poetry*. Ed. Rita Guerlac. Ithaca, N.Y.: Cornell University Press.

Hyde, Thomas. 1986. *The Poetic Theology of Love: Cupid in Renaissance Literature*. Newark, Del.: Delaware University Press.

Jacoff, Rachel. 1984. "God as Mother: Julian of Norwich's Theology of Love." *Denver Quarterly* 18:134–39.

Jacquot, Jean, ed. 1956. *Les fêtes de la Renaissance*. Paris: Editions du Centre national de la recherche scientifique.

Jaeger, C. Stephen. 1985. *The Origins of Courtliness: Civilizing Trends and the Formation of Courtly Ideals 939–1210*. Philadelphia: University of Pennsylvania Press.

Jaeger, Werner. 1945. *Paideia: The Ideals of Greek Culture*. 3 vols. Trans. (from the second German edition) Gilbert Highet. Oxford: Blackwell.

Javelet, Robert. 1961. "Intelligence et amour chez les auteurs spirituels du XIIme siècle," part 1. *Revue d'ascétique et de mystique* 37:273–90.

————. 1962a. "Thomas Gallus et Richard de Saint-Victor mystiques," part 1. *Recherches de théologie ancienne et médiévale* 29:206–31.

————. 1962b. "Intelligence et amour chez les auteurs spirituels du XIIme siècle," part 2. *Revue d'ascétique et de mystique* 38:429–50.

————. 1963. "Thomas Gallus et Richard de Saint-Victor mystiques," part 2. *Recherches de théologie ancienne et médiévale* 30:88–121.

————. 1967. *Image et ressemblance au douzième siècle, de Saint Anselm a Alain de Lille*. Strasbourg: Editions Letouzey & Ane.

Jeaneau, Edouard. 1973. *'Lectio philosophorum': Recherches sur l'Ecole de Chartres*. Amsterdam: Adolf Hakkert.

Johnson, Harold J., ed. 1987. *The Medieval Tradition of Natural Law.* Studies in Medieval Culture 22. Kalamazoo, Mich.: Medieval Institute Publications.

Johnson, Mark, ed. 1981. *Philosophical Perspectives on Metaphor.* Minneapolis: University of Minnesota Press.

Jolivet, Jean. 1980. "Remarques sur les *Regulae theologicae* d'Alain de Lille." In *Alain de Lille, Gautier de Châtillon, Jakemart Giélée et leurs temps: Actes du Colloque de Lille*, Oct. 1978, 83–99, ed. H. Roussel and F. Suard. Lille: Presses Universitaires de Lille.

————. 1975. "Vues medievales sur les paronymes." *Revue internationale de philosophie* 29:222–42.

Kantorowicz, Ernst H. 1957. *The King's Two Bodies: A Study in Mediaeval Political Theology.* Princeton, N.J.: Princeton University Press.

————. 1970. "De Pugna: La letteratura longobardistica sul duello giudiziario." In *Rechtshistorische Schriften*, ed. Helmut Coing and Gerhard Immel, 255–71. Karlsruhe: C. F. Muller.

Kaske, R. E. 1958. "*Sapientia et Fortitudo* as a Controlling Theme in *Beowulf.*" *Studies in Philology* 55:423–57.

————. 1988. *Medieval Christian Literary Imagery: A Guide to Interpretation.* Toronto Medieval Bibliographies 11. Toronto: University of Toronto Press.

Kelly, Donald R. 1984. *History, Law and the Human Sciences: Medieval and Renaissance Perspectives.* London: Variorum Reprints.

Kevane, Eugene. 1964. *Augustine the Educator: A Study in the Fundamentals of Christian Formation.* Westminster, Md.: The Newman Press.

Kibre, Pearl. 1969. "The Quadrivium in the Thirteenth Century Universities (with special reference to Paris)." See *Arts liberaux* 1969.

————. 1981. "The Boethian *De institutione arithmetica* and the Quadrivium in the Thirteenth-Century University." In *Boethius and the Liberal Arts*, ed. Michael Masi. Berne: P. Lang.

Kleinz, John P. 1944. *The Theory of Knowledge of Hugh of Saint Victor.* Philosophical Studies 87. Washington, D.C.: Catholic University of America Press.

Klibansky, Raymond; Panofsky, Erwin; and Saxl, Fritz. 1979. *Saturn and Melancholy.* Nendeln/Liechtenstein: Kraus Reprint.

Krestowsky, L. 1947. *La laideur dans l'art a travers les âges.* Paris: Editions du Seuil.

Kristeller, P. O. 1961. "Un 'Ars dictaminis' di Giovanni del Virgilio." *Italia médiévale e umanistica* 4:181–200.

Kritzeck, James. 1964. *Peter the Venerable and Islam.* Princeton Oriental Studies 23. Princeton, N.J.:Princeton University Press.

Lacroix, Benoit. 1959. "Hughes de Saint-Victor et le conditions du savoir au moyen âge." In *An Etienne Gilson Tribute*, ed. Charles F. O'Neill, 118–34. Milwaukee: Marquette Uniersity Press.

Le Goff, Jacques. 1957. *Les intellectuels au moyen âge.* Paris: Editions du Seuil.

Leanza, Sandro. 1974. "La classificazione dei libri salomonici e i suoi riflessi sulla questione dei rapporti tra Bibbia e scienze profane, da Origene agli scrittori medioevali." *Augustinianum* 14:651–66.

Leclercq, Jean. 1943–45. "Le 'De grammatica' de Hugues de Saint-Victor." *Archives d'histoire doctrinale et littéraire du moyen âge* 14:263–322.

————. 1948a. "L'humanisme bénédictin du VII au XII siècle." *Studia anselmiana* 20:1–20.

————. 1948b. "Smaragde et la grammaire chrétienne." *Revue du moyen âge latin* 4:15–22.

————. 1953. "Contemplation et vie contemplative du *vie* au *xiie* siècle," *Dictionnaire de spiritualité, áscetique et mystique* 2, part 2. Paris: Beauchesne (1929–48).

————. 1962. *The Love of Learning and the Desire for God: A Study of Monastic Culture*. Trans. Catharine Misrahi. New York: New American Library.

————. 1963. *Otia monastica: Etudes sur le vocabulaire de la contemplation au moyen âge*. Studia Anselmiana 51. Rome.

————. 1964. "Aspects spirituels de la symbolique du livre au XIIe siècle." In *L'homme devant Dieu: Mélanges offerts au Pere Henri de Lubac* 2:64–75.

————. 1975. "Le thème de la jonglerie dans les relations entre Saint Bernard, Abelard et Pierre le Venerable." In *Pierre Abelard–Pierre le Venerable*, 671–87. Les courants philosophiques, littéraires et artistiques en occident au milieu du XIIe siècle, Abbaye de Cluny, 2–9 July 1972. Paris: Editions du Centre national de la recherche scientifique.

Lecoy de la Marche, Albert. 1886. *La chaire française au moyen âge*, specialement au XIIIe siècle. 2d ed. Paris: Renouard.

Leeuw, Gerardus van der. 1963. *Sacred and Profane Beauty: The Holy in Art*. Trans. David E. Green. Nashville and New York: Abingdon Press.

Leff, Gordon. 1968. *Paris and Oxford in the Thirteenth and Fourteenth Centuries: An Institutional and Intellectual History*. London: John Wiley & Son.

Lehmann, Paul. 1963. *Die Parodie im Mittelalter*. 2d ed. Stuttgart: A. Hiersemann.

Leupin, Alexandre. 1989. *Barbarolexis: Medieval Writing and Sexuality*. Cambridge, Mass.: Harvard University Press.

Licitra, Vincenzo. 1977. "Il mito di Alberico di Montecassino iniziatore dell'*Ars dictaminis*." *Studi medievali*, 3d ser. 18:1175–93.

Lindberg, David, ed. 1978. *Science in the Middle Ages*. Chicago and London: University of Chicago Press.

Little, A. G. 1926. "The Franciscan School at Oxford in the Thirteenth Century." *Archivum franciscanum historicum* 19(1926): 803–74.

Livesey, Steven J., and Rouse, Richard H. 1981. "Nimrod the Astronomer." *Traditio* 37:203–53.

Lloyd, A. C. 1971. "Grammar and Metaphysics in the Stoa." In *Problems in Stoicism*, ed. Anthony Arthur Long, 58–74. London: Athlone.

Lottin, Odon. 1931. *Le droit naturel chez Saint Thomas d'Aquin et ses predécesseurs*. Bruges: Ch. Beyaert.

————. 1942–49. *Psychologie et morale aux XIIe et XIIIe siècles*. 3 vols. Gembloux: J. Duculot, Editeur.

Lourdaux, W. and Verhelst, D., eds. 1979. *The Bible and medieval culture*. Louvain: University Press.

Lovejoy, Arthur O. 1960. *The Great Chain of Being: A Study of the History of Ideas*. New York: Harper and Row.

Lubac, Henri de. 1959–61. *Exégèse médiévale: Les quatre sens de l'écriture*. Paris: Aubier.

————. 1960. "Saint Gregoire et la grammaire." *Recherches de science religieuse* 48:185–226.

Lutz, Cora E. 1956. "Remigius' Ideas on the Origin and the Classification of the Seven Liberal Arts." *Medievalia et humanistica* 10: 32–49.

MacCarthy, Joseph M. 1976. *Humanistic Emphases in the Educational Thought of Vincent of Beauvais.* Leiden: E. J. Brill.

MacDonald, Ronald R. 1987. *The Burial-Places of Memory: Epic Underworlds in Vergil, Dante and Milton.* Amherst, Mass: University of Massachusetts Press.

McGarry, Daniel D. 1948. "Educational Theory in the Metalogicon of John of Salisbury." *Speculum* 23:659–75.

MacIntyre, Alasdair. 1988. *Whose Justice? Which Rationality?* Notre Dame, Ind.: University of Notre Dame Press.

McKenzie, Kenneth. 1914. "Per la storia dei Bestiarii italiani," *Giornale storico della letteratura italiana* 64:359–71.

McKeon, R. 1952. "Rhetoric in the Middle Ages." In *Critics and Criticism, Ancient and Modern*, ed. R. S. Crane, 260–96. Chicago: University of Chicago Press.

———. 1964. "The Status of the University of Paris as *Parens Scientiarum.*" *Speculum* 39:651–75.

Mahoney, Edward P. 1987. "Lovejoy and the Hierarchy of Being." *Journal of the History of Ideas* 48:211–30.

Maier, Anneliese. 1983. *Scienza e filosofia nel medioevo: Saggi sui secoli XIII e XIV.* Trans. with an introduction by Massimo Parodi and Achille Zoerle. Biblioteca di cultura medievale. Milan: Jaca Book.

Man, Paul de. 1979. "Autobiography as Defacement." *MLN* 94:919–30.

Mandonnet, Pierre. 1976. *Siger de Brabant et l'averroisme latin au XIIIe siècle.* Geneve: Slatkine Reprints.

Marigo, Aristide. 1916. "Cultura letteraria e preumanistica nelle maggiori enciclopedie del dugento, lo 'Speculum' ed il 'Tresors.'" *Giornale storico della letteratura italiana* 68:1–42; 289–326.

Maritain, Jacques. 1961. *Creative Intuition in Art and Poetry.* The A. W. Mellon Lectures in the Fine Arts. Cleveland and New York: Meridian Books.

———. 1962. *Arts and Scholasticism and the Frontiers of Poetry.* Trans. Joseph W. Evans. New York: Scribner's Sons.

Marrou, Henri-Irenée. 1958. *Saint Augustin et la fin de la culture antique.* Paris: Editions E. De Boccard.

———. [1956] 1982. *A History of Education in Antiquity.* Trans. George Lamb. [London]. Reprint. Madison, Wis.: University of Wisconsin.

———. 1969. "Les arts liberaux dans l'antiquité classique." See *Arts Liberaux* 5:27.

Maurer, Armand. 1981. "Siger of Brabant on Fables and Falsehood in Religion." *Mediaeval Studies* 43:515–30.

Mazzotta, Giuseppe. 1986. *The World at Play in Boccaccio's Decameron.* Princeton, N.J.: Princeton University Press.

———. 1988a. "Humanism and Monastic Spirituality in Petrarch." *Stanford Literature Review* 5(1–2):57–74.

———. 1988b. "Vico's Encyclopedia." *The Yale Journal of Criticism* 1:65–79.

Menendez Pidal, Ramón. [1924] 1957. *Poesia juglaresca y Juglares.* Revista de filologia espanola. Madrid: Centro de estudios historicos.

Menocal, Maria Rosa. 1987. *The Arabic Role in Medieval Literary History: A Forgotten Heritage.* Philadelphia: University of Pennsylvania Press.

Merlo, Grado G. 1989. *Eretici e eresie medievali*. Bologna: Il Mulino.

Michaud-Quantin, Pierre. 1966. "Les petites encyclopédies du XIIIe siècle," *Cahiers d'histoire mondiale* 9:580–96.

———. 1970. *Etudes sur le vocabulaire philosophique du moyen age*. Lessico intellettuale europeo 5. Rome: Ed. dell'Ateneo.

Michel, Alain. 1980. "Rhetorique, poetique et nature chez Alain de Lille." In *Alain de Lille, Gautier de Chatillon, Jakemart Gielee et leur temps*, textes reunis par H. Roussel et F. Suard. Actes du Colloque de Lille, Oct. 1978. Lille: Presse universitaires de Lille.

———. 1982. *La parole et la beauté: Rhetorique et esthetique dans la tradition occidentale*. Les belles lettres, collection d'etudes anciennes. Paris.

Miller, David L. 1970. *Gods and Games: Toward a Theology of Play*. New York and Cleveland: The World Publishing Company.

Mohrmann, Christine. 1951. "Credere in Deum." In *Melanges J. de Ghellinck* 1:277–85. Gembloux: J. Duculot.

Monterosso, Raffaello. 1956. *Musica e ritmica dei trovatori*. Milan: Giuffré.

Mroz, Sister Mary Bonaventure. 1941. *Divine Vengeance: A Study in the Philosophical Background of the Revenge Motif as It Appears in Shakespeare's Chronicle History Plays*. Washington, D.C.: Catholic University of America Press.

Murphy, J. 1971. "Alberic of Monte Cassino: Father of the Medieval *Ars Dictaminis*." *American Benedictine Review* 22:129–46.

———. 1974. *Rhetoric in the Middle Ages*. Berkeley: University of California Press.

Nardi, Bruno. 1947. *S. Tommaso d'Aquino: Trattato sull'unità dell'intelletto contro gli averroisti* (trans. with a commentary and historical introduction). Florence: Vallecchi.

———. 1959. "L'amore e i medici medievali." In *Studi in onore di Angelo Monteverdi* 2:517–42. Modena: Società Tipografica Editrice Modenese.

Nemetz, Anthony. 1956. "Logic and the Division of the Sciences in Aristotle and St. Thomas." *The Modern Schoolman* 33:91–109.

Newman, Francis X. 1963. *Somnium: Medieval Theories of Dreaming and the Form of Vision Poetry*. Ph.D. Diss., Princeton University, Princeton, N.J.

North, J. D. 1988. *Chaucer's Universe*. Oxford: Clarendon Press.

O'Daly, Gerard. 1987. *Augustine's Philosophy of Mind*. London: Duckworth.

O'Donnel, J. Reginald. 1969. "The Liberal Arts in the Twelfth Century with Special Reference to Alexander Nequam (1157–1217)." See *Arts Liberaux*: 127–35.

Olson, Glending. 1982. *Literature as Recreation in the Later Middle Ages*. Ithaca, N.Y., and London: Cornell University Press.

———. 1986. "The Medieval Fortunes of 'Theatrica.'" *Traditio: Studies in Ancient and Medieval History, Thought and Religion* 42:265–86.

Ordo: IIo colloquio internazionale del lessico intelletuale europeo. 1979. Atti a cura di Marta Fattori e Massimo Binachi, Rome, 7–9 Jan. 1977. Lessico intelletuale europeo 20. Rome: Edizioni dell'Ateneo & Bizzarri.

Ovitt, George, Jr. 1987. *The Restoration of Perfection: Labor and Technology in Medieval Culture*. New Brunswick, N.J.: Rutgers University Press.

Owst, G. R. 1961. *Preaching in Medieval England*. 2d ed. Oxford: Oxford University Press.

Paetow, L. J. 1910. *The Arts Course at the Mediaeval Universities with Special Reference to Grammar and Rhetoric*. The University Studies 3, no. 7. Urbana-Champaign, Ill.: University of Illinois Press.

Paré, Gerard. 1947. *Les idees et les lettres au XIIIe siècle: Le roman de la rose*. Montreal: Bibliotheque de philosophie.

Paré, G.; Brunet, A.; and Tremblay, P. 1933. *Les écoles et l'enseignement: La renaissance du XIIe siècle*. Publications de l'institut d'études médiévales d'Ottawa 3. Paris: J. Vrin.

Pasquini, Emilio. 1987. "La santità nella letteratura italiana del Trecento." In *Santi e santità nel secolo XIV*, 25–53. Atti del XV Convegno internazionale. 15–17 Oct. 1987. Assisi: Edizioni scientifiche italiane.

Peck, George T. 1980. *The Fool of God: Iacopone da Todi*. Tuscaloosa, Ala.: University of Alabama Press.

Pedersen, Jorgen. 1955–56. "La recherche de la sagesse d'apres Hugues de Saint-Victor." *Classica et medievalia: Revue danoise de philologie de d'histoire* 16 (fasc. 1–2): 91–133.

Pegis, Anton. 1934. *St. Thomas and the Problem of the Soul in the Thirteenth Century*. Toronto: St. Michael's College.

Pelikan, Jaroslav. 1978. *The Christian Tradition: A History of the Development of Doctrine*. 5 vols. Chicago: University of Chicago Press.

Pepin, J. 1976. *Mythe et allégorie: Les origines grecques et les contestations judeo-chretiénnes*. 2d ed. Paris: Etudes augustiniennes.

Perrot, Maurice. 1895. *Maitre Guillaume de Saint-Amour, l'Université de Paris et les ordres mendiants au XIIIe siècle*. Paris: Firmin-Didot.

Petrocchi, Giorgio. 1965. *La letteratura religiosa*. In *Storia della letteratura italiana*, 627–85. Milan: Garzanti.

Phelan, G. B. 1932. "The Concept of Beauty in St. Thomas Aquinas." In *Aspects of the New Scholastic Philosophy*. New York: Benziger Brothers.

Pieper, Josef. 1952. *Leisure: The Basis of Culture*. Trans. Alexander Dru. New York: Pantheon.

———. 1957. *The Silence of St. Thomas*. Trans. John Murray and Daniel O'Connor. New York: Pantheon.

———. 1958. *Happiness and Contemplation*. Trans. Richard and Clara Winston. New York: Pantheon.

Pinckaers, S. 1958. "La nature vertueuse de l'espérance." *Revue thomiste* 58:405–52 and 623–44.

Piper, Ferdinand. 1851. *Mythologie der Christlichen Kunst*. 2 vols. Weimar: Landes-industrie-comptoir.

Poirion, Daniel. 1973. *Le roman de la rose: Connaisance des lettres*. Paris: Hatier.

———. 1980. "Alain de Lille et Jean de Meun." In *Alain de Lille, Gautier de Chatillon, Jakemart Gielee et leur temps*, textes reunis par H. Roussel et F. Suard, 136–63. Actes du Colloque de Lille, Oct. 1978. Lille: Presse universitaires de Lille.

Poque, Suzanne. 1984. *Le langage symbolique dans la prédication d'Augustin d'Hippone*. 2 vols. Paris: Etudes augustiniennes.

Portelli, J. P. 1982. "The 'Myth' that Avicenna Reproduced Aristotle's 'Concept of Imagination' in *De Anima*." *Scripta mediterranea* 3:122–34.

Potter, G. R. 1936. "Education in the Fourteenth and Fifteenth Centuries." *Cambridge Medieval History* 8:688–717.

Pouillon. H. 1946. " La beauté, proprieté transcendentale chez les scolastiques (1220–1270)." *Archives d'histoire doctrinale et littéraire du moyen âge* 15:263–327.

Quilligan, Maureen. 1977. "Words and Sex: The Language of Allegory in the *De planctu naturae*, the *Roman de la rose*, and Book III of *The Faerie Queene*." *Allegorica* 2:195–216.

Radding, Charles M. 1988. *The Origins of Medieval Jurisprudence: Pavia and Bologna 850–1150*. New Haven, Conn. and London: Yale University Press.

Rahner, Hugo. 1972. *Man at Play*. New York: Herder & Herder.

Rajna, Pio. 1928. "Le denominazioni *trivium* e *quadrivium* (con un singolare accessorio)." *Studi medievali*, n.s. 1:4–36.

Rashdall, Hastings. 1936. *The Universities of Europe in the Middle Ages*. 3 vols. Ed. M. Powicke and A. B. Emden. Oxford: Clarendon Press.

Reau, Louis. 1955–59. *Iconographie de l'art chrétien*. 3 vols. Paris: Presses universitaires de France.

Reeves, Marjorie. 1969. *The Influence of Prophecy in the Later Middle Ages: A Study in Joachism*. Oxford: Oxford University Press.

Riché, Pierre and Lobrichon, Guy. 1984. *Le Moyen Age et le Bible*. Paris: Beauchesne.

Rijk, Lambert Marie de. 1985. *La philosophie au moyen âge*. Leiden: E. J. Brill.

Robilliard, J.-A. 1939. "Les six genres de contemplation chez Richard de Saint-Victor." *Revue des sciences philosophiques et théologiques* 28:229–33.

Roques, René. 1954. *L'univers dionisyen: Structure hierarchique du monde selon le Pseudo-Denys*. Theologie 29. Paris: Aubier.

———. 1958. "Connaissance de Dieu et théologie symbolique d'apres le *In hierarchiam coelestem sancti dionysii* de Hugues de Saint-Victor." *Recherches de philosophie* 3–4:187–266.

———. 1962. *Structures théologiques de la gnose a Richard de Saint-Victor: Essais et analyses critiques*. Bibliothèque de l'école des hautes études, section de sciences religieuses, 72. Paris.

Rosen, Stanley. 1988. *The Quarrel between Philosophy and Poetry*. Studies in Ancient Thought. New York–London: Routledge.

Rovighi Vanni, Sofia. 1967. "Le disputazioni dei filosofanti." In *Dante e Bologna nei tempi di Dante*, 179–92. Bologna: Commissione per i testi di lingua.

Ryan, Christopher J. 1983. "Man's Free Will in the Works of Siger of Brabant." *Medieval Studies* 45:155–99.

Ryan, Mary Bride. 1958. *John of Salisbury on the Arts of Language in the Trivium*. Washington, D.C.: Catholic University of America Press.

Sabra, A. I. 1980. "Avicenna on the Subject Matter of Logic." *Journal of Philosophy* 77:757–64.

Sanfor, Eva M. 1949. "Famous Latin Encyclopedias." *Classical Journal* 54:462–67.

Santayana, George. 1955. *The Sense of Beauty: Being the Outline of Aesthetic Theory*. New York: Dover.

Santi, Enrico M., ed. 1990. *Canto general*, by Pablo Neruda. Madrid: Ediciones Catedra.

Scheindlin, Raymond P. 1976. "Rabbi Moshe Ibn Ezra on the Legitimacy of Poetry." *Medievalia et humanistica* 7:101–15.

Schiller, J. C. F. 1954. *On the Esthetic Education of Man*. Trans. R. Snell. London: Routledge and Kegan Paul.

Schullian, Dorothy M. 1970. "Notes and Events." *Journal of the History of Medicine* 25:77–80.

Se Boyar, G. E. 1920. "Bartholomaeus Anglicus and His Encyclopaedia." *Journal of English and German Philology* 19:168–89.

Shaw, J. E. 1949. *Guido Cavalcanti's Theory of Love: The Canzone d'amore and Other Related Poems*. Toronto: University of Toronto Press.

Simone, Franco. 1949. "La 'reductio artium ad sacram Scripturam' quale espressione dell'umanesimo medievale fino al secolo XII." *Convivium*, n.s. 2:887–927.

Smalley, Beryl. 1984. *The Study of the Bible in the Middle Ages*. Oxford: Basil Blackwell.

Spargo, E. J. M. 1953. *The Category of the Aesthetic in the Philosophy of Saint Bonaventure*. Philosophy Series 11. New York: Franciscan Institute of St. Bonaventure.

Spariosu, Mihai I. 1989. *Dionysus Reborn: Play and the Esthetic Dimension in Modern Philosophical and Scientific Discourse*. Ithaca, N.Y., and London: Cornell University Press.

———. 1991. *God of Many Names: Play, Poetry and Power in Hellenic Thought from Homer to Aristotle*. Durham, N.C., and London: Duke University Press.

Spearing, A. C. 1976. *Medieval Dream Poetry*. Cambridge: Cambridge University Press.

Spitzer, Leo. 1963. *Classical and Christian Ideas of World Harmony*. Ed. Anna Granville Hatcher. Baltimore: The Johns Hopkins University Press.

Stahl, William H. 1971. *Martianus Capella and the Seven Liberal Arts*. New York: Columbia University Press.

Steenberghen, Fernand van. 1955. *Aristotle in the West: The Origins of Latin Aristotelianism*. Trans. Leonard Johnston. Louvain: E. Nauwelaerts.

———. 1966. *La philosophie au XIII siècle*. Louvain-Paris: Publications universitaires.

———. 1974. *Introduction a l'étude de la philosophie médiévale: Recueil de Travaux offerts a l'auteur par ses collègues*. Philosophes médiévaux 18. Louvain: Publications universitaires.

———. 1977. *Maitre Siger de Brabant*. Philosophes medievaux 21. Louvain: Publications universitaires.

Stephens, Walter. 1984. *Giants in Those Days: Folklore, Ancient History and Nationalism*. Regent Studies in Medieval Culture. Lincoln and London: University of Nebraska Press.

Stickler, Alfonso M. 1977. *Il giubileo di Bonifacio VIII: Aspetti giuridico-pastorali*. Rome: Alfonso dell' Elefante.

Stillinger, Thomas. 1992. *The Song of Troilus: Lyric Authority in the Medieval Book*. Philadelphia: University of Pennsylvania.

Stock, Brian. 1972. *Myth and Science in the Twelfth century: A Study of Bernard Silvester*. Princeton, N.J.: Princeton University Press.

Svoboda, K. 1933. *L'esthétique de Saint-Augustin et ses sources*. Brno and Paris: Belles Lettres.

Szittya, Penn R. 1986. *The Antifraternal Tradition in Medieval Literature*. Princeton, N.J.: Princeton University Press.

Tacchella, Enrico. 1980. "Giovanni di Salisbury e i Cornificiani." *Sandalion* 3:273–313.

Tatarkiewicz, Wladyslaw. 1970. *Medieval Aesthetics*. Vol. 2 of *History of Aesthetics*, 3 vols., ed. C. Barrett. The Hague/Paris: Mouton.

Tateo, Francesco. 1960. *'Retorica' e 'poetica' fra medioevo e Rinascimento*. Bari: Adriatica.

Tega, Walter. 1983. *L'unità del sapere e l'ideale enciclopedico nel pensiero moderno*. Bologna: Il Mulino.

Thillet, Pierre. 1978. "Réflexions sur la paraphrase de la *Rhetorique* d'Aristote." In *Multiple Averroes: Actes du colloque international organise a l'occasion du 850e anniversaire de la naissance d'Averroes*, ed. J. Jolivet, 105–12. Paris: Belles Lettres.

Thorndike, Lynn. [1923–58] 1958–60. *A History of Magic and Experimental Science*. 8 vols. Reprint. New York: Columbia University Press.

Thouzellier, Christine. 1927. "La place du 'Periculis' de Guillaume de Saint-Amour dans les polémiques universitaires du XIIIe siècle." *Revue historique* 156:69–83.

Tierney, Brian. 1964. *The Crisis of Church and State, 1050–1300*. Englewood Cliffs, N.J.: Prentice Hall.

Toccafondi, Eugenio Teodolfo. 1969. "Il pensiero di san Tommaso sulle arti liberali." See *Arts Liberaux*: 639–51.

Torrell, J.-P. 1974a. "Hugues de Saint-Cher et Thomas d'Aquin: Contribution a l'histoire du traité de la prophetie." *Revue thomiste* 74:5–22.

———. 1974b. *Theorie de la prophetie et philosophie de la connaissance aux environs de 1230: La contribution d'Hugues de Saint-Cher* (critical edition with introduction and commentary). Spicilegium Sacrum Lovaniense, Études et documents, 40. Louvain.

Toschi, Paolo. 1978. *Il contributo dei giullari*. Rome: Bulzoni.

Trimpi, Wesley. 1983. *Muses of One Mind: The Literary Analysis of Experience and Its Continuity*. Princeton, N.J.: Princeton University Press.

Trout, John. 1979. *The Voyage of Prudence: The World View of Alan of Lille*. Washington, D.C.: Catholic University Press of America.

Ullman, Walter. 1975. *Law and Politics in the Middle Ages*. Ithaca, N.Y.: Cornell University Press.

Vance, Eugene. 1987. *From Topic to Tale: Logic and Narrativity in the Middle Ages*. Minneapolis: University of Minnesota Press.

Vasoli, C. 1968. *La dialettica e la retorica dell'umanesimo*. Milan: Feltrinelli.

Vauchez, A. 1977. *La spiritualité du moyen âge occidental*. Paris: Presses universitaires de France.

Vecchi, Giuseppe. 1951. *Per la storia delle scienze nel medio evo*. Bologna: Azzoguidi.

Verbeke, Gerard. 1983. *The Presence of Stoicism in Medieval Thought*. Washington, D.C.: The Catholic University of America Press.

Verdier, Philippe. 1969. "L'iconographie des arts liberaux dans l'art du moyen âge jusqu'à la fin du quinzième siècle (23 plances)." See *Arts Liberaux*: 305–55.

Verger, Jacques, and Jolivet, Jean. 1982. *Bernard-Abelard ou le cloître et l'école: Douze hommes dans l'histoire de l'église*. Paris: Fayard et Mame.

———. 1984. "L'exégèse de l'université." In *Le moyen âge et la Bible*, 199–232. Bible de tous les temps. Sous la direction de Pierre Riche and Guy Lobrichon. Paris: Editions Beauchesne.

Viarre, Simone. 1975. "Cosmologie antique et commentaire de la création du monde." In *La cultura antica nell' Occidente latino dal VII all' XI secolo* 22:541–73. Settimane di studio del Centro italiano di studi sull'alto medioevo.

Wack, Mary F. 1990. *Lovesickness in the Middle Ages: The Viaticum and Its Commentaries*. Philadelphia: University of Pennsylvania Press.

Waddell, Helen. 1989. *The Wandering Scholars*. Ann Arbor Paperbacks. Ann Arbor, Mich.: The University of Michigan Press.

Wagner, David L., ed. 1983. *The Seven Liberal Arts in the Middle Ages*. Bloomington, Ind.: Indiana University Press.

Walsh, Katherine, and Wood, Diana. 1985. *The Bible in the Medieval World: Essays in Memory of Beryl Smalley*. Oxford: Basil Blackwell.

Walzer, Richard. 1962. *Greek into Arabic: Essays on Islamic Philosophy*. Oriental Studies 1. Oxford: Cassirer.

Watson, Gerard. 1986. "Imagination: The Greek Background." *Irish Theological Quarterly* 52:54–65.

Weber, Edouard-Henri. 1970. *L'Homme en discussion a l'université de Paris: La controverse de 1270 a l'université de Paris et son retentissement sur la pensée de S. Thomas d'Aquin*. Bibliotheque thomiste 40. Paris: J. Vrin.

———. 1974. *Dialogue et dissensions entre Saint Bonaventure et Saint Thomas d'Aquin a Paris*. Bibliothèque thomiste 41. Paris: J. Vrin.

Wedel, T. O. 1920. *The Medieval Attitude to Astrology, Particularly in England*. Yale Studies in English 60. New Haven, Conn.: Yale University Press.

Wedin, Michael V. 1988. *Mind and Imagination in Aristotle*. New Haven, Conn., and London: Yale University Press.

Weisheipl, James A. 1964. "Curriculum of the Faculty of Arts at Oxford in the Early Fourteenth Century." *Mediaeval Studies* 26:143–85.

———. 1965. "Classification of the Sciences in Medieval Thought." *Mediaevel Studies* 27:54–62.

Wells, James M. 1968. *The Circle of Knowledge. Encyclopaedias Past and Present*. Chicago: Newberry Library.

Wenzel, S. 1967. *The Sin of Sloth: Acedia in Medieval Thought and Literature*. Chapel Hill, N.C.: University of North Carolina Press.

Wetherbee, Winthrop. 1969. "The Function of Poetry in the 'De planctu naturae' of Alain de Lille." *Traditio: Studies in Ancient and Medieval History, Thought and Religion* 25:87–125.

———. 1972. *Platonism and Poetry in the Twelfth Century: The Literary Influence of the School of Chartres*. Princeton, N.J.: Princeton University Press.

———. 1976. "The Theme of Imagination in Medieval Poetry and the Allegorical Figure 'Genius.'" *Medievalia et humanistica* 7:45–64.

Wieruszowski, H. 1967. "Rhetoric and the Classics in the Italian Education of the Thirteenth Century." *Studia gratiana* 11: 169–208. Reprint. In *Politics and Culture in Medieval Spain and Italy*. Rome: 1971.

Wilks, Michael, ed. 1984. *The World of John of Salisbury*. Studies in Church History, Subsidia, 3. Oxford: Blackwell.

Wilpert, J. 1929. *I sarcofagi cristiani antichi*. Rome: Pontificio istituto di archeologia cristiana.

Wind, Edgar. 1948. *Bellini's Feast of the Gods*. Cambridge, Mass.: Harvard University Press.

Wippel, J. F. 1977. "The Condemnations of 1270 and 1277 at Paris." *The Journal of Medieval and Renaissance Studies* 7:169–201.

Witt, Ronald. 1982. "Medieval 'Ars dictaminis' and the Beginnings of Humanism: A New Construction of the Problem." *Renaissance Quarterly* 35:1–35.

Wolfson, Harry A. 1935. "The Internal Senses in Latin, Arabic, and Hebrew Philosophic Texts." *Harvard Theological Review* 28:69–133.

The World of John of Salisbury. 1984. Ed. Michael Wilks. Studies in Church History, Subsidia, 3. Oxford: Blackwell.

Yanal, Robert. 1982. "Aristotle's Definition of Poetry," *Nous* 16:499–525.

Yates, Frances A. 1972. *The Art of Memory*. Chicago: University of Chicago Press.

Zambelli, Paola. 1982. "Albert le Grand et l'astrologie," *Recherches de théologie ancienne et médiévale* 49:141–58.

Zarb, S. 1938. "Le fonti agostiniane del trattato sulla profezia di S. Tommaso d'Aquino," *Angelicum* 15:169–200.

Ziolkowski, Jan. 1985. *Alan of Lille's Grammar of Sex: The Meaning of Grammar to a Twelfth-Century Intellectual*. Speculum Anniversary Monographs 10. Cambridge, Mass.: Medieval Academy of America.

Zolla, Elemire. 1978. *I mistici dell'Occidente*. 8 vols. Milan: Rizzoli.

Zumthor, Paul. 1972. *Essais de poétique médiévale*. Paris: Seuil.

Zwart, Ansar. 1927. "The History of Franciscan Preaching and of Franciscan Preachers (1209–1927): A Bio-bibliographical Study." *The Franciscan Education Conference* 9:247–587.

INDEX

CPSIA information can be obtained at www.ICGtesting.com
Printed in the USA
BVOW09s1704310714

360943BV00021B/639/P